Making mediation work for you

a practical handbook

Kate Aubrey-Johnson is an accredited mediator and barrister at Garden Court Chambers in London. She is an active member of the wider mediation community and a community mediator for CALM (Community and Legal Mediation). In addition to her work as a mediator and barrister, Kate provides training and seminars on special educational needs, young people's rights and youth justice. Kate is a member of Garden Court Mediation (accredited to the Civil Mediation Council) and has written widely on developments in mediation.

Helen Curtis is an accredited mediator and restorative justice facilitator dealing with high conflict cases. She incorporates these mediation skills in her legal practice as a barrister. Helen is also a mediator for LawWorks and a restorative justice facilitator and mediator with CALM. She speaks on mediation at seminars and conferences and is a member of Garden Court Mediation.

Available as an ebook at www.lag.org.uk/ebooks

The purpose of the Legal Action Group is to promote equal access to justice for all members of society who are socially, economically or otherwise disadvantaged. To this end, it seeks to improve law and practice, the administration of justice and legal services.

Making mediation work for you

a practical handbook

Kate Aubrey-Johnson

with Helen Curtis

Legal Action Group
2012

This edition published in Great Britain 2012
by LAG Education and Service Trust Limited
242 Pentonville Road, London N1 9UN
www.lag.org.uk

While every effort has been made to ensure that the details in this text are
correct, readers must be aware that the law changes and that the accuracy
of the material cannot be guaranteed and the author and the publisher
accept no responsibility for any loss or damage sustained.

The right of the author to be identified as author of this work has been
asserted by her in accordance with the Copyright, Designs and Patents
Act 1988.

British Library Cataloguing in Publication Data
a CIP catalogue record for this book is available from the British Library.

Crown copyright material is produced with the permission of the
Controller of HMSO and the Queen's Printer for Scotland.

This book has been produced using Forest Stewardship
Council®(FSC®) certified paper. The wood used to produce
FSC certified products with a 'Mixed Sources' label comes
from FSC certified well-managed forests, controlled sources
and/or recycled material.

Print ISBN   978 1 903307 93 9
ebook ISBN   978 1 908407 19 1

Typeset by Regent Typesetting, London
Printed in Great Britain by Hobbs the Printers, Totton, Hampshire

For Jonah and Erin

Foreword

by The Rt Hon the Lord Woolf

The number of books being published dealing with mediation is growing rapidly. However, *Making mediation work for you* is breaking new ground. It is designed to assist those who find themselves involved in disputes which do not involve substantial commercial issues but are among the ordinary citizens who can nonetheless be seriously affected by a dispute. In most cases the individual concerned is able to resolve the dispute without being sucked into litigation, which he can neither afford nor control. Although the sums involved may not be vast by standards of commercial litigation, to the individual involved the issues can be critical.

In the past the individual could seek legal aid, but now situations where legal aid is available have been seriously curtailed by a series of statutes, the latest of which is the Legal Aid, Sentencing & Punishment of Offenders Act 2012. Its effect has been truly dramatic. In these situations in which direction does the individual turn? Fortunately LAG (Legal Action Group) has always been deeply concerned to assist the individual in this situation. Consistent with its policy, it has published this excellent book written by Kate Aubrey-Johnson with Helen Curtis. Both are Accredited Mediators and barristers and they have produced a book which is easy to understand and informs the reader, whether or not a lawyer, precisely what needs to be known about mediation in order that mediation can provide a solution.

No matter what the nature of a dispute, this book should provide all the ammunition needed to conduct a successful mediation. It deals simply and clearly with the hazards of mediation. It should become the standard companion of mediators engaged in the type of disputes to which I referred. It should also help those who will benefit if mediation is used to resolve those disputes. It will be a blessing to those who in the past would have depended upon legal aid to provide a solution to the problems with which they are faced. It provides a way in which the citizen can, even without legal aid, find a way of resolving his or her problem.

The first edition deserves to be followed by many more so that in the changing world of dispute resolution members of the public will always be able to benefit from its assistance.

Harry Woolf
May 2012

Acknowledgments

Thank you to Helen Curtis who has spent an immense amount of time helping me devise a handbook which would be practical and useable to readers. Her commitment to mediation resonates throughout the book. The chapter on workplace mediation reflects her particular interest in making the workplace a more productive environment where individuals are better skilled to address conflict as issues emerge.

My particular thanks to Margaret Doyle, Carey Haslam, Elena Noel, Rajeev Thacker and Martin Wright who made considerable contributions to the content of this book and have undoubtedly made this book more authoritative and useful to readers. Any errors are, of course, my own.

Anna Wood and Crispin Aubrey had the 'privilege' of seeing the book in its unpolished form, and so I am grateful to them for making it readable. I would also like to thank the kind and generous 'test readers' Rosie Aubrey, John Beckley, Polly Bradford, Spencer Hird, Clara Johnson, Isobel Leaviss, Catrin Lewis, Dr Mary Malescka, Chloe Mawson, Sharon Love, Suzanne Lowe, Corinne Rechais, Julian Rendall, Letitia Stenning, Kathy Torman and Rajeev Thacker.

And to the panel of contributors who have brought the book to life through their answers to some frequently asked questions: Sir Henry Brooke, Margaret Doyle, Lavinia Shaw-Brown, John Kendall, Paul Randolph, Heather Allen, Carey Haslam, John Sturrock, Tony Allen, Beverly-Ann Rogers, Margaret Pendlebury, Christopher Richards, Marilyn Webster, Carolyn Graham, Elena Noel, Lesley Saunders and Lawrence Kershen – your answers speak for themselves, thank you.

My thanks to Bolton Mediation, Confidential and Local Mediation (CALM), Commercial and Medical Dispute Solutions (CMDS), Core Solutions, the Family Mediators Association (FMA), LawWorks, Mediation Works, Oxfordshire Family Mediation, the Public Law Project, the Tim Parry Jonathan Ball Foundation for Peace and UK Mediation for allowing their work to be reproduced in this book.

I believe the benefits of mediation in the UK are yet to be fully realised. This book, I hope, will offer the mediation profession and the different specialist fields the impetus needed to continue to strive for the highest standards and integrity in mediation. Members of the public are increasingly looking for the profession to have a clearly defined set of skills, ethical codes and shared practice. With a united voice, we will be able to work with government to ensure mediation goes hand in hand with informed decision-making and, when appropriate, high quality legal advice and that the expansion of mediation is never allowed to erode access to justice.

Mediation has the potential to make us into collaborative decision-makers, to value ongoing relationships and to look for creative and mutually beneficial outcomes rather than seek to blame or attribute fault. All of this will build stronger communities and better relationships within our families, neighbourhoods, schools, workplaces, businesses and government; it can provide people with the skills to positively address conflict which is part and parcel of our everyday lives.

I am lucky enough to be part of a progressive chambers which saw the promise of mediation, I want to thank Garden Court Chambers and Garden Court Mediation for providing me with a space to grow.

It leaves me to thank Esther Pilger and LAG who saw the potential of a mediation handbook and nurtured it into existence.

Finally, thank you to Sue, Crispin, Meg, Rosie and, most of all, Lewis. Without their unwavering support this book would not have been written.

Kate Aubrey-Johnson
May 2012

Contents

Table of cases

Case studies

Chapter 11: Community mediation

Frequently asked questions

Chapter 6: Mediation skills, strategies and techniques

Chapter 7: Concluding the mediation: writing the agreement

Chapter 8: Civil mediation

Chapter 9: Family mediation

Chapter 10: Workplace mediation

Chapter 11: Community mediation

Chapter 12: Training, accreditation and ethics

Abbreviations

ACAS	Advisory, Conciliation and Arbitration Service
ADR	alternative or appropriate dispute resolution
AIM	All issues mediation
ASBO	anti-social behaviour order
ATE insurance	after the event insurance
BATNA	Best alternative to a negotiated agreement
BIS	Department for Business Innovation and Skills
BTE insurance	Before the event insurance
Cafcass	Children and Family Court Advisory and Support Service
CAMS	Court of Appeal Mediation Service
CBT	cognitive behavioural therapy
CEDR	Centre for Effective Dispute Resolution
CFA	Conditional fee agreement
CIArb	Chartered Institute of Arbitrators
CIPD	Chartered Institute of Personnel and Development
CLS	Community Legal Service
CMC	Civil Mediation Council
CMD	case management discussion
CPD	Continuing professional development
CPR	Civil Procedure Rules
DRC	Dispute Resolution Commitment
DRS	Dispute Resolution Service (Northern Ireland)
EAT	employment appeal tribunal
EHRC	Equalities and Human Rights Commission
EMS	Equalities Mediation Service
ENE	early neutral evaluation
FDR	financial dispute resolution
FGC	Family group conference
FHDRA	first hearing dispute resolution appointment
FJC	Family Justice Council
FMA	Family Mediators Association
FMC	Family Mediation Council
HMCTS	HM Courts and Tribunals Service
HMRC	HM Revenue and Customs
HR	human resources
IMI	International Mediation Institute
LGO	Local Government Ombudsman

LSC	Legal Services Commission
MIAM	Mediation Information and Assessment Meeting
MISCC	Mediation Information Service in Civil Cases
MLATNA	Most likely alternative to negotiated agreement
MOJ	Ministry of Justice
NAO	National Audit Office
NFM	National Family Mediation
NGO	non-governmental organisation
NMH	National Mediation Helpline
NVC	non-violent communication
OCN	Open College Network
ODR	Online Dispute Resolution
PCC	pre-claim conciliation
PMN	Peer Mediation Network
PPC	professional practice consultant
PPS	parent partnership service
SCMA	Standing Committee of Mediation Advocates
SEN	special educational needs
SENDIST	Special Educational Needs and Disability Tribunal
SMART	specific, measurable, achievable, realistic and time-limited
SMN	Scottish Mediation Network
SOCA	Serious Organised Crime Agency
SOLACE	Society of Local Authority Chief Executives
SPCP	School of Psychotherapy and Counselling Psychology at Regent's College London
TCC	Technology and Construction Court
TKI	Thomas-Kilmann Conflict Mode Instrument
WATNA	Worst alternative to negotiated settlement
YMN	Young Mediators Network
YOT	youth offending team
ZOPA	zone of potential agreement

Glossary

Adjudication	An independent third party considers evidence provided by both parties and makes a determination. This is usually done on paper.
Alternative or Appropriate Dispute Resolution (ADR)	Ways of attempting to resolve disputes so as to avoid court proceedings.
Agreement to mediate	This is a legally binding document signed by the parties (or their legal advisers). Also called a pre-mediation agreement or mediation agreement.
Arbitration	A formal process where an impartial third party (the arbitrator) makes a judgment about which party is at fault and the decision is usually legally binding. Arbitrators are usually experts in the subject of the dispute.
Conciliation	An independent and impartial person (the conciliator) helps parties to reach a resolution. The conciliator may recommend solutions but the parties remain responsible for any agreement.
Confidentiality	Anything said or done during the course of mediation is not shared with others.
Counterclaim	A claim brought by a defendant in response to a claimant's claim, which is included in the same proceedings as the claimant's claim.
Damages	A sum of money paid as compensation to the claimant.
Expert Determination	An independent expert in the subject matter of the dispute makes an expert decision which is usually legally binding on the parties.
Early neutral evaluation (ENE)	Where an independent person, a lawyer or an expert in the subject, gives an opinion on the merits of a dispute. Their opinion is not binding on the parties.
Joint meeting	Where the parties agree to meet together to attempt to resolve their dispute. The process may involve a combination of joint sessions, where the parties are in the same room together, and separate sessions.

Legal adviser

A barrister or a solicitor (both can also be described as a lawyer) who provide legal advice, write letters on behalf of their clients and draft legal documents. If a party attends court their lawyer will usually speak on their behalf.

Limitation period

The period within which a party must start court proceedings. The time limit varies for different types of claim.

Litigation

Settling a dispute according to legal rights and responsibilities and using court proceedings.

Med-Arb

Mediation is first attempted to mediate and then arbitration is used if no agreement is reached

Mediation

A voluntary and confidential process in which an independent and impartial third party (the mediator) assists parties to explore reaching an agreement.

Mediation settlement agreement

The agreement reached during a mediation, it is usually written down and signed by the parties or legal advisers. Also called a mediation agreement or Memorandum of Understanding (MoU).

Negotiation

The parties or their legal advisers reach an agreement between themselves.

Ombudsman

Investigate and resolve complaints about organisations and government bodies.

Opening statement

The opportunity for parties to set out the issues as they see them and explain the impact the dispute has had on them. Also called uninterrupted speaking time.

Parties

The people who are directly affected by the dispute and who attend the mediation. This term is also used to describe the claimant and defendant in legal proceedings.

Pre Action Protocol

Statements of best practice about what parties should do before issuing legal proceedings.

Position statement

A written document prepared for the mediator in civil mediation summarising the background facts and core issues in each party's case.

Reality testing

Where the mediator asks questions to test the validity of a party's position or assertion.

Re-framing

Where the mediator uses neutral words to rephrase something a party has said and to identify the specific issue or a shared problem.

Roundtable meeting (joint settlement conference)

A discussion between lawyers seeking to reach a negotiated settlement (parties may also participate).

Separate meetings	Private meetings with the mediator where discussions remain confidential, unless parties wish the information to be shared.
Stay	A stay halts court proceedings for a specified period of time or indefinitely. The proceedings can be continued if a stay is lifted or ends.
Tomlin Order	A court order which enables the terms of the agreement to remain confidential and the parties to enforce the agreement without issuing new proceedings.
Without prejudice	Negotiations with a view to settlement, which cannot be relied upon in as evidence in legal proceedings.

PART I

Introduction to mediation

CHAPTER 1

What is mediation?

Key points

- The core principles of mediation are that it is a voluntary, confidential, *without prejudice* process in which parties try to reach a consensual agreement.
- Mediators are facilitators who are impartial and independent.
- While the mediation process is flexible, most mediations follow a similar structure.
- Mediation methodology encourages parties to engage with the emotional aspects of a dispute, generate creative solutions and widen the options for agreement.
- Mediation finds practical solutions rather than focusing on whether a party was 'right' or 'wrong'.
- The origins of mediation are drawn from a number of disciplines: non-adjudicative dispute resolution, conciliation, principled negotiation, psychology and the principles of alternative dispute resolution (ADR).
- The mediation movement in the UK includes civil, community, family and workplace mediation.

What is mediation?

1.1   Mediation can involve two or more individuals, groups, businesses or organisations who have had a disagreement and have been unable to resolve the issues between themselves.[1] The parties meet with an independent/neutral third party who facilitates discussions. In most mediations, parties meet together face-to-face and are taken through the mediation process, which encourages them to reach an agreement. Mediation can be used to resolve disputes which arise in a wide variety of situations, such as:

- anti-social behaviour;
- boundary disputes;
- bullying in the workplace;
- clinical negligence;
- community care;
- construction disputes;

1 This book will generally refer to a mediation process involving two parties for ease of reference. Mediation is also suited to resolving disputes in which there are multiple parties.

- consumer relations;
- contractual difficulties;
- divorce and separation;
- employment and management relationships;
- financial services;
- inheritance and trusts;
- judicial review;
- licensing;
- neighbour disputes;
- personal injury;
- planning issues;
- professional negligence;
- relationship breakdown;
- special educational needs;
- technology and intellectual property.

1.2   Mediation can provide practical, long-term solutions which would not be available through alternative grievance or complaints procedures, or through the courts. The mediation process can improve communication, restore relationships and build greater understanding between parties. The dispute may involve a noisy neighbour or a contractual breach, a failure of a public authority to meet a statutory obligation, parents unable to agree on when they see their children or a teenager wishing to leave home; mediation can provide an effective means of finding a solution which is satisfactory to both parties.

> 'Mediation' means any structured process, however named or referred to, whereby two or more parties to a dispute attempt by themselves, on a voluntary basis, to reach an agreement on the settlement of their dispute with the assistance of a mediator.[2]

1.3   People facing an unresolved conflict or going through the court system may find mediation offers an appropriate way of resolving their dispute.

The principles of mediation

1.4   Mediation is a flexible process and different disputes require different approaches. The process used in the UK shares the following fundamental principles.

---

2   EU Directive on certain aspects of mediation in civil and commercial matters 2008/52/EC 21 May 2008 ('EU Mediation Directive'), article 3(a) – appendix G.

Voluntary

> Mediation is ...a voluntary process in which a neutral third party assists disputing parties to reach a consensual solution to their dispute.[3]

1.5   The decision to mediate is voluntary. This means parties who attend mediation are free to leave at any time. When parties decide to mediate they are also attempting to determine the outcome themselves without the decision being imposed by, for example, a judge, an adjudicator or an ombudsman. Consequently, they invest a significant personal and often financial commitment to reaching a successful outcome. At present there is no mandatory requirement to use mediation to resolve disputes in the UK.

> It is often said the hallmark of ADR [alternative dispute resolution] procedures, and perhaps the key to their effectiveness in individual cases, is that they are processes voluntarily entered into by the parties in dispute with outcomes, if the parties so wish, which are non-binding. Consequently the court cannot direct that such methods be used but may merely encourage and facilitate.[4]

1.6   The EU Mediation Directive provides for mediation to be 'a voluntary process in the sense that the parties are themselves in charge of the process and may organise it as they wish and terminate it at any time'.[5] Increasingly parties pursuing legal proceedings are required to have given the possibility of mediation proper consideration. For example, referral to mediation will become automatic in small claims.[6] In higher value claims there is the possibility of costs sanctions against a party who unreasonably refuses to mediate.[7] In some instances a strong judicial recommendation may be given, and proceedings may be stayed pending consideration of mediation.[8] In other situations, ADR contract clauses may require parties to first consider mediation.[9] In private family law cases, compulsory mediation information and assessment meetings (MIAMs) have been

---

3   H Genn, *Judging civil justice*, Cambridge University Press, 2010 p82.
4   *Civil Procedure 2012*: The White Book (Sweet and Maxwell, 2012) Vol 2 para 14-6.
5   EU Mediation Directive, recital (13) – see appendix G.
6   *Solving disputes in the county courts: creating a simpler, quicker and more proportionate system: a consultation on reforming civil justice in England and Wales – the government response*, TSO, February 2012 p11, para 24.
7   See paras 8.98–8.107 on costs sanctions.
8   See para 8.44 and CPR 26.4(2).
9   See paras 8.66–8.67.

introduced for parties initiating court proceedings.[10] By April 2013, legal aid changes will limit public funding in private family law cases to mediation only (with limited exceptions).[11]

Private and confidential

> Mediation ... is a without prejudice, voluntary and private dispute resolution process, in which a neutral person (the mediator) helps the parties to reach a negotiated agreement. It is also as confidential as the law will allow.[12]

1.7　Mediation is confidential, with certain exceptions,[13] Its private and confidential nature can be as important for resolving disputes arising from family breakdowns as it is in commercial litigation.

1.8　If an agreement is reached, parties decide whether or not they wish it to remain confidential. In legal disputes there are mechanisms to enable parties to enforce the agreement even where it has not been disclosed to the court.[14] In exceptional situations the mediator may have a duty to disclose what has been said during a mediation, such as where confidential discussions lead the mediator to believe someone would face a substantial risk of serious harm, or that a criminal offence has been or will be committed.[15] In family cases, financial information disclosed during the mediation process may be used in any subsequent court proceedings. This is described as open financial disclosure.[16]

Non-binding and without prejudice

> Mediation takes the form of assisted without prejudice negotiation.[17]

1.9　The voluntary and non-binding nature of mediation means that parties are not compelled to reach an agreement and options for an agreement can be discussed without binding themselves to a particular outcome. There is no consequence on the parties if they are unable to agree

---

10　Practice Direction 3A, Family Procedure Rules 2010 SI No 2955 – appendix K. Also see paras 9.8–9.9 and 9.63–9.66.

11　Legal Aid, Sentencing and Punishment of Offenders Act (LASPOA) 2012 Sch 1, Part 1, para 14, see paras 9.59–9.62 on the impact of legal aid changes.

12　Chartered Institute of Arbitrators, *Mediation rules*, available at www.ciarb.org/.

13　See paras 7.31–7.45.

14　See para 7.22 on Tomlin orders, and appendix E.

15　See paras 7.34–7.36 and 12.59–12.60.

16　See paras 9.31–9.33.

17　*Brown v Rice and Patel and ADR Group* [2007] EWHC 625 (Ch) para 13.

(other than financial loss where the mediation is self-funded). Mediated agreements are only binding if both parties wish them to be.

1.10   The description of the mediation process as *without prejudice* means that anything said during the mediation cannot then be used as evidence in any legal proceedings which are being considered or already started.[18] This allows parties to talk openly about options for agreement. Parties are able to suggest new and creative possibilities for agreement without jeopardising their chance to go (or to go back) to court if an agreement isn't reached. A mutually agreeable outcome is often one which could not have been reached in court.

1.11   In civil mediation, if parties reach an agreement it is often drafted into a legally binding document, which brings the legal proceedings to an end. The original claim or counter claim cannot then be reinstated even where the other party does not comply with what has been agreed. If properly drafted, mediation agreements are capable of being legally enforceable.[19]

1.12   In most other fields of mediation, any agreement reached is not legally binding on either party. This enables parties to work collaboratively to resolve a dispute without forfeiting their right to go to court if the agreement does not resolve the issues. In community mediation, for example, parties may reach a confidential written agreement or statement of future conduct. In family mediations, parties reach a 'memorandum of understanding'.

Parties control the outcome

> Mediation is always a voluntary process in the sense that a mediator cannot impose a settlement on the parties and is there to encourage and facilitate the reaching of a mutually acceptable settlement to the dispute.[20]

1.13   During a mediation, while the mediator assists and facilitates the process, the parties are responsible for generating options for agreement and the terms of any settlement reached.[21] The mediator does not offer their opinion on the merits of either party's case or seek to determine or impose any outcome. They do not make suggestions or recommend proposals for agreement (but may pass offers between

---

18 With the exceptions highlighted at para 1.8.
19 See paras 7.17–7.24.
20 Legal Services Commission (LSC), *Funding Code*, Part C3C-102.
21 This book will discuss facilitative mediation – there are styles of mediation, see paras 1.33–1.34.

the parties if requested to do so). Any agreement reached must be mutually acceptable to all parties and will have been created by them.

Informed decision-making

1.14 It is integral to the mediation process that parties are able to make informed choices, about what to propose by way of agreement and whether to reach a settlement. Mediators encourage parties to explore their positions so that any agreement reached can reflect their needs and interests.[22] Mediators also encourage parties to consider the likely alternatives to reaching a mediated agreement to objectively assess any offer on the table.[23] When a dispute involves legal rights and entitlements, parties should seek legal advice before commencing mediation. Parties may have a legal adviser present during the mediation (or available on the telephone), or be given the opportunity at the end of the mediation to consult a legal adviser before reaching a legally binding agreement.

Creative outcomes

1.15 Mediation invites parties to widen the potential options for agreement and explore new possibilities and ideas. Mediated settlements can be reached where direct negotiations have failed by getting the right people in the same room and breaking down barriers to communication. The time spent by a mediator encouraging parties to explore their own needs, as well as those of the other party, enables participants in mediation to make practical proposals. Such offers may have added-value[24] as they may have huge significance to one party but can be provided with minimal inconvenience to the other. It may involve looking at previously unconsidered options and widening the options for agreement.

Case study 1: Resolving a dispute over a car warranty

Jack has run a successful second hand car business for the past 12 years and, as an added bonus, he gives all customers a three-month warranty as standard. Katie recently purchased a Vauxhall Astra for £2,000 from Jack's garage, which seemed a great deal.

---

22 See paras 1.40–1.41, 4.54 and 6.62.
23 See paras 4.55.
24 See paras 1.44–1.45 and 4.57–4.61.

Unfortunately, exactly three months after buying the car, it developed a banging noise, which ground the car to a halt. Katie had to be rescued from the motorway and the Astra was towed to a nearby garage. They told her that the engine was beyond repair and it would cost her £1,200, including labour, to have the Astra repaired.

Katie was unable to contact Jack's garage over the phone, so decided to settle the matter face to face, in a pledge to see how Jack could compensate her. After the two met, heated words were exchanged and Katie was escorted from the premises. Unhappy with the car, she decided to have an independent mechanic see what had caused the engine failure. He found that there was insufficient oil in the engine and suggested that the car had been run at high speeds, over long periods. Katie had been advised to check the oil levels when she bought the car. She also knows her 20 year old son sometimes borrows the car, and tends to drive fast and at times recklessly.

At the *joint meeting* after both parties had vented their frustrations, it was clear that neither were particularly bothered about the other's feelings. Jack agreed that although Katie was warned about the oil levels, he did not want an unhappy customer and offered to replace the engine free of charge. Katie agreed to this proposition, as she just needed to get her car back on the road. She also agreed not to contact the local press, as Jack had agreed to do the work for free.

Katie wanted to avoid taking the matter to court, concerned that it would cost her more in lawyer's bills and legal advice, than it would to pay for a new car.[25] Mediation seemed like the sensible option. Jack was also very interested due to the confidentially aspect. If this story was leaked to the papers or local news, he could have been branded a 'Wheeler Dealer'.[26]

---

25 In low value civil claims, parties can contact their community mediation service who may provide free mediation, or access the civil mediation directory which offers fixed fee civil mediation – see para 8.13. Alternatively, by lodging a small claim, parties are entitled to free mediation provided by Her Majesty's Courts and Tribunals Service – see para 8.12.

26 Case study provided by UK Mediation: www.ukmediation.net.

The mediator

1.16 Mediators undertake specialist training.[27] A mediator may work on his or her own or in pairs, either with a lead mediator or as co-mediators.[28] This book describes the facilitative mediation model; other mediation processes include settlement, evaluative and transformative approaches.[29]

Facilitator

Mediators avoid taking sides, making judgements or giving guidance. They are simply responsible for developing effective communications and building consensus between the parties.[30]

1.17 The mediator's role is to manage the mediation process, to facilitate discussions between the parties and to work towards a consensual resolution of their dispute. Facilitative mediation – in contrast to other models of ADR such as arbitration, conciliation or early neutral evaluation (ENE) – does not involve any evaluation or adjudication by the mediator in terms of expressing an opinion or recommending any particular agreement or outcome. The facilitative model of mediation is the most commonly used style of mediation in the UK.[31]

Impartial third party

A structured discussion facilitated by a neutral third party.[32]

1.18 A mediator is required to act, and be seen to act, with impartiality at all times. The mediator is a facilitator and not a judge, expert or arbitrator. Their role is to ensure that each party fairly participates in the mediation process. While the mediator remains impartial and non-judgmental, the mediator controls the mediation process and will, if required, intervene to address power imbalances or ensure fairness.

1.19 The mediator is sometimes described as a 'third party neutral'. Some practitioners resist the use of the word 'neutral' on the basis

27 See paras 12.18–12.32 (civil), 12.33–12.41 (family), 12.42–12.45 (workplace), 12.46–48 (community).

28 This book will refer to a sole mediator for ease of reference when describing the mediation process. Increasingly, mediators are co-mediating or working alongside an assistant mediator.

29 See paras 1.33–1.34.

30 See www.civilmediation.org/about-mediation/29/what-is-mediation.

31 See paras 1.30–1.32.

32 K Mackie, D Miles, W Marsh and T Allen, *The ADR practice guide: commercial dispute resolution*, 3rd edn, Tottel, 2007.

that mediators will remain non-judgmental and impartial and have no vested interest in the outcome of the dispute even where they may not *feel* neutral. Equally, 'impartiality' might suggest that mediators play a passive role, when in fact they take an active part in directing a process which encourages parties to reach an agreement. It is fundamental that parties do not perceive the skill and expertise of the mediator in their specialist field as guiding or directing a particular outcome.

1.20   In facilitative mediation, the mediator does not give their legal opinion or provide other professional guidance. There are several court-annexed schemes where judges have been trained as mediators.[33] Using a mediator should never be seen as an alternative to seeking legal or other professional advice.

Independent

1.21   Mediators should be independent of the parties and have no interest in reaching a particular outcome. The EU code of conduct for mediators[34] requires mediators to disclose any connection or relationship with either party, whether a personal or business relationship, direct or indirect, financial or otherwise. Where there is any potential conflict of interest the mediator should withdraw to preserve the integrity of the mediation process.

1.22   It is not uncommon for one party to fund the mediation, and this can threaten the perception of the mediator's independence. The appointed mediator should be independent of the person paying his or her fees and carefully assess whether the potential power imbalance can be managed within the mediation process. Mediation may also be offered by 'in-house' mediators to address a workplace dispute or as part of the complaints process, such as an issue arising between patient and a hospital.[35] Where an in-house mediation process is used, it remains important to select a mediator who does not know either party or has not had had any involvement in the dispute in order to ensure the mediator's independence.[36]

---

33   For example, the Technology and Construction Court's Court Settlement Process (CSP) – see para 8.33; financial dispute resolution (FDR) in family cases – see para 9.48; judicial mediation in employment tribunal cases – see paras 10.56–10.59.

34   Para 2.1 – appendix H. Also see Family Mediation Council (FMC) Code of Practice paras 5.1.1–5.1.7 – see appendix J.

35   See para 8.16 and 'In-house mediation schemes' at para 10.25.

36   Parties can request a neutral venue and an external mediator.

The mediation process

1.23 The mediation process follows a similar format whether it involves a civil, family, workplace or community dispute.[37] It starts with an initial screening process and assessment of suitability for mediation followed by *pre-mediation meetings* which can take place face-to-face or on the telephone. This is an opportunity for a mediator to familiarise himself or herself with the issues and the parties and gain a greater understanding of the factors which are most significant to each side. An *agreement to mediate* is usually signed at the outset of the process, with some exceptions – such as some types of workplace and community mediation, where this level of formality would not be appropriate.

1.24 Most mediations involve a *joint meeting* between the mediator and the parties. Unless it is a telephone or online mediation, the mediator and the parties would usually meet face-to-face. The *joint meeting* begins with *the opening*. First the mediator and then the parties speak. The mediator talks about the mediation process, the mediator's role and setting the *ground rules*. The ground rules are agreed by the parties, for example, only one person speaking at a time. The purpose of the ground rules is to ensure that the mediation process is fair, impartial and safe and that both parties are heard. Each party is then given the opportunity to explain the dispute from their perspective. This is described as the *opening statement* or *uninterrupted speaking time*. It may be the first time either party has set out the issues which matter most to them, and heard the other party's grievance.

1.25 The mediator then takes the parties through a structured, facilitated discussion described as *the exchange*, in which the mediator asks carefully directed questions to explore all the issues and encourages parties to identify their interests. This includes identifying areas of common ground, as well as any 'green shoots' (such as an apology or acknowledgement) which may provide the basis for an agreement. The stages of the discussion start with *exploring the issues*; this includes identifying the underlying interests which enable parties to *generate options for agreement*. Once the parties have a good understanding of the areas of agreement and disagreement, they are ready to start making offers and counter-offers, working towards an agreement.

1.26 Many mediators choose to conduct the entire process in a *joint meeting*. Civil mediators often begin with a *joint meeting* (sometimes

---

37 See chapter 5 for a fuller exploration of the mediation process.

described as a *plenary*) and then it is common for parties to move to separate rooms. The mediator then speaks in private with each party and conveys messages back and forth (sometimes described as *caucusing* or *shuttle mediation*). When appropriate, the mediator may encourage parties to continue with a *joint meeting*. This model enables a process of open and frank discussion with the mediator without compromising a party's legal case.

1.27   The mediator encourages the parties to generate options and formulate a written agreement. In mediations where no lawyer is present, the mediator will usually help the parties make the written record of the agreement; where lawyers are present the agreement is drafted by the legal representatives. All mediations share the same objective – to reach an agreement, if one is possible. But where an agreement is not reached, the process may still assist by narrowing the issues and improve communication between the parties so that they are able to resolve the dispute between themselves.

Variations to the process

1.28   There are number of variations to this overview of the mediation process:

- *Parties:* There may be two or more parties.
- *Mediators:* There may be one mediator, two co-mediators or a lead mediator working with an assistant mediator or co-mediators.
- *Number of mediation meetings:* The most common format is for the mediation process to take place on one day (for a fixed period of time), although pre-mediation meetings may take place beforehand. Mediations can last several days. Family mediation takes place over a series of up to six meetings.
- *Telephone and online mediation:*[38] In addition to face-to-face meetings, mediation can take place over the telephone or online.

1.29   For the purposes of this book, when the mediation process is discussed it is assumed there are two parties and a sole mediator. Mediation is also suited to resolving disputes where there are multiple parties. It is common practice for mediators to work in pairs as co-mediators or for mediators to use an assistant or trainee mediator.

---

38   See paras 5.68–5.71.

The mediation model

Pre-mediation meetings

The mediator will introduce himself or herself and have the opportunity to establish an understanding of the issues, build rapport with the parties and gain their trust. Pre-mediation meetings may take place on the same day as the *joint meeting*, or beforehand.

The joint meeting

Most mediations involve a *joint meeting* (or series of meetings) which takes place at a neutral venue with all parties present.

The opening

The *joint meeting* will begin with the *mediator's opening*, when the mediator explains his or her role and the mediation process and sets the ground rules. Then each party has the opportunity to set out their views in their *opening statement* or *uninterrupted speaking time*.

The exchange: exploring the issues and getting to interests

The parties exchange their views and clarify issues. The mediator uses a number of techniques, including *re-framing*[39] and *reality testing*,[40] to help the parties explain their positions and identify their interests. In some mediations this takes place in a *joint (plenary) meeting*; in civil mediation the parties will leave the *joint meeting* to go to their private meeting rooms. The mediator will then have *private (caucus) meetings* with each party. Moving between the parties is what is sometimes described as *shuttle mediation*.

The problem solving and settlement stage

The mediator will help parties *generate a wider number of options for agreement*, including looking for any *added value* solutions.[41] Where an agreement is reached it is usually written down and signed. The parties can decide whether or not it will be legally binding and the agreement is signed.

Closing the mediation

The mediator will bring the mediation to an end by providing a copy of the agreement to all those involved in the mediation, or read it aloud. If no agreement has been reached, they will identify where the issues have been narrowed and partial agreement has been reached. The mediator will remind parties that anything that has been said during the process remains confidential and cannot be used in future proceedings. The mediator may conduct follow-up meetings.

---

39 See paras 6.32–6.33.
40 See paras 6.34–6.35.
41 See paras 1.44–1.45 and 4.57–4.61.

Styles of mediation

1.30   There are a number of approaches to mediation. This book focuses on the facilitative model of mediation, which is the approach predominantly (but not exclusively) used in the UK.

Facilitative mediation

1.31   The mediator's role is to manage the mediation process. The mediator may challenge and test each party's beliefs and positions but does not express an opinion on the strengths and weaknesses of the case or impose solutions on the parties. The mediator plays no active role in determining the outcome. Parties decide for themselves a workable agreement.

1.32   The key features of facilitative mediation are that the mediator conducts the process and helps the parties generate their own consensual solutions.

Other styles of mediation

1.33   There are a number of differenct styles and approaches used by mediators.

- In *evaluative mediation* the mediator uses a similar process to facilitative mediation but will provide his or her expert opinion with a view to enabling the parties to reach a settlement.
- In *rights-based mediation* the mediator ensures that any mediated agreement reflects the parties' statutory rights and legal entitlements.
- In *settlement mediation* the mediator focuses more on reaching an agreement and less on exploring emotional and psychological issues. Encouraging parties to compromise in order to reach an agreement, the mediator is likely to be directive, persuasive and interventionist.
- In *therapeutic mediation* a therapeutic approach is used to address the underlying causes of the problem with a view to resolving the dispute.
- In *transformative mediation* the focus is on improving the communication between the parties rather than on achieving settlement.[42]

---

42 See the Institute for the Study of Conflict Transformation at www. transformativemediation.org.

Hybrid model

1.34 'Med-arb' is a combination of mediation and arbitration, though each process is kept separate. Mediation is attempted first, and if no agreement results, the dispute will go to arbitration where a binding decision will be issued. In some cases the same person acts as mediator and arbitrator; in others a different neutral person is brought in to arbitrate.

Mediation methodology

> Skilled mediators are now able to achieve results satisfactory to both parties in many cases which are quite beyond the power of lawyers and courts to achieve.[43]

1.35 The mediation process is informal and flexible – it will vary depending on the parties, the subject matter and the nature of the dispute – but there are some important underlying themes. The mediation process encourages parties to generate creative solutions to their dispute. This can widen the options for agreement and can also include elements which otherwise would not have been considered. Such elements of a potential agreement can be of little or no cost to one party, but invaluable to the other. In some cases, the mediation does not result in an agreement, but by narrowing the issues, identifying common ground and improving communication, relationships can be restored and the potential for future resolution is established.

Engaging with the emotion

1.36 Mediation provides parties with an opportunity to talk about the emotional impact of the dispute. Being able to 'let off steam', be listened to and have the chance to share the emotional impact of the dispute, can allow parties to have their feelings acknowledged and legitimised and thus enable them to move on. By sharing their story they are psychologically able to move forward; this paves the way to thinking about reaching an agreement.

1.37 Many people who go through the court process feel they never got their 'day in court'. In civil cases, claimants often envisage that the court process will be an opportunity publicly to set out their grievance and prove someone 'right' or 'wrong'. In reality, most civil trial processes rely on evidence given in written witness statements and

---

43 Brooke LJ in *Dunnett v Railtrack plc* [2002] EWCA Civ 303, para 14.

any live evidence focuses on discrete areas. Often the areas which have a high emotional value for the party are those which lawyers do not consider relevant and which never get aired in court. By contrast, mediation provides the opportunity to speak directly to the person or people they hold responsible for the dispute.

1.38   Mediation can reach agreements where direct negotiations have failed. The mediation process places a significant emphasis on giving parties the chance to 'tell their story', to vent their frustrations and anger. This can overcome psychological blockages to reaching a resolution and help parties objectively to reflect on their position and be more open to reaching an agreement.

Case study 2: SEN case study – an apology and restored relationship

Communication between Mr and Mrs P and the school attended by their 13-year-old son, T, had deteriorated. T had Down's syndrome and other complex needs, including difficulties with communication. The school, a mainstrem secondary school, had excluded T after he hit one of the other pupils. Mr and Mrs P did not deny that T had hit the boy, but said that the school's treatment of their son amounted to disability discrimination.

His parents felt that the school had not taken T's disabilities into account when considering the appropriate action to take after the incident. The school argued that T's behaviour was not due to his special educational needs, and therefore the school had not discriminated against him because of his disabilities.

The solicitors for the school had used mediation before and felt that it would be a good way to resolve the disagreement and produce a satisfactory outcome for all. The parents' solicitors also agreed that mediation was the best way forward, so, after checking with the two parties that they were also happy to attend mediation, a mediation session was arranged.

At the mediation, the school's head teacher stated that some mistakes had been made by the school regarding T's exclusion and apologised to the parents. She agreed to provide disability discrimination training for all staff. The parents accepted that it had not always been easy to get in touch with them, which had contributed to the deterioration in communication between themselves and the school. They agreed to withdraw their claim on the basis that the school agreed to welcome T back and remove any reference to the expulsion from his record. The school's representatives were also content with the outcome and felt satisfied to have been able to avoid a lengthy and stressful legal process in such a productive way.[44]

Improving communication

> Family mediation is a process in which those involved in family breakdown ... appoint an impartial third person to assist them to communicate better with one another and reach their own agreed and informed decisions ...[45]

1.39 Going to court or tribunal can polarise parties or leave people feeling unheard, worsening an already strained relationship between the parties. Having a grievance resolved through a complaints procedure or an ombudsman may resolve the specific issue but leave parties feeling they want an apology or to address ongoing problems. Mediation aims to provide strategies to improve communication between the parties. Discussing the emotional impact of the dispute can reveal underlying tensions and issues central to the disagreement or dispute. Borrowing skills from non-violent communication (NVC)[46] and cognitive behavioural therapy (CBT),[47] parties are taught to separate the impact and emotion from the actual event or observation (also described as separating the people from the problem).[48] All of these skills can enable parties to communicate more effectively.

Interests not positions

1.40 Mediation invites parties to identify their interests and needs rather than simply setting out their position. It takes as a starting point that parties' positions may appear incompatible, but by exploring their

---

44 Case study from the London SEN Mediation Service. Reproduced with permission of Public Law Project and originally published in V Bondy and M Doyle, *Mediation in Judicial Review: A practical handbook for lawyers* (2011): www.publiclawproject.org.uk/documents/MJRhandbookFINAL.pdf.
45 Family Mediation Council (FMC) Code of Practice – see appendix J.
46 See paras 1.48, 1.54 and 4.35–4.37.
47 See paras 6.59–6.60.
48 R Fisher and W Ury, *Getting to yes*, 2nd edn, Random House, 1999 pp17–40; see also para 4.53.

true interests and needs may reveal a mutually compatible or 'win-win' solution.[49]

1.41 To take a well-used example, two children are arguing over an orange, so their positions are the same and apparently incompatible: they both want the orange. Traditional negotiation techniques using positional bargaining usually end up with one side 'caving in' or both sides compromising, so that neither actually gets what they really want. The automatic reaction of a parent (or a judge) is to intervene to reach a 'fair' outcome and to reach a compromise by cutting the orange in half and giving each child half. However, if one child wants the orange zest for making a cake and the other wants the juice of the orange to make a drink, neither child will have received a satisfactory outcome. By communicating effectively and looking at a party's underlying interests it may be revealed that they have compatible interests.

Future focused

1.42 Mediation encourages parties to explore how they would like things to be in the future. This may mean literally placing a financial value on certainty and an end to a legal dispute, or devising a practical solution to shared childcare. Mediation is less concerned about resolving liabilities for past events than formulating a pragmatic solution. It is focused towards finding an outcome for both parties which addresses their ongoing interests and needs. This does not mean that liability or responsibility is unimportant or not addressed, rather there is a subtle and important shift of emphasis away from fixed determinations of right or wrong towards a more fluid solution-focused approach to resolving the dispute.

1.43 While mediation is sometimes criticised for failing to hold parties to account or resolving liabilities for past events, it can be effective at formulating a pragmatic solution for the future. It is fair to say that one reason mediation is able to reach agreement is because contentious issues are sometimes side-stepped in order to find consensus. Alternatively, issues which appear central to the agreement are re-examined once the underlying interests are identified.

---

49 This concept of principled negotiation is described in the seminal text – R Fisher and W Ury, *Getting to yes*, 2nd edn, Random House, 1999.

Added value solutions

1.44   An important part of the mediation process is that the parties generate ideas, so that any settlement reached will have been formulated
and tailored by them. Barriers to agreement are more likely to be
overcome by self-generated solutions rather than a proposal imposed
or suggested by a third party, judge or arbitrator.

1.45   In some cases, something of little or no monetary value can be
offered as part of the agreement. Gestures of goodwill or a written
apology, for example, may be of no financial value to one party but
have huge significance to the other. The structure of payments or the
offer of a share in equity rather than a lump sum may facilitate an
agreement to be reached when the principles are agreed but the prac-
ticalities have been a stumbling block. These options provide added
value[50] which would not have been available in a court-determined
agreement and enable parties who were previously deadlocked to
reach an agreement.

The emergence of mediation

Roots and branches

1.46   It is useful, for our understanding of the mediation process, to look
at the origins of the mediation model which is now well established
in the UK. Mediation has a rich history, both as an ideology and a
practice.[51]

Non-adjudicative dispute resolution

1.47   The origins of mediation can be seen in the Confucian approach
to dispute resolution. Confucianism was being used in China over
3,000 years ago as an alternative to an adjudicative legal system.
Within Confucianism there is a greater emphasis on the preserva-
tion of social order; where the focus is on improving communication,
building empathy and restoring relationships rather than attributing
blame or fault.

1.48   Going to a third party to help us resolve our disputes is not new.
Across cultures and throughout history, village elders and community
leaders have mediated disputes. In social and religious movements,
which aspire to social cohesion and harmony, the non-violent resolution

---

50 Also see paras 4.57–4.61.
51 Carrie Menkel-Meadow (ed), *Mediation: theory, policy and practice*, Ashgate, 2001.

of conflict is desirable. Principles of conflict resolution through a negotiated, non-adversarial process underpin community models of social
justice and social transformation. The principles of NVC, closely associated with the Quaker movement, inform the mediation process.[52]

Conciliation

1.49   Conciliation is sometimes described as a 'form of mediation' and
has developed as an alternative to the court process. It is now used
primarily in employment disputes and was the term used to describe
early models of mediation used in the family courts and community
mediation.

1.50   Conciliation is a voluntary, private and confidential process using
an independent third party. It differs from facilitative mediation
because conciliators have an evaluative role. Conciliation is used
when an employee is making, or could make, a specific complaint
against their employer to an employment tribunal. If an agreement
is reached it is legally binding on both parties. Conciliation is provided free in employment disputes by ACAS (the Advisory, Conciliation and Arbitration Service). Collective conciliation refers to talks
between representative groups (often trade unions) and employers,
facilitated by an independent third party.

1.51   Conciliation differs from mediation in that the conciliator may
intervene more, by narrowing the issues, recommending solutions
and encouraging parties to make concessions. Parties might choose
not to meet together but the conciliator will encourage parties to see
each other's point of view and to identify their own list of objectives.

Principled negotiation

1.52   The doctrines of 'principled negotiation'[53] underpin many of the
approaches taken by mediators. The mediation process incorporates
these core principles:

- Explore parties' true interests to examine what each party actually needs, rather than arguing over positions.
- Separate people from the problem and divest the emotion
  from the situation. Even in commercial and business disputes
  emotions will have a part to play; understanding this and
  separating the emotion from the issues will be important in
  getting to the heart of the problem.

---

52 See paras 1.54 and 4.35–4.37.
53 For more detailed description of principled negotiation see R Fisher and
    W Ury, *Getting to yes*, 2nd edn, Random House, 1999; and see paras 4.51–4.61.

- Find options for mutual gain, encouraging parties to suggest solutions that are advantageous to both sides. This may involve thinking differently about what issues are under discussion and widening the options for an agreement by examining how a solution satisfactory to both sides might be delivered.
- Negotiate using objective criteria for determining an agreement.

Psychology and psychotherapy

1.53 Psychology teaches us that conflict is not a negative phenomenon. The use of psychology in mediation is examined by Strasser and Randolph[54] who identify that conflict is part and parcel of the human condition. The mediator should not seek to eradicate conflict. Parties may need help from a third party to resolve their dispute and the positive benefits of mediation (which addresses underlying issues, improves communication and restores relationships) provide a social 'bonding' function.[55]

> In the psychotherapeutic paradigm of mediation, the aim in conflict solving is to transcend the antagonistic and emotional stance and move the parties from their initial confrontational position to a more reasonable position.[56]

1.54 Mediators use a wide range of psychological and psychoanalytical approaches, from an awareness of their own body language to active listening, from the use of CBT[57] to the principles of non-directive counselling. Psychology can also benefit a mediator's understanding of how people respond to conflict. A psychological analysis of disputes is that they involve an unmet need or an emotional hurt, and the mediator's role is to uncover it. NVC (also known 'compassionate communication'), as developed by psychologist Marshall Rosenberg in the 1960s, focuses on uncovering the needs and feelings which shape our positions and demands in order to seek alternative solutions to conflict situations in which all needs are met.[58] The unmet

---

54 F Strasser and P Randolph, *Mediation: a psychological insight into conflict resolution*, Continuum, 2004.
55 See paras 2.21–2.25.
56 F Strasser and P Randolph, *Mediation: a psychological insight into conflict resolution*, Continuum, 2004, p24.
57 Cognitive Behaviour Therapy – see paras 6.59–6.60.
58 M B Rosenberg, *Nonviolent communication ... a language of compassion*, PuddleDancer Press, 2002; see the Center for Nonviolent Communication at www.cnvc.org. See paras 4.35–4.37.

need is not always apparent from the issues in dispute but may be a significant barrier to the parties resolving the dispute.

Alternative dispute resolution

1.55   The use of mediation as a formal alternative to resolving legal disputes emerged in the US at the start of the twentieth century. This led to greater acknowledgement of mediation in the UK, which by the late twentieth century saw the growth of court-annexed schemes and encouragement through legal protocols of the need to consider mediation. This increase in the use of alternative or appropriate dispute resolution (ADR) has acted as a catalyst for the growth of mediation. Mediation is the most commonly used of the different methods of ADR.[59]

The growth of mediation in the UK

Mediation in England and Wales

Family mediation

1.56   In the family courts, mediation (or 'conciliation' as it was then known) emerged before the Second World War with a focus on preserving marriage. During the 1970s, there were a number of court-annexed conciliation services for family disputes established across the UK, their remit widening to disputes over custody and access.[60] In 1974 the Finer Report made recommendations to encourage conciliation rather than adversarial relations between divorcing and separating couples. Although these recommendations were not adopted, independent family mediation services began to emerge and the National Family Conciliation Council was established in 1981. In 1985, the Booth Committee[61] led to greater use of court-annexed family mediation conducted by district judges or welfare officers.

1.57   Family mediation is now encouraged for all separating and divorcing couples and, once the changes to family legal aid are implemented, it will be the only publicly funded remedy for most separating couples in private family law cases.[62] Family mediation is also used to resolve other family issues including those relating to the

---

59 See para 8.7 for different types of ADR.
60 *The Finer Report of the Committee on One Parent Families*, Cmnd 5629, HMSO, 1974.
61 Booth Committee *Report of the Committee on Matrimonial Causes*, HMSO, 1985.
62 See paras 9.59–9.62.

care of an elderly relative or a teenager leaving home.[63] The Family Mediation Council (FMC) was set up in 2007 with the aim of over- seeing minimum standards of professional conduct for family medi- ation, which is self-regulated.[64]

Community mediation

1.58 Community mediation services began to emerge in the late 1980s and early 1990s. Many were established to address neighbour dis- putes, including noise nuisance, racial harassment, criminal dam- age and aggressive or anti-social behaviour. Their work has expanded to address disputes within families, workplaces and schools, and between victims and offenders.

1.59 Community mediation services usually rely on trained volunteer mediators. Most community services are used by referral agencies such as housing associations, local authorities and the police. Com- munity mediation was represented by an umbrella organisation, Mediation UK, until 2006.

Civil mediation

1.60 In the late 1980s, as community and family mediation were becom- ing established in the UK, the use of mediation gained credibility as a form of ADR in a legal context. It was then a relatively new form of ADR, but began to be used more widely in the early 1990s, primarily in personal injury and clinical negligence cases. It was not until Lord Woolf's reforms to the civil justice system, including the introduc- tion of the Civil Procedure Rules (CPR) in 1999, that ADR, and in turn mediation, was placed at the heart of the civil justice system.

1.61 Lord Woolf's reforms introduced a codified system of rules to gov- ern the civil courts. The CPR embodied active case management and set out a new approach to civil justice which encouraged people to con- sider going to court proceedings only as a last resort. The pre-action protocols required parties to explore alternative methods of resolving their dispute, including mediation. People going to court could no longer afford to ignore whether their dispute could be resolved using mediation as judges were given the power to impose costs sanctions on those parties who unreasonably refused to mediate.[65] Once a case has been brought to court, the CPR encourages the active manage- ment of cases and judges can direct parties to consider ADR.

63 See paras 11.16–11.18 and 11.74.
64 See paras 12.33–12.41.
65 See paras 8.98–8.107 and rule 44.5(3)(a)(ii).

1.62   Heralded as a cheaper, quicker and more effective remedy than the legal process for non-family legal disputes, the introduction of the CPR has encouraged a significant growth of civil and commercial mediation in England and Wales. Reflecting this, in 2003 the Civil Mediation Council (CMC)[66] was formed to act as an independent body to promote civil and commercial mediation.

1.63   Since 2005, there have been a number of court-based (sometimes described as 'court-annexed') schemes. Free small claims mediation is now available in defended small claims cases, mostly conducted on the telephone by salaried court mediators. Mediation is offered by a large number of providers and accreditation is overseen by the CMC. For parties with limited means, LawWorks[67] is a charity working throughout England and Wales which offers a free service for people unable to afford mediation in civil disputes.

Workplace mediation

1.64   Workplace mediation seeks to restore working relationships and to promote good management and organisational culture. Workplace mediators aim to become involved in resolving workplace disputes at an early stage to increase the opportunity to restore a good working relationship. They may be employees (who have no connection to either party) who act as in-house mediators, or from an external mediation provider.

1.65   Workplace mediation has seen a gradual increase in profile since changes brought about by the Employment Act 2008.[68] Workplace mediators are self-certified and can voluntarily register with the Civil Mediation Council (CMC).[69]

Recent developments

1.66   Since the change of government in May 2010, mediation has achieved even greater prominence. In April 2011, the government introduced compulsory Mediation Information and Assessment Meetings (MIAMs) in private family law cases.[70] By April 2013, automatic referral to small claims mediation will have been introduced and the government continues to explore ways to increase knowledge about

---

66   See www.civilmediation.org.
67   See www.lawworks.org.uk.
68   See para 10.3.
69   See paras 12.42–12.45.
70   See paras 9.8–9.9 and 9.63–9.66.

the use of mediation as a mechanism for resolving disputes.[71] The government has also renewed its commitment to ADR in the Dispute Resolution Commitment (DRC)[72] which requires government departments and agencies to be proactive in the management of disputes, and to use appropriate forms of dispute resolution in order to avoid costly litigation.

1.67   Alongside these domestic developments, the EU Mediation Directive[73] has now been implemented and applies to all EU cross-border disputes. It can be seen as a blueprint for future domestic legislation on the enforcement of mediation agreements and mediation confidentiality in civil and commercial cases.

Mediation in Scotland

1.68   In Scotland, the mediation community has its own code of practice and the Scottish Mediation Register[74] lists all registered mediators who meet its requirements, a process which is overseen by an independent Standards Board and administered by the Scottish Mediation Network.[75] Accreditation is also offered by the Law Society of Scotland for family and commercial mediators.[76]

Mediation in Northern Ireland

1.69   Given its recent history, mediation has played an important role in Northern Ireland. Mediation Northern Ireland[77] is a leading provider of community mediation. The Law Society of Northern Ireland runs the Dispute Resolution Service (DRS)[78] to provide accredited civil mediators from its panel of solicitors and barristers. The Labour Relations Agency[79] provides mediators to assist parties involved in a workplace conflict or dispute.

71 *Solving disputes in the county courts: creating a simpler, quicker and more proportionate system – the government response*, TSO, February 2012 pp11–12, paras 24–28.
72 See www.justice.gov.uk/guidance/mediation/dispute-resolution-commitment.htm.
73 See appendix G.
74 See www.scottishmediation.org.uk/find-a-mediator.
75 See www.scottishmediation.org.uk.
76 See www.lawscot.org.uk/members/membership-and-registrar/accredited-specialists/mediation.
77 See www.mediationnorthernireland.org.
78 See www.lawsoc-ni.org/role-of-the-law-society/resolving-disputes/.
79 See www.lra.org.uk/index/resolving-disputes/mediation-2.htm.

International mediation

Mediation around the world

1.70   The US, Canada and Australia have a long history of mediation and the UK has borrowed heavily from their experience in developing its practices, particularly in civil mediation. The North American experience has explored a number of initiatives to increase the use of mediation: in the US, the concept of the multi-door courthouse, where all new civil claims are screened and directed to appropriate forms of dispute resolution without automatically entering the court process; and in Canada, the introduction of mandatory court-annexed mediation.[80]

1.71   Since the implementation of the EU Mediation Directive in May 2011, an increasing number of European countries, including Germany and Italy, have introduced mandatory mediation. Across Europe in Belgium, Bulgaria, Croatia, France, Ireland, the Netherlands, Poland, Portugal, Romania, Slovenia, Spain and Sweden there is increasing court-regulated mediation and mediation legislation. Throughout the world, mediation is gaining greater prominence. Countries including Brazil, China, Hong Kong, India, Japan, New Zealand, Nigeria, Russia, Singapore, South Africa and UAE have established mediation practices.

International dispute resolution

> Third party mediation has proven to be one of the most important means at the disposal of the United Nations to prevent and resolve deadly conflicts around the world.[81]

1.72   Mediation is frequently described as having played a significant role in the resolution of international conflicts. International diplomacy has always relied on intermediaries enabling discussions where parties are unable to meet face to face. More recently, prominent figures such as US presidents, the secretary-general of the UN and retired politicians have sought to broker agreements between states in conflict or between governments and opposition groups. Over the past decade, the UN has increased efforts to support the development of

---

80   See R G Hann and C Baar, *Evaluation of the Ontario Mandatory Mediation Program (Rule 24.1): final report – the first 23 months*, March 2001 – available at www.attorneygeneral.jus.gov.on.ca/.

81   *Politically speaking*, Bulletin of the United Nations Department of Political Affairs, Summer 2007.

the use of mediation in international diplomacy and this has seen a shift towards the professionalisation of the international mediator.[82]

1.73   In 2008, the UN Department of Political Affairs established a Mediation Support Unit – its work to promote mediation includes the UN Standby Team of Mediation Experts, an 'on call' group of experts that can be deployed individually or as a group to assist mediators in the field.[83] Many non-governmental organisations (NGOs) and charities use mediation as a conflict resolution technique to bring parties to the negotiation table or to support international diplomatic efforts, in particular in small, neutral countries, such as Norway and Switzerland.[84]

Frequently asked questions answered by Sir Henry Brooke

1.74   The following questions have been answered by Sir Henry Brooke, a former Appeal Court judge who became a practising mediator after his retirement and has mediated more than 180 disputes and was chair of the Civil Mediation Council (2007–2012).

Isn't mediation just about compromise?

In civil cases, most disputed claims are compromised before trial, often after great expense has been incurred, much irrecoverable management time has been consumed by businesses, and many individual litigants subjected to considerable stress. A mediation is an occasion when the parties can meet with the help of an experienced third party neutral, whose role is to guide them to an agreed solution of their dispute which they both regard as a fair outcome once they have a clearer appreciation of the strengths and weaknesses of their case. Experience shows that an agreed solution is far more likely to result in immediate payment, thereby averting the further expense and delay and stress which often follows the delivery of an imposed solution by a court before the payment of the sum adjudged due (including legal costs) is actually forthcoming.

82 *A more secure world: our shared responsibility*, Report of the Secretary-General's High-level Panel on Threats, Challenges and Change, United Nations, 2004.

83 See www.un.org/wcm/content/site/undpa/mediation_support.

84 The Swiss organisation SwissPeace and the Norwegian Refugee Council are notable examples, providing expert technical advice, training and mediation support to the EU, UN and national governments.

How can the situation be described as 'win-win' if I don't get everything I want?

I do not use language like 'win-win'. Most cases are settled before trial, and in a long professional lifetime I have seen many litigants starting with ambitious demands and then being willing to accept less when they understand the risks involved in holding out for too much. I have witnessed again and again the pleasure on the faces of all parties when they have reached a solution at the end of a mediation which they consider acceptable and fair.

Mediation is a soft option – I want them hung out to dry!

Everyone is different, and mediation is not to everybody's taste. But I know, from my direct experience, of a great many cases where a party was unwilling to accept the reasonable terms that were available at the end of a mediation and then fared disastrously when they took the dispute on to court. If they can afford it, all well and good, but many litigants cannot afford to lose, and for them mediation offers an ideal way of limiting the risks they run.

CHAPTER 2

Why choose mediation?

> ### Key points
> - Mediation is effective because it shifts the focus, overcomes psychological barriers and produces pragmatic outcomes.
> - Mediation can be cheaper and quicker than the alternatives.
> - Mediation has high satisfaction and success rates.
> - Mediation can reach successful outcomes which are beyond those reached by other forms of dispute resolution.
> - There are limitations to mediation, and parties should be well-informed when making the decision to go ahead.
> - Mediation is a form of alternative dispute resolution (ADR), so parties should consider all options for resolving the dispute when they decide to proceed.

Is mediation an effective remedy?

> Mediation can bring about earlier resolution in cases which are destined to settle and can, on occasions, identify common ground which conventional negotiation does not reach.[1]

2.1   Mediation has the potential to provide more constructive, creative outcomes than would be available through the court process or other conventional remedies. It is also a flexible and inclusive process. Parties remain in control of the outcome and it does not prejudice their opportunity to seek an alternative remedy. But that is only half the story. Commentators have raised concerns about the impact of mediation on access to justice and whether it 'does what it says on the tin'.[2] There also continues to be a surprisingly low take up of mediation. So, does mediation provide the benefits it is claimed to offer? The government is keen to herald 'mediation as often quicker, cheaper and less confrontational than going to court',[3] but does it represent a faster, cost effective alternative way of resolving disputes?

---

1   Jackson LJ, *Review of civil litigation costs: final report*, December 2009, p49, para 4.3.32.
2   See, for example, H Genn et al, *Twisting arms: court referred and court linked mediation under judicial pressure*, Ministry of Justice Research Series 1/07, 2007 p198.; Lord Neuberger MR, *Gordon Slynn Memorial Lecture: Has mediation had its day?* November 2010 para 8.
3   MOJ Press Release, 23 February 2011.

People choose mediation because it is ...

Flexible – Mediation lacks the formality of other dispute resolution processes, making it accessible to everybody. It can be used as easily for reaching agreements between separating couples as for multi-party, complex commercial disputes.

Empowering – Parties enter the process voluntarily and retain control over the outcome.

Creative – Mediation reaches agreements which can provide wide-ranging solutions tailored to the parties' needs and which could not be reached through the courts or other forms of dispute resolution.

Without prejudice and non-binding – If an agreement cannot be reached it does not affect a party's entitlement to take a case to court or pursue an alternative remedy.

Is it quicker?

2.2   Once parties agree to resolve a dispute, civil mediations can be organised relatively quickly and sometimes at very short notice.

Even on a very conservative estimate, mediated settlements occurred several months earlier than among non-mediated cases.[4]

2.3   In small claims (cases with a claim value of £5,000 and less), it takes an average of 29 weeks for a case to be heard in court, with the target to process claims within 15 weeks from case allocation to court hearing. By comparison, the average length of time for a case to be settled through mediation is 5.2 weeks.[5] In higher value claims, much will be determined by when in the mediation process parties decide to mediate.

2.4   In fast-track cases a contested civil trial can take up to 30 weeks to reach court.[6] If requested, and with the co-operation of the parties, a mediation can be organised within a matter of days (although in practice there can be delay in getting everyone to agree). The very

---

4   H Genn, The Central London County Court Pilot Mediation Scheme Evaluation Report for LCD 1998, p2; also see H Genn et al, *Twisting arms: court referred and court linked mediation under judicial pressure*, MOJ Research Series 1/07, 2007 p22.

5   L Bello, *Small claims, big claims: consumers' perceptions of the small claims process*, Consumer Focus, October 2010 pp29 and 39.

6   This is the maximum delay from directions to trial date.

existence of a dispute between the parties, underlying communications breakdown and feelings of distrust can play out in the administration of the mediation, with parties being uncooperative over the choice of mediator, date and time. This can cause delays in setting up the process.

2.5   Mediation does not always take place at an early stage of civil proceedings, so although it can be quicker than alternative remedies that is not always the case. Equally, a large number of civil cases are settled out of court without the need ever to go to mediation.[7] In some cases, an unsuccessful attempt at mediation may actually delay a resolution, or cause a delay so that a party is out of time to lodge a claim.[8]

2.6   In family cases, where there may be up to six mediation meetings, the average time for a case to be completed is three to four months. This compares to nearly four times as long for court cases on similar issues.[9] In workplace disputes, the timescale of mediation will be responsive to the urgency of the issues and the ability of the parties to make themselves available. Community mediations are generally arranged within four to eight weeks of the referral. For disputing neighbours or an unhappy employee, an alternative resolution might be a drastic step, such as moving house or leaving a job. In such cases mediation has the potential to offer a swift result.

2.7   When comparing alternative forms of dispute resolution – a legal challenge, a complaint to an ombudsman or an internal complaints process – mediation provides practical solutions addressing wider issues and (because settlements are consensual) it has higher rates of compliance than court-imposed settlements.[10] Even where a court hearing or formal complaint has been dealt with swiftly, having to enforce a remedy causes further delay. Unlike mediation, the alternatives are unlikely to engage with underlying issues and creative outcomes, so there may be further litigation or time needed to address the underlying issues. Parties who attend mediations can walk away with a signed agreement which represents an acceptable outcome to a previously unresolved dispute and the vast majority will have no further delay (or cost) in enforcing the outcome.

7 See para 2.10.

8 See paras 2.38 and 8.64–8.65.

9 The average time for a mediated case to be completed is 110 days, compared to 435 days for court cases on similar issues – *Legal Services Commission; Legal aid and mediation for people involved in marital breakdown*, National Audit Office, March 2007.

10 See paras 2.19–2.20.

Is it cost-effective?

2.8   On the face of it, mediation is cheaper for parties than going to court in terms of legal fees or other expenses. There are an increasing number of ways to access mediation for free – the small claims mediation service (low value civil cases), judicial mediation in employment cases, community mediation providers, as well an increasing number of civil mediation schemes make no charge to the parties.[11]

2.9   In civil and family mediation, the basic fees will cost an average of £500 per party (with higher rates where more than one mediator is involved). There may, however, be additional costs such as venue and administrative charges, as well as paying a legal adviser (and any expert) to prepare for and attend the mediation – or potentially to review the agreement and draft a legally binding document. In high-end commercial cases, mediators can charge £2,000–3,000 per day (and higher) with additional fees for legal advisers, experts and administration (although these costs may be proportionate to the value of the contested issue and the fees incurred when attending court).[12]

2.10   If an agreement is reached at mediation, this will save parties the considerable legal costs which would otherwise have been incurred if the matter continued to a contested trial. In one study, 90 per cent of legal advisers whose cases had reached mediated settlements, whether for claimant or defendant, thought cost savings had been made.[13] It is hard to calculate the precise savings, however, because a high proportion of cases reach settlement without the need for mediation. In defended small claims cases, around half of cases are settled before the hearing date.[14] In personal injury cases, it is estimated that 95 per cent are settled without the need for formal mediation.[15] In family cases, 90 per cent of private law cases are resolved without the need to go to court.[16] The cost of resolving a dispute using

---

11   In small claims, the HMCTS mediation service is only accessed once parties have paid their claim fee. See paras 5.64–5.66 and 8.12.

12   See paras 3.74–3.81.

13   H Genn et al, *Twisting arms: court referred and court linked mediation under judicial pressure*, Ministry of Justice (MOJ) Research Series 1/07, 2007 pp22 and 180.

14   V Reid and M Doyle, *Small claims mediation – does it do what it says on the tin?* Ministry of Justice (MOJ) June 2007 p7.

15   Evidence submitted by Trust Mediation Limited, cited in Jackson LJ *Review of civil litigation costs: final report*, December 2009 p358, para 36.2.11.

16   The Justice Committee Report: Operation of the Family Courts 2011 para 92.

mediation is estimated to be £535–£753, compared with between £1,682–£2,823 for cases going to court.[17]

2.11   There are financial cost savings to be made with the increased use of workplace mediation. There are direct savings which include avoiding the cost of defending a claim in the employment tribunal, which is estimated to cost an average of £3,800 for businesses and £1,500 for claimants.[18] The indirect savings are a workplace with less absenteeism, greater loyalty and increased productivity, although these cost savings are more difficult to quantify.

2.12   The cost-savings of community mediation are considerable. When compared with legal interventions, mediation costs around £121 (rising to nearly £500 in some complex cases) while anti-social behaviour orders (ASBOs) cost around £2,250 and repossession actions approximately £9,000.[19] In an earlier study, mediation was estimated to cost between £81 and £251 compared with £800 for a housing transfer and nearly £4,000 for a possession order.[20]

2.13   These projected savings make the assumption, of course, that the mediation was successful at bringing the dispute to an end, and in the majority of cases that will be so. But for some parties, mediation may prove a more costly and time-consuming option than pursuing more conventional options. In court-annexed mediation, there is also the considerable cost of administering the process, which requires greater use of court resources than a comparable contested claim. If parties do not reach an agreement, mediation may have caused delay in reaching a resolution and (for privately funded mediations) been a costly expenditure. For parties involved in civil proceedings, the increased costs are estimated to be £1,000 to £2,000.[21] This may not be a wasted cost. Mediation can address misunderstandings and false impressions, clarify and narrow the issues which can save the parties both time and money. In some cases, where no agreement is reached at mediation, the groundwork is laid to enable parties to resolve the issue in the following weeks and months.

---

17   See para 9.62 for an analysis.

18   *Resolving workplace disputes: a consultation*, BIS, January 2011, p19.

19   *The role of mediation in tackling neighbour disputes and anti-social behaviour*, Scottish Executive Social Research 2003 para 8.

20   J Dignan, A Sorsby, J Hibbert *Neighbour disputes – comparing the cost-effectiveness of mediation and alternative approaches*, Centre for Criminological and Legal Research, University of Sheffield, 1996. Also see para 11.8.

21   H Genn et al, *Twisting arms: court referred and court linked mediation under judicial pressure*, MOJ Research Series 1/07, 2007 p iii.

What is a successful outcome?

2.14 When assessing whether mediation is an effective remedy, parties may ask how successful it is at resolving the dispute. It is tempting to look at settlement figures alone. In practice, mediation offers wider benefits to parties who may feel the consequential impact of unresolved conflict. Judging success should also take into account the perceptions and experiences of the parties themselves. Court proceedings, for example, are criticised for leaving people feeling unheard and polarised. Exploring levels of satisfaction may be as important as whether mediation reached an 'agreement', as well as the potential economic and social benefits to wider society.

What is a successful mediation?

Mediation can produce a number of beneficial outcomes:

- narrow the issues;
- enable parties to off-load and voice grievances;
- overcome psychological blockages and misunderstandings;
- prevent further polarising of positions;
- build empathy and greater understanding between the parties;
- improve communication;
- provide longer-term solutions.

Settlement rates

2.15 Parties considering mediation will want to know the likelihood that a resolution will be reached. In the UK, settlement rates for civil mediation range between 70 and 90 per cent.[22] These rates, however, only tell part of the success story. Even where mediation does not achieve an outright settlement, it may narrow the areas of disagreement, clarify the issues and create a better understanding between the parties.

2.16 A number of factors influence the chances of reaching a settlement. The attitude or motivation of the parties, the contribution of their legal advisers, the skill of the mediator, the opportunity for

---

22 For example, 73 per cent settlement rate for small claims mediation – *Solving disputes in the county courts: creating a simpler, quicker and more proportionate system*, Consultation Paper CP6/2011, March 2011, para 141, p88. In commercial mediation, mediators report a 90 per cent success rate (70 per cent settle on the day and 20 per cent shortly after) – *The Fifth Mediation Audit*, CEDR, May 2012, p7. The judicial mediation pilot in employment tribunals had a 72 per cent success rate – see para 10.57.

parties to exchange views and reassess their own position and their willingness to negotiate and compromise are all seen as factors more likely to lead to agreement.[23] When assessing the outcomes of mediation, research has shown that the process starts the ball rolling and removes the emotional obstacles to an agreement. If no agreement is reached at mediation, it is commonplace for a settlement to be reached in the weeks after the mediation has taken place.[24]

Satisfactory outcomes

2.17   Participants in mediation often have positive experiences. Consumer satisfaction is high: 83 to 98 per cent were satisfied with the mediation process according to one survey, whether or not it resolved their dispute.[25] Although this may be a misleading figure as satisfaction with the small claims court process generally is also high, and 'litigants' satisfaction may reflect not objectively fair outcomes but their lowered expectation or lack of awareness of what they are entitled to receive or what other procedures might offer'.[26]

2.18   In many cases mediation reaches solutions not achievable through other forms of dispute resolution. Straightforward apologies or the opportunity for parties to exchange views, overcome misunderstandings and improve communication are not always measured in statistical analyses. Reaching outcomes that restore relationships, and agreements which put in place mechanisms and procedures to prevent the same dispute arising again, provide long-term solutions and are cost saving.

23 H Genn et al, *Twisting arms: court referred and court linked mediation under judicial pressure*, MOJ Research Series 1/07, 2007 pp147–149. See also paras 2.39–2.42.

24 'Monitoring the effectiveness of the government's commitment to ADR 2002–2004', DCA Research Paper, 2005.

25 L Bello, *Small claims, big claims: consumers' perceptions of the small claims process*, Consumer Focus, October 2010, p36.

26 L Wissler, 'Mediation and adjudication in the small claims court: the effects of process and case characteristics', *Law and Society Review*, vol 29, no 2, 1995 p352.

Case study 3: Building dispute

Paul and his wife Suzie decided to have an extension built. Paul gathered many quotations, and enlisted the help of Sam, who had been recommended to him by a friend. Sam agreed to charge £5,000 less than most of the other firms and was able to start immediately. In order for Paul to save more money, he decided to draft the plans for the extension. They both agreed that payment would take place during key points throughout the project.

As the project progressed, some key problems were encountered. Sam realised that Paul had underestimated the number of sockets required and failed to account for damp proofing, which was essential due to a nearby embankment. A joke developed about Paul continually asking Sam, 'Can you just...?' Close to the completion date, Sam gave Paul his bill for the penultimate payment. It was £4,300 more than agreed, taking into account all of the 'Can you just...?' extra jobs. Paul would not pay the bill and Sam refused to complete the work without payment.

As both parties were adamant that the other was in the wrong, it was suggested that they use mediation instead of the small claims court. This way a resolution could take place without the need for court action and a quick resolution was highly likely.

Following mediation and after receiving an itemised bill from Sam, Paul suggested that he pay £2,500 of the extra £4,300 of the 'Can you justs...?' He believed that this was a fair deal after seeing the itemised bill and it would mean that the job was completed for a better price than any of his original quotes. Sam agreed to complete the work for £2,500, as he would still make a good profit on the work and agreed that he should have made Paul aware that the project was going to run well over budget.

Both parties stuck to the agreement.[27]

Compliance

2.19   One measurable benefit of mediation not highlighted as often as its speed and cost-effectiveness is compliance with the resulting agreement. Because parties reach their own agreements, compliance is higher for mediated agreements than court-imposed settlements. In a consumer study of small claims, 87 per cent of mediated cases received full payment, as opposed to 69 per cent of cases won in

27   Case study provided by UK Mediation – www.ukmediation.net.

court.[28] Ministry of Justice research found that only 4 per cent of mediated cases required enforcement action, compared with 19 per cent where a judicial order was made.

2.20   In small claims cases where the judge ordered one party to pay a sum of money, only 27 per cent of parties had received their award in full shortly after the hearing. A further 32 per cent had not received their money within a month of the final hearing.[29] Enforcement action can be costly and potentially futile.

Benefits to the wider community

Benefits to participants

2.21   People who have been through a successful mediation process will have seen the benefits of reaching consensual agreements. An increased awareness of how to communicate more effectively, empathy and reaching mutually beneficial outcomes has the potential to reduce conflict and make parties better at addressing it when it arises in the future. This prevents more complex disputes arising and creates more cohesive societies.

Economic benefits

2.22   Enabling parties to resolve their disputes at an early stage (without going to court or seeking other forms of dispute resolution) saves money. Not only does it save the parties money, it has a significant cost savings to the public purse. Reducing the number of cases which pass through the civil justice system means a consequential reduction in publicly funded legal representation, although the cost of administering mediation should not be overlooked. It has been estimated that civil mediation saves the UK an annual £2 billion. The cost of the mediation services that help achieve these savings is estimated at only £20 million.[30]

2.23   There are also other consequential economic benefits to the wider community. By addressing neighbourhood disputes at an early stage, mediation prevents the situation from deteriorating so that parties don't resort to more extreme and destructive behaviour. The impact of anti-social behaviour on communities cannot be underestimated. Environmental health investigations of noise complaints or police

---

28 L Bello, *Small claims, big claims: consumers' perceptions of the small claims process,* Consumer Focus, October 2010 p37.

29 V Reid and M Doyle, *Small claims mediation – does it do what is says on the tin?* MOJ, June 2007 p9.

30 *The Fifth Mediation Audit,* CEDR, May 2012, p11.

investigations, for example, are all costly. Criminal proceedings and sending people to prison is expensive, both as a fiscal expenditure and in terms of the wider impact on a local community.

2.24   Mediation can help to build a culture of more collaborative problem-solving which has wider economic benefits by improving overall productivity and leading to better economic performance. For the business community, a country that builds a reputation as a place where disputes are minimised and resolved quickly, creatively and cheaply will be a more attractive place to work and invest in.

Benefits to society

2.25   Mediation has wider, less tangible benefits. By restoring relationships and improving communication, it increases business and commercial performance as well as workplace, social and personal relationships. If mediation means that parties overcome the psychological impact of a dispute and generate longer lasting agreements, it creates a more peaceful and harmonious society. There are also other consequential benefits to the national health and well-being. Reducing stress has knock-on cost savings for both the NHS and businesses through a reduction in absenteeism from stress-related ill health.

Case study 4: Workplace grievance

J was a senior manager in a charity. His colleague, P, held a more junior position but was an established member of staff having worked in the organisation for many more years than J. P accused J of undermining and bullying behaviour and had lodged a formal grievance against him.

The charity proposed mediation and J and P agreed. The mediation process enabled both parties to understand each other's positions more fully and various incidents which may have led to communication break down were explored in some detail. The mediation succeeded in reaching an agreement, J agreed to receive management training and the grievance was withdrawn by P.[31]

For a charity, with pressure to avoid unnecessary expenditure, the cost of using an external mediation provider was an investment worth making. It avoided the threat to their reputation and the expense of an employee bringing a claim for constructive dismissal against them as well as enabling their employees to restore their working relationship.

---

31   Case study provided by Commercial and Medical Dispute Solutions (CMDS) – www.cmds.org.uk.

Why mediation works

> [M]ediation often succeeds where previous attempts to settle have failed.[32]

2.26   Parties may ask why mediation is able to reach an agreement when other attempts to resolve a dispute have failed. Direct negotiations may have broken down or previous attempts at face-to-face discussions may have resulted in deadlock or an escalation in tensions.

Shift of focus

2.27   The involvement of the mediator as a neutral third party enables individuals to overcome impasse and deadlock because it invites them to move away from their fixed positions and widen the options for agreement. It is not uncommon for parties who have adopted a positional bargaining approach to make incremental concessions but be unable to close the final gap.

2.28   As a third party in the room, the mediator is able to absorb some of the tensions and frustration in these situations. Their presence enables people to communicate more effectively and avoid point-scoring or a combative and aggressive approach. In civil mediation, this removes the adversarial approach of litigation. Mediators can prevent discussion from deteriorating into a style of negotiation which can escalate tensions and polarise views. Through face-to-face discussions they are able to employ techniques which de-escalate tensions by reframing negative or antagonistic remarks. By encouraging parties to separate the facts and events from their assumptions about behaviour and motive, they are able to uncover misunderstandings which may have triggered or escalated the dispute.

Flexibility

2.29   The mediation process is flexible. It can happen at a place and time convenient to the parties and accommodate disabilities and additional or special needs. It is possible to mediate a vast array of disputes, ranging from playground bullying to international conflicts. In particular, mediation can be effective in multi-party or multi-agency disputes where other forms of dispute resolution have failed to achieve a practical outcome.

---

32   Dyson LJ in *Halsey v Milton Keynes General NHS Trust* [2004] EWCA Civ 576 para 20.

2.30   The fact that mediation can occur quickly without any formal process having to be followed means that it can be an effective form of dispute resolution. It could be used, for example, to avoid a construction project being de-railed where a conflict has arisen between contractors, or where a breach of contract is alleged it can enable commercial and business relationships to return to normal.

Overcoming psychological obstacles

2.31   Mediation enables parties to listen and be listened to and have the impact of a past event acknowledged. This can allow them to off-load and overcome psychological obstacles to reaching agreement. Even in commercial or corporate disputes, psychology often creates a barrier to reaching a negotiated settlement.

2.32   At the most basic level, it is important to explore why a parties have been unable to resolve their dispute. Individuals and organisations pursue unresolved disputes for a number of reasons, including:

- to redress a wrongdoing;
- to make a point;
- to punish the other side;
- to have the other party 'judged' as wrong;
- to be vindicated;
- as a point of principle.

2.33   Conventional dispute resolution often fails to address or acknowledge these psychological issues. The process of mediation may enable parties to shift beyond these positions and explore what outcomes would actually address their underlying needs and interests. Exploring these issues can enable them to reach an agreement.

Creative, practical solutions

2.34   The mediation process encourages parties to generate wider options for agreement and solutions with added value. Mediators may educate or coach parties so that they are able to negotiate more effectively and explore win-win or mutually beneficial outcomes. Concessions or offers may have little or no cost to one party, for example, but would have huge significance to the other. Widening the options for agreement and providing added value could include offering an apology or giving an undertaking to change a practice or policy or adapting the timescale of any settlement and its terms. The detail of any agreement can often provide added value, such as paying in instalments rather than a lump sum, and therefore overcome barriers to its achievement.

2.35   In contrast to an adversarial or adjudicative process, mediation empowers parties to think creatively about possible solutions. It also enables them to reach agreements or make offers which are outside the legal or procedural framework. For many parties, reaching a practical solution which puts in place the steps which will ensure what has been agreed is actually implemented is essential to reaching a consensual agreement. The certainty of outcome and implementation cannot be ensured by other dispute resolution processes.

Case study 5: Separating couple

Sam and Jane had separated when Anita was 4 months old; Sam had not seen his daughter since then. By the time she was 2, there were contested court proceedings in respect of both contact and financial provision. Contact was awaiting completion of a psychological report on Sam; their barristers suggested that the issue of finance alone be referred to mediation to reduce costs, costs on each side already being £7,000.00. Over six mediation sessions, an agreement was reached over finance and sufficient trust was gained for there to be both discussion and conclusion in respect of contact arrangements, all proceedings being withdrawn.

Jane: 'This time a year ago I would never have dared hope that I would be where I am now. The consequences of the on-going legalities had it not taken the route of mediation, don't bear thinking about ... Best of all, Anita is a happy, well-balanced child, with at least some form of contact with her father – something I am sure would not have evolved had we not had you both to guide us through a legal and personal nightmare ...'.[33]

---

33 Case study provided by the Family Mediators Association (FMA) – www. thefma.co.uk.

The limitations of mediation

'Just' outcomes

> The outcome in mediation is not about just settlement, it is just about settlement.'[34]

2.36 There is some evidence to suggest that the financial agreements reached in civil mediation are of lower value than the amount parties would have received if they had gone to court and won; in small claims, mediated cases settle for about 55 per cent or two-fifths of the original claim.[35] This may be partly to do with the possibility that the original claim figure was inflated or unrealistic.[36] While claimants should be wise to the fact that mediation may result in a lower settlement, such results could also be misleading. How do you assess whether a claim would have been successful in court, and the value? Equally the cost savings that may have been achieved from resolving the matter could off-set the reduced damages.

2.37 Comparing settlement amounts may also overlook the less tangible benefits of the process, such as 'closure', a restored relationship, an apology or a practical outcome such as the method and timing of payment. For separating couples, reaching an agreement without legal proceedings destroying their strained relationship may enable parents to overcome obstacles to shared contact with their children. For a mother, this may off-set the less favourable financial settlement she obtained through mediation.

> ... mediation is a facilitative process, designed to arrive at a mutually acceptable outcome rather than the legally correct result; accordingly mediation ... carr[ies] with it the risk that claimants would be under-compensated ...[37]

2.38 In legal cases, parties will be reliant on their legal adviser to help weigh up whether they have achieved a 'just' settlement. This is particularly important in cases where complex calculations such as compensation for future needs are being considered, for example, care needs in personal injury cases or pension entitlements in employment claims.

---

34 H Genn, *Judging Civil Justice – The Hamlyn Lectures 2008*, Cambridge University Press, 2010, p117.

35 H Genn et al, *Twisting arms: court referred and court linked mediation under judicial pressure*, MOJ Research Series 1/07, 2007 pp21–22.

36 L Bello, *Small claims, big claims: consumers' perceptions of the small claims process*, Consumer Focus, October 2010 p39.

37 H Genn, *Judging Civil Justice – The Hamlyn Lectures 2008*, Cambridge University Press, 2010.

Provided a party receives high quality legal advice, they will be making any decision freely and without pressure. Other factors may be weighed in the balance – the fact that the defendant is more likely to comply with the terms of the settlement, underlying issues may have been addressed and the considerable stress of ongoing legal proceedings and living with unresolved conflict will have been brought to an end. There are risks, however, that a party who has not received legal advice may undertake mediation and agree to a settlement that is considerably less than their entitlement or allow the time within which a claim needs to be lodged to elapse.[38]

Quality of the mediator or the mediation process

2.39   Research suggests that outcomes at mediation can be influenced by the skills and ability of the mediator.[39] Where the mediator lacks the confidence to manage the process, or use the *joint meeting* effectively to allow parties to express their feelings and explore underlying interests, there may be some mediations where parties leave the process feeling the situation between them has worsened. It may also be the case that some parties enter the mediation process with ulterior motives[40] – in such cases there is the potential that the mediation process will be used to identify weaknesses in the other party's case and gain tactical advantages. It takes a skilled mediator to identify cases where this arises and draw them to an end.

2.40   Not all mediation processes enable parties to find creative outcomes and explore underlying issues. In small claims telephone mediations, for example, the parties may not speak directly with each other at all. In civil mediation, the use of 'shuttle mediation'[41] means there is little or no dialogue between parties. In time-limited mediation, some participants have observed that pressure placed on them during the mediation process was positive (and necessary for parties to settle their issues). Others felt the time pressure had a negative effect.

2.41   For certain types of cases, a time-limited settlement-focused process might be appropriate, as is used by the small claims mediation

38   See paras 8.64–8.65.
39   H Genn et al, *Twisting arms: court referred and court linked mediation under judicial pressure*, MOJ Research Series 1/07, 2007 p iii; Justice Select Committee, 6th Report, Operation of the Family Courts, June 2011, para 123.
40   See paras 4.43–4.44 on the importance of good faith.
41   See paras 5.13–5.14.

service. Where parties have a financial dispute and they are looking for a quick and pragmatic settlement.

> I expected to have to pay some money but probably paid a little more than I'd anticipated beforehand ... I was happy at the end of the day, it was a settlement and the thing was put to bed which was fine.[42]

2.42 Parties have described the small claims mediation process as a 'mild form of bullying', 'sophisticated head banging ... and I'm not sure it's that sophisticated either'. '[P]arties felt coerced rather than empowered', and felt that an unreasonable amount of pressure was placed upon them to find a settlement.[43]

Power imbalances

2.43 Baruch Bush and Folger[44] have evaluated mediation in the UK and identified four distinct rationales:

- 'satisfaction' – mediation as a process is 'satisfying human needs and reducing suffering for parties to individual disputes';
- 'social justice' – mediation builds stronger community ties, for example tenants involved in a neighbour dispute may be united in a shared grievance with their landlord;
- 'transformative' – mediation can help people gain greater self-respect, self-reliance and self-confidence;
- 'oppression' – mediation increases/magnifies imbalances of power, for example in cases where an individual is challenging a public authority or for some women in family mediation.[45]

2.44 The benefits of mediation are widespread and far-reaching, but the oppression rationale cautions against its use without safeguards to protect vulnerable parties and avoid imbalances of power. It is important that a large company is not able to use mediation to encourage an uninformed party to settle potentially costly litigation for a derisory sum; or a husband to agree to provide an ex-partner with ongoing

---

42 M Doyle, *Evaluation of the Small Claims Mediation Service at Manchester County Court*, 2006 p90.

43 J Enterkin and M Sefton, *An evaluation of the Exeter Small Claims Mediation Service*, DCA Research Series 10/06, 2006 p71.

44 RA Baruch Bush and JP Folger, *The promise of mediation: the transformative approach to conflict*, Jossey-Bass, 2005. See also C Harrington and S Merry, 'Ideological production: the making of community mediation', 1988 22(4) *Law and Society Review* 709; and J Auerbach, *Justice without law*, Oxford University Press, New York, 1983 p57.

45 The authors identify that the 'neutrality' of the mediator has the potential to address power imbalances.

financial support which is substantially below than that which a court would order. It is not the role of facilitative mediators to ensure parties receive a 'just' outcome from mediation.

2.45   Mediation does have some safeguards against the risks of power imbalances. It is voluntary – parties who are concerned about a potential imbalance of power do not have to participate. In many cases the agreements reached are non-binding. In family and community mediation in particular, the screening process should reveal power imbalances and any other welfare concerns. Alternatively, where the agreement would be binding and involve legal rights and entitlements, parties are always encouraged to receive high quality legal advice.

Access to justice

> Mediation is a complement to justice. It cannot ever be a substitute for justice.[46]

2.46   Mediation is the most commonly used form of alternative dispute resolution (ADR). This is because it is cost-effective, non-binding and can achieve successful outcomes quite beyond the scope of legal proceedings. However, mediation is not always the most appropriate form of dispute resolution. Parties who are unwilling to work collaboratively can obstruct the process, so that however many incentives and deterrents are put in place, it will remain an ineffective remedy. A careful balance must always be struck between encouraging parties to consider mediation and preserving its voluntary nature.

> ... to oblige truly unwilling parties to refer their disputes to mediation would be to impose an unacceptable obstruction on their right of access to the court.[47]

2.47   Preserving the voluntary nature of mediation is essential to ensuring that power imbalances do not undermine its effectiveness as a tool for dispute resolution.[48] It ensures that individuals have access to justice against parties who are more powerful than themselves: large companies and government agencies; employers and landlords; bullies and aggressors.

---

46 Lord Neuberger MR, The Gordon Slynn Memorial Lecture, *Has mediation had its day?* November 2010, p14.

47 Dyson LJ in *Halsey v Milton Keynes NHS Trust* [2004] EWCA Civ 576.

48 See paras 2.43–2.45.

In spite of the considerable benefits which mediation brings in appropriate cases, I do not believe that parties should ever be compelled to mediate.[49]

Frequently asked questions answered by Margaret Doyle

2.48 The following questions have been answered by Margaret Doyle, who is an independent mediator specialising in equalities and discrimination disputes, including education and consumer issues. She is a consultant in dispute resolution and works with the legal advice sector and a number of ombudsmen schemes as well as managing ADRNow, a website offering accessible information on dispute resolution.

Why would you recommend a friend use mediation to resolve a dispute?

I wouldn't necessarily recommend it. I'd start with helping them think about what they want to achieve. Is it an apology, an acknowledgement, financial redress, a change in procedure, a legal ruling, revenge? Then I'd help them identify what process is most likely to enable them to achieve that. If they want revenge, they won't get that in mediation, or in court, or from an ombudsman.

I'd also help them explore whether the other side would engage in mediation in good faith – is there likely to be some degree of trust and willingness to discuss with an open mind. Then there are practical issues to consider – urgency, cost, who needs to attend. There are lots of factors to consider – it's not one size fits all!

That said, I would wholeheartedly recommend that my friend use mediation if she wants control over the outcome and she wants to have her say and be heard. It is the only dispute resolution process that provides such a powerful opportunity for the parties to understand each other and to reach sustainable agreements.

---

49 Jackson LJ, *Review of civil litigation costs: final report*, December 2009 p361, para 36.3.4.

How do I decide whether my case is suitable for mediation?

First, ask yourself a series of questions.

- Is your problem urgent – do you need to get someone to do something or stop doing something immediately? If so, mediation won't be your first choice – you might need an injunction, or the police.
- Do you want to mediate? Are you interested in discussing the issues with the other side, hearing their position, clarifying yours?
- Is what you want achievable in mediation – or are you more likely to get what you want by using another process?
- Do you have access to independent advice if you need it? Remember that a mediator can't advise you or the other party.

If the answers to those questions indicate that mediation might be suitable, then weigh up the cost – can you afford to mediate? Whether or not mediation is cheaper than other options depends on the context. There are lots of ways to pay for mediation, and lots of different providers with different fee ranges. Again, if you can get independent advice, this can help you identify what types of mediation providers there are for your dispute, and what the charges are. You can also look on www.adrnow.org.uk, a website run by Advice Services Alliance, which gives objective information on dispute resolution.

Mediation is voluntary, so it is only suitable if both parties are willing to give it a try. You will need to identify whether the other side will participate in good faith and will send the right people to the mediation, people who have the authority to make a binding settlement. The mediator or mediation service can help you with this.

How will I know if I got a fair outcome?

What's a fair outcome? It's a serious question. Mediators generally say that a 'fair' outcome is one the parties agree to. In a sense it's relative – if you start with the premise that a decision to mediate is based on what you want to achieve, then it follows that you will judge the outcome against your expectations. Of course, your expectations might be unrealistic, in which case you can achieve a fantastic outcome that you feel isn't fair – and that can happen in court as much as in mediation.

But you might also achieve far more than you expect in mediation – such as long-term changes in behaviour or procedures, a genuine apology, an explanation of what went wrong, improved communication, even a repaired relationship.

A fair outcome isn't necessarily the same outcome you'd get in court, although it can be useful to have a sense of the legal strength of your case. Individuals and organisations make pragmatic decisions about what they can live with – they settle hopeless cases, they weigh pros and cons, they set their own priorities. The fundamental safeguard to ensure fairness, in my view, is that parties are well informed and know what their options are before they make any decision that closes the door to other dispute resolution routes.

Also, fairness can be related to how someone achieves an outcome, their experience of taking part in the process, and not just the outcome itself.

Isn't mediation an opportunity for large companies to avoid their legal obligations and make deals behind closed doors?

Yes! I know I shouldn't say this, but the reality is that confidentiality of settlements is usually more attractive to respondent organisations than it is to individual complainants. It's an incentive to settle – whether that's settling through negotiations conducted by lawyers, or settling with the help of a mediator. Organisations – whether they are companies or public-sector bodies – see a reputational risk in being involved in disputes, and they see a commercial risk in being seen as buying off claimants.

But it is also an opportunity to hold large companies to account, to increase access to justice, if mediation makes it less daunting for individuals to challenge institutions. Furthermore, it's not a given that all aspects of a mediated agreement remain confidential, particularly where there is a wider public interest and where procedural changes have been agreed that will affect others. Part of the mediation discussion is about what both parties agree can be made public – which might be the entire settlement agreement, aspects of the settlement, or a public statement.

PART II

The mediation process

CHAPTER 3

How to set up a mediation – the practicalities

continued

> ## Key points
> - The prerequisites to mediation are that there is another party to the dispute, there is a willingness to mediate and the remedy sought is achievable through mediation.
> - Legal advice (or expert advice) should be sought before parties seek to reach a binding agreement in mediation and cease litigation.
> - Encouraging the other party to mediate can be challenging. A mediation provider may be able to bridge the gap.
> - The steps to setting up a mediation include jointly selecting a mediator (or mediation provider), the time and date, the venue and who will attend the mediation.
> - Jointly selecting the mediator or mediation provider is something parties should undertake with care and consideration.
> - The screening process, particularly in family and community mediation, ensures that the mediation process can take place safely without putting the parties or mediator at foreseeable risk.
> - Parties are usually asked to sign a pre-mediation agreement before the mediation process begins.

Choosing mediation

3.1   If a person or organisation finds themselves in an unresolved dispute with another party or parties, what steps do they need to take if they wish to consider mediation as a way of resolving their issues?

Routes to mediation

3.2   Parties arrive at mediation when they:

- suggest mediation as a way of resolving a dispute;[1]
- have been referred to a mediation provider by a third party;[2]
- have been required to consider mediation by a policy or contract clause;[3]
- have been invited to respond to an offer to mediate.[4]

1   See paras 3.17–3.22.
2   See para 3.23.
3   See paras 8.66–8.67.
4   See paras 3.24–3.38.

3.3   In civil mediation, judges are increasingly encouraged to actively manage cases and this includes identifying those cases where mediation may be suitable.[5] Parties are responsible for finding a mediation provider, a service formerly provided by the National Mediation Helpline (NMH) which has been replaced by the Civil Mediation Online Directory.[6] There are also a number of free or low-cost schemes.[7]

3.4   In family cases, it is envisaged that separating couples will first try to resolve issues between themselves and if unable to resolve their issues, they then approach a mediator (rather than going to court).[8] As a way of trying to bring about this change of mindset, the government has made attending a Mediation Information and Awareness Meeting (MIAM) a pre-requisite to court proceedings in private family law matters.[9]

3.5   In workplace disputes, parties may be offered the opportunity to mediate through an in-house scheme or referred to an external mediation provider.[10]

3.6   In community mediation, some mediation services are able to offer free mediation to all local residents.[11] Other community mediation services provide mediation, usually free of charge, through referrals from a third party agency such as local authority or housing officer.[12]

Timing of mediation[13]

3.7   As a general rule, mediating at an early stage is more effective because parties have not yet become entrenched in fixed positions. The reality is, however, that parties may not feel ready to meet together until the issues have clarity or the intense feelings of anger or resentment have subsided. As a result, mediation commonly occurs when disputes have been ongoing for some time. Mediation requires the voluntary participation of parties, and the decision whether to mediate can be re-considered at any stage.

---

5 See paras 8.34–8.50 on CPR and active case management.
6 See para 3.47.
7 See paras 8.10–8.33.
8 *Family Justice Review: final report*, November 2011 p162.
9 See paras 9.63–9.66.
10 See paras 10.25–10.28.
11 For example, Ealing Mediation Service accepts self referrals from any local resident – see http://ealingmediation.org.uk/Starting-Mediation.
12 See paras 11.4–11.6 and 11.31.
13 Also see paras 8.37–8.50 (civil), 9.40–9.50 (family), 10.19 (workplace), 11.61–11.62 (community) on when to mediate.

The earlier the better

> Mediation should be attempted as early as possible.[14]

3.8   Most mediators agree that settlements are more easily reached before the dispute has developed into a long-running feud or lengthy litigation. If the underlying desire is to restore relationships and improve communication, this can be done most effectively at an early stage while there is an opportunity to de-escalate a tense or highly charged situation. This has clear advantages – for example, in workplace or construction disputes, being able to mediate at an early stage enables an employee to remain in the workplace or a building project to continue. It is easier to explore creative and practical outcomes which legal proceedings cannot achieve such as apologies, provision of a reference or future work. Where legal proceedings have begun, costs are immediately incurred and continue to rise. If parties delay in mediating, high costs may have accrued, and this can present a barrier to a mediated resolution as parties have a primary need to recover their legal expenses. Where third parties, such as housing officers, refer parties to mediation swiftly, a deterioration in a neighbour dispute can be avoided, saving time and expense.

3.9   Parties who mediate at an early stage are more likely to reach agreement,[15] the higher settlement rates may reflect the fact that the issues were less difficult to resolve or that the circumstances enabled parties to work collaboratively. There is also an element of self-selection – parties who choose mediation may be more co-operative and therefore more likely to reach an agreement.

Can it be too soon to mediate?

3.10   In some cases it may be too early to mediate. In family cases where relationship breakdown has left one party more greatly affected than the other, the emotional hurt can create resentment and it would not be appropriate for the more emotionally vulnerable party to be considering long-term decisions.[16]

3.11   In civil proceedings, parties are usually only able to mediate once they have sufficient information about the other party's case and evidential certainty. In a few cases, encouragement to mediate too early may require parties to invest in legal advice or expert opinion when

14 Legal Services Commission (LSC) Funding Code, Part C, 3C-102, para 9.
15 See, for example, N Gould, C King and P Britton, *Mediating construction disputes: an evaluation of existing practice*, King's College London, Centre of Construction Law and Dispute Resolution, 2010 p14.
16 See para 9.43.

subsequently the case will prove to be groundless and parties will have explored mediation unnecessarily.

Evidential certainty or clarity of issues

> Broadly, when a case is ready for settlement negotiations, it is ready for mediation.[17]

3.12   Mediation may be premature if the issues between the parties are vague or uncertain. There may be factual or legal matters that require clarification, and things may be clearer once a formal, official or legal procedure is commenced, for example:

- an official complaint;
- a formal complaint, grievance or disciplinary process;
- legal advice has been sought;
- tribunal or court proceedings are initiated.

3.13   These processes may clarify issues, and be a motivating factor in encouraging a party to consider mediation and provide an incentive for resolution. Parties should be aware, however, that formalising the dispute may also be perceived as an aggressive, litigious stance which can intimidate the party on the receiving end and deter efforts to find a resolution.

3.14   In civil mediation, there are *settlement phases* triggered by stages of the trial process when mediation should be (re)considered. For example, at the pre-action protocol (letter before claim), post-permission or allocation questionnaire; case management conference; and pre-trial review stages.

Litigation or conflict fatigue

3.15   Mediation is often only considered once a situation has deteriorated or litigation has been underway for some time. Just as making a dispute formal by making a complaint or issuing legal proceedings may provide impetus to resolve matters, parties are often only willing to consider mediation once the reality of an impending trial or hearing is imminent. Parties often try mediation when they feel they 'have nothing to lose'.

3.16   Where there has been a long-standing issue between the parties and alternative attempts to resolve issues or find a remedy have failed

---

17 See Court Mediation Service Manual, March 2009 p7 – available at www.judiciary.gov.uk/.

to reach agreement, parties come to mediation because they want to bring an end to the dispute. This means, even at a late stage, or once the parties have become embittered and entrenched, parties enter mediation actively seeking a solution which increases the chances of it being effective.

Case study 6: Probate dispute – it's never too late

In the week before a final hearing, which followed two years of litigation, all parties attended a mediation at the suggestion of the judge. The case involved five siblings and their parents' will. The primary issue was whether the youngest brother had acquired a beneficial interest in the family home. The judge had already ruled on this issue, now remained the resolution of costs, apportionment of the equity including whether the estranged brother would be entitled to occupier's rent.

The siblings attended the mediation with mixed levels of reluctance. After a brief opening session, where only the lawyers spoke, the parties returned to their separate rooms. The mediation lasted over four hours. The imminent prospect of a trial, the escalating costs and the fact that costs considerations may have forced the parties to appear as litigants in person generated pressure which was used constructively to explore an agreement. The necessity of a trial was ultimately avoided and the agreement reached represented a mutually acceptable division of the assets.

Initiating the mediation process

Proposing mediation

3.17   Having decided that mediation would be an appropriate way to resolve a dispute, parties have two options: to propose mediation directly, or to contact a mediation provider who will then contact the other party.[18] Encouraging parties to find out more about the process is important – research has shown that parties who do not pursue mediation would have done so if they had known more about it.[19]

---

18   See para 3.22.
19   National Audit Office, *Legal aid and mediation for people involved in family breakdown*, March 2007 p15 – available at www.nao.org.uk/.

Isn't agreeing to go to mediation a sign of weakness?

3.18   An offer to mediate is proactive and assertive. However, it is reasonable to anticipate that the other party may treat the offer of mediation with some suspicion, scepticism and possibly as an indication of weakness. For this reason, it may be helpful for a party clearly to set out their reasons for using mediation. This is also why requesting a mediation provider to contact the other party may prevent an offer of mediation from being misconstrued or worsening an already tense situation.[20]

3.19   In legal proceedings, inviting another party to mediate suggests that a case has been well-prepared; that a party has a good measure of the strengths (and weaknesses) of their case and of the likely outcome if the matter proceeds to trial; and that they are looking to avoid the further delay and expense of ongoing legal proceedings.

How to propose mediation?

3.20   In contrast to civil litigation, mediation is a collaborative form of dispute resolution. Parties can use their offer to mediate to signify a genuine interest in reaching a mutually acceptable agreement. Where appropriate, it can be helpful to mention that mediation is an opportunity to explore practical outcomes that cannot be achieved through legal proceedings. This may minimise any concern the other party may feel that the offer to mediate is not genuine.

3.21   The proposal should be in writing, setting out the reasons why mediation is appropriate in this particular case and the statutory guidance or legal framework which encourages the use of appropriate or alternative dispute resolution.[21]

Using a mediation provider to approach the other party

3.22   It may be more effective for an independent mediation provider to approach the other party directly and seek to persuade them of the benefits of mediation.[22] A lack of knowledge of mediation often means parties (and their legal advisers) are not convinced that it is worth considering. A mediation provider may also be able to address any

---

20 See para 3.22 on using a mediation provider; and paras 3.25–3.29 on encouraging an unwilling party.
21 See para 8.51 on proposing mediation.
22 See paras 3.25–3.29 on encouraging an unwilling party to mediate.

concerns and overcome psychological issues which would otherwise mean parties fail to give the proposal reasonable consideration.[23]

Referral to mediation

3.23 A court may refer parties to mediation (or actively encourage them to consider an alternative form of resolving the dispute). Parties may also be referred to mediation by a clause in a contract.[24] Some parties are referred to mediation by their employer – this may be to an external mediation provider if an internal mediation scheme is not in place. Others may be offered mediation by third party agencies such as housing associations or the local council.

Responding to an offer to mediate

> Whilst ADR should always be considered at the outset and prior to issuing proceedings, ADR should be re-considered on an ongoing basis.[25]

3.24 An offer to mediate should always be carefully considered. It is, of course, open to parties who are invited to mediate to say 'No'. Parties should be mindful that in civil cases an unreasonable refusal to mediate carries cost sanctions.[26] In civil cases, the reasons for refusing mediation should be recorded in writing.[27] The fact that mediation can take place and be effective at any stage of a dispute means that the decision whether to mediate needs to remain under consideration throughout the litigation process.

Encouraging unwilling parties to mediate

3.25 Where one party has indicated a willingness to mediate, or both parties have been referred to mediation, the mediator or the appointed member of staff within the mediation provider will get in touch with the other party or parties. This usually marks the beginning of the process of mediation.

3.26 The mediator or administrator has to find a delicate balance between setting out the advantages of mediation, while remaining impartial. Their initial task is to 'listen' and answer questions about

---

23 See paras 4.77–4.78 on making the first offer; para 6.69 on reactive devaluation.
24 See para 8.66.
25 LSC Funding Code: Decision Making Guidance 3C-102, para 9.
26 See paras 8.98–8.107 on costs sanctions.
27 See paras 8.52–8.65 on responding to an offer.

the mediation process. They will encourage parties to discuss any anxieties they may have about the mediation process and allow parties to off-load where appropriate. They may discuss possible strategies to overcome the party's concerns.[28] Throughout, open and non-judgmental language will be used to reassure parties of the mediation provider's neutrality.

3.27   Mediators or administrators must be careful not to disclose any information from a conversation with one party to another party, unless they have obtained the party's consent. Where it would be helpful to explain to an unwilling party the initiating party's reasons for pursuing mediation, this must first be discussed with the initiating party. Mediators or administrative staff can 'anticipate some resistance, ignorance or suspicion'[29] as parties are likely to be distrustful of another party's motives.

3.28   The mediation provider can ascertain factors that may make mediation a more appropriate remedy, such as the need for a quick resolution of the issues, the need for a practical solution and the fact that alternative remedies will not address the underlying issues. Other factors include the avoidance of adverse publicity or damage to their reputation, cost-savings and the desirability that the relationship between the parties be restored.

3.29   In some cases, mediation providers may advise parties that mediation is unlikely to be an effective remedy.

Concerns raised by legal advisers and parties[30]

3.30   In many cases, parties are unfamiliar with the mediation process and will have concerns about participating in a mediation, which can be addressed by an experienced administrator or mediator. Alternatively, the mediation provider may suggest the parties speak directly to a mediator who may be able to talk through any concerns.[31] In family mediation, a more formal process of a Mediation Information and Assessment Meeting (MIAM) can enable parties to speak with a mediator about any of these issues. Concerns raised by legal advisers and parties include the following:

---

28   See paras 3.22, 3.30–3.33 and 8.56–8.65.
29   L Boulle and M Nesic, *Mediator skills: triangle of influence*, Bloomsbury Professional, 2010 p22.
30   See also paras 8.56–8.65.
31   See para 3.40.

The issues can be resolved more simply

3.31   There are situations where parties are able to resolve issues between themselves or through their lawyer to lawyer negotiations. In such cases, mediation is not necessary. Likewise, a straightforward application to court to obtain an injunction, or enter summary judgment,[32] may resolve matters. Mediation should always be considered where there is an ongoing relationship with the other party and where there are wider issues which could helpfully be resolved. Combining mediation with court proceedings can be effective – for example, obtaining an injunction or issuing proceedings and then proposing mediation.

Mediation is unlikely to succeed

3.32   Parties may already have tried to resolve their issues and failed. They may have tried to speak with one another or had lawyer-to-lawyer negotiations which have made the situation between the parties worse or ended in stalemate. Mediation can achieve outcomes that are not otherwise possible by speaking face-to-face because the presence of a third party facilitates communication. The mediation process is also designed to overcome psychological obstacles and help parties reflect upon their needs and underlying interests so that offers are objectively considered. This can also produce solutions which are more collaborative and address wider issues than direct negotiations.

3.33   In some cases, parties may be concerned that the parties' positions are so fixed, that there is no room for compromise. Mediation uses principled (interest-based) negotiation techniques[33] which encourage parties to look outside the fixed positions presented by each party. Mediation, unlike positional negotiation or litigation, discusses the parties' needs and goals to achieve pragmatic, creative outcomes. Practical solutions can increase the likelihood of reaching an agreement and it can be important to remind parties that these may not be available if they pursue litigation or a more formal process.

One party is in an unfair bargaining position

3.34   Parties may have concerns that there is a power imbalance or an unequal bargaining position. Power imbalances may change over time. In civil proceedings, one party may feel they are in an unfair position because there has been inadequate disclosure and they do

---

32   Civil Procedure Rules 1998 (CPR) Part 24.
33   See paras 4.51–4.61 on principled bargaining.

not fully understand the other party's case – this can be addressed by setting out requests for information before mediation takes place. Alternatively, a power imbalance in a family mediation created when one party separates from the other is likely to diminish over time.

3.35   In other situations, steps can be taken to address inherent power imbalances. Where parties are in an unequal bargaining position – such as an individual or small voluntary not-for-profit organisation challenging a large corporation or public body, or where one party has far greater economic resources than the other – mediation may be more effective once legal proceedings have been issued. For example, after the claimant has successfully sought summary judgment, defended a strike out or permission has been granted in a judicial review case. In a neighbour dispute, a party who indicates that they feel unconfident about attending a mediation may be reassured by the possibility of bringing a friend as a 'supporter'.[34] Different processes can be used to address concerns.[35] Co-mediation, in particular, is an effective approach at addressing imbalances or where one party is more articulate or vocal.

Ulterior motive

3.36   If mediation is proposed by one party, the other party may be suspicious of their motive. In civil cases, a party may use the mediation process to place pressure on a party to settle or to scope potential witnesses and ascertain more information about the other party's case. In other mediations, one party may have a hidden agenda for attending mediation and no intention of reaching an agreement. Rather than refusing to mediate, issues such as a party's lack of 'good faith' can be considered when preparing for mediation.[36]

Public interest and publicity

3.37   A party may be concerned whether any agreement reached will be confidential and remain private and off-the-record. As a general rule, mediation agreements remain confidential, but parties can decide to include in the settlement agreement an agreed public statement or press release.[37] Alternatively, where a civil case would have created a legal precedent and benefited other parties in a similar position, it

---

34   See para 3.89 on the role of a supporter.
35   See para 3.38.
36   See paras 4.43–4.44.
37   See para 7.15.

is possible to ask, as part of the mediated agreement, that the public body, company or business review the policy or procedure that has brought about the dispute.

Case study 7: Housing dispute – achieving the unimaginable

A block of flats was substantially refurbished including the replacement of all the windows. As part of this process, satellite dishes which had been attached to the external walls of individual flats were repositioned to allow the scaffolding to be erected. A number of tenants complained. Once the work was complete, the local authority refused to reinstate the satellite dishes because they asserted the tenants had been in breach of their tenancy agreements to have installed them. Legal proceedings were commenced by the local authority seeking injunctions against those tenants who had reinstated their satellite receivers.

On the face of it, this case could appear totally unsuited to mediation since the local authority and tenants had opposing and incompatible views. A joint mediation was arranged, some of the tenants who faced legal proceedings and the local authority attended, as well as the satellite provider who was invited as an interested third party. The mediation produced an settlement which included the Local Authority giving permission for the satellite provider to erect a central receiver on the roof of the building enabling internal cables to be used to connect individual flats. The agreement reached would never have been achieved through legal proceedings.

Practical difficulties

3.38   If parties are based in separate parts of the country, telephone or online mediation may be suggested. Where one party is anxious about a face-to-face meeting with the other party, then talking through the issues and raising the possibility of the parties remaining in separate rooms may meet those concerns. In situations where there are multiple parties and a number of issues, the mediation process can be adapted so that a series of mediation meetings may take place over a period of time.

Pre-mediation information

3.39   Mediation is provided by:

- mediation provider organisations;
- dispute resolution consultants;
- mediation schemes;
- independent mediators.

3.40   All mediation providers, whether they are community, workplace, family or civil, understand the importance of supporting parties to make a positive decision to mediate. When parties initially contact a mediator they may not be certain they want to mediate, they will have concerns and are likely to want the process explained. Providers invest considerable resources in speaking to parties and, where it is required, encouraging unwilling parties to mediate.[38] This is usually an informal service over the telephone. Many commercial mediation providers advertise a *free* 'no commitment' service where a mediator or mediation administrator speaks to parties, explains the mediation process and discusses whether the dispute is suitable for mediation.

Screening for suitability

3.41   There are a number of issues which need to be considered before a party can mediate:

a) *Is the other party willing to mediate?* Is there another party to the dispute? Are there other third parties who are involved and who should also attend? Are the other party's whereabouts known and are contact details available? Has the other party been approached or has mediation been proposed?

b) *Are there any reasons why mediation is unsuitable?* Are there any risk factors or power imbalances which would make mediation unsuitable?[39] Is the remedy or outcome sought achievable through mediation? Is another form of dispute resolution service more appropriate?[40]

c) *Other considerations:* Is legal advice required? Is the mediator or mediation provider independent and impartial?

---

38 See paras 3.22 and 3.25–3.38.

39 This is an issue parties may wish to discuss with the mediator at a mediation information meeting – see paras 3.42–3.44.

40 All mediation providers should be able to signpost parties to alternative forms of dispute resolution or professional help where appropriate.

Mediation information meetings

3.42   As a first step, parties often want to know more about mediation. Primarily for this reason, Mediation Information and Assessment Meetings (MIAMs) are now a procedural requirement in family cases. There was also a pilot scheme offering a Mediation Information Service in civl cases.[41] Although the government does not anticipate introducing a similar procedural requirement in civil cases,[42] information and advice is usually provided informally and free of charge over the phone in all fields of mediation.[43]

What are mediation information meetings?

3.43   In family cases, MIAMs are meetings between a mediator and the parties. The mediator explains the process of mediation as well as discussing other alternatives to going to court. The mediator will find out more about the parties and their circumstances and assess their suitability for mediation by screening for domestic abuse and other safeguarding checks.[44]

3.44   In civil cases, a mediation information session (MIS) is a meeting with a mediator. It is a chance for the mediator to educate the parties and their legal advisers about the mediation process, to allay fears, build confidence in the process and assess the suitability of the case for mediation. The mediator will ensure that there is no conflict of interest and may direct the parties to alternative dispute resolution (ADR) processes or professional help if appropriate.

Setting up the mediation

3.45   Parties and the mediator or mediation provider will have to decide the following:

a)   Is the dispute suitable for mediation?

b)   Do the parties need legal advice?

---

41   Ministry of Justice Mediation Information Service in Civil Cases (MISCC) Pilot, June 2011–March 2012 in Birmingham, Manchester and London.

42   *Solving disputes in the county courts: creating a simpler, quicker and more proportionate system – the government response*, TSO, February 2012 p11, para 25.

43   See para 3.40.

44   See paras 9.8–9.22 for a fuller explanation.

c) The mediation model – face-to-face, telephone, online, co-mediation? What combination of meetings is required – how many? how long?[45]
d) Who will be the mediator?
e) Who will attend?
f) What are the costs and who pays?
g) What is the time and date for the mediation meeting(s)?
h) What is the venue?

An *agreement to mediate* is then signed by everyone attending,[46] including the mediator (in workplace and community mediation a written agreement may not always be used).

Finding a mediator

Civil mediation

3.46   The *small claims mediation service* is a free service, run by Her Majesty's Courts and Tribunals Service (HMCTS), available to all parties in defended small claims cases. The service is free to use and parties who reach a settlement can receive a refund of their hearing fee. If the case doesn't settle, then the case is listed for a small claims hearing and the contents of the mediation remain confidential. As from April 2013, all small claims up to £5,000 will be automatically referred to mediation.[47]

3.47   The *Civil Mediation Online Directory*[48] is a searchable database listing mediation providers across England and Wales, accredited by the Civil Mediation Coucil. The Directory is provided by the Ministry of Justice (MOJ) and replaces the National Mediation Helpline (NMH).[49] The Directory provides a fixed-fee scheme for cases up to £50,000, with fees for higher value cases agreed with the provider. For parties who are prevented from accessing mediation because the cost is prohibitive, *LawWorks* is a charitable organisation which offers free civil and commercial mediation where at least one party

---

45 See paras 5.16–5.20.
46 This will include participants at the mediation such as experts or supporters who will not be party to any settlement or agreement but will be bound by confidentiality. See paras 3.102–3.105.
47 For more about the Small Claims Service see paras 5.64–5.66 and 8.12.
48 See www.civilmediation.justice.gov.uk.
49 Until October 2011, the NMH provided members of the public and legal advisers with a well-resourced website and telephone helpline.

is on a low income.[50] There are also other low-cost or specialist mediation schemes.[51]

3.48   Parties can approach *mediation providers* directly and there are numerous *independent mediators* who have their own websites and have established specialist areas of work. The Bar Council also compiles a list of barrister-mediators,[52] and the Law Society accredits civil and commercial mediators.[53] For senior commercial mediators, the Chambers & Partners directory[54] provides another source of information.

Family mediation

3.49   Parties wishing to find a family mediator can use the online search facility, Find a mediation service,[55] which replaces the Family Mediation Helpline and its associated website. Alternatively, the *Legal adviser finder*[56] website locates local mediators who have contracts to provide publicly funded mediation, using the *family mediation* option. Family mediators are regulated by the Family Mediation Council (FMC) and all mediators found on these websites have met the FMC training accreditation requirements.[57] The Family Justice Review has recommended the creation of an online information hub and helpline[58] which, if created, would be an opportunity to provide greater access to information about family mediation.

Workplace mediation

3.50   The use of mediation is increasingly available in the resolution of workplace disputes. The Civil Mediation Council runs a voluntary registration scheme and provides a database of workplace mediators.[59] Many large employers, such as the NHS, have in-house mediation schemes. Representative bodies and organisations also offer in-house

50 See www.lawworks.org.uk.
51 See paras 8.10–8.33.
52 See www.barcouncil.org.uk/.
53 See www.lawsociety.org.uk/.
54 See Chambers and Partners UK – Dispute Resolution: Mediators available at www.chambersandpartners.com/.
55 See www.familymediationhelpline.co.uk.
56 See http://legaladviserfinder.justice.gov.uk.
57 See paras 12.33–12.41. Also see paras 9.51–9.55 for other considerations when choosing a family mediator.
58 *Family Justice Review: final report*, November 2011 para 114.
59 See http://cmcregistered.org.

schemes. The Bar Council, for example, provides an Arbitration and Mediation Service[60] free-of-charge as part of its members' services for disputes arising within barristers chambers.

Community mediation

3.51   There is no longer an online database of community mediation organisations.[61] Community mediation schemes are often funded by, or work closely with, local authorities. The local council's website is therefore a good place to start.[62]

Scotland

3.52   In Scotland, the Scottish Mediation Register provides an online searchable database of mediators as well as a telephone helpline.[63]

Choosing a mediator

Mediation has a greater chance of settling the case if all parties believe in the mediator's reputation, personality and qualifications.[64]

How to choose a mediator?

3.53   Most parties choose their mediator based upon the mediator's reputation and word of mouth. For parties using mediation for the first time and who are self-funding the mediation process, choosing a mediator can be a daunting task. It is important to choose a mediator whose skills are appropriate to the particular dispute and whose approach meets the needs of the parties concerned. For parties accessing a free mediation scheme or who have been referred to mediation, the selection of the mediator may be done by the mediation provider.

Jointly selecting a mediator

3.54   Parties will benefit from investing time in selecting their mediator. Mediators vary in quality as well as style and approach. It can be common practice in civil disputes to exchange a list of preferred mediators, but the risk is that parties end up with the 'least objectionable'

---

60 See www.barcouncil.org.uk/for-the-bar/introduction-to-member-services/ arbitration-and-mediation-service/.
61 This was formerly provided by Mediation UK which ceased to exist in 2006.
62 For a list of community mediation providers see appendix A.
63 See www.scottishmediation.org.uk/find-a-mediator; tel: 0131 556 1221, 9–5 Mon–Fri.
64 LJ Berman quoted in A Goodman, *Mediation advocacy*, 2nd edn, XPL, 2010 p48.

rather than their favoured choice. For this reason, parties may find it helpful to exchange the particular skills or expertise they require. There may be additional considerations when choosing a family mediator.[65]

Choosing between a mediator and a mediation provider

3.55   The first consideration is whether to choose an independent mediator or a mediation provider.

3.56   Independent mediators offer the assurance that they will remain the mediator throughout the process. An independent mediator may not be able to offer the administrative support of a venue which an organisation may be in a position to provide. They may be cheaper when compared with those mediation providers who charge an administration fee, but that is not necessarily the case. Independent mediators may have specialist subject-matter expertise which is important to parties.[66]

3.57   Mediation providers range from not-for-profit mediation services to specialist mediation schemes, and include large mediation training organisations and small commercial providers of mediation services. Mediation providers may offer administrative support and a venue, but it can come at a cost.[67] Some mediation providers offer mediation as part of a wider dispute resolution service so are able to tailor their service to meet the parties' needs. Low-cost or free-to-use mediation schemes[68] may be a cost-effective option, but this does not prevent a party asking questions about the mediator or indicating a preference.

3.58   The larger, most established mediation providers often offer mediator training courses. One consideration when using large mediation providers is whether the proposed mediators will be recent trainees eager to get exposure to the field of mediation but lacking expertise and experience.

3.59   All mediators or mediation providers ought to have basic structures in place such as adherence to a code of conduct, minimum standards of accreditation and ongoing training, a system of peer review or mentoring, a complaints policy and professional indemnity insurance (up to the value of the dispute). All should also have a complaints procedure. Civil Mediation Council (CMC) accredited provid-

65   See para 9.55.
66   See paras 3.66–3.69 on subject matter expertise.
67   See paras 3.79–3.81 on administrative fees.
68   See paras 8.10–8.33.

ers, accredited family mediators and workplace mediators registered with the CMC *must* have these structures in place.[69]

Factors to be considered when choosing a mediator

3.60   The following factors, which will be explored in more detail, may be considered when choosing a mediator:

- style and personality;
- qualifications and experience;
- subject-area or specific expertise;
- approach and ethos;
- location;
- cost.

Style and personality

3.61   The mediator's style, interpersonal skills and personality are perhaps the most important considerations. Communication, rapport, empathy and the mediator's ability to inspire trust have all been described as a mediator's strengths.[70] The ability of the mediator to manage the mediation process and shift the conflict dynamic may make them more effective than their familiarity with the subject area of the dispute. Much of this comes down to the mediator's personality and explains why most mediators are selected from personal recommendation.

3.62   In some cases, where one party has a strong or dominant character, a mediator with status and authority may be chosen. In fact, all facilitative mediators can address power imbalances between parties. Where a party is vulnerable, a mediator with a more measured and sensitive approach may be needed to ensure the party's effective participation while having the skills to ensure that the mediation process is fair. Some parties select the mediator to complement their own style – a confident and authoritative party may be balanced by the softer touch of a more personable and creative mediator.[71]

---

69   See paras 12.16–12.17.

70   A Bucklow, 'The "everywhen mediator": the virtues of inconsistency and paradox: the strength, skills, attributes and behaviours of excellence and effective mediators' (2007) 73 *Arbitration* 40.

71   LJ Berman quoted in A Goodman, *Mediation advocacy*, 2nd edn, XPL Publishing, 2010 p49.

Qualifications and experience

3.63 There is no government regulation of mediators in England and Wales, Scotland or Northern Ireland, but there are commonly agreed standards for training and accreditation in the four fields of mediation: civil, family, workplace and community – these are explored in chapter 12. It is helpful to look at the training undertaken by a mediator to understand the type of approach they may adopt.[72]

Experience

3.64 A mediator's approach, skill and knowledge are considered some of the factors which determines successful outcomes at mediation.[73] Mediation skills develop over time and with experience. It is important to ascertain how experienced the mediator is, and parties are free to ask how many mediations they have undertaken.

Success rates

3.65 Parties should be cautious about relying too heavily on a mediator's 'settlement rate' as a measure of their effectiveness as a mediator. It is undoubtedly the case that some mediators are more effective than others.[74] It is one of several factors to take into consideration. High success rates may suggest that the mediator places greater emphasis on encouraging settlement rather than allowing parties to reach an agreement that addresses their underlying needs.

Subject-matter expertise

3.66 It remains a significant debate within the mediation community whether or not the mediator needs to have a background knowledge of the subject-area of the dispute. And, in a civil dispute, whether the mediator should have legal expertise.

Legal expertise

3.67 This has been described as the choice between an 'expert mediator or mediator expert'.[75] A facilitative mediator's skills can be applied to any dispute, and an experienced mediator with the appropriate style and approach but no knowledge of the background issues may be the best candidate. On the other hand, a skilled mediator who is familiar

---

72 See para 3.70.
73 H Genn et al, *Twisting Arms: court referred and court linked mediation under judicial pressure*, MOJ Research Series 1/07, 2007 p198.
74 See paras 2.15–2.17.
75 F Strasser and P Randolph, *Mediation: a psychological insight into conflict resolution*, Continuum, 2008 p95.

with the issues in a particular dispute may offer insight and sensitivity and be able to grasp complex legal or technical concepts quickly.

Specialist knowledge

3.68   In certain cases, subject-matter expertise can be particularly valuable. This is never a substitute for receiving high quality legal advice, but will ensure that the mediator is familiar with the practical issues which are likely to arise in a particular situation, as well as being familiar with the terminology and jargon in a particular field. Mediators are able to provide guidance to parties on the general legal and procedural framework, for example in special educational needs (SEN)[76] or equalities mediation.[77]

3.69   For some parties, finding a mediator who has a particular expertise or specialist knowledge will be essential to establishing trust in the mediation process. Examples of specialisms include:

- faith and religion;
- languages spoken;
- cultural sensitivity or awareness;
- knowledge of a particular issue, such as honour killing, cross-cultural marriage and intergenerational disputes arising in particular communities.

Approach and ethos

3.70   This book describes a facilitative approach to mediation, where mediators assist the parties to reach an agreement but do not impose a settlement or express their opinions or judgment on a particular outcome. Mediation training covers a number of different approaches. Some mediators have been trained in mediation from a negotiation and settlement perspective, while others have been trained to bring a therapeutic or psychological insight to understanding conflict:

- *Settlement-focused:* A settlement-orientated mediator may be described as good at 'banging heads together' or possessing 'a natural authority'. Particularly in civil mediation, some parties favour a more directive approach.[78] Mediators may spend time talking with the parties about the 'value' of settlement, particularly where legal costs have escalated and reaching a mediated agreement makes financial sense.

76   See paras 8.30–8.32.
77   See para 8.17.
78   See paras 5.56–5.57.

- *Psychotherapeutic:* Mediators use their understanding of the psychology of conflict to inform their approach and explore the underlying reasons for conflict. Mediators are trained to observe conflict from a psychotherapeutic perspective (see, for example, the mediator training provided by the School of Psychotherapy and Counselling Psychology at Regent's College London[79]).
- *Counselling/coaching:* Some trained mediators have a background in counselling or life coaching. This means they bring additional skills to their role as a mediator, are emotionally aware and are confident in exploring the parties' emotions and feelings.

Co-mediation

3.71   There are a number of advantages of co-mediation. In large complex cases, the mediators may be able to help parties achieve a settlement more quickly. Two mediators may be able to work together to address power imbalances and other issues that would be less easily managed by a sole mediator without being perceived as partial. If parties wish to benefit from the skills of an experienced lawyer–mediator as well as having a mediator with counselling skills, for example, this can be achieved by using co-mediation. Co-mediation can be more costly, but if it reaches a resolution or an agreement it will be money well spent.

3.72   In family mediation, the use of co-mediation is well-established. Most community mediations are conducted by co-mediators.

Location

3.73   The mediator's geographic location may be important and parties may wish to choose a mediator who is local to them. This may because they do not wish to travel to the mediation or to avoid paying the mediator's travel costs. If practical obstacles such as a disability would mean that it would be difficult for the parties to meet, telephone or online mediation could also be considered.[80]

---

79 See www.spc.ac.uk.
80 See paras 5.64–5.71 for some alternative approaches to mediation.

How much will mediation cost?

3.74   When considering the cost of mediation, the mediation fees are usually split equally between the parties. In some cases, one party may offer to pay the costs. Workplace mediation, for example, is usually funded by the employer. In other cases, mediation may be funded by a party who has accepted liability or has far greater resources than the other party. If parties are entitled to public funding (legal aid), then the mediation will usually be funded.[81] Parties on a low income can consider whether a mediation scheme is available which may offer free or low-cost mediation.[82]

The mediator's fee[83]

3.75   The mediator's fees will usually be determined by the complexity of the case and the experience and expertise of the mediator. Some mediators and providers publish their rate, others do not. Parties may find that the mediator's fee is negotiable.

3.76   The mediator's fee generally covers their attendance at the mediation, and then an hourly rate if the mediation continues beyond the agreed time. The fee will usually include preparation and pre-mediation telephone calls or meetings with the parties – this is particularly important as pre-mediation contact with the parties is likely to increase the prospects of reaching an agreement. In some cases a mediator may charge their travel costs.

Assistant mediators

3.77   In certain situations, the mediator may request an assistant mediator. Assistant mediators usually play a less active role and there may be no costs consequences for parties.

Cancellation fees

3.78   Most mediators and mediation providers have a cancellation policy which entitles them to retain a proportion of the fee where the mediation is cancelled prior to the mediation – for example, half the fee if the mediation is cancelled within seven days. This is both a commercial necessity for the mediator and may also operate to establish a firm commitment from the parties to work towards the mediation.

---

81 See paras 8.78–8.80 on public funding.
82 See paras 8.11–8.33.
83 Also see para 2.9 on mediator's fees.

Other mediation costs in civil mediation

3.79 When considering the cost of mediating, in addition to the mediator's fee each party may have to pay the following costs:

- arrangement fee;
- venue costs (may or may not include refreshments/catering);
- legal adviser (preparation and attendance);
- expert (preparation and attendance).

3.80 The arrangement fee is the amount charged for the administration of the mediation by the mediation provider. Not all individual mediators or providers charge a fee. Some mediation providers include the provision of a venue with suitable facilities including refreshments and catering.[84] Questions parties may wish to ask a mediator or mediation provider are as follows:

- What are your fees?
- Do you charge an administration fee?
- Do your mediator's rates include preparation (including pre-reading) and pre-mediation meetings or telephone consultations/calls?
- Is the venue included in the price?
- What is your cancellation policy?
- Do you charge VAT?

3.81 Parties should remember that if the mediation involves a financial settlement, then the mediation fees and other expenses can be part of the settlement, or the mediation fee will be recoverable as part of the successful party's costs if the matter is not resolved by mediation.[85]

Who will attend the mediation?

3.82 Parties should consider carefully who they would like to attend the mediation. This should be shared at an early stage which enables both parties to be made aware of who will be attending and raise any objections or concerns.

The party or parties

3.83 The party (or parties) who attend the mediation should be the people who are affected by the dispute. They are described as the *parties*,

---

84 See paras 3.101–3.102.
85 See paras 8.89–8.85.

participants or *disputants*. It is important that the party (or parties) have the *authority to settle*, which means that they are able to sign any legally binding agreement. Individuals who have detailed knowledge of the dispute may not be decision-makers. In these situations, where the permission or authority of another person is required, arrangements should be made for them to be available at the end of the telephone. Otherwise, there is a real risk that the time spent narrowing the issues and working towards a settlement may not result in a final agreement.

Person with the authority to settle

This is the person who has the authority to make a decision that brings the dispute to an end and, where appropriate, can be legally binding. In most cases, the parties are the people who have the dispute. In the case of organisations or public authorities, this may mean a person attending the mediation (or being available on the telephone) who has not been involved in handling the dispute but has sufficient seniority or decision-making authority. In civil disputes, insurers may be required to authorise any settlement, and where costs issues arise, a partner or senior practitioner's authorisation may be needed.[86]

It is possible for the person at the mediation to be authorised to reach an agreement.[87] It may be equally important, in some disputes, for a third party or '*supporter*' to be present to enable the decision-maker to reach a final outcome.

Before the mediation, the mediator should check that the parties have thought carefully about who should attend.

Additional representatives and third parties

3.84   In some situations, people other than the immediate decision-makers can make a real contribution to the mediation process. Finding innovative solutions may require the participation of individuals who have day-to-day knowledge of the issues or who will be responsible for the practical implementation of any agreement. Alternatively, if an apology is sought then that might influence who attends.

---

86 See para 8.93 on costs issues in civil mediation.

87 This can present difficulties. If the decision-maker is not present at the mediation, they are not party to all the discussions that take place and may not appreciate what has caused their representative to rethink their position.

3.85   Both parties should actively engage in considering whether it would be beneficial for any other people, other than those directly involved in the dispute, to attend.

Legal advisers

3.86   Legal advisers play an essential role in mediation[88] and parties are encouraged to seek legal advice where a legally binding agreement may be created. In particular, where issues of legal costs arise, it will be essential for a legal adviser to have sufficient authority to agree their fees during the mediation.[89]

3.87   It is not usual for legal advisers to be present in family, workplace or community mediations. In family mediations legal advisers may attend, but more commonly meet separately with their client to review a *memorandum of agreement* and draft a legally binding document when appropriate.

Experts

3.88   In appropriate cases, experts may attend if they will assist the mediation process and be able to provide their expert opinion to assist parties reach an agreement.

Supporters

3.89   If a party wishes to bring a friend, relative or supporter to the mediation, they are often described as 'supporters'. A supporter will usually remain silent and take no active role in the *joint meeting*, unless invited to do so. The other party should also be informed that the supporter will be attending and who they are. In some cases, a party may object, and the mediator should seek to resolve this during the pre-mediation communication. The supporter should sign the *agreement to mediate* so that they are bound by the confidentiality.

Assistant mediators/observers

3.90   It is common practice for mediation providers to ask parties for their permission for either an observer or an assistant mediator to be present at the mediation. Observations of mediations are a component of the training and accreditation requirements for newly qualified mediators. In mediations involving multiple parties, assistant

---

88 See paras 4.6–4.7 and 4.94.
89 See para 3.83 on 'authority to settle' and para 8.93 on recovery of costs.

mediators are often used to assist a lead mediator. Acting as an assistant mediator may also bridge the gap for recently qualified mediators
seeking to develop their skills.

Effective participation

3.91 Mediation providers should ask parties questions to ensure that they
will be able effectively to participate in the mediation process. Various
steps can be taken to assist parties and meet their needs, such as:

- provision of an interpreter (including British Sign Language
  interpreters);
- regular breaks;
- presence of a friend or support worker (also called
  'supporters'[90]);
- considerations in terms of timing and venue.

Finding a suitable time and date

3.92 Arranging a date for the mediation will involve taking into consideration the parties' needs.

Timing

3.93 When the date and time of the mediation are arranged, parties' religious and cultural beliefs may need to be considered, such as what
day of the week to schedule the mediation. The timing of the mediation should consider personal needs such as childcare or work commitments. The aim is to ensure as few distractions as possible. Even
discussing these issues enables parties to feel more comfortable and
encouraged that their needs at mediation will be met.

Duration/length

3.94 Mediations are usually scheduled for a fixed length of time. Participants attending the mediation should be encouraged to make
arrangements in case the mediation continues beyond its scheduled
time. Mediations may last into the evening.

90 See para 3.89.

Finding a suitable venue

3.95 In many cases the mediator or mediation provider will use their own office for the mediation or they may have the use of a venue, this may even be a room in the local court. In some cases providers will have a specially designed ADR suite.

3.96 Alternatively, the mediation provider[91] or parties will need to identify a suitable venue. In a certain situations, such as a boundary dispute, this may require the mediation to take place at the location of the dispute. The venue should, ideally, be neutral. In practice the mediation may be held in the lawyer's, local authority's or employer's offices, but wherever possible this should be avoided. It is worth suggesting whether a neutral law firm or business may be able to provide offices on a reciprocal basis. In appropriate cases a suitably located municipal building, community college or local hall may hire out rooms.

Accessibility

3.97 It is important that the venue is accessible for the parties, with parking arrangements and good public transport links. The mediator or mediation provider may ask the parties questions regarding a suitable location and time of the mediation. For a vulnerable party, meeting in a less formal space, such as a community centre, or finding a venue local to where they live are important considerations. Other additional needs such as having a wheelchair accessible building, having suitable child facilities (such as play materials), a prayer room and a breastfeeding room should also be considered.

Rooms

3.98 Where possible, the mediation should take place in a comfortable and accessible venue. This includes separate waiting areas and arrangements for parties to arrive and leave separately.[92] There should be a minimum of two rooms. An additional room enables the mediator to speak with the parties separately, this is sometimes described as a 'breakout room'. In civil mediation, at least three rooms are required (and more if there are additional parties), separate rooms for each party and a large room suitable for a *joint meeting*.

---

91 If you are using a mediation provider, this is something that should be part of their service.

92 This is a requirement for LSC Family Mediation Quality Mark. See LSC Quality Standard, 2nd edn, September 2009 p26, para C4.1.

3.99　　Consideration should be given to ensure that private meetings cannot be overheard – soundproofing or non-adjacent private rooms may be appropriate. There should be adequate space within rooms and sufficient seating to ensure that the mediator or any of the parties does not need to stand. Comfortable seating and daylight (rather than an internal, airless room) are more conducive to creating the right atmosphere at mediation.[93]

Facilities

3.100　Ideally the rooms will have flipcharts and pens and paper. It is also helpful to have access to a computer or laptop, photocopier or printer so that any agreement can be copied and read by all the participants.

Refreshments

3.101　Tea, coffee, water and fruit juice or soft drinks should be available during any mediation lasting longer than a couple of hours, particularly where it is anticipated to last all day. Alternatively, parties can be advised to bring refreshments and breaks can be provided.

3.102　Many mediators make arrangements for lunch to be provided. This has the advantage of enabling the mediator to work with the parties without a formal break for lunch. Further refreshments may be needed if the mediation lasts into the early evening.

Agreement to mediate

3.103　Once all the arrangements have been made, it is good practice for the parties to sign an *agreement to mediate*, which may also be described as a mediation agreement, or pre-mediation agreement.[94] A formal document should always be signed by all participants where parties have recourse to legal remedies if the mediation does not reach an agreement.

3.104　The *agreement to mediate* is intended to create a legally binding contract between all participants in the mediation. It will identify the parties, the mediator(s) and the nature of the dispute. The terms of the agreement will generally include:

- that all parties will co-operate in good faith in the mediation;
- that mediation is voluntary and parties can leave at any time;

93　For a helpful checklist when organising the venue, see Core Solutions's *Guide to Mediation Services*, available at www.core-solutions.com.

94　See appendix C for an example agreement to mediate.

- that the mediation process is confidential – the parameters of the confidentiality may be set out in some detail;
- that participants agree not to call a mediator to give evidence in court about the dispute, or what happened, what was said or what was done at the mediation;[95]
- that any settlement or agreement reached during the mediation must be in writing and signed by the parties;
- that the mediator will not give legal advice;
- that the mediator will observe a code of conduct;
- that the mediator may terminate or adjourn the mediation at their discretion;
- provision for payment of mediator's fees and any costs of the mediation;
- consequences of non-payment of fees, late cancellation or postponement of the mediation;
- the law and jurisdiction governing the agreement;

Other terms may be included such as:

- that the parties will attend with the authority to settle;
- that the mediation provider undertakes to make the necessary preparations for the mediation (setting out the responsibilities);
- that the arrangements for the exchange of information between the parties prior to the mediation;
- that the parties will not record/tape the mediation.

Who signs the agreement

3.105   The *agreement to mediate* is intended to bind all parties, legal advisers and the mediator (and the mediation provider) as well as any other attendees such as supporters or experts. Either everyone who attends signs the agreement, or the agreement specifies that 'each representative signing the agreement is deemed to be agreeing to the provisions of the agreement on behalf of the party he/she represents and all other persons present on that party's behalf'. All those attending should be named in the agreement.

---

95   See paras 7.31–7.33.

Checklist: Setting up a mediation

✓

☐ Agree a mediator
☐ Agree a date
☐ Agree a venue
☐ Agree who should attend
☐ Sign agreement to mediate
☐ Exchange of written information[96]

Frequently asked questions answered by Lavinia Shaw-Brown and John Kendall

3.106   The following questions have been answered by Lavinia Shaw-Brown and John Kendall. Lavinia Shaw-Brown runs the pro bono mediation provider, LawWorks Mediation, is an accredited civil and commercial mediator and has experience particularly in dealing with litigants in person. Following a career with a major City law firm, John Kendall practised as a mediator for 12 years. He was a founder of LawWorks Mediation.

Isn't agreeing to go to mediation a sign of weakness?

No, because even a strong case can be won more quickly and cheaply by mediation than by an application to the court for judgment which can be subject to appeal. In every case, however strong you think it is, there are unavoidable downsides and serious risks in going to court. The unavoidable downsides are the amounts of time and nervous energy that will be consumed, and the costs of pursuing one's own case, not all of which can ever be recovered. The serious risks arise from the inherent uncertainty of all litigation, which can lead, at the very least, to having to pay the other side's costs. The risks of litigation are much greater for those unable to afford a lawyer. A mediation meeting can give you a final settlement without those downsides and risks, and it may well be worth trading a small percentage of a strong claim for that finality.

No, because mediation offers the opportunity to meet the other party (as well as their lawyer) and to speak face-to-face. If you have a strong case, that will show in the exchanges. Taking personal

---

control of your dispute, rather than letting a court decide for you, can be seen as a sign of strength not weakness. It also often leads to greater satisfaction with the outcome.

How do I know if the mediator will be any good?

First, check that the mediator is fully accredited in the right type of mediation for your dispute. In civil mediation, some individual accredited mediators are listed on the Civil Mediation Council's website,[97] although this shows they have completed an accredited foundation training course, not how up-to-date their practice is. A more helpful guide may be the list of accredited civil mediation providers[98] who must ensure their panel of mediators meet annual accreditation requirements set by the Civil Mediation Council, which includes a requirement to have recent mediation experience. In family mediation, look for mediators who have completed the LSC competency. Other lists of annually accredited mediators include the Scottish Mediation Register.[99]

Second, ask for a copy of the mediator's CV and look at the extent of their practice and what types of case they have taken and how recently, rather than their settlement rate.

Ultimately, it is a personal relationship so it is important that you 'like the look of' the mediator. Perhaps the best guidance can come from regular users of mediation who can tell you who they would recommend. It may be possible to speak to the mediator before deciding.

Is it important that I find a mediator who has expertise in the subject-matter of the dispute?

When selecting a mediator, some people think that you need a mediator whose expertise is in the particular sector in which the dispute is taking place. While the mediator should have some familiarity with the context of the dispute, the danger of appointing a sector expert is that parties will look to that person for answers to the legal and technical issues rather than assistance in reaching a deal.

---

97   See www.civilmediation.org/members-search.
98   See www.civilmediation.org/about-cmc/15/accredited-mediation-providers; also listed in appendix A.
99   See www.scottishmediation.org.uk/find-a-mediator.

CHAPTER 4

Preparing for a mediation, negotiation techniques and mediation advocacy

continued

Key points

- Making the most of mediation means preparing effectively.
- Mediation works best when parties and legal advisers who attend a mediation are flexible and collaborative.
- Mediation uses principled (interest-based) negotiation techniques, which includes using objective criteria and finding solutions with 'added value'.
- Parties should be able to discuss issues openly and frankly and enter the process in 'good faith'.
- Participants may find it helpful to use the NVC.
- Effective mediation advocates are forward-focused, able to assess whether mediation is in a party's best interests and advise parties on the value of any proposed agreement.

Preparing for a mediation

> [Mediation] offers a cathartic pseudo 'day in court' to parties; it gets cards on the table and all parties around the table.[1]

4.1   Mediations are most effective when parties come prepared. Preparation includes being able to set out the issues in the dispute, and also thinking about what outcome parties hope to achieve. Parties will only reach an outcome that they feel is 'fair' if they have spent time thinking about what this means to them. Legal advisers can play an important role in helping parties reach this stage. Understanding the role negotiation techniques play within the mediation process also helps parties make informed decisions.

4.2   When parties have both decided to mediate, the process of setting up a mediation requires them to jointly select a mediator or provider and agree on a time, date and venue for the mediation.[2] In many civil cases the parties will also have to pay the fee and sign an *agreement to mediate*. The pre-mediation process then begins, which involves:

- preparing for the mediation;
- exchange of written information (civil mediation);
- *pre-mediation meetings* or telephone discussions.[3]

---

1 H Genn, 'The Central London County Court – pilot mediation scheme evaluation report', Lord Chancellor's Department Research Series No 5/98, 1998 p3.
2 See paras 3.45–3.105.
3 See paras 5.3–5.8.

4.3   A fundamental element of mediation, and what distinguishes it from other forms of dispute resolution, is that the parties will take an active role in deciding the outcome. Each participant (mediator, party, legal adviser) has different roles and responsibilities within the mediation process.

What to expect at a mediation

Stages of a mediation

4.4   The general stages to expect are as follows:

- The mediator will invariably have already made contact with the parties to help them prepare for the mediation.[4]
- There may be *pre-mediation meetings*, and in family and community mediation these take place before the parties decide to mediate.
- The mediation meeting will then take place.
  - Parties arrive at the venue and wait in separate rooms or waiting areas before being greeted by the mediator.
  - Parties will usually be invited by the mediator into a *joint meeting* with the other party (in some processes there will be separate meetings before a *joint meeting* takes place).
  - The *joint meeting* begins with the opening – first the mediator speaks, followed by the parties' opening statements or uninterrupted speaking time.[5]
  - The mediation then follows a number of stages: First, the exchange, which is an opportunity to share information, express views and clarify the issues. These may be in joint sessions or in private confidential sessions. Towards the end of the exchange parties will start to identify interests and needs which will help them generate options for agreement. Offers and counter-offers are then made before jointly drafting an agreement.

The mediation process is discussed in detail in chapter 5.[6]

---

4   See paras 5.3–5.8.
5   See paras 4.26–4.30.
6   Also see paras 1.23–1.27 for a brief overview.

The roles of the participants

The role of the mediator

4.5 The mediator is responsible for managing the mediation process. The mediator guides the parties through the stages of a mediation but doesn't impose a solution or decide what, if any, agreement should be reached by the parties. The mediator may suggest an agenda to help facilitate the discussions, and ask the parties questions designed to enable them to examine the strengths and weaknesses of their account. The mediator facilitates communication and may intervene to manage power imbalances and, at times, act as an educator or coach in relation to communication skills, negotiation techniques, the value of reaching a settlement and reframing issues to remain forward-focused. The mediator does not, however, express their opinion on the merits of either party's position or determine what might form a 'fair' agreement.[7]

The role of the parties

4.6 The parties determine the outcome of the mediation. They decide what issues they wish to discuss and the extent to which they are prepared to think creatively about finding a solution. Parties are at the centre of the mediation process; they are required to play an active role and can expect to be asked challenging questions which may explore why they have reached a particular position or viewpoint as well as examine their underlying interests and needs. Parties work co-operatively and collaboratively with each other to find a mutually agreeable settlement. The settlement is not suggested or imposed, it is created by them. Parties are responsible for whether or not an agreement is reached.

The role of the legal adviser

4.7 Not all mediations will involve a legal adviser. Generally speaking, in any case where mediation is intended to reach a legally binding agreement it is preferable that the parties either have received legal advice beforehand or attend with a legal adviser. The legal adviser is usually a solicitor or barrister who may also be described as a *mediation advocate*.[8] Their role is to support the party to reach a fair outcome. The solicitor or barrister will provide legal advice, ensure that any agreement is legally correct and is a 'just and equitable' outcome

---

7 The exception is evaluative or rights-based mediation processes.
8 See paras 4.83–4.85.

according to the merits of the party's case and what they want to achieve.

4.8　The legal adviser provides guidance on the strengths and weaknesses of a party's position and the likely outcome if the matter were to be contested in court. He or she will usually help summarise the main facts, the issues to be mediated and provide the mediator with core documentation. The legal adviser may assist with negotiation, discuss strategies and explore ways to widen the options for agreement. In some cases an expert may fulfil a similar role, providing guidance and advice on a likely outcome if the matter were to be adjudicated or resolved through another form of dispute resolution.

How to prepare for a mediation

General preparation

4.9　In preparation for a mediation, all participants should spend time thinking about the following:[9]

- First, the mediation process gives parties the opportunity to air their grievances, so parties should think about setting out the background and the different issues, as well as anything they may want to 'get off their chest'. In legal mediations, a written document called a case summary or *position statement*[10] is prepared.
- Second, mediation is outcome-focused, so parties should think about what they want to achieve from mediation, both in terms of the process and the outcome.
- Third, mediation is often chosen when attempts to resolve issues informally or through face-to-face discussions or negotiations have failed, therefore parties need to think about different or creative ways a resolution could be found.

Gather all the information

4.10　It can be a useful exercise to put all the bits of paper or documents into a file and write thoughts down on paper. Reading through the papers and preparing a core document bundle is invaluable. It may also help to clarify the issues and focus on what is really important. This is more appropriate in legal cases than community or workplace disputes. In some cases this will reveal that there has been inadequate

9　Some mediators or mediation providers will provide participants with a pre-mediation checklist or questionnaire – see appendix D.

10　See para 4.19.

disclosure or that further documentation is needed. As mediation is only a fair and balanced process when both parties are in a position to make informed decisions, mediators will expect legal advisers to co-operate with requests for further information or disclosure.

What is it you really want to say?

Clarifying your point of view

4.11 The mediation meeting usually commences with all the participants meeting together in a *joint meeting*. The mediator will make some opening remarks explaining their role and how the parties may wish to use their time, reinforcing that the mediation process is confidential and setting ground rules.[11] The parties – or if they prefer or are uncomfortable about it, their lawyers – are then given the opportunity to make an opening statement or speak for a period of time, uninterrupted.[12] This is a chance for parties to explain their point of view and the issues which they feel need to be resolved, as well as the impact the dispute has had. There are a number of questions which provide a helpful prompt for all parties preparing for a mediation, such as:

- What are the facts or any chronology that the mediator will need to know?
- What are the issues that have had the most impact?
- What are the important facts or events that explain the background to the dispute?
- What are your feelings about those facts and events?
- What are the issues between yourself and the other party?
- What matters to you most?
- What have you been told is irrelevant and still believe is important?
- What is the most difficult issue?
- What issue(s) do you anticipate the other party is going to raise and how will you respond?

Worries and anxieties

4.12 Preparing for a mediation involves anticipating what may be said by the other party during a mediation. Most mediations involve a personal element. Whether it is a civil, workplace, community or family dispute, there are likely to be strong emotions. Feelings can be expressed in the mediation process without being confrontational

11 See paras 5.25–5.34.
12 See paras 5.35–5.39.

or aggressive, but parties will be best equipped to hear the other party talking about the impact of the dispute if they have thought about this in advance. Some useful questions include:

- What do you want to ask to the other party?
- What do you think they will want to ask you?
- What issues, incidents or behaviour might they raise which you will find difficult?

Managing expectations

4.13   Parties will benefit from having a realistic idea of what mediation can achieve. Expecting an apology or a climb down by the other party may or may not be a remote possibility. Equally, parties who remain fixated upon achieving the 'best possible' outcome (the best result if matters proceeded to court or an alternative resolution, which may only be a remote possibility) need to be reminded that such a result is unlikely to be proposed by the other party, or may not be something the other party could offer. While it is helpful for parties to be clear about what they wish to achieve from the mediation process, this includes having realistic expectations about what the other party will find an agreeable outcome.[13] The mediation process may involve both parties being willing to compromise or being flexible to some degree, or alternatively, may involve a party explaining the reason for being unable to compromise.

What do you want to achieve?

Clarifying what it is that you want to achieve

4.14   The following list is a useful starting point for all parties preparing for a mediation:

- What are the possible options for agreement?
- What is the other party likely to want from you?
- Is there anything you can offer the party by way of a proposal or a concession to make an agreement possible (eg an apology, a change in policy, etc)?
- How will you feel if an agreement is reached at mediation?
- What will happen if an agreement is not reached at mediation?

---

13   See para 4.16.

The value of reaching an agreement

4.15 There are many agreements reached at mediation that could not be imposed by a court or other alternative dispute resolution processes, such as adjudication or arbitration. Courts do not have the power, freedom or flexibility that the parties have to find their own solution. It can be helpful for parties to have thought about the following questions:

- How much impact the dispute has had on them, emotionally and/or financially?
- What would be the benefit in terms time and money if an agreed solution could be found?
- What additional negative outcomes can be avoided by reaching an agreement – such as avoiding adverse publicity, a formal complaint or permanent record of a grievance, or simply the stress of litigation?
- What positive outcomes can be reached for the parties by deciding the outcome for themselves?

What will the other side want?

4.16 It is a useful exercise for a party to put themselves in the other party's shoes and ask what sort of agreement they will be looking for. When parties have thought about what the other party wants to achieve (not just what they want for themselves), they can start to suggest potential solutions. Useful questions to consider include:

- What outcomes would be acceptable to the other side?
- What can I offer to the other party to make an agreement possible?

Steps to reaching a 'good outcome'

4.17 Mediation encourages parties to use principled (interest-based) negotiation techniques. This requires parties to:

- separate people from the problem;[14]
- identify interests and needs;[15]
- assess the strengths and weaknesses of their position;[16]
- consider potential options for agreement and exploring 'added value' or alternative solutions.[17]

---

14 See para 4.53.
15 See para 4.54.
16 See paras 4.55–4.56.
17 See paras 4.57–4.61.

Checklist: What to take to a mediation

What to take to a mediation will depend on the issues under discussion. For advisers attending a mediation, they should consider whether they will need:

✓

☐ A notepad and pen
☐ A calculator
☐ A laptop computer (confirm there will be access to photocopying and printing facilities)
☐ A copy of the *agreement to mediate*
☐ All relevant documentation and a copies of your position statement
☐ A draft agreement[18]

Exchange of information

Civil mediation

4.18   In civil mediations, parties will usually prepare a mediation brief which includes a position statement and core documentation. In order to prepare this documentation, legal advisers need to be clear about the legal advice they are providing to their client. Legal advisers, solicitors or barristers, attending the mediation should be prepared for the following questions:

- What are the prospects of succeeding at trial?
- In money claims, what is an accurate value of claim or counterclaim (including interest)?
- What would be the best outcome for the client?
- What benefits can be achieved through mediation rather than an alternative process? What negative outcomes can be avoided by reaching a mediated settlement (including any added value options)?
- What are the costs to date? What are the estimated costs to trial? (This is not always disclosed before the mediation, but the legal adviser needs to bring this information to the mediation.)[19]

---

18 See example mediation agreements – appendix E.
19 See para 4.22.

Writing a position statement

4.19 A position statement or case summary provides the mediator with a summary of the issues, the party's position and the background to the dispute. A mediation brief should be just that, brief. While preparation for a mediation increases the likelihood of reaching a satisfactory settlement, being thoroughly prepared does not mean arriving at a mediation weighed down with bundles of documents. The purpose of drafting a position statement is to consolidate the issues. It is a concise and short document setting out the details of the dispute in simple and clear terms. See the checklist below for what to include in a position statement.

Checklist: What is usually included in a position statement

✓

- ☐ **Who the parties are:** Who is involved in the dispute and who will attend the mediation (the parties, legal team, supporters, experts).
- ☐ **A brief outline of the facts:** What events gave rise to the dispute, and any other information necessary for the mediator to understand the dispute. A chronology can be helpful; if possible, this should be agreed with the other side.
- ☐ **An overview of any legal proceedings:** Include any significant developments, as well as any *without prejudice* or Part 36 offers.[20]
- ☐ **The issues to be mediated:** List the issues and the party's position or views in relation to each issue.
- ☐ **The potential outcomes:** Set out what the party wishes to achieve from mediation. Include suggestions on how the dispute could be resolved and potential options for agreement.
- ☐ **A list of key documents:** The documents can be attached as a bundle – a joint bundle will usually be prepared.

Cross-service of position statements

4.20 When providing the position statement to the mediator, parties should anticipate that this material may be disclosed to the other party. It is common practice for the mediator to ask parties to exchange their mediation bundles. Alternatively, parties may wish to prepare a joint document setting out an agreed summary or outline of facts.

---

20 See para 8.88 for an explanation of Part 36 offers.

Confidential material

4.21   Parties wishing to provide the mediator with confidential or sensitive material can do so in a separate document. This may arise when a party has taken a particular position in relation to an issue, but involves information or documentation they do not wish the other party to see. The most prudent course is to include this information in a separate confidential brief; alternatively, clearly state which sections of the position statement are confidential and not to be disclosed to the other party.

Legal costs

4.22   Mediators may ask legal advisers to prepare a schedule of costs and bring it along to the mediation. In some cases, they may be asked to exchange them in advance – however, this information may remain confidential at the outset of the mediation and discussed initially in separate meetings. The information is then available, and can be disclosed, if parties are moving towards agreement and need to consider the legal costs. In certain cases, where the 'costs issues' are central to the issues in dispute and the possibility of reaching an agreement, mediators may request parties to exchange this information in advance of the mediation.

Family mediation

4.23   In mediations involving property and finance, mediators will request financial information which they can review before the first joint meeting.[21]

Workplace mediation

4.24   The process of referring or commissioning a workplace mediation usually involves the employer or organisation to providing information about the dispute to an external mediation provider or in-house mediation service.[22] The parties would provide further information about the dispute at the *pre-mediation meeting*.

Community mediation

4.25   In community mediation, if there is a referral from a third party agency, some information about the background of the dispute may be provided in order for the mediation provider to undertake a risk assessment. The parties would not normally be expected to provide

21 See paras 9.31–9.33.
22 See para 10.32.

any written information – they will have an opportunity to discuss the issues with the mediators at a *pre-mediation meeting* or home visit.

Attending a mediation

Those attending mediations should always:

- *Listen* to what the other party has to say.
- *Be fair and reasonable* – Only offer something that would be fair to the other side as well as yourself or your client.
- *Put themselves in the other party's shoes* – Try to think of settlements or outcomes that would be attractive to the other party.
- *Wherever possible, be polite and courteous* – If the mediation dissolves into abusive or antagonistic language it will undermine the strength of the argument, although it may be important for the other party to see the strength of feeling coming from your side.
- *If possible, avoid being adversarial* – Being adversarial can demonstrate a lack of openness, or can suggest an unwillingness to work co-operatively, and creates mistrust.
- *Be wise* – Think carefully before putting an offer on the table or making a concession – the settlement has to be pragmatic and fair. It is important to avoid suggesting something that a party will later regret.
- *Go prepared* – Spend time before the mediation considering what would be a fair outcome.
- *Be flexible* – Have an open mind and be prepared to have frank discussions.

Presenting an opening statement

4.26 The *opening statement* (uninterrupted speaking time) is an opportunity for each party to speak without being interrupted. It can be presented by the party, the legal adviser, or both. It is helpful when preparing to ask the mediator how long each party will be invited to speak for. The purpose of the opening is to allow each party to set out their point of view and the impact of the dispute, and it is an opportunity for the other party and the mediator to hear this account. It can also be a long-winded process if parties have not prepared in advance and are unable to keep what they say succinct and focused.

4.27   Parties (and legal advisers) are encouraged to:

- Speak normally using everyday language and avoid reading from notes. Instead use a list of key points or prompts. Remember, this is an opportunity not to be missed!
- Make eye contact with the other party. It is them and not the mediator who needs to be persuaded.
- Remain focused and stick to the point – it may only be necessary to mention the key facts very briefly, as all participants will be only too well acquainted with them!
- Explain the issues in order of importance and, where necessary, explain why they have personal and emotional significance (even where that may differ from the legal position or the primary focus of the mediation).
- Try to stick to your own agenda and only respond to points made by the other party if they are relevant.
- Acknowledge the impact the dispute has had on the other party (and apologise if it is appropriate).
- Explain why you have come to mediation and what you hope to achieve (this is not necessarily the moment to start setting out more detailed proposals).
- Make any concessions or proposals (which signal your intention to work collaboratively).
- Be passionate and persuasive.

4.28   Additional considerations for legal advisers:

- Don't try to score points or exaggerate your client's position.
- Think carefully before conceding a legal point; alternatively, indicate concessions which could be made in principle for the purposes of the mediation.
- Emphasise your best arguments and likely outcome if legal proceedings continue – avoid repeating what is set out in the position statement.
- Only respond to points raised in the other party's position statement if really necessary and try not to attack the other party.
- Use your client's language – unless you wish specifically to address the other party's legal advisers.

4.29   The opening statement may be the first time a party has had to explain why the issues are so important to them. For those parties who come to mediation as an alternative to legal proceedings or other forms of redress, this is their 'day in court'. This creates a tension between the legal adviser who wishes to present the arguments and a party who will benefit from explaining the impact of the dispute.[23]

4.30   It is very important that the parties prepare well for the opening session. It can be a cathartic process, enabling them to overcome any emotional or psychological blockage that has prevented them from putting the dispute behind them. It may be difficult to sit and listen to the other party telling their story. However, generally it leaves parties feeling more able to enter discussions about reaching an agreement.

Addressing the other party in joint meetings

4.31   Depending on the type of mediation, after the opening statement the parties may go to separate rooms or remain in the *joint meeting*. The initial process will be an exchange of views and information gathering to clarify the issues and explore parties' underlying interests. Legal advisers and parties can assist this process in a number of ways:

- Listening to what the other party is saying, making notes of contentious issues rather than interrupting (see 'active listening'[24]).
- Using language that is co-operative and non judgmental.
- De-personalising assertions and statements (see non-violent communication[25]).
- If appropriate, avoiding giving short answers – providing detail and clarification to avoid misunderstandings. Givving a fuller explanation demonstrates openness and encourages collaboration.
- Asking questions of the other party to gain a better understanding of their position.

4.32   Parties can request time to discuss proposals with their legal adviser or supporter. In legal mediations, parties should be mindful of disclosing tactical strategies or sensitive information to the other party, but ultimately they will reap what they sow. Those parties who fully engage in the mediation process are more likely to get a meaningful and practical outcome even where they may have given the other party greater insight into the strengths *and* weaknesses of their case.

23 See para 5.39.
24 See para 4.33.
25 See paras 4.35–4.36.

Active listening

4.33　Active listening is the use of non-verbal techniques to indicate to the speaker that the listener is attentive to what is being said.[26] This means the listener:

- uses open body language, and does not fold their arms (which may be taken as a sign of a 'closed' attitude) or frown to indicate that they disagree with something that has been said;
- makes eye contact where appropriate;
- does not interrupt the speaker.

Empathy

4.34　Demonstrating empathy can be a powerful way to break down mistrust and encourage the other party to offer concessions and suggest creative options for agreement. This can be achieved by acknowledging the other party's position and feelings. For example, by saying 'I understand that it must have been very frustrating for you ...', or 'I heard what you said when you were talking about ...'.[27]

Non-violent communication (NVC)

4.35　Michael Rosenberg's non-violent communication (NVC) strategies[28] (compassionate communication) de-personalise the language we use and avoid making accusations or being confrontational. When communicating during the mediation, it can be helpful for parties, legal advisers and mediators to use these strategies to communicate effectively:

- Observation: 'When I see / When you ...'
- Feelings/impact : 'This makes me feel ... / This causes difficulties because ...'
- Needs: 'I need ...'
- Requests: 'In future / Would you be willing to / Could you ...'

4.36　To give two examples:

- Rather than saying, 'You drop the kids off late every week, it drives me mad!', a party could say: 'When you drop off the kids, if you are late this is difficult because it disrupts plans or arrangements I have made. What I need is to know when the

---

26　See paras 6.27–6.29.
27　See paras 6.36–6.38 on empathy.
28　M B Rosenberg, *Nonviolent communication ... a language of compassion,* PuddleDancer Press, 2002 p6.

children will be home. In future, could we have an agreement that you'll text me if you are going to be late.'

- Instead of saying, 'These pleadings are hopeless, this is a waste of time!', the legal adviser could say: 'The pleadings fail to provide any detail, this is a problem because I need to know the case I am defending, could you provide a particularised statement of case.'

4.37 The re-phrasing in these examples can leave the listener with a positive, forward-focused message. NVC principles focus on uncovering the needs and feelings which shape our positions and demands. Understanding this enables parties to seek alternative solutions to conflict situations in which all needs are met. This mirrors interest-based or principled negotiation techniques.[29]

Speaking with the mediator in separate meetings

Benefits of separate meetings

4.38 Mediation works best when there is a relationship of trust between the participants and the mediator. In private meetings, everything said between the party and the mediator is confidential. Parties may feel able to be candid about any weaknesses in their case or off-load and express their frustrations. It may be an opportunity for the mediator to empathise with the party and acknowledge their grievances. The mediator may also ask challenging questions and 'reality test'[30] the strengths and weaknesses of a party's position without undermining the party in the presence of the other side.[31]

Relationship with the mediator

4.39 There is no reason why the legal adviser or the parties cannot be totally honest and open with the mediator during private meetings. Legal advisers attending mediations are required by their code of conduct not to mislead the other party or the mediator – the Code of Conduct for barristers states:

> 708.1 A barrister instructed in a mediation must not knowingly or recklessly mislead the mediator or any party or their representative.[32]

---

29 See paras 4.51–4.61.
30 See paras 6.34–6.35.
31 See paras 6.34–6.35 on reality testing.
32 Code of Conduct of the Bar of England and Wales, 8th edn para 708.1 – available at www.barstandardsboard.org.uk/regulatory-requirements/the-code-of-conduct/.

And the Code of Conduct for solicitors states:

> O(5.1) [A solicitor must] not attempt to deceive or knowingly or reck-lessly mislead the court;[33]

4.40   Private meetings are totally confidential and this gives the parties the freedom to use the mediator as a sounding board. This can help parties assess the strengths and weaknesses of their claim or any pro-posed settlement, without worrying that they are jeopardising their position or losing face. In the same way, the mediator will test a par-ty's position by probing or reality testing their assertions. Of course, there will be parties who lie or mislead the mediator as to their true position, and provide misleading bottom lines.[34] It is hard to see what this achieves. Mediators are bound by the confidentiality of what they are told in private meetings and are aware this cannot be used to steer the negotiations.

Making offers and proposals

4.41   There are a number of strategies that are suited to mediation[35]

- Making multiple or alternative offers at the same time (and trying to avoid incremental concessions, which undermines credibility).
- Ensuring that any concessions remain 'in principle' for the purposes of the mediation and will not need to be upheld if the mediation fails to reach agreement.
- Exploring trade-offs, such as, 'What would it take to drop the requirement for X?', or 'If we offered A would you be prepared to undertake to do B?'.
- Exploring practical solutions that 'future-proof' any agree-ment, ensuring the underlying issues are addressed to avoid the same issues arising

Finalising the agreement

4.42   The agreement will usually be written down. In non-legal media-tions, the mediator will work with the parties to record the agree-ment. In legal mediations, it is usually drafted by the legal advisers. It can therefore be extremely helpful for at least one legal adviser to bring a laptop computer and for the venue to have printing facilities.

---

33   Solicitors Regulation Authority (SRA) Code of Conduct 2011 para O(5.1) – available at www.sra.org.uk/solicitors/handbook/code/content.page.
34   See paras 4.66–4.67 on the risks of using bottom lines.
35   Also see paras 4.75–4.81 on negotiation pitfalls.

If neither party has a legal adviser present at the mediation, an agreement in principle may be written down and a legal document drafted by lawyers after the mediation. Mediation agreements are considered in more detail in chapter 7.[36]

The importance of good faith

4.43   It is essential to the integrity of the mediation process and for all parties attending mediation that each party has attended voluntarily and in good faith.

Parties who enter a mediation in bad faith

Parties may use mediation to achieve a tactical advantage. This may be more common in civil mediation, where the legal framework incentivises alternative dispute resolution and imposes costs sanctions on those who unreasonably refuse to mediate.[37] In reality, given that mediation itself may be an additional layer of costs, it is unlikely that this will be the motivating factor (even if there is an element of this at play). Alternatively, parties may wish to mediate to test the strength of the other side's legal case, assess the other party as a witness or get access to sensitive material. Commonly described as a 'fishing exercise'. Mediators, legal advisers and parties should be alert to this.

4.44   Potential safeguards include:

- Being upfront – tell the mediator about any concerns that the other party is only attending the mediation for tactical reasons.
- If you want to speak at the *joint meeting*, thinking carefully about what you wish to say. It may be possible to read a prepared statement. (Legal advisers may discuss what the party wishes to say in advance. The most cautious advocate would read the statement on the client's behalf).
- In civil mediation, where a party feels that an offer or proposal has not been reasonably considered, it is open to the party to make a Part 36 offer which would be revealed to the judge when considering costs.[38]

---

36   See paras 7.9–7.29.
37   See paras 8.98–8.107 on costs sanctions.
38   See para 8.88 on Part 36 offers.

Self-represented parties

4.45   One of the core strengths of mediation is that it is informal and parties are offered the opportunity to come together to resolve their disputes in a less adversarial way. There are no formal rules or procedure. Unrepresented parties may, if agreed by all concerned, bring friends or relatives (who may be described as 'supporters').[39] So they are not as disadvantaged as they may be in court, particularly where the other party has a lawyer who will be familiar with court procedures and process. Most mediations in family, community and workplace disputes have no legal advisers present (even where legal advice has been sought). In civil mediation, the reverse is generally true – most parties will have sought legal advice and their legal adviser will attend the mediation and may take a prominent role. It follows that most agreements reached in civil mediations are legally binding.

Litigants in person

In legal proceedings, individuals or groups attending court without a legal adviser and speaking on their own behalf are described as 'representing themselves' and are also referred to as *unrepresented* or *self-represented parties*.

Do I need a lawyer?

4.46   The primary issue for litigants in person is whether to seek legal advice. Where legal rights are engaged or the mediation agreement will be a legally binding document, *it is prudent to have received legal advice*. The determining factor is usually cost. If there is an imbalance of power created by one side being represented and the other not, the first step is to discuss this with the mediator or explore options for receiving free legal advice.[40] But in any event a mediator is trained to be alive to power imbalances and can, if necessary, halt a mediation and recommend that a party seeks legal advice before resuming the mediation at a later stage.

4.47   If cost is an issue, parties can ask for their legal adviser to remain at the end of a telephone to discuss any proposed agreement. This can present difficulties if a party changes their position as the legal adviser is not part of all the discussions that have taken place during the mediation. They may not therefore appreciate what has caused

---

39 See para 3.89.
40 See appendix B.

their client to rethink their original position or deviate from original instructions. Alternatively, the party can reach an agreement in principle and ask to have a legal adviser look through the agreement before it is drafted in its final legally binding form.

Use of negotiation strategies in mediation

Negotiation techniques

4.48   Mediation can be described as a *structured* or *assisted negotiation*, so it can be helpful for mediation advocates and parties entering mediation to have an understanding of negotiation techniques. Mediation encourages parties to make informed choices and use principled or interest-based decision-making.[41]

4.49   If parties have compatible interests then principled negotiation can help them reach an agreement that meets both their needs. In contrast, positional bargaining is all about 'success' and 'winning'. If one party has a much stronger case, positional bargaining will get them a quick and (objectively) better outcome. It will not, however, address any underlying conflict, or restore their relationship with the other party and it may be costly to enforce any agreement.

Positional/competitive bargaining

4.50   Some key features of positional bargaining are:
- extreme opening offers and use of bottom lines;
- a sequence of small concessions;
- competitive tactics such as bluffs, threats and stonewalling;
- the outcome is victory for one party and loss for another, or a compromise.

Advantages:
- It can be a quick and straightforward way to reach agreements.
- It can achieve a successful outcome for the stronger party.

Disadvantages:
- It can be an inefficient negotiation strategy, with the potential for neither party to get what they want, for there to be a 'winner and loser' or for a stalemate to be reached.
- It can damage ongoing relationships between the parties.

---

41   See R Fisher and W Ury, *Getting to yes*, 2nd edn, Random House, 1999; also see paras 4.51–4.61.

Principled/collaborative (interest-based) bargaining

4.51   Some key features of principled bargaining are:

- focuses on underlying interests and needs;
- looks for mutually acceptable solutions;
- avoids negotiation tactics, takes a 'cards on the table' approach;
- explores 'added value' solutions and options for mutual gain.

Advantages:

- Produces creative, mutually beneficial outcomes.

Disadvantages:

- May lengthen the process of reaching a decision.
- Could encourage a party to reveal sensitive information.
- Potential for stronger party to exploit a collaborative approach.

4.52   There are four core principles of principled negotiation as described in *Getting to yes* by Roger Fisher and William Ury:[42]

- separate the people from the problem;
- focus on interests not positions;
- use objective criteria for bargaining;
- invent options for mutual gain.

Separate the people from the problem

4.53   Positional bargaining values the ongoing relationship between the parties. Parties should therefore be mindful of avoiding antagonistic or aggressive language. Parties and legal advisers will be most effective if they listen, demonstrate empathy and de-personalise their assertions.[43]

Focus on interests not positions

4.54   By encouraging parties to think about their real interests and underlying needs, they can look at more creative and mutually agreeable solutions. Shifting the focus from a fixed position to an underlying interest prompts questions such as:

- What is it that the party really wants?
- What does the party think is important?

---

42 2nd edn, Random House, 1999 p15.
43 See paras 4.35–4.37.

Objective criteria for bargaining

4.55   It can be helpful for parties objectively to reflect on the strengths and weaknesses of their position. One technique used in principled negotiation is to anticipate what the alternative outcomes will be if an agreement is not possible. These provide a benchmark from which parties can assess the merits of any proposed settlement which arises during mediation. Mediators may ask the parties what is their:

- *BATNA – Best alternative to a negotiated agreement:* What is the best outcome they will achieve if no agreement is reached through mediation? What is the likelihood of this happening?
- *WATNA – Worst alternative to negotiated settlement:* What is the worst outcome if no agreement is reached through mediation? What is the likelihood of this happening?
- *MLATNA – Most likely alternative to negotiated agreement:* If no agreement is reached, what is the most likely outcome? Entering mediation with a clear idea of the 'most likely' outcome can help prevent parties becoming fixated upon achieving the 'best possible outcome'.

4.56   Another negotiator's tool is described as the 'ZOPA' (zone of potential agreement) – this is the area where both parties' interests overlap. It can be helpful for mediators to focus parties on the potential for agreement and identify the common ground.

Invent options for mutual gain – the 'added value' principle

4.57   Once parties have identified their underlying needs and interests, it is possible to think creatively about generating options for mutual gain. This can produce commercially intelligent solutions and pragmatic outcomes which would not have been achieved through legal proceedings or conventional negotiations.

4.58   This is most simplistically demonstrated by the concept of the 'mythical fixed-pie'.[44] Try drawing four straight lines that connect all nine dots.

4.59   Here are some of the most common attempts at a solution:

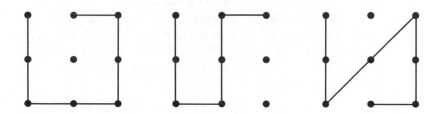

4.60   Most people assume that that the lines should not go outside the dots. In fact, the answer lies in looking beyond that self-imposed assumption:

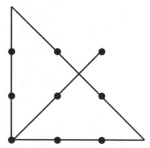

4.61   Direct negotiations often fail because they remain focused on the fixed areas of potential agreement. Mediation can involve creative problem-solving. It is often difficult for parties involved in a dispute – be it a contractual dispute or a marital breakdown – to think beyond

44   This is a frequently cited example, see M H Bazerman and M A Neale, *Negotiating rationally*, The Free Press, 1992 pp18–19.

their fixed positions. Mediators help parties see beyond this notional fixed pie and encourage parties to look for added value solutions and mutually beneficial resolutions. Legal advisers and parties can anticipate this aspect of negotiation and think about added value options to propose during mediation. The benefit may be cost-saving for one party and of added value to the other. For example, parties can devise creative ways to pay a debt, such as:

- timing: lump sum or staged payments, immediate or deferred payment;
- method: cash, cheque, standing order, banker's draft, dividends, payment to third party;
- non-monetary alternatives: delivery of goods, provision of a service.

Case study 8: The redundancy dilemma

A large manufacturing firm was facing financial difficulties and sought to reduce running costs by making 12 employees redundant. This was strongly resisted by the workforce who argued the cost savings were not necessary, it resulted in low morale and a number of staff were signed off on sick leave. Mediation was proposed, and three staff representatives agreed to meet with managers.

After a series of pre-mediation meetings a joint meeting was held. At the joint meeting the atmosphere was initially very tense, but during the opening statements the managers were able to explain why the financial difficulties had arisen, and explained why cost savings needed to be put in place swiftly to avoid all staff losing their jobs. The staff representatives were asked to keep the information confidential as it was commercially sensitive.

During the mediation, the staff representatives agreed to a joint discussion about the possible options to achieve the proposed cost savings. The mediator encouraged parties to think about options which would address the concerns of the workforce. This led to a proposal that all staff would finish early on Fridays, resulting in a slight reduction in pay across the entire workforce (including managers) which would achieve sufficient cost savings. Following the mediation, an agreed statement was made to staff who accepted the proposals.

Negotiation styles

Different negotiation styles

4.62   Mediation seeks to improve communication between parties, encouraging openness and collaboration. The stage at which offers start being made inevitably invokes negotiation strategies. Parties, legal advisers and mediators should be mindful of the different negotiation styles.

4.63   Individuals take different approaches when negotiating. The way different people behave is influenced by:

- how assertive they are – how much they want to satisfy their own needs, how much they want to win or reach their goal;
- how co-operative they are – how much they want to keep a good relationship with the other person and how much they want to meet the other person's needs.

4.64   Parties can be seen to have one of several different 'conflict styles', for example: withdrawing, forcing, compromising, smoothing or confronting.[45] When parties are aware that people have different conflict styles, they may have greater self-awareness when mediating. This also enables a party to adapt their approach and style to make the chances of reaching agreement more likely. Mediators will encourage parties to be 'collaborators'.

Animals are sometimes used to characterise the different conflict management styles:

- Withdrawing – the 'turtle' withdraws into their shell to avoid conflict. They give up their personal goals as well as their relationships.
- Forcing – the 'shark' tries to overpower opponents by forcing others to accept their desired outcome and is less concerned about preserving relationships.
- Compromising – the 'fox' is prepared to give up some of their goals if the other person is also prepared to give up some of theirs. Valuing their own goals as well as others and concerned with maintaining relationships.

---

45   See also the Thomas-Kilmann Conflict Mode Instrument (TKI) – KW Thomas and RH Kilmann, *The Thomas-Kilmann conflict mode instrument*, CPP Inc, 2002, which defines conflict modes as accommodating, avoiding, compromising, competing or collaborating.

- Smoothing – the 'teddy bear' values relationships over their own goals. They avoid conflict and try to smooth over conflict so that it does not damage the relationship.
- Confronting – the 'owl' value their own goals and relationships. They see conflict as a problem to be solved and look for solutions which achieves their goals and the goals of the other person.

Soft, hard or firm negotiators

4.65 *Soft* negotiators start with an 'opening offer' which is akin to 'testing the water', anticipating a margin within which they will then manoeuvre. They do not anticipate that their 'opening offer' will be accepted, and predict that it will trigger a response that will provide them with greater insight into the other party's position. Soft negotiators will be content to make sequential concessions. Soft negotiators can be *accommodating*, willing to concede to reach agreement. The risks associated with this approach are that *soft* negotiators are overly/ too co-operative and conciliatory, eager to compromise in order to reach an agreement and mindful of being 'liked' by others. Mediators have to be watchful to ensure parties who are *soft negotiators* are not exploited by the other party to achieve an unfair outcome.

4.66 *Hard* negotiators make proposals which take little account of the other side's position. Hard negotiators can also be *aggressive* negotiators and seek to engage negotiation tactics to give themselves an unfair advantage. Their objective is to get the best outcome for themselves, they disregard ongoing relationships or the interests of the other party. Such negotiation tactics include:

- misleading bottom lines;
- threat of walking out;
- stand-offs and ultimatums;
- making unrealistic or excessive demands;
- misrepresenting the importance of a particular issue;
- last minute add-ons.

4.67 The risks associated with these strategies are that an agreement is reached, but the other party is left feeling aggrieved or cheated. Relationships are irretrievably broken down, the opportunity is lost to find an agreement in which longer term commercial or personal interests are met. Alternatively, the negotiation ends in stalemate. Parties who have given a misleading 'bottom line' or an ultimatum do not want to 'lose face' and are unwilling to move from their fixed position.

4.68   *Firm* negotiators may start with an offer which has been carefully considered and reflects their 'true' *bottom line* – an offer they
consider reasonable and therefore leaves little room for negotiation.
Firm negotiators will make little or no concessions. Firm negotiators
may also be *avoiding*: parties who dislike conflict and do not actively
engage with discussions. This can be an effective strategy if the other
party is accommodating. Mediators should seek to manage power
imbalances caused by different negotiating styles.

4.69   The risk of *firm* negotiation is that taking a firm stance has the
potential to derail negotiations, as it signals a lack of flexibility and
may be perceived by the other party as a lack of 'good will'. Mediators
may need to spend longer with firm negotiators to encourage a more
flexible approach and to look at more creative solutions.

Reading the signals

4.70   Legal advisers and parties will try to interpret the 'signals' given during negotiations. The ability to 'read' such signals is determined by
the style of negotiation being used by the other party. An awareness
of different styles of negotiation (as well as negotiation pitfalls[46])
will therefore enhance parties' ability to participate confidently in a
mediation.

Left-brainers and right-brainers

4.71   Some neurobiologists who study brain functioning suggest that individuals whose right hemisphere of the brain is dominant process
information and respond in different ways to those who are left-brain
dominant. Right-brain dominant people are more emotional and
intuitive, while left-brain dominant people respond in sequential,
logical ways.

4.72   Hard and firm negotiators place greatest emphasis on the substance of the agreement, looking for structured and reasoned offers
and counter-offers. Soft and collaborative negotiators are more
concerned about relationships, a sense of what is 'just' and global
outcomes. Neurobiologists may suggest that these different negotiation styles are influenced by left-brain and right-brain dominance.
By understanding the importance of the substance and form of an
agreement, mediation can achieve settlements that respect these different approaches.

46 See paras 4.75–4.81.

> ## Case study 9: Selling a business – two different perspectives
>
> Ten years ago, Sadat had set up a business investing his life savings. Five years ago he had become ill, and his friend Steve had taken over as manager. They decided to sell the business; but were unable to agree on how to divide the assets? Sadat is a 'right brainer' and was never particularly good at numbers, he just felt he should get a greater share. Steve is a left-brainer, he wanted to itemise and catalogue the contributions each had made to the business and divide the assets accordingly.
>
> At mediation, a global settlement was reached which apportioned a lump sum to Sadat reflecting his initial investment and then divided the remaining assets according to the equitable approach Steve favoured. This awarded Sadat a greater share and Steve felt his contribution had been acknowledged. Both appeared relieved at the end of the mediation. Some misunderstandings were ironed out and they subsequently resumed their friendship.

Addressing power imbalances

4.73 Mediation seeks to minimise the use of positional negotiation tactics by using an interest-based approach and challenging parties who adopt such positions through strategies such as reality testing. Mediators will discuss with advocates and parties the risks that such tactics carry and how they may weaken their position. Mediators will explain that such posturing creates distrust and can ultimately polarise and entrench positions and mean the other party who was initially willing to compromise is more likely to 'dig their heels in'. For example:

Party A   I think you should take what's on the table, if you go to court a judge is never going to award you as much as this. If you are going to be unreasonable I'll just leave now.

Party B   If you feel like that, let's go to court and let a judge decide.

Mediator   Perhaps Party A could explain why the deal is such a good one and why it is in Party B's interests to accept it.

4.74 The mediator's options include:

- In a separate meeting, challenge a party if a tactical device is being used – ask what they hope to achieve, explore their interests and goals.

- Discourage the use of bottom lines and ultimatums.
- Reality test fixed positions.
- Encourage parties to adopt an interests-based approach.
- Keep all options on the table, to avoid anyone feeling 'backed into a corner'. The mediator doesn't prescribe how an agreement is reached, but can recommend that different approaches to reaching agreements can remain under consideration (for example, exploring a global or 'all-in' settlement alongside a more systematic resolution of individual issues or heads of claim).

Negotiation pitfalls

Defendant bias

4.75　One challenge for legal mediation is the fact that defendants are 'loss adverse' and would rather take the risk of going to court and 'losing' than paying out an at early stage – whereas claimants would rather settle at an early stage than risk the uncertainty of going to court.

> ...the claimant is more likely to accept an offer rather than risk going to trial and lose everything (risk aversion). However the defendant would tend to choose the option of proceeding to trial, preferring to gamble in order to avoid the certain loss (loss aversion).[47]

4.76　This is borne out by research that claimants tend to achieve lower levels of recovery in mediated cases than non-mediated cases.[48] Research shows defendants are less willing to consider mediation[49] and are more likely to overestimate their likelihood of reaching a favourable outcome following a trial.[50] In legal mediation, it therefore important that legal advisers are able to given their clients robust advice about likely outcomes and litigation risk.

47　F Strasser and P Randolph, *Mediation: a psychological insight into conflict resolution*, Continuum, 2008 p33.

48　See, for example, H Genn, *Twisting arms: court referred and court linked mediation under judicial pressure*, Ministry of Justice (MOJ) Research Series 1/07, May 2007 p22.

49　H Genn, *Twisting arms: court referred and court linked mediation under judicial pressure*, MOJ Research Series 1/07, May 2007 p ii.

50　See, for example, R Kiser, *Beyond right and wrong: the power of effective decision making for attorneys and clients*, Springer, 2010.

Making the first offer

4.77 When making the first offer in mediation, parties should be mindful that the other party needs to understand why the offer is being made. This is particularly so when offers are being communicated by a mediator who is moving between two parties in separate rooms (as is commonplace in civil mediation). There is a risk that the other party may reject the offer because they think it must be 'too good to be true', there is a hidden catch or because of 'reactive devaluation'.[51]

4.78 Reactive devaluation can cause parties to dismiss proposals or offers on the basis of who is making the offer, believing that everything being offered by the other party (including what may appear a reasonable proposal) is not good enough. For this reason, mediators will often ask parties to set out their reasons for making an offer or concession. They may suggest that offers are made in a *joint meeting* (rather than through the mediator) so that parties can provide this explanation. Explaining why an offer or concession is being made, or sandwiching the more contentious aspect of an offer between two concessions, may prevent an offer being dismissed without proper consideration.

Use of negotiation tactics

4.79 We've already seen that where parties have used negotiation tactics, such as 'bottom lines' or issuing ultimatums, they risk undermining the negotiation process.[52] Parties and legal advisers should be mindful of this.

4.80 It is also important to consider whether there can be 'give and take' during negotiations. If one party perceives that they are making all the concessions or compromising on a previously immoveable position, they may feel they are 'losing face'. The desire to 'save face', retain dignity and self-worth in the eyes of others, peers, colleagues or clients may present a psychological obstacle to reaching an agreement. Even where, objectively, a party is being offered a good outcome, the fear of 'losing face' may prevent them taking it.

51 See para 6.69.
52 See paras 4.66–4.67.

The risk of 'meeting in the middle'

> each party is left wondering whether they might have achieved more had they pursued their claim further and not compromised so soon.[53]

4.81 One approach commonly relied upon in positional bargaining is 'splitting the difference'. It can help close the gap in negotiations and, if used appropriately, is a useful negotiating device. The danger with this approach is that both parties feel they have 'lost' and that they have conceded too much. There is also a risk that parties have not started the negotiation with a fair starting figure or bottom line. Discussions become 'anchored' at an unfair starting point which is more favourable to one party than the other.

> Splitting the difference may well reward the 'biggest liar', in that the point of compromise will favour the party who made the more extreme opening demand.
>
> ...
>
> Mediators should be alert to the problem of only one party is offering to come halfway to cross the gap; the danger is that the other party will then split the remaining difference, and so on. For example, if there is a last gap of £10,000 and one party offers to move £5,000 the other might respond with an offer of only £2,500. [54]

Mediation advocacy

4.82 Mediation advocacy is a term often used to describe the role of a legal adviser during a mediation. The principles of mediation advocacy are conventionally drawn from a legal or civil mediation context, although the underlying principles apply equally to all participants at a mediation.

Who is a mediation advocate?

4.83 A mediation advocate is any legal adviser, solicitor or barrister who is able to advise their client as to when, and when not, to mediate, and is confident to represent their client's interests during a mediation.

---

53 F Strasser and P Randolph, *Mediation: a psychological insight into conflict resolution*, Continuum, 2008 p75.

54 L Boulle and M Nesic, *Mediator skills: triangle of influence*, Bloomsbury Professional, 2010 p198.

4.84   For legal advisers who are litigators and who are familiar with an adversarial approach, mediation requires a change of mindset. It requires the legal adviser to shift their attention beyond, 'what can a legal challenge achieve for my client?' towards a future-focused or outcome-based approach which takes account of wider commercial, personal and practical needs. Practitioners who are new to the profession may embrace this approach more readily, as it is embedded in the Civil Procedure Rules (CPR), and Appropriate or Alternative Dispute Resolution (ADR) is on the syllabus of law degree courses and vocational training.

4.85   Mediation advocacy is developing into a specialist field in England and Wales. The Standing Committee of Mediation Advocates (SCMA)[55] is working alongside the International Mediation Institute (IMI)[56] to establish an accreditation scheme. This may create the impression that only specialist lawyers can represent their clients at a mediation. This is not true. Any legal adviser who has a good understanding of the strengths and weaknesses of their client's case, has taken the time to understand and uncover their client's interests and is willing to work collaboratively can represent their client in a mediation. The existence of the field of mediation advocacy does, however, acknowledge that it draws upon different skills from those of a litigator.

When should a legal adviser advise parties to mediate?

4.86   Parties may require advice on whether to mediate and if so, when.[57] Solicitors are under a duty to act in their clients' best interests and this includes considering alternatives to court proceedings.[58] Advisers need to look beyond the factual and legal framework and examine their clients' underlying interests, needs and goals. Mediation takes a holistic approach which can achieve outcomes beyond the scope of the relevant legal or procedural framework. Frequently, formal and legal processes can only undo or provide financial compensation for past mistakes without providing practical outcomes and certainty.

---

55 See www.mediationadvocates.org.uk.
56 See http://imimediation.org.
57 See paras 3.7–3.16.
58 SRA Code of Conduct 2011 para O(1.12): Solicitors must ensure that '*clients are in a position to make informed decisions about the services they need, how their matter will be handled and the options available to them*' (formerly the Solicitors' Code of Conduct rule 2.02(1)(b))– available at www.sra.org.uk.

The following considerations may be useful when advising a client whether to mediate:

- What does my client want to achieve?
- Do the legal issues and wider considerations lend themselves to an alternative form of dispute resolution?
- Are we ready to negotiate? If so, then why not mediate?
- Are there any reasons why mediation will achieve a result that court proceedings could not?
- Are there any reasons why mediation may place my client in a worse position?[59]

Best interests

4.87　Many cases involve 'points of principle' and may have potential implications for a wider pool of people. It is important, however, that legal advisers examine what their client really needs in order to decide whether to mediate. This will involve taking into consideration wider commercial, personal and practical needs as well as the impact of ongoing litigation and uncertainty.

4.88　The following are some of the reasons given by parties as to their motivation to pursue a dispute:

- to redress a wrongdoing;
- to make a point;
- to punish the other side;
- to prove that the other party 'is in the wrong';
- to have the other party 'judged' as wrong;
- to be vindicated;
- as a point of principle;
- to recover legal costs.

4.89　There is usually a mismatch between what motivates a party who has a dispute, what they are likely to achieve and the outcome that would address their underlying needs and interests. Exploring the outcomes parties are seeking can sometimes reveal whether mediation would be an opportunity to address underlying issues. Legal advisers need to have the confidence to recommend mediation to their clients.

Thinking creatively

4.90　On the face of it, many cases may appear unsuitable for mediation. The case of *Cowl*[60] is a good example. It was a case involving the

59　See paras 3.30–3.37 and 8.54–8.65.
60　*Cowl and others v Plymouth City Council* [2001] EWCA Civ 1935.

closure of a care home. The residents sought to judicially review (challenge the legality of) the council's decision to close the home. The parties were criticised during the legal proceedings for not considering ADR, in particular mediation, because the legal challenge could only achieve a ruling that the original decision was unlawful and would not achieve the desired outcome for the residents. Ultimately, the residents pursued a lengthy complaints process which resulted in overturning the council's decision.

Legal adviser's preparation for mediation

4.91   The legal adviser will explain to their client what to expect at the mediation. This is an opportunity to discuss strategies and any additional areas of agreement where 'added value' offers or requests could form part of the mediation.[61]

4.92   The adviser will need to know the following additional information:

- the client's financial position;
- whether there are any implications of a financial agreement, eg impact on benefits entitlements, statutory charge;[62]
- if appropriate, whether the client is prepared to apologise or make any concessions;
- any additional needs or interests which can form part of the bargaining position;
- practical actions the other party can be asked to take;
- any potential 'added value' solutions which would cost the client very little or nothing, but could make the agreement possible, eg payment by instalments, the offer of a service.

4.93   The legal adviser should have a clear understanding of the strengths and weaknesses of the client's case, as well as detailed knowledge including:

- amount claimed (and counterclaimed), including interest calculations;
- schedule of costs, including projected costs if matters proceed to trial;
- the alternatives to a negotiated agreement (BATNA, WATNA and MLATNA).[63] The legal adviser may be expected to say in percentage terms the likelihood of each of these outcomes;
- the client's essential and desired outcomes (interests).

61 See paras 4.57–4.61.
62 See paras 8.94–8.97.
63 See para 4.55

Attending a mediation as a legal adviser

Legal adviser's approach

> Mediation is a team game. The client must be involved in the process from start to finish.[64]

4.94   The legal adviser's role is to advise the party and support them during the mediation.[65] For legal advisers, it can be a challenge to avoid the temptation to score points with their client by taking an antagonistic and robust stance. It can be helpful to remember that taking a confrontational approach may actually undermine the client's negotiating position. Experience shows that it is in the client's interests to listen carefully to the other party and not to react to emotional outbursts.[66]

Joint meetings

4.95   *Joint meetings* are important, as they get the parties in the same room, however uncomfortable or difficult it may be. Whether the party communicates directly, or through their lawyer, this is a chance to explain why they are there and what they actually want. *Joint meetings* allow the emotion of the dispute to be communicated. This may be the first time that parties have told their side of the story in their own words and explained why certain issues are so significant to them. The legal adviser and party will need to decide who will speak during *joint meetings.*[67]

Separate meetings

4.96   Everything said in separate, private meetings is confidential. In shuttle mediation, mediators will assume everything they are told is confidential unless a party expressly requests that information is conveyed to the other party. Legal advisers may wish to confirm with the mediator the information he or she has been given permission to disclose.

Top tip: Make use of time the mediator is spending with the other party in private meetings, by continuing to discuss the possible options for agreement.

---

64   A Goodman, *Mediation advocacy*, 2nd edn, XPL Publishing, 2010 p100.
65   See paras 4.7–4.8.
66   See para 4.33 on active listening.
67   See paras 4.29 and 5.39.

Assessing the value of the deal on the table

4.97 A criticism of mediation is that it provides no guarantee of a 'fair' outcome.[68] Legal advisers are fundamental to ensuring that a party achieves a settlement that reflects their legal position as well as their wider interests. On the other hand, legal advisers may not be able properly or fully to assess the value to their client of not having to endure the stress of continued or protracted litigation. Mediators encourage parties objectively to assess their options and explore the alternatives to a mediated settlement. Parties will often be focused on the best possible outcome if mediation does not yield a settlement. Legal advisers will be expected to offer guidance and be realistic and objective about the likely outcome if a mediated agreement is not reached.[69] Legal advisers should be prepared to help their client assess the wider benefits of a proposed agreement as well as safeguarding their client's interests, and be mindful that there are no guarantees when a party goes to court.

Knowing when to say it isn't working

4.98 Legal advisers need to be alert to the risks of mediation. Mediation may be costly in that it adds a further expense if no agreement is reached. However, even in those circumstances it is highly likely to have narrowed and clarified the issues. A legal adviser's preparation for mediation is likely to be useful if legal proceedings proceed.

4.99 Mediation needs to be a balanced process and if the legal adviser perceives that the other party is paying 'lip service' to mediation by attending but not taking an active role, then this will not be achieved. Parties can leave at any time, and legal advisers should feel confident to do so if they perceive that the other party is not acting in good faith. In these situations, mediators are often in the best position to decide if the mediation needs to be brought to an end, and can discuss this with parties.

---

68 See, for example, H Genn, *Judging civil justice*, Cambridge University Press, 2010 p117.

69 See paras 4.55 and 4.93.

Frequently asked questions answered by Paul Randolph

4.100   The following questions have been answered by Paul Randolph, a highly experienced mediator, trainer and author on mediation. Paul has mediated in a very large number and wide variety of disputes, and his special area of expertise is in the psychology of conflict, a subject upon which he has lectured throughout the UK, Europe and Asia.

What three things would you advise a party to do before a mediation?

First, analyse what you really wish to achieve in the mediation process – not just in terms of the financial or practical outcome, but also in terms of the emotional and 'principled' aspects of the dispute.

Second, consider carefully what you are really prepared to offer or concede in the mediation process in order to achieve these aspirations.

Third, ensure that your legal adviser, or any other person attending the mediation with you or assisting you in the decision-making process, fully understands your aspirations and concessions, and your reasons for having them.

Mediation usually means claimants settling for less – what can I do to achieve a fair outcome?

You do not need to compromise if you do not wish to do so. It is an understandable, but often a false, concern on the part of claimants that they will be forced to accept less than that to which they are entitled. Every offer of settlement emanating from the other side can – and should be – fully analysed, both by you and by any other person assisting you:

- What will be the benefits if I accept what is on offer?
- What will be the effect upon me if I reject it?

In this way you can ensure that you achieve an outcome that is fair from your own perspective.

How should a legal adviser prepare for a mediation?

Assist their client in making the analyses above.

What if I do not wish to come face-to-face with the other party or be in the same room as them?

There are no rules of procedure which oblige you – or the mediator – to follow one form of process or another. If you do not feel comfortable about facing or being with the other party, you can make this concern known to the mediator. He or she should accommodate that concern, and ensure that your fears are addressed. A good mediator should be flexible and sympathetic to your position.

continued

> ## Key points
> - This chapter describes the facilitative mediation process.
> - Most mediations will involve *pre-mediation meetings* and a *joint meeting* between the parties. These meetings may take place on the same day or a different day. There is variation in the processes used in civil, family, workplace and community mediation.
> - The 'mediation' commonly describes the parties meeting together in a joint meeting.
> - The joint meeting follows a number of stages: the opening, the exchange, the problem solving and settlement stage, closing the mediation. This provides a flexible framework but does not have to be rigidly followed.
> - There are alternative models which include time-limited, telephone and online mediation.

Introduction

The golden rule is that there are no golden rules.[1]

5.1   This chapter explores what parties (and legal advisers) can expect to happen at a mediation. It explains the processes followed during a facilitative mediation, whether conducted by a sole mediator, co-mediators or a lead and assistant mediator. Mediation is a fluid process and it is not envisaged that these stages will be followed rigidly – instead they provide a framework within which the mediator will operate.

5.2   The term 'facilitative mediation' is used describe a mediation process where the mediator does not express any judgment about the underlying merits of the dispute and who does not make decisions about whether either party is 'right' or 'wrong' (as opposed to an evaluative mediator or a hybrid process such as med-arb[2]). This does not mean that facilitative mediation is a passive process. An effective mediator makes judgments and recommendations about the process, coaching parties to make the best use of the negotiation process within a mediation, assisting parties to make progress and helping them to take account of the likely alternative outcomes if no agreement is reached, which may involve directing parties to assess

1   George Bernard Shaw.
2   See paras 1.33–1.34.

and reassess the risk of litigation or consequences of not reaching an agreement.

Pre-mediation meetings

5.3   Once the parties have agreed to mediate, there are a number of considerations to be taken into account when setting up the *mediation meeting*,[3] as well as preparing for the process itself.[4] Pre-mediation meetings help the mediator learn more about the dispute and enable the parties to prepare for the mediation as well as talk about the impact of the dispute on them.

5.4   In most mediations, initial communication with the parties will have been undertaken by administrators or caseworkers from the provider or providing organisation. The pre-mediation meeting may therefore be the first direct communication between them and the parties. This is an opportunity for the mediator to start to build a relationship of confidence and trust with the parties and establish a different atmosphere of conflict resolution which shifts the focus away from the antagonistic, adversarial or combative approaches that they may have become caught up in. By explaining and demonstrating their independence and impartiality, the mediator should be able to illustrate his or her ability to create a safe space, and to listen with equal attention and interest to each point of view.

Practical arrangements

5.5   Pre-mediation (or preliminary) meetings are arranged with each party separately. The meetings enable the mediator to establish a good understanding of the issues in the dispute and the factors that hold greatest significance or importance for each of the parties. Pre-mediation meetings are a valuable opportunity to establish good rapport with the parties and to build their trust in the mediation process. Parties usually meet the mediator face-to-face. In family mediation, parties attend Mediation Information and Assessment Meetings (MIAMs).[5] In community mediation, mediators meet the parties at *pre-mediation meetings* or home visits.[6] At the conclusion

3 See para 3.45 for a list of steps to set up a mediation, also see paras 3.46–3.105.
4 See paras 4.9–4.25.
5 See paras 9.8–9.22.
6 See paras 11.39–11.40.

of these meetings, parties will decide whether to proceed to mediation. In workplace mediation, a series of pre-mediation meetings may be needed before the parties are ready to meet in a joint meeting. In civil mediation, the mediator may conduct the pre-mediation meeting over the telephone. An introductory email can be used to confirm what has been discussed and make additional suggestions about preparation.[7] In civil mediation, detailed information will be provided by the parties in their position statements and document bundle.[8] This enables the mediator to learn more about the party, clarify the issues and discuss what they expect to achieve.

5.6   Where parties are legally represented, the mediator's primary point of contact will be with the legal advisers. If at all possible, the mediator will want to develop a direct relationship with the parties. Where one party is self-represented they may speak directly with that party but communicate with the legal adviser for the other party. For this reason, the mediator may write separate emails or letters to the lawyers and the parties. Mediators will be sensitive to the tension which may exist between them and a legal adviser, with the lawyer seeking to protect his or her client's position and not necessarily wanting the client to speak directly with the mediator in the lawyer's absence.

Preparing the parties

5.7   The *pre-mediation meeting* will prepare parties for what to expect at the joint mediation meeting and give them an opportunity to think through what is likely to happen. This includes, for example, questions such as: how it will feel to be in the same room as the other party? what is the other party likely to say? what impact will that have? and what do they really want from mediation? The meeting enables the mediator to explain more about the mediation process and enhances their understanding of each party's position. It is also a chance to support the parties preparing for the mediation, ensure that they have a realistic expectation of the mediation process and encourage them to start thinking creatively about what can be achieved.

5.8   Pre-mediation meetings are useful for parties to be able to offload, receive empathy and be listened to. This can be cathartic and start to erode psychological impasses to shift the dynamic towards a more collaborative settlement and process.

7 See paras 4.9–4.17 and appendix D.
8 See paras 4.18–4.22.

Pre-mediation checklist

The following should be included in a *pre-mediation meeting* with the parties:

✓

☐ Introduce yourself and the mediation organisation you represent.

☐ Acknowledge the parties' decision to mediate.

☐ Ask permission to be able to address parties by their first names.

☐ Brief overview of mediation principles process: voluntary, confidential, *without prejudice.*

☐ Set out the mediator's role: the mediator is an impartial and independent facilitator. Mediators do not impose solutions, they help parties to explore their options and the likely alternative outcomes if no settlement is reached. They enable parties to communicate more effectively and make the best use of the mediation process.

☐ Set out the parties' role: parties should enter the process in good faith with a willingness to reach an agreement.[9]

☐ Explain that the parties need to have the authority to settle the dispute.

☐ Confirm who will be attending (party/ies, legal adviser, supporter), and explore whether there is anyone else who should attend.

☐ Where appropriate, clarify any special requirements that need to be accommodated, such as childcare, working hours, time constraints, disabilities or health issues.

☐ Discuss who will make the opening statement or speak for an uninterrupted period of time at the start of the mediation.

☐ Provide a list of questions to help parties prepare for the mediation.[10] In civil mediation parties are requested to provide a position statement or case summary and document bundle.

☐ Preparation for the mediation – encourage the parties to think about what they want to say and what they may find difficult, as well as what they want to achieve and how it might be possible.

☐ Manage expectations – think about what the other party may say or demand at the mediation and how each side reacts. Be realistic about what can be achieved.

☐ Take questions.

☐ Be positive.

---

9 See para 3.83.

10 See paras 4.9–4.17 and appendix D.

The joint meeting

Overview

5.9 The joint meeting can be described as the 'mediation appointment' or a 'face to face' meeting. In some cases there may be a series of *joint meetings*, such as family mediation. In practice, the mediator adapts and uses the process flexibly to meet the needs of the parties. The mediation may be concluded in a few hours, over the course of a day, or take place over a period days, weeks or months. The general framework of a *joint meeting* is as follows:

- the opening;
- the exchange;
- the problem solving and settlement stage;
- closing the mediation.

Joint sessions (plenary meetings)

5.10 *Joint meetings* enable a dialogue to emerge between the parties, and communication to improve and grievances to be aired. In family, community and some workplace mediations, the entire process takes place in a *joint meeting* with all participants present together. Mediators use their skills to keep the flow of the discussion moving forward. In particular, mediators can *re-frame*[11] remarks if one party makes contentious or negative points and return to the ground rules when appropriate. The *joint meeting* does not have to be continuous – mediators can invite parties to take a break, have refreshments or use breakout rooms for separate meetings.

Separate sessions (private, caucus meetings)

5.11 Separate meetings help the parties to build trust in the mediator and allow the mediator to explore the issues in more detail. They enable the mediator to ask questions about sensitive issues which may be difficult to raise in the presence of the other party. This is also an opportunity to ask challenging and probing questions and to *reality test*[12] each side's position in the absence of the other. Parties are able to speak more openly, which encourages frank discussion and allays concerns that they will compromise their legal position or reveal sensitive information by speaking in such candid terms.

11 See paras 6.32–6.33.
12 See paras 6.34–6.35.

5.12　　　In civil mediation, it is usual to have separate meetings following the initial opening session. In family, community and workplace
mediation, separate meetings are used during the *pre-mediation
meetings*. Separate meetings may be appropriate where risk factors
emerge or where the mediator needs to ask more challenging questions in order to overcome apparent intransigence or deadlock.

Shuttle mediation (caucusing)

5.13　　In mediations where separate meetings are used, the mediator may
move between two private rooms, having separate meetings with the
parties. This is described as *shuttle mediation* or *caucusing* and is commonly used in civil mediation.

5.14　　　The key features are:

- The mediator will aim to spend equal lengths of time with
  each party (although this is not always possible).
- Everything said in the separate, private meetings remains
  confidential and is not shared with the other party, unless the
  mediator is given permission to pass information on. Good
  mediators seek opportunities for progress and take the initia-
  tive to ask for permission to convey information they think
  might be useful.

Further joint meetings

5.15　　Where the parties are in separate rooms, the mediator may, at any
stage, invite the parties back into the same room in order to facilitate a *joint meeting* if they believe it would be helpful in moving the
discussion forward. Alternatively, the mediator may convene a *joint
meeting* with either the lawyers, experts or the parties only.

Variations in the process

Civil mediations

5.16　　Civil mediations usually take place over one day, for a fixed period of
time. Mediators make use of three rooms, a *joint meeting* room and
two separate rooms for the parties (with additional rooms if there
are more parties). *Joint meetings* will commonly take place around
a large oval or rectangular table. Pre-mediation meetings may take
place beforehand, often over the telephone.

5.17　　　Civil mediations generally have greater formality, mainly because
legal proceedings are likely to have already commenced (or at the

very least have been contemplated). In practice, there may well have been protracted court proceedings, so the process will be informed by the fact that the legal advisers and parties will arrive with bundles of papers which will be laid out on the tables in their separate rooms.

Family mediation

5.18   Family mediations often use a single room, with comfy chairs as this creates a more relaxed and less formal environment. The mediation takes place as a series of *joint meetings*. There is also a breakout room, which provides the opportunity to have separate meetings when appropriate.

Workplace mediation

5.19   Workplace mediations may take place on one day, with pre-mediation meetings followed by a joint meeting. Alternatively, the pre-mediation meetings take place beforehand. Similar to family mediation, a single room is used for joint meetings, with a breakout room.

Community mediation

5.20   Community mediations commonly take place at the provider's offices or in venues such as community centres. The *pre-mediation meetings* may take place at the parties' homes (described as 'home visits'). The process may take place over a single day, or with the pre-mediation meeting and *joint meeting* on separate days.

Pre-mediation arrangements

Arrival

5.21   The mediator or mediation provider will have provided parties with instructions on when to arrive at the mediation. In some cases, arrangements will have been made to ensure that they don't meet each other, either by arranging for them to arrive at different times or by taking them to separate private rooms.[13]

5.22   If the parties are taken to private rooms, the mediator will usually greet the parties separately. If it has not been possible before, this will be a chance to have a preliminary meeting and go through any pre-mediation issues. The mediator will be able to answer any ques-

---

13 See para 3.98.

tions, confirm that each party is able to stay until the end of the session and there are no pressing issues if the mediation overruns. This is also an opportunity for the parties to update the mediator on any further information or issues which may have recently arisen. Having spoken to them separately, the mediator will then usually invite the parties to join him or her in the joint meeting room.

Room layout and seating arrangements

5.23   In the *joint meeting*, the seating arrangements will have been carefully considered by the mediator, making best use of the space and existing furniture in the room.[14] The mediator will usually sit facing the parties or will place themselves at the centre, with each party on either side. Supporters, legal advisers and experts sit next to the party, where possible. The mediator will manage the seating of parties, and consider whether it might or might not be productive to have parties sitting directly opposite each other.

The opening

5.24   Most mediations include a *joint meeting* (also described as a *plenary* session). The first joint session commences with the *mediator's opening* and then the parties each making an *opening statement*, this can also be described as *uninterrupted speaking time*. The opening is an opportunity for introductions, to confirm how the day will be used and setting the ground rules. By setting the scene, the mediator establishes his or her control over the process.

Mediator's opening statement

5.25   Although there are different models and variations, a mediator's opening statement is likely to be broadly the same. The tone and pace are aimed at communicating a calm authority, making the parties feel comfortable and establishing a safe environment. This signals a shift away from confrontational or adversarial language. It also provides a focus as the parties adjust to being in the same room together.

5.26   The mediator's opening sets the tone and defines the atmosphere for what is to follow. It helps the parties build trust in the mediation process in order to create a safe environment for them to speak openly and frankly. While there are likely to be strong emotions, even in a commercial or civil dispute, it is important for the parties to feel

14   See paras 6.23–6.25 on room layout.

that there will be no loss of control even when there are emotional outbursts or tensions during the process.

Welcome and introductions

5.27 The mediator will welcome everybody and use words of encouragement to recognise that both parties have made a positive decision to try and resolve the issues between them. If appropriate, mediators may acknowledge the courage it has taken to attend the meeting, particularly when the process is unfamiliar. This represents a positive first step in finding an agreement which could put the dispute in the past.

5.28 The mediator will introduce himself or herself and then all participants introduce themselves individually (including any observers, legal representatives and supporters). This is a chance to check what the parties wish to be called. The mediator is likely to have discussed in advance whether they are happy to be addressed by their first names.

Timings

5.29 The mediator explains how long the mediation is expected to last and the possibility that it may last longer. Participants should be open about the time they have available and any time constraints they may have so that the mediator can take this into consideration.

Agreement to mediate

5.30 In most mediations, the mediator asks the parties to sign the *agreement to mediate* (or provide parties with copies of an agreement which has previously been signed). Parties will have been sent the *agreement to mediate* (also described as a pre-mediation agreement) beforehand, and had a chance to comment or amend the content. This may also be the appropriate opportunity to thank the legal advisers for providing position statements and document bundles.

5.31 In mediations where written agreements to mediate are not used, the parties are asked whether they are happy to proceed at the conclusion of the opening.

Overview of the mediation process

5.32 The mediator may give an overview of the mediation process, explaining the following:

- *Mediator's role:* Mediators provide structure to the mediation process. They help parties to use the time efficiently and explore their own positions as well as weigh up their options. In some cases, they may guide parties on different aspects of negotiation, assessing their available options and how to communicate more effectively with one another. Mediators remain impartial and are not able to give legal advice, impose a solution or tell parties what to do.

- *The mediation process:* Mediators may set out the difference between joint and separate meetings and the stages of the mediation process.
- *Participants' roles:* Parties control the outcome of the mediation, it is their process and they can decide whether to reach an agreement and what it contains. Legal advisers provide advice and guidance to their client, and make a significant contribution to the mediation. A supporter's role is to support a particular party and usually remain silent during *joint meetings* unless invited to speak.
- *Voluntary:* This means parties should not feel any pressure to reach an agreement and are free to leave at any time.
- *Without prejudice and non-binding:* Any offers or concessions made during the mediation remain confidential and are not binding unless an agreement is reached.
- *Confidentiality:* The mediator will remind the parties that the mediation process is confidential.[15] This means that parties cannot repeat what is said during the mediation unless this is agreed with the other party as part of the mediated agreement.
- *Authority to settle:*[16] It is important that the parties who attend mediation are in a position to reach an agreement, without requiring another person's approval.
- *Reaching agreements:* In civil mediations, the legal advisers will usually write any agreement. In family, workplace or community mediation, the agreements are written with the help of the mediator. The agreement will only be a legally binding document if the parties wish it to be so.
- *Ending the mediation:* Mediators can explain that there may come a time when they have to end the mediation and may not always be able to provide a reason. This is because their code of conduct requires them to bring a mediation to an end in certain circumstances. Parties who wish to leave may do so.

15 See paras 7.31–7.36 for fuller discussion on the confidentiality of mediation.
16 See para 3.83.

Mediators may ask parties to agree not to leave without speaking to them first.

- *Facilities:* Mediators will explain where to find the toilets, refreshments (if any) and fire exits, as well as other facilities such as internet, photocopying and printing facilities.
- *Note-taking:* Mediators often make written notes as a memory aid, but everything said during the mediation remains confidential.[17] It is helpful to explain this to parties to avoid the risk that note-taking is off-putting and may be perceived as judgmental or legalistic.

Introducing and agreeing the ground rules

5.33   The mediator will introduce the need for ground rules, which are an essential part of the process. Agreed by all participants, these ensure that the discussion remains balanced and fair and is not threatening or abusive. Mediators may suggest rules which in their experience have proved useful. Ground rules may include:[18]

- Only one person speaking at any time.
- Listen when the other person is speaking.
- Avoid using abusive or threatening language.
- Be respectful.

Questions

5.34   Participants should be encouraged to ask questions.

---

17   Some mediators have a practice of destroying their notes once the mediation is concluded and will choose to explain this to the parties. Most mediators and mediation providers retain a record that the mediation took place which may include the following information: names of parties, contact details, brief summary of dispute, date, time and duration of the mediation meeting(s), brief summary of whether an agreement was reached.

18   In mediations where there is no agreement to mediate, parties may be asked to consider a ground rule about confidentiality. See paras 7.31–7.32.

Checklist: Mediator's opening

✓

- ☐ Confirm how parties wish to be addressed
- ☐ Signed *agreement to mediate* (civil mediation)
- ☐ Time available
- ☐ An overview of the mediation process
- ☐ Role of the mediator
- ☐ Role of the participants (parties, legal advisers, supporters, experts)
- ☐ Authority to settle
- ☐ Voluntary
- ☐ *Without prejudice* and non binding
- ☐ Confidentiality
- ☐ Note-taking
- ☐ Facilities (toilets, refreshments etc)
- ☐ Ending the mediation
- ☐ Agreements (binding/non-binding)
- ☐ Setting the ground rules

Parties' opening statements (uninterrupted speaking time)

5.35   Parties are usually asked to make short opening statements, also described as *uninterrupted speaking time* or *presentations*. These statements set out the issues, as well as outlining personal grievances and factual background which the parties feel are relevant. This is an opportunity for parties to explain in general terms why they have come to mediation and what they hope to achieve. The mediator will give each party the chance to speak for an equal length of time, and when appropriate they may ask clarifying questions to help parties develop what they want to say.

5.36   Opening statements are an opportunity for the parties to tell their side of the story and to be listened to. They may help explain the strength of feeling about a particular issue, for example. They may also provide an opportunity for a party to acknowledge a grievance or the impact of a past incident or event. Explanations may emerge which resolve misunderstandings. The process of 'telling their story' can also be a cathartic process for parties and enable them to move away from discussing who is 'right' or 'wrong' towards a more collaborative discussion.

Choosing who speaks first

5.37   There can be a natural advantage to speaking first,[19] because the party who follows will instinctively respond to assertions already made. This means, unintentionally, the agenda will have been 'set' by the first speaker. In mediations where there is a power imbalance, or where one party is more articulate than the other, allowing the weaker party to speak first may assist the mediation process. The mediator can discuss with the parties who speaks first and offer guidance based on a range of factors such as whether both parties are represented, the parties' wishes and any fears or concerns, whether an imbalance of power (real or perceived) needs to be redressed. In civil mediation, the claimant is usually (but not always) invited to speak first. If one party is unrepresented, it would be usual for them to be invited to speak first.

5.38   Parties should be encouraged to stick to their own perception of the dispute (and resist responding to what they have just heard). Although they can still respond to matters raised by the other party if they wish, it is important they communicate the issues which matter most to them. There are also going to be further opportunities to speak during the mediation and the person who speaks first can be alternated.

Should the legal adviser or party speak?

5.39   If a party has a legal adviser, who should give the opening statement? The mediator will usually encourage the parties to speak, because it is an opportunity for them to *tell their story* in their own words. The legal adviser may resist this as they will instinctively want to maintain control over the process and their client, in particular, to manage what information is conveyed to the other party. A compromise can be reached where the legal adviser gives an opening statement and the party is invited to comment at the end or read a prepared statement. The mediator should raise the question of who will make the opening statement in the pre-mediation stage.[20] Where the advocates make the opening statements, mediators can provide parties with opportunities to address each other in a *joint meeting* at later stages in the mediation.

---

19   L Boulle and M Nesic, *Mediator skills and techniques: triangle of influence*, Bloomsbury Professional, 2010 p105.

20   See paras 4.26–4.30.

Mediator's summary

5.40   Once each party has had their uninterrupted speaking time or made
their opening statement, the mediator may summarise each side's
position (this may be achieved by summarising the core themes or
issues). A mediator may acknowledge any common ground and list
the key issues that can be used to develop an agenda for discussion. A
mediator's summary can include identifying any 'green shoots', such
as an apology or offers which may form the basis of settlement. By
summarising what has been said, the mediator checks their understanding. This provides parties with the opportunity to reflect on
their accounts and whether they have other issues they wish to raise.
It may be appropriate to acknowledge the impact or the emotional
issues in a particular dispute.

The exchange

Exploring the issues

5.41   The next phase of the mediation is where parties clarify the issues.
This may also involve an exchange of views in relation to the different issues. To initiate the discussion, the mediator may summarise
a party's position in relation to a particular issue and invite the other
party to respond. The mediator will often identify the 'easiest' or
most straightforward issue, one on which it appears that the parties
are most likely to reach an agreement.

5.42   The parties exchange information and explain the issues in order
to build a better understanding of the other side's position. This process will explore the differences between them as well as the common
ground. It also aims to separate facts from perceptions or interpreta-
tions, and certainties from uncertainties, in order to help the parties
more objectively reflect on their own positions. The exchange will
often begin in a *joint meeting* and follow on from the opening phase.
In civil mediations, the parties usually move to their separate meeting rooms and the exchange is facilitated by the mediator 'shuttling'
between their rooms.[21]

5.43   As in civil mediations, if the process of exploring the issues takes
place in separate meetings, this enables the mediator to ask questions which may challenge a party about why they hold a particular
belief or opinion. The mediator may encourage each party to develop
what has been said in relation to a particular point. He or she may

21 With further joint meetings at an appropriate stage.

also prompt parties to clarify what has been said, challenge or reality test assertions, re-frame contentious or negative remarks and summarise the parties' positions before moving on to the next issue.

Getting to interests

5.44   This is the process of examining parties' positions and exploring their feelings. The mediator will encourage the parties to talk freely and openly. They may prompt parties with questions but avoid being too prescriptive and refrain from setting their own agenda for the discussion. This is the opportunity to understand what really matters to the parties, revealing underlying interests and needs. In some cases the process of unpacking these emotions and feelings will uncover a separate event or 'hurt' which may have triggered the conflict. There are often many layers to a dispute,[22] and it can be important to get to the core interests in order to be able to start developing options for an agreement.

5.45   This process begins at the pre-mediation stage, when parties set out their positions in terms of demands or claims and mediators also start encouraging parties to identify their interests. Some questions to ask are:

- What really matters to a party?
- What does the party think is important?
- What do they really hope to achieve from mediation?

Position	Interest	Issue
'I want £20,000 and nothing less'	I want to be treated fairly and paid for work I've completed	Payment of contract
'He is late every day, he can't continue to work here as that is in breach of his contract and company policy'	Ensuring good discipline and work ethic and that all employees are treated equally	Time-keeping, working hours
'I want to see my children every weekend'	I want to maintain a relationship with my children	Overnight contact with children
'I want my neighbour evicted'	I want to be able to sleep at night without being disturbed by my neighbours	Noise issues in neighbours' flat

22 J Beer, *The mediator's handbook*, 3rd edn, New Society Publisher, 1997 p111.

5.46   The role of the mediator is therefore to help parties identify their underlying interests and needs by exploring each side's position and exposing underlying factors which may provide a greater understanding of why each party has reached a particular viewpoint. This information can then, with permission, be conveyed to the other party so as to increase their understanding and widen their perspective.

The turning point or golden thread

5.47   The mediator is always looking for the moment where there is a shared understanding. In a commercial dispute that may be when both parties agree that it makes economic sense to settle the dispute rather than initiating court proceedings; in a workplace dispute it may be the acknowledgment that the management did not handle a grievance well; in a family dispute it may be when a couple are able to acknowledge they both want what is best for their children; in a community dispute it may be an acceptance by one party that the noise caused by their faulty garage door is disturbing their neighbour. In some cases it may be a concession or an apology, in others an agreement about a less contentious issue which can build empathy and trust between the parties. This is the moment when they could be ready to move to the settlement stage.

The problem-solving and settlement stage

5.48   Parties should be aware that any settlement is not imposed or proposed by the mediator but is created from ideas they generate. In mediations where the mediator helps the parties write the agreement, this still applies.

Generating options for agreement

5.49   Once the mediator has helped the parties identify their interests (what they really need), each party can start to generate options for agreement and making requests or offers. Over time, as psychological impasses diminish, the 'exchange' may evolve into a dialogue which enables brainstorming and creative solutions to be discussed. This requires each party to think about the other side's interests, and the scope or potential for meeting this need. Mediation widens the options for agreement, exploring creative solutions which would not be available from a court, tribunal or other adjudicative process.

Before entering the negotiation or 'bargaining' phase, mediators will encourage parties to reflect on their 'interests'.[23]

Making offers and counter-offers

5.50　In most mediations, a stage is reached when the parties start to make and exchange offers for settlement. In a civil or legal dispute, this may be a formal process, in a community or family dispute proposals may be suggested throughout the discussions. Parties may have arrived at the mediation with suggestions or proposals which have the potential to form the basis of an agreement. Throughout the process, mediators acknowledge and note suggestions or ideas which may develop into a potential agreement.

5.51　The process of making offers and counter-offers will usually remain fluid and mediators often encourage parties to keep all options open. Possible solutions may initially be rejected and later reconsidered. Sometimes it may be difficult for a party to 'climb down' or make a concession on a certain issue. This may be avoided by discussing a global (all-in) settlement, or, in some situations, by an issue-by-issue approach.

5.52　If one party makes an offer while the parties are in separate meetings, the offer can be written down. The advantage of getting the party to write the offer down is that it minimises confusion or human error. In practice, this is not always possible or pragmatic. If the mediator conveys an offer, they may wish to place the offer in context to minimise the chance of it being rejected without proper consideration.[24]

Evaluating options

5.53　Parties will be guided and coached by the mediator in various techniques to enable them objectively to assess the proposals being put forward. These include:

- considering what are their alternatives to a negotiated agreement (BATNA, WATNA and MLATNA);[25]
- understanding litigation risk;[26]
- reflecting on their interests.

23　See paras 5.44–5.46.
24　See para 6.69 on reactive devaluation and paras 4.77–4.78.
25　See para 4.55.
26　See para 8.50.

The value of reaching agreement

5.54   The mediator is likely to discuss with the party the value of reaching an agreement. In essence, the mediator will be encouraging the party to be mindful of being flexible and open minded – reaching agreements requires 'give and take'. In a civil case, the value of reaching an agreement may be 'damage limitation' (avoiding costly legal proceedings). It may also be cost-saving if a party's legal adviser does not believe they will be successful at trial, or it may avoid damage to business reputation or preserve an ongoing lucrative contractual arrangement. This means, for example, that compromising over a difference of £5,000 may be worthwhile, even where the party opposes a compromise 'in principle'. In a family case, reaching a resolution and restoring communication, as well as establishing a framework for future decision-making, may be worth a compromise over a much-cherished family heirloom or whether a partner collects a child at 5.00pm or 6.30pm.

5.55   Where stumbling blocks are presented, the mediator enables parties to take a step back and look at the bigger picture, enabling them to remain focused on agreement rather than being caught up in a disagreement on a specific issue.

The evaluative mediator

Moving from facilitation to evaluation.[27]

5.56   Research has shown that civil and commercial mediators perceive a stage towards the end of a mediation where the mediator becomes more evaluative.[28] Mediators can be assertive and provide guidance to parties which assists them to reach agreements and settlements. They may ask probing questions of parties to help them to objectively assess an offer/proposal. Educating and coaching parties to communicate more effectively (such as explaining NVC principles[29]) is an important part of the mediator's role. This is quite different from a mediator offering their legal or expert opinion which may guide or steer the parties towards a particular solution. Or, may encourage

---

27   K Mackie, D Miles, W Marsh, T Allen, *The ADR practice guide: commercial dispute resolution*, 3rd edn, Tottel, 2007 p266.

28   A Bucklow, 'The "everywhen mediator": the virtues of inconsistency and paradox: the strength, skills, attributes and behaviours of excellence and effective mediators' (2007) 73 *Arbitration* 40 and A Bucklow, 'The law of unintended consequences or repeated patterns?' (2006) 72 *Arbitration* 348.

29   See paras 4.35–4.37.

parties to accept a particular proposal or suggest a solution not yet considered, which is not the mediator's role.

5.57 Expressing an opinion as to the likely outcome if the matter is not resolved at the mediation, or what a court is likely to do, is obviously contrary to the principles of facilitative mediation. It presents many risks. At what stage does the mediator become evaluative? How will the parties know? If a party feels they are being placed under pressure by the mediator, will they still feel ownership over the agreement? What happens if they regret reaching a settlement? Could the party sue the mediator for negligent advice? Would the mediator's professional indemnity insurance cover them for this liability? How would the mediator reach a judgment when they may not know all the facts? Does this create a conflict of interest, in particular, for a mediator who markets himself or herself on high settlement rates? For all these reasons, this book cautions against taking a 'strictly' evaluative role.

Writing the agreement

5.58 All mediated agreements (also described as settlement agreements) should be written in common sense and accessible language. This should apply whether the final agreement is legally binding, a non-binding agreement or a Memorandum of Understanding. Chapter 7 considers in more detail how to write mediation agreements, which should be future focused, balanced and positive.[30]

5.59 In legal mediations, the agreement is usually drafted by the legal advisers on a laptop which can then be printed and reviewed by the parties. In family, workplace or community mediation, the agreements are written with the help of the mediator. Where the agreement is handwritten, it is usually photocopied to enable parties to review it; alternatively the agreement will be read back to all those concerned. Once the agreement has been reached, it is usually signed (this is necessary if the agreement is intended to be binding) and a copy given to all the parties.

Closing the mediation

5.60 The mediation will usually end when the parties reach an agreement which has been written down and signed. It is desirable that the mediator brings the process to an end in a *joint meeting*, acknowledging the progress which has been made. This is important whether the

30 See paras 7.11–7.16.

parties have reached an agreement, been able to narrow the issues between them or acknowledge where their differences lie. Where parties have spent most of the time in separate rooms, it may be a significant step to be in the same room, and possibly shake hands.

5.61   Sometimes there is an insurmountable obstacle to reaching agreement, such as a decision-maker not being present, the parties' interests proving incompatible, a party's demand not being achievable or the scheduled time for the mediation having elapsed. Alternatively, the mediator may need to end the mediation for other reasons.[31]

Follow-up

5.62   When an agreement is reached, the mediation provider will usually contact the parties in the weeks following the mediation, to get oral feedback on their experience of the process and to confirm that there have been no difficulties with the agreement.

5.63   If an agreement is not reached, the mediator may continue to work with the parties where they are willing and there is still potential for progress.

Alternative models of facilitative mediation

Time-limited mediation – small claims mediation

5.64   Her Majesty's Courts and Tribunals Service (HMCTS) small claims mediation service conducts mediations primarily over the telephone (or face to face if requested by the parties). The mediator is a fully trained practitioner who is independent of the parties but employed by HMCTS.[32] This may be perceived as undermining the neutrality and independence of the mediator, as there is an apparent conflict of interest – the mediator is employed to divert cases out of the court system. The other notable feature is that there is no *joint meeting* during a small claims mediation.

5.65   Small claims telephone mediation usually uses a model where the mediator speaks to each party separately. This process follows the stages of a mediation: first the mediator has *pre-mediation meetings* with each party and then the joint mediation process commences as shuttle mediation, where the mediator speaks to one party and then

---

31 See paras 6.77 and 12.55–12.56.

32 When the government proposals to introduce automatic referral are implemented, external providers may also provide this service. See para 8.12.

the other, narrowing the issues and moving towards settlement. Most mediations last around an hour. There is limited opportunity for the cathartic process of making an opening statement or to address underlying issues that would usually take place during a mediation.

5.66 There have been concerns that this model of time-limited telephone mediation should properly be described as a 'court-facilitated settlement process'[33] as it does not give parties the opportunity to address their underlying grievances, explore non-monetary outcomes or restore an ongoing relationship and is better suited to money claims where any commercial relationship has ended. Small claims mediators are able to offer face to face meetings. They can assess those cases where a family relationship has broken down or an ongoing commercial relationship between two businesses would benefit from a face to face meeting or a slightly longer process to ensure parties can explore more creative solutions and explore underlying needs and feelings.[34]

Multi-disciplinary approaches

5.67 The model of mediation set out in this chapter broadly describes a process whereby parties enter a *joint meeting* which lasts for a set period of time, up to a day. Increasingly, mediators are borrowing from the different approaches used in civil, family, workplace and community mediation. Geographic and time constraints, for example, may make it practical to hold a series of pre-mediation meetings and joint meetings with parties, legal advisers, interested third parties and experts. Slowing the process, so it extends over more than a day, has the advantage of ensuring a number of decision-makers can be involved in the process and parties are given the opportunity for time to reflect on any final settlement.

Telephone mediation

5.68 In telephone mediation, parties do not actually meet face to face. Where there is a great deal of bad feeling between the parties or they do not live close to one another and there will be no ongoing relationship – or just as a cost-saving exercise – telephone mediation

---

33 V Reid and M Doyle, *Small claims mediation – does it do what is says on the tin?* MOJ, June 2007 p12. Also see paras 2.40–2.42.

34 In cases of relationship breakdown, parties may be signposted to other support services such as counselling or family therapy.

can be effective. Although the whole process takes place over the telephone, it can mirror the stages of a face-to-face mediation process. The mediator will usually speak to the parties over the phone, separately, in *pre-mediation meetings*. Using conference-call facilities, the mediator is able to open the mediation with a *joint meeting*. The mediator may then speak to the parties separately and the mediation will follow similar stages to the process already described.

5.69   Telephone mediation has cost benefits as there is no venue hire, travel expenses and it may take less time. There are fewer logistical difficulties in arranging a meeting on a convenient date. In some cases, parties remaining in a familiar environment may help facilitate reaching an agreement.

5.70   Telephone mediation has disadvantages, parties may feel inhibited by using the telephone. It may be more challenging for a mediator to build rapport with the parties. The fact that parties don't meet face to face may mean communication difficulties are less easy to overcome – for example, body language and other non verbal signals cannot be observed.

Online mediation

5.71   Much like telephone mediation, online mediation takes place without the parties actually meeting in person using Skype and other online video conferencing facilities.[35] This is an emerging field. Reflecting this trend, the European Commission is currently considering a proposal for a Regulation on Online Dispute Resolution (ODR) for consumer disputes.[36]

Frequently asked questions answered by Heather Allen

5.72   The following questions have been answered by Heather Allen who has been a civil and commercial mediator since 1994, as well as a volunteer community mediator and a health service conciliator. Alongside her mediation practice, Heather is head of the Centre for Effective Dispute Resolution's (CEDR's) Training Faculty and trains others in mediation skills both in the UK and in many other parts of the world.

35 See, for example, www.themediationroom.com.
36 http://ec.europa.eu.

How valuable is pre-mediation communication?

Some would say that there is no 'pre-mediation' and that the mediation starts at the first contact with the parties. Preparation is important, whether the parties are to meet on a day or at a series of shorter meetings, or not at all. The mediator will start to get to know the parties from the very first contact, either directly or through their representatives, and the parties will begin to gain trust and confidence in the mediator. The mediator has an important role in helping all participants to join in the mediation process as fully and comfortably as possible, describing the process and inviting questions about who should attend, how to prepare, how the meetings might be run and what might happen.

The mediator can also establish the tone for the mediation, as calm and productive. By helping the parties to co-operate, for example, by setting a start time for the mediation and listing a bundle of documents, the mediator establishes a habit and track record of agreement between the parties.

Preparation on the substantive issues will include reading the documents and anticipating any further information which might be necessary to reach an agreement. For example, suggesting an expert be on hand to provide objective information to the parties during the meetings. Preparation is always important in order to give the parties the best chance of resolving matters efficiently, effectively and as amicably as possible.

How flexible is the mediation process?

The fundamentals of mediation do not change: that it is a confidential process, that the mediator is impartial as between the parties, and that it is the parties who determine whether agreement is reached and on what terms. One of the strengths of mediation is that there is no prescribed process that must be followed, and every mediation can be designed to meet the needs of the parties and the particular circumstances of each case. Initial plans about how the mediation will be run, what issues are to be discussed, how settlement might be documented and even who might attend, can all be negotiated and renegotiated if necessary. It is important for the mediator to remain flexible in his or her use of the process, while managing the parties' expectations, giving time for process suggestions to be discussed, and keeping the parties informed about probable next steps.

How does the mediator help parties to reach agreement without telling them what to do?

The mediator works actively to enable the parties to make best use of the opportunity that mediation affords; the role demands a range of skills and techniques. In many ways it would be easier to tell the parties what to do rather than to undertake the task of the mediator, which is to assist the parties to grapple with the problem and determine the outcome for themselves.

Throughout the process the mediator will model appropriate behaviours, use positive language, accept and work with emotions, and use empathy and skilled listening to enable the parties to relax and participate fully. The mediator needs to apply strong process management skills throughout – about timing, about what meetings might take place and who might attend, and in moving through the stages to create momentum and direction towards settlement without determining the outcome or taking sides. In order to facilitate effective exchange of information, the mediator might help the parties rehearse what they want to say to the other party.

During the problem-solving stage, and especially if the parties get stuck, the mediator might help the parties to think through their strategy and the possible consequences of a suggestion or offer; they might reality test a particular stance or position in private to allow parties to consider a shift of position; they might assist parties to assess or reassess the risks they face if no settlement is reached – legal, financial, commercial, and other risks, such as to wellbeing – using challenging questions and sometimes specific risk assessment tools. The mediator uses their own negotiation experience and understanding to help the parties – all parties – to negotiate effectively, but without telling them what to offer or accept.

The role of the mediator requires skill, perseverance, and attention to the human needs of dignity, equal treatment and consideration for the individual.

CHAPTER 6

Mediation skills, strategies and techniques

continued

Key points

- The mediator is responsible for the mediation process while parties are responsible for any outcomes.
- The mediator aims to create a safe environment, so that parties feel comfortable and able to participate fully.
- The mediator's toolkit includes: self awareness, active listening, summarising, re-framing, reality testing, empathy and positivity.
- The mediator is able to use the ground rules to help ensure that the meeting runs smoothly.
- The mediator can use a private meeting (caucus) to work with the parties separately. This could include testing their views, helping them frame their offer or discussing their level of participation in the process.
- The mediator encourages parties to use an interest-based approach to find mutually acceptable outcomes, and added-value solutions.[1]
- Any agreement reached is written with the help of the mediator. In civil mediation the legal adviser will usually draft the agreement.
- The mediator will close the mediation appropriately, and the mediator or mediation provider will usually provide a follow-up service.

The mediator's role

6.1 The role of the facilitative mediator is to manage the process of mediation and enable the parties to decide any agreement or settlement reached during the mediation. The mediator moves the conversation through the stages of the mediation process. The mediator is impartial and neutral which means: not taking sides, not giving an opinion or advice, and not directing the outcome of the mediation. The mediator is not passive and takes an active role to ensure that mediation is a fair process.

6.2 Mediators support the parties to reach an agreement by:

- demonstrating good active listening;
- ensuring that both parties have equal chances to speak and be heard;

1 Discussed more fully in chapter 4 – see paras 4.51–4.61.

- helping parties to communicate effectively;
- managing power imbalances;
- guiding parties through the negotiation process.

Setting the scene and creating the right environment

Mediator functions

6.3   The role of the mediator or mediation provider is to help the parties feel that they can trust the mediation process to bring their conflict to an end. It is important that every aspect of the mediation process reinforces the principles of neutrality, independence and fairness.

6.4   Boulle and Nesic identify four mediator functions:[2]

- creating favourable conditions for the parties;
- assisting the parties to communicate;
- facilitating the parties' negotiations;
- encouraging settlement.

Communication and language

6.5   The way the mediator speaks and the language they use is an incredibly powerful tool. The mediator uses the pace, tone and volume of their voice to establish a non-judgmental and informal atmosphere.

6.6   The mediator uses language that aims to demonstrate that mediation is a co-operative and open process. For this reason mediators ask parties if they are happy to be addressed by first names, as this is intended to place everyone on an equal footing.

Safe space

6.7   Mediation providers should ensure that parties can arrive separately without meeting each other. This may involve parties arriving at different times, having separate waiting areas or being shown into separate rooms.

6.8   The mediator will invite parties to establish *ground rules*[3] which help the mediator control the process and ensure that the meeting runs as smoothly as possible. The mediator will usually propose a number of ground rules and parties are able to make additional suggestions. Within the mediation process, venting or *off-loading* can be helpful in moving towards agreement. Parties may express their

2   L Boulle and M Nesic, *Mediator skills and techniques: triangle of influence*, Bloomsbury Professional, 2010 pp12–13.
3   See para 6.26.

emotions and communicate their strongly held beliefs. Emotions may run high. As a third party, the mediator is able to de-fuse tensions by *neutralising* language and move the discussion forward by *summarising* and *re-framing*.

Accessibility

6.9 The participants and the mediator or the mediation provider[4] will need to identify a suitable, neutral venue which is appropriate to the parties' physical and personal needs. The timing of the mediation should take into account issues such as childcare or work commitments. At all times, mediation providers should consider factors that may assist parties fully participate in the mediation such as interpreters, advocates and supporters.[5]

6.10 Some parties may not have English as their first language or may have other communication needs. It is possible to arrange an interpreter, or alternatively the mediator will explore ways to ensure that parties are able to understand the mediation process and express themselves. For example, it is good practice to read the final agreement aloud. This helps parties who may have reading difficulties, and ensures that the parties have understood before they are invited to sign it.

Meeting the participants' needs

6.11 The mediator will also want to ensure that the parties feel as comfortable as possible. This includes making sure the participants can find their way around the building and know where the toilets are as well as other facilities. In full-day mediations, it is helpful to provide adequate refreshments including access to tea and coffee-making facilities to ensure parties can keep their energy levels up during the day. Where appropriate, the mediator may also invite parties to take a break and possibly leave the building for a short walk.

6.12 The rooms should ideally be sound proofed and have a flipchart, pens and paper and a calculator.[6]

---

4 If you are using a mediation provider, this is something which should be part of their service.

5 See paras 3.84–3.91 and 3.97.

6 See paras 3.98–3.102.

Pre-mediation meetings

6.13   A *pre-mediation meeting* may take place face-to-face at the mediation provider's office or the party's home, or over the telephone.

6.14   A *pre-mediation meeting* enables the mediator to learn more about the dispute and the parties. This provides the mediator with information to help structure the mediation process. The mediator will explain the mediation process and what will happen at the joint mediation meeting and start to build the parties' trust.[7]

6.15   The mediator may ask open questions to find out more about the dispute and the issues the party considers important. It can be helpful for the mediator to clarify these issues; this may reveal areas a party will find difficult to talk about or confidential or sensitive topics that they do not want to discuss during the *joint meeting*. In workplace mediation, *pre-mediation meetings* are an opportunity for the mediator to help parties prepare their opening statement for the *joint meeting*.

6.16   In some areas of mediation, the *pre-mediation meeting* takes place before parties agree to mediate. In family cases, mediation information and assessment meetings (MIAMs) are now routine.[8] In community mediation, mediators use home visits or *pre-mediation meetings* to help the parties decide whether to proceed to a *joint meeting*.[9]

The joint meeting

Planning the structure of the mediation

6.17   The mediator will usually have spoken to the parties before the *joint meeting*, so they will have some idea of the issues. Before the mediation, the mediator will plan how to structure the mediation, making decisions such as which party will be invited to speak first, and any particular issues or strategies for dealing with the parties. As part of the preparation the mediator should remain open-minded and avoid making judgments or allowing pre-conceived ideas about possible outcomes to influence how the mediation is conducted.

6.18   It may be helpful for the mediator to spend some time reviewing what worked well in their most recent mediations, the strategies that were less effective and what approach they wish to take in this particular case.

---

7   See paras 5.3–5.8.
8   See paras 9.8–9.22 and 9.63–9.66 for a fuller discussion.
9   See paras 11.39–11.40.

Practical preparation

6.19 Practical steps before the mediation meeting:

- set up the room;
- have paper and pens (and calculator);
- have all documents, including any notes from *pre-mediation meetings* (position statements, document bundles and copies of the *agreement to mediate*);
- decide the room plan – most mediators write the participants' names on a seating plan or table map (as well as memorise their names);
- be familiar with the facilities – where any separate or 'break-out' rooms are, the *joint meeting* room, where toilets are situated, how the heating/air conditioning works, refreshments (if supplied), details of computing facilities, photocopying and printing arrangements, and whom to ask if assistance is required.

Co-mediators

6.20 If you are using the co-mediation model, you will need to discuss the following with your co-mediator:

- sharing out the tasks – the opening statement, summarising the parties' accounts, setting an agenda for the exchange, writing out the agreement;
- raise any concerns or potential issues which may arise in the mediation and discuss strategies for handling them, for example, what to do if a party walks out.

Observers

6.21 An observer may be a newly qualified mediator who will adopt an observer role. Observers will not usually play an active role in the mediation sessions. They may be required to meet parties as they arrive or help with refreshments.

Assistant mediators

6.22 An assistant mediator may be a fully accredited mediator who will assist the lead mediator with the mediation process. They may or may not play an active role. The role an assistant mediator will play should be discussed in advance.

Room layout and seating arrangements

6.23   Room layout is important.[10] The main consideration is that all the participants should be able to see and hear each other. The aim is to create a sense of balance and fairness and remove barriers to communication. This can be reinforced by where the mediator positions themselves in the room. The mediator may position themselves at the 'head of the table' in the joint mediation meeting to establish their authority over the process. They may choose to position themselves facing the door, so that they can 'welcome' the parties into *their* room (and *their* process). While mediators are non-judgmental and neutral facilitators, it is important that the parties feel confident that the mediator will be able to maintain control over the process. This is particularly so, where legal advisers attend a mediation and there is potential for an imbalance of power if one advocate is more articulate and assertive or there is a self-represented party. All parties, including the advocates, need to trust the mediator to manage the mediation process fairly.

6.24   Mediators may be constrained by the room and the facilities available, but will be mindful of types of seating and whether to make use of a table. The main aim is to remove devices used by people in a position of authority to assert their authority or control, such as sitting on a higher chair or placing a desk between themselves and other people in the meeting.

6.25   One decision a mediator will need to consider is where to seat the parties if they attend with their legal adviser and/or a supporter or expert. All the members of one party should be able to sit together. If a party has a legal adviser, it is most common to seat the party nearest the mediator, then their supporter or legal adviser or expert. The purpose of this is to empower the parties, as they are the decision-makers (rather than their advocates or supporters). If the mediator is concerned about an imbalance of power between the legal advisers, seating them nearest the mediator may reassure a less confident adviser and bolster the party. If a party appears more vulnerable and wants to be seated next to their supporter, placing them between their legal adviser and the supporter would be appropriate.

10 See para 5.23.

Possible seating arrangements for a joint mediation meeting

No table

(M)

(P1)   (P2)

No table

(M)   (M)

(A)   (P)

Low table

(M)

(P1) [ ] (P2)

(A)   (A)

Oval table

(M)

(A)   (A)

(P1)   (P2)

(S)   (S)

Round table

(M)

(P1)   (P2)

(A)   (A)

(A)   (A)

M – Mediator   P – Party   S – Supporter   A – Legal adviser

Mediation skills

The mediator's 'toolkit'

Upholding the ground rules

6.26   The ground rules[11] are a simple way of ensuring that parties are listening to each other and that the conversation between the parties remains calm. While a mediator tries to ensure that their interventions remain neutral, the mediator may need to be assertive in order to manage power imbalances between parties. Assertive interventions can be achieved by returning the parties to the ground rules, which are established during the mediation opening. For example:

> Mediator   Sadat and Ronan, can I just ask you to stop for a moment. I'm finding it difficult to hear what Ronan is saying. We agreed that only one person would speak at a time. Sadat, you clearly want to respond to what Ronan is saying. Would you like some paper to make notes so that you don't forget the points you want to make?

Active listening

6.27   Active listening is important during a mediation because it creates space for parties to speak openly. The aim of active listening is to ensure that the parties feel that they have been heard and to help the mediator get a full understanding of the issues.

6.28   Active listening skills include:

- maintaining open body language;
- making eye contact;
- using encouraging behaviour, such as nodding;
- listening without interrupting;
- silence;
- summarising (to ensure understanding);

6.29   For the mediator, note-taking is important so that they are able to summarise accurately what the parties have said and keep an overview of the whole case. Mediators need to be mindful that writing notes can be distracting and take their attention away from the speaker. They will also have taken care to explain that everything said remains confidential.[12]

---

11 See para 5.33.
12 See paras 7.31–7.32.

Summarising

6.30 A function of active listening is checking that the mediator has understood what a party has said. Summarising helps the mediator achieve this, and it provides the party with an opportunity to correct any bias or misunderstanding on the mediator's part. A mediator may ask, for example:

> Mediator Does that fairly summarise what you've said?
>
> Mediator Would you agree with that?
>
> Mediator Would you like to add or change anything?

6.31 Summarising has another important use for the mediator, it can create time to think, de-fuse tensions and refocus the discussion.

Re-framing

6.32 This is the process where you take the 'sting in the tail' out of something a party has said, and rephrase it to make it future-focused and easier for the other person to hear. For example:

> Desmond If I don't get my £10,000 today I'm leaving, that's what I deserve!
>
> Mediator So you would consider £10,000 a fair settlement?

6.33 Re-framing can also be used to demonstrate that both parties have overlapping or shared interests. This may also be described as 'mutualising'. For example:

> Duran I want Rachel to live with me, I live nearest her school.
>
> Bethan That's ridiculous, she has to live with me. I'm her mother.
>
> Mediator So you are both looking for an arrangement which meets Rachel's needs and is in her best interests.

Reality testing

6.34 Reality testing is where the mediator asks questions to test the strengths and weaknesses of a party's position or assertion. Sometimes these questions may confront a party with 'contradictions, discrepancies and gaps'[13] in what they are saying, or question the validity of a party's position. Two examples:

> Mediator You've said that you'd get £30,000 damages if your legal argument is successful. how condient are you that you'll actually win on this point? Have you discussed this with your legal adviser?

13 F Strasser and P Randolph, *Mediation: a psychological insight into conflict resolution*, Continuum, 2008 p52.

> Mediator　You've told us if you can't resolve things you'll just leave and get another job. When was the last time you changed jobs? Have you thought about how long it might take to get a new job?

6.35　Reality testing may require mediators to ask challenging, probing and searching questions. This will usually be done when the other party is not present, either during a *pre-mediation meeting* or in a private meeting during the mediation.

Empathy

6.36　When emotions are running high, acknowledging the parties' feelings can diffuse tensions. Empathy enables the mediator to validate the emotional impact of the dispute without expressing an opinion about the underlying issues. It is important to distinguish between empathy (acknowledging feelings) and sympathy (feeling sorry for). Being sympathetic is generally avoided by mediators as it could be perceived as taking sides.

6.37　Mediators use open questions to help encourage the parties to express their emotions – for example:

> Mediator　How did you feel when ... happened?
>
> How would you feel if ...?
>
> What was the impact of ... on you?

6.38　The mediator is then able to empathise, using phrases such as:

> Mediator　This is clearly something you feel strongly about.
>
> You've expressed a lot of emotion about ...
>
> You've talked about how angry you felt.
>
> You've described how frustrating it has been.

Keeping positive and balanced

6.39　Mediators can bring humour and positive language to the mediation process. Demonstrating that the mediator believes that the parties will reach an agreement is a powerful tool in changing mindsets and overcoming impasses. For example:

> Mediator　You've both come here today to ... It is realistic to think that you can find a settlement today.

6.40　The mediator tries to ensure that parties speak for equal time during *joint meetings*, and also that equal time is spent in separate meetings with each party. During *joint meetings*, the mediator aims to be balanced and non-judgmental, ensuring both parties participate fully.

Self-awareness

6.41 Mediators aim to create an environment in which parties are able to speak openly and communicate effectively. They will maintain good eye contact with all the people in the room: parties, lawyers and supporters. They will use open and relaxed body language and have a confident and positive demeanour. In co-mediation, mediators are able to model good co-operative working throughout the mediation.

Body language

6.42 Mediators should be aware of the participants' body language as well as their own. This enables them to recognise parties' emotions and concerns, using both verbal and non-verbal clues, and where appropriate, these observations can be acknowledged. This may encourage a party to communicate or voice an issue; alternatively, it may address a party who is using their body language as a device to intimidate or interrupt another party. For example:

> Mediator   Rosie, I've noticed that you have your arms folded and are very quiet. Is there something you don't feel happy with?
>
> Mediator   Dylan, you are looking puzzled / have raised your eyebrows. Is there something you want to say?

Remaining impartial

6.43 Mediators aim to manage the mediation process without their opinions or judgments coming into play, which is not always easy. There are times when their impartiality is threatened. It is good practice for mediators to be aware of their own cultural and religious values, as well as how their personal beliefs and experiences which may impact upon their impartiality during mediation. A mediator's awareness of class, gender, age and race prevent this impacting upon their role.

6.44 Mediators may use a reflective diary and other reflective practices to develop their self-awareness.[14] In co-mediation or where there is an observer or assistant mediator, if invited to do so, the mediator's colleague will be able to give feedback on any perceived biases or prejudices.

Cultural sensitivity

> Understanding ... cultural patterns – both your own and the parties' – will help you adjust how you mediate to fit a particular dispute.[15]

---

14 See para 12.11 on self-reflective practices.
15 J Beer, *The mediator's handbook*, 3rd edn, New Society Publisher, 1997 p80.

6.45 Being self-aware extends to understanding that our perceptions are shaped by cultural norms. What may be considered an everyday occurrence in one culture may cause offence in another; for example, 'silence' may infer that a party is agreeing with what is being said, or it could also be a party expressing their disapproval or indifference. Direct eye contact in some cultural contexts can be polite and respectful behaviour, and looking away is evasive and disrespectful; in another culture, direct eye contact could be considered challenging and disrespectful and looking away a sign of respect.

Question bank: 'Mediation gems'[16]

It sounds like ...

Would I be right in thinking ...

I sense / I'm sensing ...

What are you wanting from mediation?

What do you think your neighbour wants from mediation?

Can you explain ...

What leads you to think ...

Tell me a bit more about ...

Questioning styles

6.46 Mediators use a mixture of open and closed questions. In some cases, focused and closed questions can appear loaded or judgmental. Generally, 'why' questions are not 'mediation-friendly', as they make people defensive and can be difficult to answer. Instead, 'what' questions ask for specific, descriptive responses in a less directive way.[17] Leading questions should be avoided as they invite the parties to respond in a way which may suggest the mediator expects or approves of a particular answer.

16 Courtesy of Heather Loebel, CALM (Confidential and Local Mediation) – www.calmmediation.org.
17 J Beer, *The mediator's handbook*, 3rd edn, New Society Publisher, 1997 p108.

Questioning style	Example	Purpose
Affirmation	'You've described a situation which sounded very difficult and frustrating for you' 'I understand that it has been difficult for you to come here today ...'	To build trust with the party and to enable them to state their grievance and be listened to so they can move on.
Acknowledging feelings	'You've talked about how angry you felt ...' 'I sense there is a great deal of tension about this issue ...'	To express empathy and sensitivity. It may enable a party to discuss an issue they feel strongly about. It may also help a party focus on settlement instead of focusing on the past.
Assertive	'You've repeated that point several times ...' 'Can I interrupt for a moment ...?'	To assert the mediator's control over the mediation process, to manage power imbalances and to ensure that each party is heard.
Checking in	'Have I missed anything?' 'How are you feeling?'	To create a positive, unassuming, inclusive atmosphere.
Clarifying	'Am I right in thinking ...?' 'Have I understood correctly?'	To check understanding; to maintain non-judgmental interventions and to minimise mediator bias
De-personalising	Rather than, 'You're selfish and never ever give in on anything': 'Sarah has expressed frustration that she feels that you seem unwilling to compromise ...'	To remove personal attacks or criticisms to reveal the underlying issues, to enable the other party to hear what is being said rather than react or become defensive.

Questioning style	Example	Purpose
Neutral and non-judgmental	Rather than, 'Why didn't you mention ... at the time?': 'Have I understood correctly that you didn't mention ... at the time?' 'What made it difficult for you to mention ... at the time?'	To remove any stigma and prevent the party feeling defensive or judged.
Neutralising	Rather than, 'He was always untrustworthy, he never did anything he said he would': 'So you felt you couldn't rely on him?'	To model good communication and de-fuse comments that may upset or antagonise the other party.
Probing	'Can you tell us more about ...' 'Can you explain ...'	To obtain greater detail and understanding of the issues.
Reflecting	'Would you agree with what was just said?' 'How do you feel about that?' 'Would that be an agreement you could live with?'	To ensure that a mediator has fully understood and to give a party has understood what is being said.

Issues that cannot be mediated

6.47   Many disputes arise where parties have different values or beliefs or there has been a different recollection or interpretation of an incident. It is helpful for mediators to identify issues that cannot be mediated to prevent parties from becoming preoccupied with something that cannot be resolved in mediation.

6.48   Issues that cannot be mediated are:

- feelings and attitudes;
- beliefs and values;
- determining the truth;
- attributing fault or liability;
- addictive or abusive behaviours.

Dealing with non-mediatable issues

6.49 When such issues arise, mediators may find it helpful to acknowledge them. For example:

Mediator   I've heard you mention several times what outcome you'd
achieve if you went to court – mediation is an opportunity to
explore solutions which are beyond the power of the court.

Mediator   We may never get to the bottom of ..., but the purpose of
mediation is to think about how things could be different in
the future.

Mediator   We can't do anything about the past, but you can make a
difference about the future.

When and how should the mediator intervene?

Pre-mediation meetings

6.50 The mediator will use the *pre-mediation meeting* (and any telephone
calls, emails or letters) to try to build rapport with the party. This
is achieved through active listening, clarifying issues and empathy.
Enabling the party to give their account of events and off-load at a
preliminary stage often has the effect of establishing a relationship of
trust with the mediator. This enables the mediator to help the party
clarify the issues and have a better understanding of what they want
to discuss at the joint meeting.

Joint meetings

6.51 The mediator will use their interventions during the joint meeting to
manage the mediation process and help the parties work towards an
agreement.

The opening

6.52 The mediator will usually speak first, using calm and clear language.
When inviting parties to start their opening statement, in non-legal
mediations, the mediator may say something such as:

Mediator   John, would you like to start?

Mediator   Would you like to talk about the situation which has brought
you here?

Mediator   Can you tell us about what's been happening?

6.53   The mediator will try to avoid interrupting once the party starts speaking. Where a party makes a particularly short opening statement, the mediator may ask additional questions to prompt a party to provide more information or to clarify an issue.

> Mediator   Can you tell us more about ...?
>
> Mediator   Could you tell us what you think are the main issues / hope to achieve from mediation / what made you come to mediation ...?
>
> Mediator   Are there any other areas of concern you wanted to raise at this stage?

Dealing with interruptions

6.54   Where a party interrupts the other party when they are speaking, the mediator will need to intervene. For example:

> Mediator   Alice, I appreciate that it is difficult to remain silent, but silence doesn't mean that you agree with everything that is being said and you will have a chance to discuss these issues in a moment.
>
> Mediator   Kath, it is still Spencer's time to speak. If you disagree with anything he has said please write it down and you can discuss it in a moment.
>
> Mediator   I'm finding it difficult to follow what is being said. I appreciate that it is difficult not to respond to issues as they are raised, but we will have plenty of time to discuss anything which concerns you.
>
> Mediator   We all agreed a ground rule that only one person would speak at a time. Are we all still happy with that?

6.55   A party's body language may cause a distraction. For example, facial expressions, fidgeting with a pen, folding arms or looking away. The mediator has to assess whether or how to intervene. On the one hand, this may be a non-verbal clue that something is not right, such as a party is uncomfortable because the room is too cold or unable to understand. On the other, the behaviour may be deliberate. If it is preventing the other party from speaking it may only need a gentle reminder, for example:

> Mediator   I'm conscious that Rajeev does not seem very comfortable. Can I check that everything is ok before we allow Marina to continue?
>
> Mediator   Rajeev, can I remind you this is Marina's chance to speak and you agreed to listen to her.

The mediator's summary

6.56   The mediator concludes the opening by summarising what the parties have said. If the parties have identified their interests, this can enable the mediator to reflect any common ground between the parties. For example:

> Mediator   Jim has outlined the issues as X, Y and Z and is seeking an equitable settlement; Isobel has outlined the issues as A, B and C and has raised her concerns about ..., and she also wants a fair settlement.

> Mediator   You have both said you are looking for a [financial] resolution which will bring the dispute to an end today and resolve the issues between you.

> Mediator   You have both said that the cost implications of ongoing court proceedings mean it is in both your interests to resolve matters today.

Setting the agenda

6.57   After the mediator has summarised the parties' opening statements they then create an agenda for the exchange. This may be done by listing the issues. Once several topics or issues have emerged, different strategies include:

- listing the issues and starting with the easiest issue first (although in some mediations taking the most difficult issue first may be appropriate);
- identifying the areas of common ground, then exploring any initial proposals or conclusions the parties can reach;
- breaking the issues down to create bite-sized chunks;
- 'parking issues' – this is the concept that if there is a sticking point in relation to a particular issue, the mediator can suggest that the parties 'park' that issue, in other words put it to one side and return to it when there is clarity on other areas or issues.[18]

---

18 See 'Moving the discussion forward', after para 6.65.

The exchange

Exploring the issues

6.58   The mediator may start the exchange in a number of different ways. They may use questions as a prompt to elicit more information and detail – for example:

> Mediator   I've set out the issues that you've talked about, Chloe, perhaps you could tell us more about ...

> Mediator   James, you wanted the opportunity to respond to some of the issues Chloe raised. Would you like to do that now?

> Mediator   Chloe, you've heard James describe the situations in relation to .... What would you like to say about that?

Separating emotions from perceptions

6.59   Mediators aim to improve understanding between the parties. In some cases, the mediator encourages parties to explore a particular incident or event and their perceptions and beliefs. For example:

Event	Impact/emotion	Perception/belief
Lawyer's letters not received by defendant	Party unaware of legal proceedings, court hearings, disclosure – causing delay and stress	Lawyers actions are malicious and contrived
Builder leaves job incomplete	Stress and inconvenience of living with an unfinished building project in the family home	Builder is selfish and unprofessional
Timing of meetings with line manager	Time pressure, concern about being late home to see children	Line manager deliberately undermining agreed working hours

6.60   The mediator's role is to help the parties separate their interpretation from the factual events, and then the mediator is able to reality test a party's beliefs.[19] This has the potential to uncover misunderstandings

---

19   This process is drawn from the principles of Cognitive Behavioural Therapy (CBT).

and, in some cases, reveal a party's underlying interests. For example:

Judy	Their lawyer deliberately mis-addresses post so that I don't receive letters.
Mediator	What makes you believe that it is deliberate?
Colin	The builder walked off the job after taking all our money. He got a better paying job and so he left.
Mediator	What explanation did the builder give for leaving? What reason have you got to disbelieve him?
Anya	My boss always waits until 5.20pm to ask me to do something. She knows I leave at 5.30pm but she doesn't have kids so she does it deliberately to make a point.
Mediator	What makes you believe that it is deliberate? Is she aware that you feel like this? Are there any other possible explanations for her behaviour?

Managing emotions

6.61 Taking part in mediation can bring up strong emotions. In some *joint meetings*, it will be valuable to let parties have an opportunity to vent their grievances, so the decision about when a mediator intervenes requires careful judgment. It is important that the mediator remains calm. Once the mediator decides they need to intervene there are a number of strategies which can be effective:

- acknowledge the impact or strength of feeling;
- use the ground rules;[20]
- re-frame issues;[21]
- create a natural break by summarising what has been said;
- ensure that both parties get to speak, summarise party A's position then asking party B how they feel about the issue;
- ask the parties whether they would like carry on or take a break.

Getting to interests

6.62 The purpose of removing the layers of the dispute helps to identify a party's underlying interests and what really matters to them.[22] The

---

20 See paras 6.54–6.55 on interruptions during the opening.
21 See paras 6.32–6.33.
22 See paras 5.44–5.46 on interests.

mediator will ask parties different questions to discern their interests, such as:

- What issue matters most to you? Can you explain why?
- What do you think is important?
- What would you like to say that you haven't been asked about?
- What do you hope to achieve from mediation?

Hidden messages

6.63　Mediators are aware that parties will have different strategies for approaching negotiation or conflict.[23] There are some particular behaviours which will signal that the party is trying to communicate a message: repetition and silence.

Repetition

6.64　If a party has repeated a point several times, it may be a sign that there is an issue of importance which may not have been fully explored or that the party thinks has not been heard. Mediators may ask:

Mediator　Polly, can you explain what makes ... is important to you?

Mediator　Stuart you've raised the issue of ... several times. Is there something you want to ask?

Mediator　Jean, you've mentioned ... but I'm not sure I know what you mean. Can I ask you to explain a bit further?

Silence[24]

6.65　In some cases silence may mean approval. More commonly in mediation, it may be a sign that a party is uncomfortable or unhappy. Parties may also just need some space to think!

23　See paras 4.62–4.64.
24　Also see paras 6.45 and 9.88 on cultural sensitivity.

Moving the discussion forward

Facilitating communication

Mediation has the potential to improve the way parties communicate between each other. It is important to highlight negative statements which can block the mediation process and not to allow misunderstandings to persist. The mediator can re-frame what is said to improve understanding, remove tensions and model good communication skills. Re-framing is about dealing with problems. The mediator keeps checking with each party that they agree with how their comments have been summarised or restated. The mediator also checks that the parties have understood what each other is saying.

Coaching and modelling

Mediators may explain to parties how different ways of communicating and negotiating may be more effective. They may help parties think through how to present offers, consider the other party's position and explore creative solutions outside the fixed positions parties have adopted. Mediators are able to model good active listening as well as negotiation techniques in the way they communicate with the parties.

'Parking' issues[25]

Certain topics may provoke high emotion or reveal complex issues. One strategy is to 'park' those issues, putting them to one side while agreement is reached on other less contentious issues. Parties may be more willing to compromise or 'let go' of these issues once some agreement is reached and the possibility of settlement is realistic.

The turning point or the 'golden thread'[26]

This the moment in the mediation when there is a shared understanding – for example, an apology or acknowledgement which starts to build empathy and trust between the parties, or an agreement or shared understanding on a certain issue.[27] When this moment emerges, the mediator acknowledges the shared understanding and uses this to move the discussion into the settlement stage.

---

25 See para 6.57.
26 See para 5.47.
27 See para 5.40.

Problem-solving and settlement

Final issues

6.66   In some cases, the mediator may encourage parties in a *joint meeting* to make any apologies or acknowledgements which have emerged in the earlier discussions. This is a chance for parties to air any final issues and raise any loose ends so that a line can be drawn under the past and helps ensure an agreement can be reached.

Generating options

6.67   Mediators use a number of different techniques for problem-solving and generating potential options for agreement. Some examples are:

- *Brainstorming:* Encourage parties to generate several suggestions (some mediators use flipcharts and other visual aids).
- *Visualising:* For example, 'If you had a magic wand, how would you see things working in the future?'
- *Thinking hypothetically:* Allowing parties to consider options without committing themselves.
- *Putting the party in the other party's shoes:* What would be a good outcome for party B? What could you offer party A that would make this a good outcome?
- *Value added:*[28] What could you offer party B to make an agreement more likely?

6.68   Legal advisers can be encouraged to think outside the framework of legal liabilities and responsibilities when exploring options. Parties can be encouraged to think creatively and practically. The mediator may ask questions such as:

Mediator   What can you offer to help resolve this issue?

Mediator   How could you address party B's concerns about ...?

Mediator   What would you want from party B to get you to agree to concede issue X?

Packaging the deal

6.69   The way offers are communicated can influence whether or not they are accepted by the other party. It is therefore important for the mediator to guide the parties when making offers to each other. Where parties are in separate rooms – for example, in civil mediations –

---

28 See paras 4.57–4.61.

how the offers are made is of particular importance. The mediator may seek permission from the party making an offer to provide an explanation and set the offer in context.[29]

Making the first move

The psychology of negotiation underpins the final stages of reaching an agreement.

'Too good to be true'
Where one party makes the first offer or proposal, there is always the risk that the other party will perceive it as 'too good to be true', or be suspicious about why the offer is being made. Even where an offer is made in good faith, a party may reject an early offer because they think they are being sold short or that there is a hidden catch.

Reactive devaluation
This is where a party rejects an offer, solely on the basis of the person who is making it without objectively assessing it.

'Losing face'
If one party perceives they are making all the concessions or compromising on a previously immoveable position, they may feel they are 'losing face'. The desire to 'save face' and retain dignity and self-worth in the eyes of others, peers, colleagues or clients may present a psychological obstacle to reaching an agreement. Even where a party is being offered an outcome which meets their interests, the fear of 'losing face' may prevent them from taking it.

Moving on from an impasse

6.70   There are a number of factors which can cause discussions to become deadlocked or break down.

Conflict blockers and obstacles to settlement

6.71   The mediator's role is to diagnose where the impasse lies, and use appropriate techniques to move on from the impasse:[30]

- *Substantive issues:* The mediator will continue to remind parties of their underlying interests, the advantages to reaching a mediated agreement and the alternatives if no agreement is reached. The mediator will encourage parties to look at the

---

29 See paras 4.77–4.78.
30 See para 9.93. Also see para 5.53 on evaluating options.

dispute in a new way – what could the other party offer to make a settlement possible? what could you offer them? if the mediation were to end now, what would you regret not asking, or saying? The mediator may use a *joint meeting* to revisit a contentious issue and allow each party to give explanations.

- *Psychological or emotional issues:* These may be a party's concern about 'losing face', or a legal adviser's reluctance to recommend an agreement which differs from their original advice. These may be addressed in a private meeting where the mediator has time to talk through the party's concerns and help the party construct reasons for accepting a proposed offer or solution. Or, the mediator may explore what one party could offer which may be of little or no financial cost but make considerable difference to the other party. Other options are an apology or acknowledgement, an explanation, an undertaking to address certain policy issues or procedures, an agreement on how to address issues which arise in the future.

- *A party's approach:* In some cases, one of the parties may be less able to be flexible, creative or open-minded about reaching a settlement. The mediator may have to be quite direct in a separate meeting, revisit the ground rules, encourage the party to talk about what they hope to achieve from mediation and reality test any unrealistic objectives. In some cases the mediator may decide it is time to bring the mediation to an end.

Accusations of lying

6.72   The mediator needs to respond to this when it arises, because accusations of lying can undermine the mediation process. It is good practice to explain that mediation does not decide whether a party is right or wrong and that there are some things we may never know. Mediation doesn't try to change the past but looks at how things will be in the future. The mediator can ask the party to explain why they have made the assertion, explore the factual background and, where appropriate, re-frame what has been said.

Last minute 'add-ons'

6.73   Where one party seeks to add another issue at a late stage, this may be designed to de-rail the whole settlement, extract a further concession or be a genuine oversight.[31] Reality testing a party's motivation

---

31   L Boulle and M Nesic, *Mediator skills and techniques: triangle of influence*, Bloomsbury Professional, 2010 p198.

can help a mediator diagnose how best to deal with it. In order to minimise the chances of this happening, it is a good idea to ask parties before the agreement starts to be written whether there are any other issues they'd wish to raise.

Dealing with a 'walk out'

6.74 Mediators should always be alert to the possibility that it is open to parties to leave the mediation process at any time. If the mediator perceives that a party is unhappy or uncomfortable, they may have a separate meeting with the party or take a break (which may also provide an opportunity to speak with the party privately). If a party does leave, the mediator should try to speak to the party and allow them to explain. The mediator may explore the consequences of walking out or the alternatives to a mediated agreement, remembering that mediation is voluntary and the party can choose to leave. Mediators may ask:

Mediator	What would it take to enable you to return to the mediation?
Mediator	You've just mentioned lots of issues to me which haven't been raised in the mediation. Before you leave would you like the opportunity to set out those issues to the other party?
Mediator	Before you leave, would you like to explain to party A why you are leaving?

Reaching agreement

6.75 In civil mediation, the agreement is usually written by the legal advisers. In family, workplace and community mediation, the mediator works with the parties to write the agreement.

6.76 All mediation agreements should be written in plain English and accessible language, this would apply whether the final agreement is a legally binding settlement agreement, a Memorandum of Understanding or a non-binding mediation agreement reached at a workplace or community mediation. Writing mediation settlement agreements is discussed in chapter 7.[32]

---

32 See paras 7.9–7.29.

Concluding the mediation

How a mediation may end

6.77   The mediation process may end in a number of ways:

- the parties reach a settlement agreement;
- one party leaves before an agreement is reached;
- the mediation ends, no agreement is reached but parties agree to have another mediation meeting;
- no agreement could be reached;[33]
- the mediator withdraws or terminates the mediation process.[34]

Closing remarks

6.78   The mediator will usually conclude the mediation in a *joint meeting*. If an agreement has been reached it is usually signed and, if possible, both parties receive a copy. If parties have been in separate rooms this is a good opportunity to meet together. The mediator will thank the participants for coming and may encourage parties to shake hands and acknowledge the change of atmosphere in the room. They may also discuss the importance of both parties working to the spirit of any agreement reached.

6.79   The mediator will invite parties to provide feedback and will remind parties about the confidentiality of the discussions which have taken place. Depending on what has been agreed, the mediator will reiterate the confidentiality of any agreement.

6.80   Whether or not an agreement is reached, it is good practice for a mediator to follow up with the parties in the weeks after the mediation. If the parties have agreed to attend further mediation meeting or negotiations are continuing, their services may continue to be required.

Feedback and complaints

6.81   All mediators should provide the parties with an opportunity to provide feedback.[35] Most commonly parties are invited to complete a feedback questionnaire. It is generally considered appropriate to give parties time to consider their response, for example, allowing parties to return the form in a stamped addressed envelope or online. There should also be an accessible and clearly published complaints policy and procedures should any issue arise.

---

33   See para 5.61.
34   See paras 12.54–12.56.
35   See paras 12.16–12.17.

Peer review and supervision

6.82 In mediations with more than one mediator or an observer, peer feedback is a valuable opportunity for a mediator to continually develop their skills and techniques.[36] Mediators should also receive regular supervision, undertake ongoing training and use self-reflective practices.[37]

Frequently asked questions answered by Carey Haslam and John Sturrock

6.83 The following questions have been answered by Carey Haslam and John Sturrock. Carey Haslam is London-based and has 20 years' experience as a practising workplace and community mediator, and as a mediation and conflict resolution trainer and consultant. John Sturrock is founder and chief executive of Core Solutions Group, based in Edinburgh, and is recognised as Scotland's leading commercial mediator, alongside an extensive practice as a coach and trainer in conflict management, mediation and negotiation.

What is the mediator's most valuable skill?

We are not sure you can identify one skill as the most valuable because it is the combination of mediation skills that makes the difference. Mediation is an art, not a science, so a mediator has to make many decisions about their interventions throughout the process.

Carey: That said, I have most often been thanked for listening. I try to actively listen both to what the parties are saying and what they are not saying. This links with the skill of asking appropriate questions which can unlock the conflict by changing the ways the parties see the situation and opening up new possibilities.

John: I agree and would also mention the ability to retain a sense of calm and presence of mind, even when matters become protracted, heated or deadlocked. Add the ability really to engage with an individual at the point where the realities of a situation need to be explored and tested.

36 See para 12.13.
37 See paras 12.9–12.12.

What are the advantages (and disadvantages) of mediating with another mediator?

Carey: Mediators hold very divergent views on this issue. I think that co-mediating is the most powerful model because two mediators can: role-model how to communicate in conflict, provide a sounding board for each other in terms of managing the mediation, input new ideas and impetus when discussions get stuck, and can minimise any potential bias towards or against one of the parties. Some mediators believe it can be helpful to mirror the make-up of the parties in the dispute (for example, using a black mediator and an Asian mediator to mediate a dispute between a black and Asian couple). A co-mediator is a valuable source of accurate feedback about your performance.

On a practical basis though, two mediators increase the costs where mediators are being paid, and it can be a challenge for some people to co-mediate because they like to be in charge and because their co-mediator may want to take the mediation in a different direction; this tension may distract the mediators from the task at hand.

John: I am one of those mediators who likes to be in charge! I think it is horses for courses. I think finding someone who complements your approach, with whom you work regularly and with confidence, enhances the prospect that co-mediation will work well. I nearly always work with an assistant mediator who can be really helpful in seeing or hearing things that I miss, acting as a sounding board and being a calming influence when the mediation gets tough.

What makes a mediator most effective?

Carey: As someone who likes to make my own decisions and does not like being told what to do, I was attracted to being a mediator by the concept of offering a process which people could use to make their own decisions and decide their own outcomes. This sense of empowerment is encapsulated in Lao Tzu's quote, 'When the best leader's work is done, the people say: "We did it ourselves."'

John: I believe that a mediator is most effective when he or she is able to establish and maintain a really good working relationship with all of the participants in the mediation. That means engaging with each of them according to their needs and interests, maintaining genuine concern for and interest in each, so that he or she is able to speak frankly and respectfully even about those matters which are most difficult.

CHAPTER 7

Concluding the mediation: writing the agreement

continued

> ## Key points
> - Mediated agreements can be binding or non-binding.
> - Agreements should be specific, clear, future-focused and balanced.
> - As a general rule the process of mediation is confidential, but there are some exceptions.
> - In legal mediations, such as civil or employment mediation, the rules of *without prejudice* privilege apply.
> - Parties can decide whether any agreement reached will be confidential. They can agree what information, if any, to tell referral agencies and interested third parties.
> - Binding agreements are enforceable as a legally binding contract.
> - Where there is a challenge to the legality of the agreement, such as fraud or duress, parties may be able to waive privilege (which means they give up their right to keep their discussion confidential).

Agreements reached at mediation

7.1   Mediation can be used to address a vast array of disputes, from organisational restructuring through to neighbourhood disagreements. Whatever the subject matter, if the parties reach an agreement at the conclusion of the process – whether a mutual understanding or a complete settlement – the terms will need to be accurately recorded in writing. Such agreements can be broadly divided into two types: those which are intended to be legally binding and enforceable by due legal process, and others which are *not* intended to be legally binding.

7.2   Agreements reached at mediation can be described as a mediated agreement, mediation settlement agreement or Memorandum of Understanding.

Binding agreements

7.3   Binding agreements are those which can be enforced through legal proceedings. The agreement will usually bring the legal case (whether current or anticipated) to an end so that the parties are unable to revive their original legal claim if a party breaches it or fails to implement it (unless the agreement specifies otherwise).

7.4   Binding agreements are most commonly reached in civil mediation and will be drafted by the legal advisers during the mediation.[1]
Where the parties need more time to reflect on the terms of the agreement, the agreement may be drafted by the legal advisers after the
mediation has concluded, although this obviously runs the risk that
any agreement may unravel.[2] In family mediation, parties reach a
'Memorandum of Understanding' at the mediation which their legal
advisers use to draft a legally binding agreement at a later stage.

Non-binding agreements

Generally

7.5   A non-binding agreement is an arrangement made between the parties in good faith. If one party chooses not to comply with the terms
of the agreement they can be reminded why the agreement was
reached. Where the mediation process has re-established a trusting
relationship there is every incentive for parties to keep to the spirit of
a mediated agreement, The agreement will usually be confidential,
so a party's failure to adhere to the agreement cannot be used by
a party or a referrer, such as a housing officer or employer, to take
action against the non-compliant party. Given the high rates of compliance with mediated agreements, the issue of 'enforcement' does
not usually arise.

7.6   In general, non-binding agreements are drafted by the mediator.
This requires a real attention to detail, and as far as possible mediators should ensure that the language reflects the actual words which
the parties have used.[3]

7.7   Non-binding agreements are usually reached in community, workplace and family mediation. In family mediation, a non-binding agreement called a Memorandum of Understanding is reviewed by a legal
adviser who can then draft a legally binding document if required.[4]

Non-binding agreements and third parties

7.8   In workplace, community and family mediation, any agreement
which is reached may indirectly affect a third party. This could be

---

1 This would include employment mediation as distinct from workplace
   mediation – see paras 10.11-10.13.
2 See para 7.27 – where an agreement is not reached, the mediator can remain in
   contact with the parties to assist in reaching a binding agreement.
3 See para 5.32 on note-taking and mediators.
4 See appendix E.

an employer, housing officer or social worker, or whoever originally referred the dispute to mediation. While the agreement is confidential, parties are usually asked whether they consent to a copy being sent to the referrer – or parties can agree what the referrer can be told about the mediation process, such as whether it resulted in an agreement or not.

How to write a mediation agreement

Creating a mediation agreement

7.9   The terms of an agreement are likely to emerge over the course of the mediation, so it is important to record all the potential areas where the parties agree, or might agree – including apologies, concessions and offers – as and when they arise. Mediators acknowledge such options for agreement as they arise and read back their notes to confirm their accuracy. In this way the agreement can emerge organically and cumulatively.

7.10   Writing agreements takes time. Mediators and legal advisers should be mindful in time-limited mediation to leave sufficient time to draft the text.

Characteristics of a mediation agreement

7.11   Agreements should be simple and easily understood. In non-legal mediations they will use everyday language and repeat the precise words used by the parties.

SMART agreements

7.12   Mediation agreements are often practical and provide detail about the steps each party will need to take to fulfill their obligations. Each issue should be set out in clear terms: who does what, where and when. As a way of ensuring that the agreement is workable, mediators often describe making an agreement SMART, which stands for:

- specific;
- measurable;
- achievable;
- realistic;
- time-limited.

Specific and clear

7.13   Any details should be set out in clear terms, and should not be conditional on something else happening. There should be clarity as to what each party is expected to do, and by when. The importance of removing any ambiguity or uncertainty is particularly important if parties want the agreement to be legally binding and enforceable.[5] This is true for straightforward goods and services disputes as much as complex multi-party commercial disputes.

Future-focused

7.14   The agreement should anticipate how parties will inform each other of any issues that may arise in the future and how they will resolve them. This may be as simple as agreeing how parties will communicate with each another or having a clause to the effect that any issues arising out of the agreement will first be approached through mediation before initiating legal proceedings.

Balanced and positive

7.15   Mediation agreements should, wherever possible, be balanced and reciprocal. Where possible, the agreement should be drafted as a positive statement, setting out what the parties 'agree to do' rather than what they will refrain from doing.

Statement on confidentiality

7.16   The agreement should set out whether or not the information contained within it is confidential. Parties can reach a settlement which is not confidential or agree to disclose the agreement to their employers (workplace mediation) or housing officer (community mediation) where it may be helpful in order to implement the agreement. Alternatively, parties can draft an agreed statement or press release so that they are able to discuss certain aspects of the agreement. This can sometimes be a practical necessity. If a statement or press release has been agreed, this should be referred to in the agreement, to avoid the risk that waiving privilege on a part of the agreement will be interpreted as waiving privilege for the whole agreement.[6]

---

5   See paras 7.17–7.24.
6   See para 7.37 on waiving privilege.

> ### Case study 10: Employment mediation – getting the wording right
>
> C was a solicitor and claimed race discrimination as a result of being unsuccessful in two applications for promotion. He was unsuccessful at the Employment Tribunal and the Employment Appeal Tribunal (EAT), but he was granted leave to appeal by the Court of Appeal. Despite a finding in favour of the employer, both the Employment Tribunal and the EAT made criticisms of the employer. The court advised the parties to use mediation. The initial value of the claim was in excess of £100,000, although by the time of the mediation a valuation of £25,000 was agreed.
>
> At the mediation, settlement was reached on the basis of a payment to C by the employer of £8,000 inclusive of costs. Virtually the whole of the mediation day was spent in negotiating the wording of an apology to be given by the employer and a joint press statement. The core issues in this case were apologies and reputation rather than financial settlement.[7]

Civil mediation agreements

Generally

7.17　In civil cases, the *agreement to mediate*[8] which parties sign at the outset of the mediation almost always provides that any settlement must be in writing and signed by the parties to be binding on them.

7.18　Considerations to be taken into account when drafting a legally binding agreement include:

- enforceability and action to be taken if the agreement is breached;
- confidentiality and publicity;
- status of any legal proceedings: withdrawn, settled or stayed;
- legal costs (including the cost of the mediation).[9]

7　Case study from the Court of Appeal Mediation Scheme. Reproduced with permission of Public Law Project and originally published in V Bondy and M Doyle, *Mediation in Judicial Review: A practical handbook for lawyers* (2011) http://www.publiclawproject.org.uk/documents/MJRhandbookFINAL.pdf.

8　See paras 3.103–3.105 on *agreements to mediate*.

9　See paras 8.89–8.90.

7.19   In most cases, an agreement brings the legal proceedings to an end and the original claim or potential claim cannot be reinstated.[10] This needs to be made clear to all parties. Defendants will be unwilling to reach an agreement if they believe they will still face the possibility of litigation; claimants may be too willing to settle if they think a break-down of any agreement would enable them to revive the original claim.

Types of civil agreements

7.20   Written settlements in civil mediations usually are drafted as:

- consent orders;
- Tomlin orders;
- settlement agreements.

Consent orders[11]

7.21   A consent order is a legally binding order which is made by a judge at the request of the parties. There are different types of consent orders – a simple consent order may set out the terms of the settlement agreement and bring the proceedings to an end. The terms of the order are not confidential and it is a public document. Parties can decide whether to include a term that parties have 'liberty to apply' to the court for enforcement purposes or if the order is breached (this avoids the need for parties to start fresh proceedings). If legal proceedings have begun, consent orders can be issued without the need for a court hearing under the Civil Procedure Rules 1998 (CPR) 23.8 and 40.6, or if proceedings have not commenced the procedure is governed by CPR Part 8.[12]

Tomlin orders[13]

7.22   If the parties wish, they may apply to the court for a Tomlin order. Tomlin orders are a special type of consent order. A Tomlin order stays proceedings on the basis of the agreement reached by the par-ties and the agreement is attached to the order as a schedule. The court is made aware that an agreement has been reached but the terms of the agreement are not placed on the court file and are not made public. This makes Tomlin orders particularly suited to medi-ation if the parties prefer the details of their agreement to remain

10   Unless the agreement specifies otherwise.
11   See appendix E.
12   Practice Direction 8A para 3.1(2).
13   See appendix E.

confidential. Parties are then able to return to court for the purpose of enforcing the terms of the agreement or to claim that the agreement has been breached without the need to commence fresh proceedings. The court is able to order enforcement of obligations agreed in the settlement, even if they could not have been ordered at trial, so long as they are not illegal.

Settlement agreements

7.23   Mediated settlement agreements[14] are contracts between the parties. If legal proceedings have been started, it could be a term of the contract that legal proceedings be withdrawn or discontinued. If legal proceedings have not been started, parties may agree to forgo legal rights against each other. It could be a term of the contract that the agreement is in 'full and final settlement of action the parties to this dispute have against each other'. Careful drafting is required in relation to potential future claims or where a relationship between the parties is continuing.

7.24   Agreements are legally binding and enforceable, provided they satisfy the rules of contract law (offer, acceptance, consideration and intention to create legal relations). It is therefore highly desirable that such agreements are drafted by lawyers. Mediators may unwittingly be fixed with legal responsibility for the efficacy and legality of terms if they draft a settlement, and may not be insured against liability for negligence in such circumstances.

Family mediation agreements

7.25   In family mediation, the agreement is usually drafted by the mediator. It is non-binding and described as a Memorandum of Understanding (in some cases mediators help draft an Outcome Summary where proposals do not meet strict legal requirements). A Memorandum of Understanding can be reviewed by each party's legal adviser. This can take place at the end of a series of mediation meetings, or before the final meeting so that a legally binding agreement drafted by the lawyers can then be discussed. Financial information is documented in an Open Financial Statement[15] which is not confidential.

---

14 This may include compromise agreements – see paras 10.11–10.14.
15 See paras 9.31–9.33.

Workplace mediation agreements

7.26   In workplace mediation, agreements are non-binding and will usually set out a road map (a plan of action) for resolving the issues. For this reason, the parties are asked whether the agreement (or a separately drafted agreed statement[16]) can be disclosed to whoever referred the case in the first place – for example, the employer, a human resources department or senior manager. This may be necessary for the agreement to be properly implemented and monitored. In some cases the employer will be expected to undertake certain actions which would be futile if the agreement remained confidential.

Community mediation agreements

7.27   Agreements in community mediations are usually non-binding and remain confidential. It is open to the parties to agree whether they can tell their friends or neighbours. The mediators may ask if the agreement can be disclosed to the referral agency or referrer, such as a housing officer. This would not be to monitor compliance but to make the referrer aware of the outcome of the mediation. Parties can agree that the only copies of the agreement will be for the parties themselves (a copy will also be retained by the mediation service).

When an agreement is not reached

7.28   Mediation is not always successful in reaching an agreement on all issues. During the process, areas of agreement and disagreement will have been identified and offers and counter-offers made. Some will be conditional and others unconditional. Where possible, mediators should suggest making a record of the stage the discussion have reached, to acknowledge where issues have been narrowed and partial agreement achieved. If binding obligations are agreed in a partial settlement, such as an offer left open for a fixed period, these should be recorded in writing and signed (if this is required by the *agreement to mediate*).[17]

16 See paras 7.8 and 7.16.
17 See para 3.104 – 'that any settlement or agreement reached during the mediation must be in writing and signed by the parties'.

7.29   In legal proceedings, offers may be left open or made as Part 36 offers.[18] The mediator may continue to work with the parties to reach an agreement and subsequent mediation meetings may be arranged. In some cases, mediators will speak to the parties over the telephone and help to convey offers and counter offers. In such cases they should make a written note of any offers, and read them back to the party who made the offer, to make sure that they are in accordance with what the party has actually offered.

Legal issues arising in mediation

7.30   The legal framework surrounding mediation is fast evolving. At present there is no UK statute governing mediation, and the government has indicated that a 'methodical review of the current domestic law, in consultation with the mediation and legal profession' is required before introducing primary legislation to codify mediation practices.[19] The EU Mediation Directive,[20] which is now incorporated into UK law and is binding only in relation to cross-border disputes arising on or after 20 May 2011, provides a helpful overview for cross-border cases, but cannot be assumed to apply to mediation of domestic disputes. This means that the legal position is defined by the common law. The issues of confidentiality and privilege,[21] the compellability of mediators to give evidence of what occurred during a mediation, the enforceability of agreements and the expiry of limitation periods while mediation is being pursued[22] have all been the subject of litigation. There has not, however, been authoritative guidance from the Court of Appeal on most of these issues.

---

18 See p242 'Guide to Costs' – Part 36 offers must observe certain formalities and are mechanisms for making written offers to settle in civil proceedings with costs consequences.

19 *Solving disputes in the county courts: creating a simpler, quicker and more proportionate system – a consultation on reforming civil justice in England and Wales: government's response,* February 2012, Cm 8274, para 27, p12.

20 Cross-Border Mediation (EU Directive) Regulations 2011 SI No 1133 and CPR 78.23–78.28.

21 See paras 7.31–7.42.

22 See paras 8.64–8.65.

Confidentiality and privilege

Generally

7.31   When parties enter into mediation, mediators often ask them to sign an *agreement to mediate* (also described as a *mediation agreement, confidentiality agreement* or *pre-mediation agreement*).[23] In mediations where parties are not asked to sign a written agreement, the mediator will explain that mediation is a confidential process at the beginning of the mediation and parties are asked to confirm whether they would agree to this ground rule.[24] Some mediators will explain that they will destroy their notes at the end of the mediation. Legal advisers will be familiar with the principle of *without prejudice* negotiations, where discussions and offers or proposals remain confidential, they do not imply any admission of liability and cannot be used in court. 'Legal privilege' means that discussions between a lawyer and their client remain confidential, unless a client decides to 'waive privilege', thereby giving up their right to confidentiality.

7.32   The importance of mediation being a confidential process is to facilitate an open dialogue, in contrast to an adversarial or positional approach to negotiation. This enables parties to brainstorm and consider new options which may be at odds with legal rights or those previously under discussion.

Definitions

Confidentiality: Anything said or done cannot be discussed with or communicated to third parties.

Without prejudice: Negotiations or discussions which cannot then be used as evidence in court without the consent of both parties.

Legal privilege: Discussions between a lawyer and his or her client which are confidential and need not be discussed.

Privilege: The right of a party to refuse to disclose a document or produce a document or to refuse to answer questions.

---

23   See paras 3.103–3.104.
24   See para 5.33.

Drafting of confidentiality clauses in agreements to mediate

7.33 Agreements to mediate include a confidentiality clause and generally include a clause confirming that the parties will not compel a mediator to give evidence in court about the dispute or what happened (what was said or done) at the mediation. This follows a judgment in *Farm Assist (No 2)*[25] which concerned the issue of whether a mediated settlement agreement should be set aside for economic duress. It was ruled that 'calling the Mediator to give this evidence would not be contrary to the express terms of the mediation agreement which, in this case, limited her appearance to being a witness in proceedings concerning the underlying dispute'.[26] For this reason, the Civil Mediation Council (CMC) has advised mediators to widen the wording of their *agreements to mediate* regarding the circumstances in which a mediator cannot be compelled to give evidence in court.[27] The confidentiality clause contained in an *agreement to mediate* can be relied on by all its signatories, including the mediator and any mediation provider.

Can a mediator (or a party) ever breach confidentiality?

7.34 Although confidentiality is an essential component of mediation, there are some circumstances in which a mediator (and a party) will be required to disclose information.[28] This could be where wider public policy considerations are concerned, and in particular there is a risk of serious harm, child protection or criminal conduct (including money laundering[29] or tax evasion). In these circumstances the mediator will terminate the mediation and may be freed from their obligation of confidentiality to the parties. The mediator should make this clear when explaining confidentiality at the beginning of the mediation session or during *pre-mediation meetings*.

---

25 *Farm Assist Ltd (in liquidation) v Secretary of State for Environment, Food and Rural Affairs (No 2)* [2009] EWHC 1102 (TCC).

26 *Farm Assist Ltd (in liquidation) v Secretary of State for Environment, Food and Rural Affairs (No 2)* [2009] EWHC 1102 (TCC), para 53(3).

27 See CMC, 'Mediation confidentiality – guidance note 1', available at www.civilmediation.org/downloads.php?f=46 – which uses the CEDR model agreement as an example: 'arising from or in connection with the Dispute and the mediation'.

28 See paras 12.59–12.60 on when can a mediator disclose confidential information.

29 See paras 12.61–12.64.

7.35   The situations where disclosure is required by law, such as a legal obligation to report to an appropriate authority, are very narrow.[30] These include:

- where the mediation is being used as an attempt to commit a crime or conceal a crime;
- where there is a risk of serious harm (physical or psychological injury);
- where child protection issues or safeguarding concerns arise.

7.36   Such wider public policy considerations may extend to a party giving evidence in court about what has been said during a mediation because it raises concerns regarding child protection or the risk of serious harm.[31]

Can parties waive without prejudice privilege?

> ... mediation takes the form of assisted 'without prejudice' negotiation and ... with some exceptions ... what goes on in the course of mediation is privileged, so that it cannot be referred to or relied on in subsequent court proceedings if the mediation is unsuccessful.[32]

7.37   As a general rule, all communication made during a mediation is *without prejudice*. Once the mediation is over, whether an agreement is reached or not, any statement made during the process cannot be used in evidence at a later stage and remains confidential. However, if both parties consent, the *without prejudice* privilege rule can be waived in certain situations.[33] The mediator has no say in whether this waiver takes place, but does have the right to enforce any contractual confidentiality obligation against the parties.[34] The main reason for waiving *without prejudice* privilege would be where the content of the mediation settlement agreement needs to be disclosed in order to implement or enforce the agreement (this may be something for parties and legal advisers to consider when writing up the agreement). Other circumstances may include a formal complaint or civil claim relating to the negligence or misconduct of the mediator.

---

30 See paras 12.61–12.64.
31 *Re D (minors)* [1993] 2 All ER 693; and paras 9.29–9.30.
32 May LJ, *Aird v Prime Meridien Ltd* [2006] EWCA Civ 1866, para 5.
33 See, for example, *SITA v Watson Wyatt* [2002] EWHC 2025 (Ch), *Chantry Vellacott v The Convergence Group* [2007] EWHC 1774 (Ch), *Earl of Malmesbury v Strutt and Parker* [2008] EWHC 424 (QB).
34 See para 7.33.

Exceptions to without prejudice privilege

> ... the court should support the mediation process by refusing, in normal circumstances, to order disclosure of documents and communications within a mediation.
>
> ... In my judgement, the court should be very slow to order such disclosure. Mediators should be able to conduct mediations confident that, in normal circumstances, their papers could not be seen by the parties or others.[35]

7.38 In very limited circumstances, the courts may admit evidence of what occurred during a mediation as an exception to the *without prejudice principle*. This will occur only in exceptional circumstances, such as occurred in *Brown v Rice and Patel*,[36] where there was a dispute over whether a binding agreement had been reached. Other exceptions may include cases of misconduct such as a fraudulent representation or duress.

7.39 It has generally been accepted that these exceptions do not extend to considering the conduct of parties during the mediation in relation to costs issues, for example when a court is assessing the conduct of a party in relation to indemnity costs or costs sanctions.[37] As summarised by Dyson LJ in *Halsey v Milton Keynes NHS Trust*:

> We make it clear at the outset that it was common ground before us (and we accept) that parties are entitled in an ADR to adopt whatever position they wish, and if as a result the dispute is not settled, that is not a matter for the Court.[38]

7.40 This has continued to be the general position adopted by the courts.[39] However, the issue of costs arose in the case of *Chantrey Vellacott v The Convergence Group*[40] where the court examined the *without prejudice* offers made during a failed mediation and concluded that one party had acted unreasonably. In this case the parties waived privilege so the court did not consider the admissibility of this evidence. Parties should be aware that in certain cases, the court may

---

35 Kirkham J, *Cumbria Waste Management and another v Baines Wilson* [2008] EWHC 786 (QB), paras 30–31.

36 *Brown v Rice and Patel and ADR Group* [2007] EWHC 625 (Ch).

37 See para 8.98.

38 [2004] EWCA Civ 576, para 14.

39 *The Wethered Estate Ltd v Michael Davis and others* [2005] EWHC 1903 (Ch); *Reed Executive plc and another v Reed Business Information and other* [2004] EWCA Civ 887; *Earl of Malmesbury v Strutt and Parker* [2008] EWHC 424 (QB); *Cumbria Waste Management and another v Baines Wilson* [2008] EWHC 786 (QB).

40 [2007] EWHC 1774 (Ch) para 228.

consider the reasonableness of a party's approach to *without prejudice* discussions (see *Earl of Malmesbury v Strutt and Parker*[41]). Whether it is ever wise to waive privilege must be a matter of judgment for the parties involved, as the judge is then free to take a view on the reasonableness of each party's approach in a way which would otherwise be impossible.

Admissibility of evidence in subsequent legal proceedings

7.41　If legal proceedings continue after the mediation process ends, it should be made clear that evidence, such as statements and expert reports, communicated during the mediation process is not privileged purely by virtue of the fact that it was referred to during the process.[42] Material will still be admissible as evidence in legal proceedings provided it meets the evidential requirements. If parties want to retain the *without prejudice* status of expert reports or other evidence this must be made explicit at the outset of the mediation. What remain privileged and confidential are the discussions, oral and written statements, including offers and counter-offers made in a genuine attempt to reach a settlement.

7.42　In family cases, financial disclosure made for the purposes of mediation is not privileged.[43]

Can a mediator be compelled to give evidence?

> ... whilst the Mediator has a right to rely on the confidentiality provision in the Mediation Agreement, this is a case where, as an exception, the interests of justice lie strongly in favour of evidence being given of what was said and done.[44]

7.43　The judgment in *Farm Assist (No 2)* suggests that, in exceptional cases such as duress or fraud, a court may override a claim to contractual confidentiality as set out in the *agreement to mediate* and the mediator can be compelled to give evidence. This decision is at odds with judgments such as *Cumbria Waste Management v Baines Wilson*,[45] which sought to protect the confidentiality of the mediation

---

41　[2008] 1 All ER 201 (CA).

42　*Aird v Prime Meridien Ltd* [2006] EWCA Civ 1866.

43　See paras 9.31–9.33.

44　Ramsey J, *Farm Assist Ltd (in liquidation) v Secretary of State for Environment, Food and Rural affairs (No 2)* [2009] EWHC 1102 (TCC) para 53(5).

45　'In my judgment, whether on the basis of the *without prejudice* rule or as an exception to the general rule that confidentiality is not a bar to disclosure, the court should support the mediation process by refusing, in normal

process, and *D (minors) (conciliation privilege)*[46] which held that only in rare cases would the public interest outweigh that of preserving the confidentiality of mediation. It also sits uneasily with the standard introduced for cross-border cases by the EU Mediation Directive.[47] Any 'interests of justice' argument is likely to be restricted to the most exceptional circumstances such as duress, fraud or serious child welfare issues.[48]

7.44   Ultimately, the case of *Farm Assist (No 2)* was withdrawn/discontinued so this issue was never fully explored. While much attention has been given to this case, it leaves behind several unanswered questions. In particular, whether a mediator who is ordered to give evidence could decline to reveal details of discussions which took place in *pre-mediation meetings* or private (caucus) meetings? Could the mediator claim what has been described by some commentators as 'mediation privilege'?[49]

7.45   There is a general consensus within the mediation community that mediators should not be compelled to give evidence, save in exceptional circumstances, as this threatens the integrity of the process. However, a careful balance has to be struck so that mediation cannot be a cover for fraud or duress, and to enable disclosure where child welfare concerns arise. This position is reflected in article 7 of the EU Mediation Directive:[50]

Article 7
Confidentiality of mediation
1. Given that mediation is intended to take place in a manner which respects confidentiality, Member States shall ensure that, unless the parties agree otherwise, neither mediators nor those involved in the administration of the mediation process shall be compelled to give evidence in civil and commercial judicial proceedings or arbitration

---

circumstances, to order disclosure of documents and communications within a mediation': *Cumbria Waste Management and another v Baines Wilson* [2008] EWHC 786 (QB) para 30.

46 (1993) 2 WLR 721.

47 See para 7.45.

48 *D (minors) (conciliation privilege)* (1993) 2 WLR 721.

49 This argument was raised in *Brown v Rice and Patel and ADR Group* [2007] EWHC 625 (Ch), paras 19–20. See also articles on mediation privilege by Michel Kallipetis QC and Bill Wood QC, 'Farm Assist: the latest developments in mediation privilege', *The Mediator Magazine*, June 2009, at www.themediatormagazine.co.uk and Sir Michael Briggs, 'Mediation privilege?', *New Law Journal*, April 2009.

50 EU Directive on certain aspects of mediation in civil and commercial matters 2008/52/EC, 21 May 2008 ('EU Mediation Directive') – see appendix G; also see CPR Part 78 section III.

regarding information arising out of or in connection with a mediation process, except:

(a) where this is necessary for overriding considerations of public policy of the Member State concerned, in particular when required to ensure the protection of the best interests of children or to prevent harm to the physical or psychological integrity of a person; or

(b) where disclosure of the content of the agreement resulting from mediation is necessary in order to implement or enforce that agreement.

2. Nothing in paragraph 1 shall preclude Member States enacting stricter measures to protect the confidentiality of mediation.

Enforceability of legally binding mediated settlement agreements

7.46　One of the advantages of a mediated settlement is that consensual agreements are more likely to be implemented, reducing the likelihood that enforcement is required. Settlement agreements may also require parties to first attempt to mediate any dispute arising from the agreement before issuing enforcement proceedings.[51]

7.47　　When necessary, a legally binding settlement agreement can be enforced.[52] If the original agreement was drafted as a Tomlin order or a consent order which included a clause allowing parties 'liberty to apply' to the court to enforce the order, a party wishing to enforce the agreement simply makes an application to the court. In other circumstances, a new set of proceedings will need to be commenced. The party issuing enforcement proceedings will usually cover the costs and, if they win, ask the court to order the other party to pay their costs.

Setting aside a mediated settlement agreement

7.48　Settlement agreements will only be set aside in exceptional circumstances, such as fraud or duress. The law of contract can be used as a guide as to when these circumstances might arise. This also raises the question of whether parties can disclose privileged discussions[53] and whether a mediator can be compelled to give evidence.[54]

51　See paras 2.19–2.20 on higher rates of compliance for mediated agreements.

52　See paras 7.21–7.24. The implementation of the EU Mediation Directive makes specific provision for enforcement of mediation agreements reached in cross-border disputes. See CPR rr78.23–78.28.

53　See paras 7.37–7.42.

54　See paras 7.43–7.45.

7.49   It is possible that an issue could turn on what a mediator conveyed on behalf of one party to the other party in a private meeting. Mediators should use great care when passing messages during 'shuttle' mediation, being careful to write down what one party wishes to be communicated on their behalf and reflecting the party's language where possible to avoid any miscommunication. In this way, a mediator also minimises the risk that they may have material evidence to give in court, as each party would be in a position to waive privilege and communicate their respective points of view.

Frequently asked questions answered by Tony Allen

7.50   The following questions have been answered by Tony Allen. Tony is a former director of CEDR and a leading civil and commercial mediator in personal injury and clinical negligence.

Is everything I say during a mediation confidential?

It will be assumed that any offers or concessions made within a mediation set up to discuss possible settlement of a dispute, remain confidential if the mediation does not reach an agreement. Every mediation should also be conducted on the basis of a written *agreement to mediate* signed by all parties and the mediator, which makes clear the extent of confidentiality. In some cases, such as community mediation, where there is no written agreement at the outset of the mediation, the mediator needs to provide very clear boundaries about the confidential nature of the process.

Depending on those boundaries, what people propose, offer or concede for the purposes of discussion during a mediation will be confidential to those who sign up to it. Mediators should encourage parties to take advantage of the confidential nature of the process to explore settlement without fearing disclosure of what they say, both in terms of *joint meetings* and also private meetings between mediator and each party. Mediators must be scrupulous to abide by such confidentiality.

The agreement made at the end of the mediation can be referred to a judge to consider its enforcement if one party fails to do what they have agreed (a rare occurrence). Parties can reinforce confidentiality as to the fact that a dispute has settled and the terms of settlement, or they may agree precisely how to authorise each other to disclose certain settlement terms to specified people. It may be important to one of the parties that they can tell people about what was agreed, in which case an agreed statement or press release could be written but the contents of the mediation process would still be confidential.

What happens when a party reaches a legally binding agreement and the next day they change their mind?

They remain bound by it. It is very important that parties carefully consider the irrevocability of any mediated settlement in this kind of claim. Advice as to the prospects of success if proceedings continue and settlement is rejected are usually available throughout the mediation from advisers. Unrepresented parties may be wise to ask for time to seek advice or for a cooling-off period or for a fixed period for accepting an offer after the mediation, and mediators should consider suggesting this to the parties.

What is the best advice you can offer to parties when they are writing a mediation settlement agreement?

In all mediations:
- Make sure that you cover all matters agreed, trying to anticipate all possible future problems that might arise.
- Include a statement about the confidentiality of the agreement or ensure this is made clear within the agreement.
- Agree how to resolve any issues that may arise in relation to the agreement and include them within it.

In settlements of civil claims:
- Remember that this is a contract that needs to meet any legal requirements for it to be legally binding. The *agreement to mediate* may also require certain formalities.
- If the truth of any contentious fact or valuation of property asserted by one party is fundamental to the acceptance of the settlement terms by any other party, recite that fact in the agreement. This will provide certainty in the event of a dispute arising from the agreement, giving the court access to it without having to enquire about what representations were made during the mediation.

What is the value of a non-binding confidential agreement?

It sets an agreed standard for future conduct, to which all involved can later turn and use as a strong indicator of what people should do. All those involved enter these agreements consensually with the intention of keeping them, and parties who make agreements voluntarily are more likely to keep to them than any agreement imposed upon them.

In workplace and community mediation, it is useful to agree what will be disclosed to the referrer, for example an employer or housing association. This is to avoid issues that may arise about how a third party is able to monitor the agreement. Alternatively, if parties choose, the agreement need not be confidential. In these circumstances, it might be taken by a court or tribunal later to be the measure of what is regarded as reasonable behaviour.

Areas of mediation

CHAPTER 8

Civil mediation

continued

> **Key points**
> - Civil mediation can be used to address a wide variety of civil and commercial disputes.
> - The agreements reached in civil mediation are legally binding and will usually bring any legal claim (or potential claim) to an end.
> - Legal advisers are usually involved in the mediation process, which can take place where there are no legal proceedings, once legal proceedings have commenced and even where litigation has been ongoing for some time.
> - Parties should consider whether to mediate and ensure they give full reasoned response if they refuse an offer to mediate.
> - The civil procedure rules provide a framework of cost sanctions for parties who unreasonably refuse to mediate. The burden is on the unsuccessful party to show that mediation had reasonable prospects of success and that the other party's refusal was unreasonable.

Introduction

What is civil mediation?

[M]ediation has a significantly greater role to play in the civil justice system than is currently recognised.[1]

8.1 Civil mediation involves the resolution of disputes where legal proceedings have begun or may be commenced. Civil and commercial disputes arise in a wide variety of contexts, such as two small businesses unable to resolve a disagreement over the interpretation of a contract, a tenant who stops paying rent because her landlord is not repairing the roof, a builder seeking to recover an unpaid bill, a student who disputes that her university has made reasonable adjustments or neighbours who are arguing over the dimensions of an extension.

8.2 Before or after a claim has been issued at court, parties have the opportunity to try to resolve their issues by using mediation. If an agreement is reached, this will usually have the effect of bringing all proceedings to an end.

---

1 Jackson LJ, *Review of civil litigation costs: final report*, December 2009 p361, para 36.3.2.

[The Court of Appeal] has made plain not only the high rate of a successful outcome being achieved by mediation but also its established importance as a track to a just result running parallel with that of the court system. Both have a proper part to play in the administration of justice. The court has given its stamp of approval to mediation and it is now the legal profession which must become fully aware of and acknowledge its value.[2]

8.3   Mediation is not a substitute for court proceedings. In appropriate cases it offers parties the opportunity to resolve their dispute avoiding the vast expense of contested legal proceedings. The shadow of litigation provides weaker parties with a stronger bargaining position and 'brings unwilling parties to the negotiating table'.[3] Mediation complements the court process but it does not replicate all of the court's powers. It does not, for example, determine a point of law, attribute fault or liability, impose an injunction or enforce an agreement. Mediation enables parties to communicate their grievances, to receive apologies or explanations, and it has the potential to restore business or personal relationships and create practical agreements, none of which a court would have been able to order.

... many disputing parties are not aware of the full benefits to be gained from mediation and may, therefore, dismiss this option too readily.[4]

8.4   One of the explanations for the relatively low take-up of mediation in civil disputes is that its benefits are not more widely known. Mediation is cost-effective in the vast majority of civil cases involving money claims, because the cost of legal proceedings and legal fees can very quickly outstrip the value of the claim or amount recoverable. Equally, in high value claims, mediation represents a cost-efficient method of resolving the dispute. In all claims, mediation can provide greater satisfaction for parties than litigation (or other processes where parties are not in control of the outcome) producing practical and long-lasting solutions. There is also an incentive to mediate, as there can be adverse costs consequences for parties who unreasonably refuse to mediate.[5]

---

2   *Burchell v Bullard* [2005] EWCA 358, para 43.
3   See H Genn, *Judging civil justice*, Cambridge University Press, 2010 p21.
4   Jackson LJ, *Review of civil litigation costs: final report*, December 2009 p355, para 36.1.2.
5   See paras 8.89–8.107 on costs sanctions.

Is there a duty to mediate?

> The value and importance of ADR [alternative dispute resolution] have been established ... All members of the legal profession who conduct litigation should now routinely consider with their clients whether their disputes are suitable for ADR.[6]

8.5 Civil mediation is voluntary. Parties are not compelled to mediate but are expected to have reasonably considered mediation before taking a case to court,[7] and to keep that decision under review.[8] In small claims cases, the government has set out proposals to introduce automatic referral to mediation for defended claims.[9]

8.6 Once court proceedings have commenced, active case management powers include being able to stay proceedings[10] in order to allow parties to attempt settlement and consider alternative forms of dispute resolution. Where parties have unreasonably refused to mediate, courts can use costs sanctions to penalise parties so that a successful party may be deprived of some or all of their costs[11] or an unsuccessful party be expected to pay the successful party's costs on an indemnity (less favourable) basis.[12]

Appropriate or alternative dispute resolution (ADR)

8.7 There are a number of forms of ADR,[13] which should all be considered when deciding how best to resolve a dispute:

- adjudication;
- arbitration;
- conciliation;
- early neutral evaluation;
- expert determination;
- formal complaints process;
- med-arb and arb-med;

---

6 *Halsey v Milton Keynes NHS Trust* [2004] EWCA (Civ) 576, para 11; see also *Dunnett v Railtrack* [2002] EWCA Civ 303.
7 See paras 8.40–8.43 on pre-action mediation.
8 See paras 8.52–8.65 on responding to an offer to mediate.
9 See para 8.12 on small claims.
10 A stay stops the court proceedings for a specified period of time or indefinitely. The proceedings can be continued if a stay is lifted or ends.
11 CPR 3.1(4).
12 See paras 8.98–8.107 on cost sanctions for refusing to mediate; parties can be ordered to pay indemnity costs.
13 See glossary for a description of these ADR processes.

- mediation;
- negotiation;
- ombudsman;
- roundtable meeting or joint settlement conference.

8.8   More specialist ADR procedures have become the industry standard in different fields. In construction, for example, large projects will use a variety of dispute resolution approaches to avoid projects being derailed by litigation, such as using Dispute Resolution Advisers, Project Mediation and Dispute Adjudication Boards. The London Olympics 2012 set up a multi-tiered dispute resolution system which included an Independent Dispute Avoidance Panel, and disputes not resolved would then be referred to an adjudication panel.[14]

8.9   Increasingly, the government is looking for more ways to keep court costs low. The Road Traffic Accident Personal Injury protocol, for example, launched in 2010, applies to low value claims ranging from £1,000 to £10,000. It deals with claims electronically and uses pre-action protocols designed to achieve low-cost and efficient outcomes for claimants. The government plans to increase the financial limit of the scheme and is working on proposals for a similar scheme for employers and public liability insurance and clinical negligence.[15]

Mediation schemes and specialisms

8.10   There are a number of specialist dispute resolution schemes offering mediation which is free or fixed-fee. In some cases they are funded by local authorities or an industry body. LawWorks[16] offers free civil mediation to parties who meet their financial eligibility criteria. Some local community mediation services[17] have funding to offer mediation to all local residents for free or at a subsidised rate. When considering whether to use these schemes or services, it will be important for parties to find out what mediation process will be used. For example, a time-limited telephone mediation of an hour

---

14   N Gould, C King and P Britton, *Mediating construction disputes: an evaluation of existing practice*, King's College London, Centre of Construction Law and Dispute Resolution, 2010 p21.

15   See *Solving disputes in the county courts: creating a simpler, quicker and more proportionate system – the government response*, TSO, February 2012 p10, paras 15–17.

16   See www.lawworks.org.uk/lw_mediation.

17   See appendix A.

may be inadequate to address the issues of a long standing boundary dispute, but may be an appropriate solution to resolving a money claim where there is no ongoing relationship between the parties.[18]

Court-based mediation schemes

8.11   There are three general schemes which provide mediation within the civil court system: small claims mediation service, Civil Mediation Online Directory and Court of Appeal Mediation Service (CAMS).

Small claims mediation service

8.12   In small claims cases, mediation is offered to parties who have issued a claim. They are currently given the option on the allocation questionnaire to first consider mediation. As of April 2013, parties will be automatically referred to mediation in defended claims up to £5,000.[19] The small claims mediation service is currently a free service covered by the court fee paid to issue a claim (any additional hearing fee is refundable if an agreement is reached and the court is notified in writing at least seven days before the trial date).[20] The mediation service is currently provided by trained HMCTS (Her Majesty's Courts and Tribunals Service) mediators and has had an impressive track record with high settlement and compliance rates.[21]

Civil Mediation Online Directory

8.13   This offers fixed fee mediation for civil cases up to £50,000, with fees for higher value cases agreed with the provider.[22] While not strictly a court-based scheme, parties in civil cases will be referred to the Directory if mediation is considered by the court to have a reasonable prospect of success in their case. The Civil Mediation Online Directory[23] is a searchable database listing mediation providers across England and Wales, accredited by the Civil Mediation Council. The Directory is provided by the Ministry of Justice (MOJ) and replaces the National Mediation Helpline.

18   See paras 5.64–5.66.
19   *Solving disputes in the county courts: creating a simpler, quicker and more proportionate system – the government response,* TSO, February 2012 p10, para 24.
20   Civil and Family Court Fees, Form EX50 (HMCTS, April 2011, p4) available at http://hmctsformfinder.justice.gov.uk.
21   See paras 2.15–2.20 and 5.64–5.66 for an analysis.
22   See paras 3.47–3.48.
23   See www.civilmediation.justice.gov.uk.

Court of Appeal Mediation Service

8.14   The CAMS scheme operates in the Court of Appeal, Civil Division for non-family cases (a similar scheme is available for family cases[24]). Under a new pilot scheme, all personal injury and contract claims up to the value of £100,000 with permission to appeal will automatically be referred to the scheme (unless a judge exceptionally directs otherwise).[25] Currently, the Civil Appeals Office should refer cases to the scheme where mediation has been recommended by the judge and where at least one party has agreed to mediate. Mediations can take place anywhere in England and Wales at the parties' convenience and are almost always completed within 3 months of referral (which means the appeal does not need to be stayed whilst mediation is undertaken). A panel of Court of Appeal approved mediators provide the fixed-fee mediation scheme, administered by CEDR, the fee for a mediation is £850 plus VAT per party.[26] Under the pilot scheme, LawWorks will provide pro bono legal advice for self representing parties who qualify for legal help (and pro bono mediators where there are two unrepresented parties).[27]

Specialist areas of mediation

Chancery cases

8.15   Chancery cases lend themselves well to mediation and the process is used extensively to facilitate resolution of, for example, property disputes of all kinds, trust and estate disputes, company, partnership and professional negligence cases as well as commercial cases heard in the chancery division. Many chancery cases involve family or close business relationships and therefore involve the toxic mix of money and high emotion. Mediation provides a forum in which both can be addressed with the opportunity, if appropriate, for family members and former business associates to have difficult conversations in a safe environment. This often assists finding a commercial resolution, sometimes leads to the rebuilding of relationships and invariably provides a sense of personal closure.

---

24   http://www.justice.gov.uk/courts/rcj-rolls-building/court-of-appeal/civil-division/mediation.

25   http://www.judiciary.gov.uk/media/media-releases/2012/news-release-mediation-pilot-court-of-appeal.

26   CAMS is administered by CEDR Solve, www.cedr-solve.

27   LawWorks – www.lawworks.org.uk.

Consumer disputes and complaints processes

8.16 Mediation has the potential to address complex and long-term complaints.[28] Organisations are investing in mediation as a form of dispute resolution before disputes require more formal or litigious processes. For example, the Bar Council offers a mediation service for barristers to resolve disputes arising in chambers between barristers or between barristers and clerks.[29] The NHS has pioneered a number of mediation processes to help its patients receive more meaningful outcomes in response to complaints. IDRS, now operated by CEDR Solve, manages a number of consumer schemes.[30]

Equalities and human rights

8.17 Equalities mediation can used by any individual who feels they have been treated unfairly because of disability, race, religion or belief, sexual orientation, gender (including gender reassignment), or age, and by any organisation, company or individual who has received a complaint about discrimination. Until March 2012 the Equalities Mediation Service (EMS)[31] was provided free of charge by the Equalities and Human Rights Commission (EHRC). Parties will continue to be able to access equalities mediation, from providers such as Mediation Works.[32]

HM Revenue and Customs (HMRC) and Serious Organised Crime Agency (SOCA)

8.18 The HMRC Dispute Resolution Unit has issued draft guidance[33] on the use of ADR in large and complex cases. There are amendments to Part 45 of the Civil Procedure Rules (CPR) to provide for a scale of fixed costs that will be awarded in cases where HMRC successfully obtains judgment in respect of unpaid tax.

8.19 In civil confiscation, mediation has the advantage of ensuring compliance with an agreed order, avoiding lengthy and complicated litigation (especially where third parties claim an interest in

---

28 See, for example, para 8.28.
29 See www.barcouncil.org.uk/for-the-bar/introduction-to-member-services/arbitration-and-mediation-service.
30 See www.idrs.ltd.uk.
31 www.equalities-mediation.org.uk/.
32 www.mediation-works.co.uk/equalities.
33 27 June 2011, available at www.hmrc.gov.uk/practitioners/adr-draft-guidance.pdf.

the assets) and parties are more likely to agree to a process which is confidential. A pioneering mediation led to one of the largest sums recovered, an £18 million confiscation order was achieved through a mediated settlement.[34]

Housing and planning

8.20   Rent arrears, disrepair claims, neighbour disputes and allegations of anti-social behaviour can quickly escalate and threaten tenancies. For local authorities, housing associations and private landlords legal proceedings are costly. Many local authorities offer mediation provided by community mediation services, as they realise the benefits of resolving issues when complaints first arise. In rent arrears and disrepair cases, mediation can find flexible, creative and constructive solutions, although landlords may be unlikely to consider mediation without the pressure of court proceedings. Tenancy deposit schemes[35] are required to have dispute resolution processes but more commonly use adjudication.

8.21   Mediation has been used effectively in the statutory planning process, creating a dialogue between applicants or developers and statutory consultees, local communities and objectors. In some cases it can narrow the issues, in others consensus can be found which results in cost-effective, creative resolutions and reduces the time to determine applications.

8.22   For further information see:

- *Mediation in planning: a short guide;*[36]
- *A guide to the use of mediation in the planning system in Scotland.*[37]

Media law and intellectual property

8.23   Disputes arising in the music, entertainment and sports industry lend themselves to mediation as parties are often looking to restore working relationships and are looking for a quick resolution which is kept out of the public eye and does not damage their reputation. The Intellectual Property Office (IPO) Mediation Service[38] uses in-house mediators

---

34   *Director of Assets Recovery Agency v Creaven* [2005] EWHC 2726 (Admin).
35   The Deposit Protection Service, Tenancy Deposit Solutions, The Tenancy Deposit Scheme.
36   National Planning Forum, 2011 – available at www.natplanforum.org.
37   The Scottish Government, March 2009 – available at www.scotland.gov.uk/.
38   www.ipo.gov.uk/mediation.pdf.

and can provide a venue for mediations. In 2006, the Gowers Review of Intellectual Property[39] recognised that mediation could be more widely used.[40] Mediation is also promoted by World Intellectual Property Organisation (WIPO) through mediation rules and guidance.[41]

Personal injury cases

8.24　There is a perception that personal injury cases are unsuitable for mediation. Although the vast majority will settle without the need for mediation, in the remaining cases mediation is considered beneficial to parties as it provides them with 'closure'. While there is no national mediation scheme, specialist mediation services exist. In clinical negligence cases, mediation may be better suited once liability is agreed and expert reports have been obtained. A major liability insurer has stated:

> From an insurer's perspective mediation is a constructive way of seeking to bring about resolution of a case. It provides an opportunity to risk assess the merits of a particular claim and make decisions based on that assessment. Mediation can be carried out earlier in the process; one does not need to have all the evidence completely together in order to form a view that may lead to settlement.
> The consensual approach to mediation also means that both parties come out of mediation with a resolution that is satisfactory to them.[42]

And a solicitor has commented:

> Our own experience is that mediation is very popular with individuals who have benefited from its cathartic process in personal injury claims.[43]

Public authorities and judicial review

8.25　Many practitioners in judicial review and claims against public authorities consider mediation unsuitable, primarily because public authorities are perceived to be unwilling or unable to reach a compromise or review a policy. Mediation has, however, achieved remarkable and far-reaching results, most commonly because it has

---

39　www.official-documents.gov.uk/document/other/0118404830/0118404830.pdf.
40　Gowers Review of Intellectual Property (2006) recommendation 43, p 12.
41　http://www.wipo.int/amc/en/mediation/.
42　Jackson LJ, *Review of civil litigation costs: final report*, December 2009 p360, para 36.2.16.
43　Jackson LJ, *Review of civil litigation costs: final report*, December 2009 p360, para 36.2.15.

the potential to enable multiple parties to work collaboratively and to find alternative solutions not available to the courts. It is particularly suited to community care, disability and discrimination cases and where there are multiple parties who would benefit from meeting together or where roundtable discussions have broken down.

8.26 For further information see:

- *Mediation in judicial review: a practical handbook for lawyers;*[44]
- *The effective use of mediation by local authorities in judicial review.*[45]

SOLACE Mediation Scheme

8.27 The Society of Local Authority Chief Executives (SOLACE) Mediation Service[46] offers fixed fee mediation to local authorities using a small panel of specialist mediators. The service is administered by CEDR and their rates are £1,250 plus VAT.

Local Government Ombudsman Mediation

8.28 The Local Government Ombudsman (LGO) for England is currently running a pilot offering mediation to complainants who have sought redress from the LGO.[47] It is proving particularly effective in complex complaints or for serial complainants where there have been recurring issues. In these types of cases, mediation is offered as an alternative to the complaints procedure.

Government's Dispute Resolution Commitment (DRC) 2011

8.29 The DRC[48] aims to encourage government departments and agencies to be more proactive at managing potential disputes and preventing the need for formal mechanisms; to adopt appropriate dispute resolution mechanisms (including ADR contract clauses) and avoid litigation. This replaces the Alternative Dispute Resolution Pledge 2001.

---

44 Varda Bondy and Margaret Doyle, The Public Law Project, 2011 – available at www.publiclawproject.org.uk/documents/MJRhandbookFINAL.pdf.
45 Nabarro LLP, 2009 –available at www.nabarro.com/Downloads/Effective_use_ of_mediation_by_Local_Authorities_in_Judicial_Review.pdf.
46 See www.solaceenterprises.com.
47 See www.lgo.org.uk/guidance -inv/settling-complaints/mediation.
48 See www.justice.gov.uk/courts/mediation/dispute-resolution-commitment.

Special educational needs (SEN)

8.30 The SEN Code of Practice places a legal duty on local authorities in England and Wales[49] to offer an independent dispute resolution service for parents who have a dispute with their child's school or the local authority (council) about SEN provision.[50] Most councils have chosen to fund an independent mediation provider to deliver this service. Local Authorities must inform parents, schools and others about this service and how they can access it. Parents can appeal against decisions to the Special Educational Needs and Disability Tribunal (SENDIST) Service, which now forms part of the First-tier Tribunal but they must also be offered the chance to try mediation (or another form of dispute resolution). Mediation can run alongside the appeals process, and parents who have a right of appeal can continue to exercise that right at any stage.

8.31 Parties are usually able to make a self-referral to these organisations; it may be helpful to contact the local parent partnership organisation.[51] Parent partnership services (PPSs) are statutory services offering information advice and support to parents and carers of children and young people with SEN.

8.32 The following organisations provide specialist SEN mediation services:

- KIDS London SEN Mediation Service;[52]
- Global Mediation (South East);[53]
- Mediation Works (North East);[54]
- Midlands SEN Mediation (Midlands);[55]
- The Together Trust (North West);[56]
- Wessex Mediation (South West);[57]
- Special Education, Dispute Avoidance and Resolution Service (Northern Ireland);[58]

49 In Scotland, every local authority must make mediation available to parents and young people free of charge (Education (Additional Support for Learning) (Scotland) Act 2004).
50 2001, *SEN Code of Practice*, Department for Education and Skills, 2001 paras 2.24–2.30. Available at www.education.gov.uk/publications.
51 See www.parentpartnership.org.uk.
52 See www.kids.org.uk/mediation.
53 See www.globalmediation.co.uk/our-services/education/special-education-needs.
54 See www.mediation-works.co.uk/sen.
55 See www.midlandssenmediation.com.
56 See www.togethertrust.org.uk/education/disagreement-resolution-service.
57 See www.wessexmediation.co.uk.
58 See www.education-support.org.uk/parents/special-education/dars/.

- Mediation Works (North East);[59]
- Midlands SEN Mediation (Midlands).[60]

In Scotland, specialist SEN mediation services can be found on the Scottish Mediation Register.[61]

Technology and construction disputes

8.33   The use of mediation is well established in the resolution of construction disputes as part of a spectrum of dispute resolution techniques, which includes a formal procedure for the adjudication of disputes,[62] long before they reach the courts.[63] Once legal proceedings are contemplated, the Technology and Construction Court (TCC) 'Construction and Engineering Pre-Action Protocol' is the most far-reaching of all the protocols. It envisages a pre-action meeting where parties meet to consider whether some form of ADR would be more suitable than litigation.[64] The TCC Court Settlement Process (CSP) offers judicial mediation. Parties may also use independent mediation providers. Mediation of construction disputes has been evaluated and proven to generate considerable cost savings.[65]

Case study 11: Getting added value

The claimant was a failed asylum seeker and was injured by the control and restraint techniques used by immigration officers during her attempted deportation. She claimed damages from the Home Office for her injuries. Her claim for £35,000 damages was settled through mediation and the Home Office agreed to suspend her removal order for two months while she recovered.[66]

---

59 www.mediation-works.co.uk/sen.
60 www.midlandssenmediation.com/.
61 See www.scottishmediation.org.uk/find-a-mediator. Also see footnote 49.
62 Housing Grants, Construction and Regeneration Act 1996.
63 For a helpful overview see N Gould, C King and P Britton, *Mediating construction disputes: an evaluation of existing practice*, King's College London, Centre of Construction Law and Dispute Resolution, 2010 pp14–21.
64 TCC, 'Construction and Engineering Pre-Action Protocol' para 5.4.
65 N Gould, C King and P Britton, *Mediating construction disputes: an evaluation of existing practice*, King's College London, Centre of Construction Law and Dispute Resolution, 2010 p63.
66 Reproduced with permission of Public Law Project and originally published in V Bondy and M Doyle, *Mediation in Judicial Review: A practical handbook for lawyers* (2011) http://www.publiclawproject.org.uk/documents/MJRhandbookFINAL.pdf.

If the claimant had sought to pursue contested legal proceedings, it is likely she would have been deported before proceedings had been concluded. This would have made it hard for her legal representatives to represent her and the outcome she achieved at mediation could never have been ordered by the courts.

The civil mediation process

How civil mediation works

8.34 The vast majority of civil disputes settle without the need for a contested hearing. The decision to mediate is therefore primarily motivated by the desire to save time and costs where direct negotiations have failed, and the ability to reach confidential, flexible and constructive outcomes which court proceedings (and direct negotiations) are unable to achieve. Some of the advantages and disadvantages of civil mediation are as follows:

Advantages	Disadvantages
Quick resolution	Complex facts or lack of legal precedent makes strength of case difficult to assess
Costs saving	If unsuccessful, parties incur additional expenditure[68]
Restored relationship	Potentially disclose sensitive information
Avoids damage to reputation,[67] prevents adverse precedent and costs sanctions	Defendant bias and loss aversion may result in lower settlements for claimants

---

67 See paras 7.31–7.45 for a discussion of confidentiality of mediation and mediated agreements.
68 This may not be a wasted cost if issues are narrowed or a partial agreement is reached.

8.35   Mediations usually take place over the course of a day. Anything said or done during a mediation remains confidential,[69] so settlements can be discussed in an informal way without conceding any issues or making formal admissions. Parties wishing to discuss commercially sensitive information or a tactical approach to their case can discuss this with their mediator in a private meeting, without the other party being present. Mediation is voluntary and non-binding, so parties can go to mediation and still pursue legal proceedings if an agreement is not reached. Parties can choose to mediate before court proceedings are even contemplated or at any stage of the legal process.

8.36   Once a party is considering legal proceedings, they must have regard to the CPR. This is described as a 'procedural code with the overriding objective of enabling the court to deal with cases justly'.[70] When considering whether alternative forms of dispute resolution are appropriate, parties should take into account the likely costs of litigation when balanced against the complexity of the issues and the amount of money at stake.[71] Courts are required to actively manage cases and encourage all parties in civil cases to co-operate with each other, which includes considering alternative methods of resolving their dispute.[72] In future, small claims cases will be automatically referred to mediation.[73]

69 See paras 7.31–7.32.
70 CPR (57th update October 2011) 1.1, Part 1.
71 Practice Direction – Pre-Action Conduct, para 6.2.
72 Relevant sections of the CPR are set out in the table below.
73 See para 8.12.

> ## Civil Procedure Rules
>
> The following is a summary of relevant parts of the CPR:
>
> The overriding objective of the Civil Procedure Rules encourages the use of alternative dispute resolution (ADR). The CPR define ADR as a collective description of methods of resolving disputes otherwise than through the normal trial process. Consequently mediation is only one method of ADR that the court is encouraged to promote.
>
> Rule 1.4(1) obliges the court to further the overriding objective of enabling the court to deal with cases justly by actively managing cases.
>
> Rule 1.4(2)(e) defines 'active case management' as including 'encouraging the parties to use an alternative dispute resolution procedure if the court considers that appropriate and facilitating the use of such procedure'.
>
> Rule 26.4(1) provides that 'a party may, when filing the completed allocation questionnaire, make a written request for the proceedings to be stayed while the parties try to settle the case by alternative dispute resolution or other means'.
>
> Rule 26.4(2) sets out that proceedings may also be stayed where 'all parties request a stay', or, 'the court, of its own initiative, considers that such a stay would be appropriate'.
>
> Rule 44.5(3)(a)(ii) requires the court, in deciding the amount of costs to be awarded, to have regard to the conduct of the parties, including in particular 'the efforts made, if any, before and during the proceedings in order to try to resolve the dispute'. This enables the court to penalise parties who have failed to consider mediation in appropriate cases.

The timing of mediation

When to mediate

8.37   There is no 'right time' to mediate (likewise research has shown that there are no uniform criteria for identifying a case which will be suitable for mediation).[74] Every case will have different considerations.

---

74 H Genn et al, *Twisting arms: court referred and court linked mediation under judicial pressure*, Ministry of Justice Research Series 1/07, 2007 p198.

There are a number of factors which indicate 'when' mediation would be appropriate in a civil case:[75]

- it would be a proportionate way to resolve the dispute, taking into consideration legal costs of going to court when compared with mediation;[76]
- the factual and legal framework is clear;
- an added value outcome could be achieved by the parties reaching an agreement together (rather than having a decision imposed upon them);[77]
- there is an ongoing relationship between claimant and defendant, where restoring confidence and improving communication will avoid issues arising in future;
- the underlying issues would not be resolved by a legal challenge;
- there are multiple parties or the settlement sought requires decisions by people who would not be a party to the legal proceedings and could attend mediation;
- there is an obstacle to settlement being reached by negotiation;
- there would be a value in the parties meeting face-to-face.

8.38　Every case needs to be considered on its own facts and legal complexity. There are certain areas of law which lend themselves to early resolution (mostly without the need for mediation). But where cases are not easily resolved at an early stage, defendants (in some cases justifiably) may not be prepared to open a dialogue until a judge rules the applicant has an arguable case, for example, at the permission stage. In disputes where expert reports are required, settlement may only be reached once proceedings are well-established and the issues are clarified by the exchange of pleadings or disclosure.

8.39　A balance needs to be struck. On the one hand, encouraging parties to mediate pre-action, may 'force parties to incur substantial costs at an early stage ("front-loading")'.[78] Defendants may make 'nuisance' pay-outs to avoid litigation costs or incur costs in a case which would ultimately fall away. Equally, it may unfairly pitch claimants against

---

75　See paras 3.7–3.16.

76　If a party is seeking injunctive relief or summary judgment, mediation may not offer a cost effective alternative.

77　There are some vulnerable clients who may find the mediation process challenging. In such cases round-table discussions may be more appropriate, or ask the other party to consider a lawyer-only mediation.

78　N Gould, C King and P Britton, *Mediating construction disputes: an evaluation of existing practice*, King's College, London, 2010 p28.

risk averse defendants.[79] On the other hand, all these concerns are almost always outweighed by the potential costs saving and added value of mediation. A change of mindset is required in order to encourage legal advisers and parties to properly consider mediation at an early stage. Experience shows that once a party or legal adviser has achieved a good outcome at mediation they are likely to see ways in which it can achieve 'better' outcomes for their clients in a wide range of cases.

Pre-action mediation

8.40   Whenever legal proceedings are contemplated, the legal adviser should discuss with their client (claimant or defendant) whether mediation would be an appropriate way to resolve the dispute.[80] The Pre-Action Conduct (Practice Direction) provides general guidance to enable parties to settle the issues between themselves without the need to go to court, encouraging parties to exchange information and to consider ADR:

> 6.1 ... before starting proceedings the parties should–
> (1) exchange sufficient information about the matter to allow them to understand each other's position and make informed decisions about settlement and how to proceed;
> (2) make appropriate attempts to resolve the matter without starting proceedings, and in particular consider the use of an appropriate form of ADR in order to do so.
> 6.2 The parties should act in a reasonable and proportionate manner in all dealings with one another. In particular, the costs incurred in complying should be proportionate to the complexity of the matter and any money at stake. The parties must not use this Practice Direction as a tactical device to secure an unfair advantage for one party or to generate unnecessary costs.[81]

8.41   There are separate pre-action protocols in a number of specialist fields which set out uniquely tailored steps to help parties avoid litigation or unnecessary costs:

- clinical disputes;
- construction and engineering disputes;
- defamation;

---

79   See para 4.75 on defendant loss aversion.

80   Solicitors Regulatory Authority (SRA) Code of Conduct 2011, O(1.12): Solicitors must ensure that '*clients* are in a position to make informed decisions about the services they need, how their matter will be handled and the options available to them' (formerly the Solicitors' Code of Conduct rule 2.02(1)(b)).

81   Pre-Action Conduct (Practice Direction) – see appendix I.

- disease and illness claims;
- housing disrepair;
- judicial review;
- personal injury claims;
- possession claims (based on rent arrears/mortgage arrears etc);
- professional negligence.

8.42   The pre-action protocols contain standard wording on ADR:

> The parties should consider whether some form of alternative dispute resolution procedure would be more suitable than litigation, and if so, endeavour to agree which form to adopt. Both the Claimant and Defendant may be required by the Court to provide evidence that alternative means of resolving their dispute were considered. The Courts take the view that litigation should be a last resort, and that claims should not be issued prematurely when a settlement is still actively being explored. Parties are warned that if this paragraph is not followed then the court must have regard to such conduct when determining costs.[82]

8.43   The clear advantage of mediating at an early stage is that parties have not become fixed in entrenched positions and there is greater flexibility to reach an agreement because neither party has built up legal costs. Claimants should be aware that defendants can be unresponsive to offers to mediate and be unwilling to consider making concessions.[83] In these cases, a claimant may seek to persuade a defendant of the advantages of early resolution – alternatively, they may wish to re-affirm their offer to mediate once proceedings have been issued. Equally, if a limitation period is imminent, claimants should issue their claim first (which protects their legal position) and then continue to pursue mediation.[84] Parties proposing mediation may want to identify why mediation would be worthwhile at an early stage.

Mediation during civil proceedings

> The trick in many cases is to identify the happy medium: the point when the detail of the claim and the response are known to both sides, but before the costs that have been incurred in reaching that stage are so great that a settlement is no longer possible.[85]

---

82 For example, Pre-Action Protocol for the Resolution of Clinical Disputes, Clinical Disputes Forum para 5.1.
83 See paras 3.17–3.22 on proposing mediation.
84 See paras 8.64–8.65.
85 *Nigel Witham Ltd v Smith and Isaacs* [2008] EWHC 12 (TCC) para 32.

8.44   The duty to consider whether to mediate remains throughout civil proceedings. At all times, parties must act in the spirit of the over-riding objective of the Civil Procedure Rules which encourages the use of alternative dispute resolution (ADR). While there is no explicit duty to mediate, parties are expected to justify any decision not to do so. In addition, where a judge forms the view that a case is suitable for mediation, or parties wish to consider mediation, he or she may order proceedings to be stayed.[86]

8.45   The CPR define ADR as 'a collective description of methods of resolving disputes otherwise than through the normal trial proc-ess'.[87] A mechanism to encourage greater use of ADR, including mediation, is the standard ADR order:[88]

> 1. On or before [*] the parties shall exchange lists of 3 neutral individuals who are available to conduct ADR procedures in this case prior to [*]. Each party may [in addition] [in the alternative] provide a list identifying the constitution of one or more panels of neutral individuals who are available to conduct ADR procedures in this case prior to [*].
> 2. On or before [*] the parties shall in good faith endeavour to agree a neutral individual or panel from the lists so exchanged and provided.
> 3. Failing such agreement by [*] the Case Management Conference will be restored to enable the Court to facilitate agreement on a neutral individual or panel.
> 4. The parties shall take such serious steps as they may be advised to resolve their disputes by ADR procedures before the neutral individual or panel so chosen by no later than [*].
> 5. If the case is not finally settled, the parties shall inform the Court by letter prior to [disclosure of documents/exchange of witness statements/exchange of experts' reports] what steps towards ADR have been taken and (without prejudice to matters of privilege) why such steps have failed. If the parties have failed to initiate ADR procedures the Case Management Conference is to be restored for further consideration of the case.
> 6. [Costs].
> Note: The term 'ADR procedures' is deliberately used in the draft ADR order. This is in order to emphasise that (save where otherwise provided) the parties are free to use the ADR procedure that they regard as most suitable, be it mediation, early neutral evaluation, non-binding arbitration etc.

---

86 CPR 26.4(2).
87 CPR, Glossary – available at www.justice.gov.uk/courts/procedure-rules/civil/glossary/.
88 Admiralty and Commercial Court Guide, 9th edn, 2011 appendix 7.

8.46   It is also open to the court to make an Ungley order (as it has become known). This is an order originally devised by Master Ungley in clinical negligence cases to provide a deadline for parties to properly consider ADR.[89]

> The parties shall by [date] consider whether the case is capable of resolution by ADR. If any party considers that the case is unsuitable for resolution by ADR, that party shall be prepared to justify that decision at the conclusion of the trial, should the judge consider that such means of resolution were appropriate, when he is considering the appropriate costs order to make.
>
> The party considering the case unsuitable for ADR shall, not less than 28 days before the commencement of the trial, file with the court a witness statement without prejudice save as to costs, giving reasons upon which they rely for saying that the case was unsuitable.

8.47   The Court of Appeal has approved the use of this type of order more widely in civil litigation (and it is also cited with approval in Lord Jackson's Review of Civil Litigation Costs[90]):

> This form of order has the merit that (a) it recognises the importance of encouraging the parties to consider whether the case is suitable for ADR, and (b) it is calculated to bring home to them that, if they refuse even to consider that question, they may be at risk on costs even if they are ultimately held by the court to be the successful party.[91]

Can it be too soon?

8.48   Parties who have a dispute involving civil liabilities and duties need to have been advised about the strengths and weaknesses of their legal position in order to make informed choices during mediation. This enables parties to reach a fair and reasonable agreement. To do so, the factual and legal positions need to be relatively clear. In 'money claims', it is usually cost-effective to mediate a dispute even where there is some ambiguity. For example, if a dispute is concerned with £10,000 owed to a builder and the client counter-claims for £6,000, the legal fees will very quickly dwarf the sums sought. Even where some uncertainty remains, parties will be better placed to mediate an agreement and reach a resolution more quickly.

---

89   Master Ungley's direction on ADR. Pre-Action Protocol for the Resolution of Clinical Disputes, Clinical Disputes Forum para 5.1.

90   Jackson LJ, *Review of civil litigation costs: final report*, December 2009 p361, para 36.3.4.

91   Dyson LJ, *Halsey v Milton Keynes NHS Trust* [2004] EWCA (Civ) 576, para 33.

Is it ever too late to mediate?

8.49   Many cases settle at the door of the court. If lawyers are unable to resolve matters through direct negotiation in the weeks leading up to trial, but parties wish to explore settlement, mediation may offer a better process than the pressured atmosphere of a court waiting room.

Case study 12: Building contracts and the costs swamp

This is a story of a house renovation project gone sour. The builder, Mr Burchell, issued proceedings for approximately £18,000 for unpaid work. The home owners, Mr and Mrs Bullard, counterclaimed for a sum over £100,000. At the conclusion of heavily contested legal proceedings which had lasted several years, the builder was awarded £18,327.04 and the owners £14,373.15 on their counter-claim. Ultimately, the defendants, Mr and Mrs Bullard, were order to pay £5,025.63. This was overshadowed by legal costs were around £185,000.

The trial judge observed that the costs had 'swamped' the litigation. The Court of Appeal held that this kind of dispute lent itself to ADR and that the merits of the case favoured mediation. In principle, the defendants should be penalised with costs sanctions for unreasonably refusing the builder's offer to mediate.[92]

Five years later, another 'sad case about lost opportunities for mediation'.[93] Home owner Mrs Rolf sued her former builder Mr De Guerin after a breakdown between the parties over the construction of a garage and a loft. The judge ruled that Mrs Rolf's husband's habit of interfering with activities on the site amounted to a repudiatory breach entitling Mr De Guerin to walk off the site. Mrs Rolf's claim at trial was for over £70,000 and she was ultimately awarded £2,500 for defective or unfinished work.

In this case, Mr De Guerin had refused an offer by Mrs Rolf of mediation. The Court of Appeal found that 'wanting his day in court' was not an acceptable reason to refuse to mediate and could be taken into account in awarding costs.[94]

---

92   *Burchell v Bullard* [2005] EWCA Civ 358.
93   Rix LJ, *Rolf v De Guerin* [2011] EWCA Civ 78, at para 1.
94   *Rolf v De Guerin* [2011] EWCA Civ 78.

8.50   There are a number of reasons why parties consider mediation once legal proceedings are well established:

- *Litigation fatigue*: Parties who have been involved in legal proceedings for some time, who are aware that the issues they think are important may not be aired, and realise that there is uncertainty and litigation risk.
- *Consolidation of issues*: In some cases, it is only once pleadings have been exchanged, full disclosure has been made or expert opinion has been sought, that the issues are sufficiently certain to enter settlement discussions and mediation.
- *Litigation risk*: The inherent uncertainty of what outcome will be achieved following a trial, as well as the costs considerations.
- *Adverse costs consequences*: The potential risk that a court will impose cost sanctions for an unreasonable refusal to mediate.

Proposing mediation

8.51   An invitation to another party to consider mediation should be persuasive and demonstrate a genuine desire to resolve the issues through mediation. The information contained in an offer to mediate may include:

- the reasons why the case is suitable for mediation;[95]
- any outcomes mediation can achieve that would not be achievable through court proceedings (or another form of dispute resolution);
- relevant paragraphs of the Pre-Action Protocol and CPR and case-law;
- that an Ungley order[96] or ADR order[97] will be sought;
- the next steps to setting up a mediation, which may include proposing named mediators or mediation providers, and a time-frame during which mediation could take place.

Responding to an offer to mediate

Decisions not to mediate

The profession can no longer with impunity shrug aside reasonable requests to mediate. The parties cannot ignore a proper request to

95   See para 8.37.
96   See para 8.46.
97   See para 8.45.

mediate simply because it was made before the claim was issued. With court fees escalating it may be folly to do so.[98]

8.52 Parties should anticipate having to justify a decision not to mediate. This is because if the matter proceeds to trial, the judge will need to decide who pays the costs of the legal proceedings. In making this decision, the judge is entitled to take into consideration what efforts the parties made to resolve the matter. A party should set out their reasons in writing – this ensures that the refusal is genuine. It also enables concerns to be addressed and possibly overcome.[99]

8.53 The decision to mediate can (and should) be reconsidered. Where a party requires a legal precedent, a judge could be invited to give a preliminary ruling on a point of law. In a case where an injunction is required, mediation can run alongside court proceedings. Once the injunction is obtained there may be scope to resolve the underlying issues through mediation.

Reasons why mediation is premature

8.54 The following reasons may suggest it would be too soon to mediate:

- a settlement can be reached through direct negotiation;
- there is insufficient information adequately to assess the merits of the case at this stage;
- there is no legal precedent and the legal issues are uncertain;
- a settlement would not be in the public interest;
- an injunction is required.

Reasons why mediation is unsuitable

8.55 In some cases mediation is unsuitable:

- a party considers they have a cast-iron case;
- a legal precedent is needed to clarify the law or inform policy;
- the remedy sought could not be achieved by a consensual agreement between the parties;
- a public decision is required;
- imbalance of power between the parties;
- there is no reasonable prospect of success at mediation;
- other settlement methods have been attempted;
- cost of mediation is disproportionately high;
- delay.

98 Ward LJ in *Burchall v Bullard and others* [2005] EWCA Civ 358.
99 See *PGF v OMFS* [2012] EWHC 83 (TCC) at para 44; see para 8.107.

Cast-iron case[100]

8.56   Even where a party considers that they have a cast-iron case, mediation may still provide a cost-effective outcome where the cost of
legal proceedings is disproportionate to the amount sought or recoverable. Parties should consider what other benefits could be achieved
from mediation. Alternatively, they should seek summary judgment
or apply to strike out the claim.

Legal precedent

8.57   Unless a case is being brought in the wider public interest as a 'test
case', there are few cases where a party's interests are served by funding expensive legal proceedings to achieve greater legal certainty or a
new legal precedent. All too often, judgments that establish the legal
position in relation to a particular issue become disassociated from
the party's best interests. Obtaining a meaningful, practical outcome
may be the right approach for a party and mediation should be considered even where the law is not certain.

Public decision

8.58   Going to court and receiving a judgment which is accessible to members of the public is not the only way to achieve a public decision.
Settlement agreements can include press releases and agreed public
statements,[101] as well as an undertaking to review or amend a policy.

Imbalance of power between the parties

8.59   Mediation is most effective when both parties enter the process being
flexible and willing to compromise. When there is a power imbalance
between the parties – such as an individual or small organisation in a
legal dispute with a large multinational company or public body – it
may be understandable that a party feels they would receive a 'fairer'
outcome by going to court. Skilled mediators will seek to address
unfair pressure being placed on a 'weaker party' and so any concerns
should be addressed directly to the mediator. A 'weaker party' may
also achieve a more balanced bargaining position by issuing proceedings, seeking permission (in a judicial review), or successfully resisting a strike out. Once the other party accepts their opponent has an
arguable case, the risk of adverse publicity and escalating costs may
make settlement more desirable.

---

100 See para 8.105 – *S v Chapman* [2008] EWCA Civ 800.
101 See para 7.15.

No reasonable prospect of success in mediation[102]

8.60   It is almost impossible to say that mediation has no reasonable prospect of success unless a party seeks an outcome which the other party will never agree to or is unable to agree to – for example, it would require a third party's agreement. Even where at first blush parties appear to have incompatible positions, mediation can achieve successful outcomes by widening the issues under discussion and exploring practical outcomes.

8.61   In some cases, however, a party will seek to limit the scope of a mediation and to exclude certain issues from discussion or negotiation. By narrowing the areas of discussion, mediation may become impractical, particularly where a party perceives a lack of good faith.

Other settlement methods have been attempted

8.62   It is reasonable to reject mediation on the basis that other settlement methods have been unsuccessful;[103] however, the Court of Appeal has been keen to emphasise that 'mediation often succeeds where other settlement attempts have failed'.[104] The burden lies with the unsuccessful party to show that mediation could have been successful.[105]

Cost

8.63   Mediation must be a proportionate method of resolving a dispute, and so in cases where the cost would be disproportionately high it might reasonably be refused.[106] Given the large number of free and low-cost mediation schemes, this is unlikely to arise.

Delay

8.64   Where a party embarks upon mediation before proceedings have been issued, they should, if at all possible, ascertain the time limit for bringing a legal case. 'Limitation periods' are the length of time a potential litigant has to commence court proceedings – after that

---

102   'Whether mediation had a reasonable prospect of success' was listed by the Court of Appeal as a possible reason for reasonably refusing mediation – *Halsey v Milton Keynes NHS Trust* [2004] EWCA Civ 576, para 23.

103   'Other settlement methods have been attempted' was listed by the Court of Appeal as a possible reason for reasonably refusing mediation – *Halsey v Milton Keynes NHS Trust* [2004] EWCA Civ 576, para 20.

104   *Halsey v Milton Keynes NHS Trust* [2004] EWCA Civ 576, para 20.

105   See paras 8.98–8.107 on costs sanctions; *Halsey v Milton Keynes NHS Trust* [2004] EWCA Civ 576, para 13.

106   'Cost of mediation is disproportionately high' was listed by the Court of Appeal as a possible reason for reasonably refusing mediation – *Halsey v Milton Keynes NHS Trust* [2004] EWCA Civ 576, para 21.

time expires they are barred from bringing a case.[107] If the 'limitation period' runs out when a party is trying (unsuccessfully) to reach a mediated settlement, they will not be entitled to take the matter to court. It is also clear that pursuing mediation should never be used by a potential defendant to delay (or avoid) making a decision as to their legal responsibilities. In *Robinson*, the local authority were criticised for failing to determine a homelessness application for a 17-year-old while the family sought to mediate.[108]

8.65   Mediations can be arranged relatively quickly, but where a trial date may be delayed, it might be reasonable to refuse to mediate.[109] Alternatively, if a limitation period is about to expire, proceedings can be issued to protect the claimant's position whilst attempts at mediation continue. As an exception to this general rule, EU cross-border disputes are protected from limitation issues by the EU Mediation Directive.[110]

Mediation contract clauses

8.66   A commercial or government contract can specify how the parties will resolve disputes that arise in the delivery of the contractual obligations. Some contracts will specify time-frames within which to seek dispute resolution. If mediation is specifically identified as the form of dispute resolution which should be pursued, the contract can only require parties to *attempt* resolution using mediation (it cannot bind them to reach a settlement). The value of such clauses is that it is designed to create a shift in mindset away from a 'litigation culture' towards more collaborative problem solving.[111]

Enforceability of mediation contract clauses

8.67   An inherent contradiction can arise where parties have a contractual obligation to attempt a consensual, voluntary process such as mediation. Compelling parties to participate in a process which requires

---

107 Subject to a discretionary extension of time in certain circumstances.

108 *Robinson v Hammersmith and Fulham LBC* [2004] EWCA Civ 1122. Also see paras 11.16–11.18 on homelessness mediation.

109 'Delay to trial date' was listed by the Court of Appeal as a possible reason for reasonably refusing mediation – *Halsey v Milton Keynes NHS Trust* [2004] EWCA Civ 576, para 22.

110 For cross-border disputes within the European Union, parties can rely on article 8 of the EU Mediation Directive, which states that a limitation period should not be able to expire during a mediation. The relevant sections of the CPR dealing with the European Directive are rule 78.23–78.28 and the associated Practice Direction.

111 See appendix F.

co-operation is self-defeating. Courts will only uphold mediation contract clauses that are drafted with sufficient clarity and certainty.[112] Such clauses should not compel parties to mediate (or prevent parties from being able to go to court) – instead they set out a series of steps which parties should follow which encourage resolution before commencing legal proceedings.[113] This may provide a prescribed time frame before a claim is issued during which parties should attempt ADR procedures or mediation.[114]

Setting up a mediation

8.68   The practical steps to setting up a mediation are considered in chapter 3. Parties need to:

- jointly select a mediator or mediation scheme and agree who pays;
- agree a time, date, venue;
- agree who will attend;
- pay the mediator's or mediation provider's fee;
- sign the *agreement to mediate*.

Who pays for the mediation?

8.69   In most cases the fees for the mediation are split equally between the parties and are paid by the parties in advance. The fees will be set out in the *agreement to mediate*, which will be signed in advance of the mediation.

8.70   In some cases one party pays the mediation fees; this may be appropriate if liability has been accepted. Although it is possible for one party to pay the cost of mediation, it has an associated risk. It suggests a power imbalance where both parties are not entering the process on an equal footing. These risks can be addressed to a large extent, provided parties are legally represented and there is evidence from both parties of good faith and a genuine desire to settle the case.

---

112   See, for example, *Walford v Miles* [1992] 1 All ER 453; *Halifax Financial Services v Intuitive Systems* [1999] 1 All ER Comm 303 – where the terms were considered to lack sufficient clarity or certainty to be enforceable.

113   For a useful overview see K Mackie, D Miles, W Marsh and T Allen, *The ADR practice guide: commercial dispute resolution*, Tottel, 2007 pp151–166.

114   See appendix F.

How to find a mediator?

8.71   Parties should always consider whether a specialist mediation scheme is available which may offer free or low cost mediation.[115] Chapter 3 considers how parties can find a civil mediator.[116]

Mediation fees and funding

8.72   The cost of a mediation includes:

- the mediator's fee;
- arrangement fee;
- venue costs (may or may not include refreshments/catering);
- legal adviser (preparation and attendance);
- expert (preparation and attendance).

8.73   If parties are unable to pay their own legal fees, they can seek public funding, enter into a conditional fee agreement or have their costs paid under an insurance policy.

Mediator's fees

Claims up to £5,000

8.74   Parties with lower value claims can access the small claims mediation scheme.[117] This service is *free* and is included within the court fee (the hearing fee is refundable if mediation resolves the claim). Although parties would also be entitled to access services at the Online Civil Mediation Directory rates, it may be cost-effective to lodge a small claim.

Claims up to £50,000

8.75   The Civil Mediation Online Directory[118] provides fixed-rates for mediation provided by mediation providers accredited with the Civil Mediation Council (CMC). The Directory rates are as follows:

---

115 See paras 8.10–8.33.
116 See para 3.48. Parties may also approach their local community mediation
     service.
117 See para 8.12.
118 See www.civilmediation.justice.gov.uk and see para 8.13.

Claim value[119]	Fees (per party)	Length of session	Extra hours (per party)
£5,000 or less	£50 + VAT £100 + VAT	1 hour Up to 2 hours	£50 + VAT
£5,000 to £15,000	£300 + VAT	Up to 3 hours	£85 + VAT
£15,000 to £50,000	£425 + VAT	Up to 4 hours	£95 + VAT

8.76 Most mediation providers also offer fixed-fee day rates. These vary from £500 per party per day upwards. Parties may feel that less time pressure on reaching a resolution would be beneficial to parties and wish to arrange a mediation for a slightly more expensive fee in order to increase the time available and therefore chances of reaching a settlement.

Claims over £50,000 or non-monetary claims

8.77 Fees range from around £500 to £1,500 per party per day, and commercial mediators can charge £2,000 to £3,000 (and higher) per party. The complexity of the case, the value of the claim (if any) and the experience and expertise of the mediator determine the 'fixed length' of the mediation and the fee charged. Only some mediation providers list the fees on their website or marketing material. It is worth comparing different providers or individual mediators in order to get a competitive rate. Any additional time will be charged at an hourly rate.

> **Top tip:** Civil mediation providers often incrementally increase their charges for mediations according to the value of the claim – these prices may be open to negotiation, the length of time the mediator spends preparing the case and at the mediation remains the same.

Public funding

8.78 If a party receives public funding, civil mediation[120] may be funded as a disbursement under Legal Help or Legal Representation. No specific limitation on a certificate is required in order to attend or fund

119 Based on the amount claimed or counter-claimed, whichever is higher.
120 Described as 'non-family mediation' in the LSC Funding Code: Decision Making Guidance Part C para 3C-100.

mediation. However the cost of mediating must be reasonable. In practice, most legal advisers will seek prior authority.

> 2. No prior authority is necessary to mediate a non-family dispute but, like all fees, the cost of mediating must be reasonable in all the circumstances ...As a general starting point, non-family mediators will need to justify any rates in excess of prescribed basic remuneration rates for lawyers providing county court advocacy under certificates for Legal Representation.
>
> ....
>
> 4. It is clearly important that a mediator is chosen whose skills are appropriate to the nature of the dispute. Clearly for complex cases requiring a commercial mediator, the fees of the mediator will be higher than for community disputes.[121]

8.79　Basic remuneration for county court advocacy is per hour £58.50,[122] which falls below the Civil Mediation Online Directory rates. Since the LSC encourages legal advisers to consider the use of mediation,[123] applications for mediator's fees at higher rates are likely to be approved. Civil mediators are expected to be on a CMC-accredited mediation provider panel, or have appropriate training and expertise.[124] Funding for mediation includes a legal adviser's preparation time (which may include drafting a position statement and preparing an opening statement) and attendance at the mediation.[125]

8.80　If a publicly funded party unreasonably refuses an offer to mediate, this can result in funding being limited to preparation for and participation in mediation.[126]

Conditional fee agreements (CFAs)

8.81　Parties who are unable to fund their own legal costs can find a legal adviser who will offer representation under a conditional fee agreement (CFA), most commonly on a 'no win, no fee' basis. Under a CFA, claimants are not liable for the solicitor's fee if they lose, but agree to be liable for any disbursements which are incurred, such as an expert report and mediation.[127] CFAs require an initial assessment

---

121　LSC Funding Code: Decision Making Guidance Part C para 3C-100.
122　Community Legal Service (Funding) (Amendment No 2) Order 2011 SI No 2066.
123　LSC Funding Code: Decision Making Guidance Part C para 3C-102.
124　LSC Funding Code: Decision Making Guidance Part C para 3C-101 (6).
125　LSC Funding Code: Decision Making Guidance Part C para 3C-105.
126　LSC Funding Code: Decision Making Guidance Part C para 3C-103 and C43.2(vi)(e) of the Code Procedures.
127　This will depend on the definition of 'disbursement' in the agreement.

of the strength of a case. If the claimant wins, lawyers can charge an uplift on top of their base costs (the percentage uplift is calculated in relation to the risk undertaken by the claimant's lawyers). Otherwise known as a 'success fee', this is payable by the unsuccessful defendant. If a claimant loses, however, they are liable for the defendant's costs. To avoid this risk, a party can purchase 'after the event' (ATE) insurance.[128]

8.82   It has been argued that the CFA framework can place an unfair burden on defendants. Reflecting this, the *Jackson Review* recommended limiting the recoverability of success fees and ATE insurance premiums which would mean parties pay any success fee and insurance premium from their damages.[129] The government has taken these changes forward in the Legal Aid, Sentencing and Punishment of Offenders Act (LASPOA) 2012. Once brought into force, the percentage uplift will be subject to a maximum limit[130] and the insurance premiums paid by claimants will only be recoverable in limited situations.[131]

Insurance

8.83   Settling is the most cost-effective method of dealing with a case, so insurers may be persuaded to fund mediation in appropriate circumstances.

Before the event (BTE) insurance

8.84   Parties may have legal expenses insurance as part of their household or motor insurance policy. If the insurer is funding the litigation, they will be liable for any the other party's costs if they lose the case. Insurers will wish to be regularly updated in relation to costs issues and may attend mediation or be contactable to agree any settlement.

After the event (ATE) insurance

8.85   Parties in a CFA-funded case can insure against the risk of having to pay their opponent's costs and their own disbursements if they lose. While there is no obligation to purchase ATE insurance, if the claim

---

128 See para 8.85.

129 Jackson LJ, *Review of civil litigation costs: final report*, December 2009 p xvi, paras 2.1–2.4. The proposals recommend a complimentary increase of ten per cent in general damages awards and a maximum limit on the amount that lawyers may deduct for success fees of 25 per cent.

130 Legal Aid, Sentencing and Punishment of Offenders Act (LASPOA) 2012, Part 2, s44.

131 LASPOA 2012 s46.

is lost the other side will pursue the claimant for their costs. In the event of winning the claim, the uplift and the insurance premium is currently recoverable from the defendant, but this will no longer be the case once the changes introduced by LASPOA 2012 come into force.[132]

Costs issues

8.86   The opportunity to resolve civil disputes without significant legal costs is a principal reason parties choose mediation. This is not to say that legal costs will not already have been incurred by the time parties are prepared to mediate. Legal costs and expenses include:

- court fees;
- solicitors' and barristers' fees;
- disbursements;
- expert reports;
- ADR procedures.

8.87   In some cases, the legal costs may not be particularly high, but will represent a significant expenditure for either party. In other cases, the costs may be disproportionate to the sums of money in dispute – for example, a contractual dispute over £15,000 where both parties' costs exceed this figure. Where considerable costs have accumulated, this may represent a greater challenge than resolving the substantive issues.

8.88   If the matter proceeds to trial, the costs consequences of Part 36 offers are complex (see 'Guide to costs' below). Simply put, the regime favours accepting early offers and penalises parties who get outcomes following a trial which are less favourable than (or equal to) a Part 36 offer to settle the case.

---

132 See para 8.82.

Guide to costs – a brief overview of costs in civil proceedings[133]

Whether the claimant or the defendant, parties will want to recover their legal costs if they 'win' or successfully defend their case.

Costs rules are, however, fairly complex. Parts 43–48 of the CPR, supplemented by the Costs Practice Directions, contain guidance on how the courts should determine costs issues.

The costs rules only apply for certain types of civil case. Legal costs and expenses are not recoverable in:

• small claims (unless a successful party can show unreasonable conduct on the part of the losing party);
• lower and upper tribunal cases;
• employment tribunals (except in exceptional circumstances).

Costs follow the event

The usual principle when deciding costs is that 'costs follow the event' (CPR 44.3(2)(a)). This means that, in broad terms, the losing party has to pay the legal costs of the successful party, as well as covering their own legal costs.

Who is the 'winning party'?

Deciding who the successful party is and how much of their costs should be paid by the other party is not a straight-forward matter. The judge will balance a number of factors including (CPR 44.3(4)):

• the conduct of all the parties;[134]
• the extent to which the party succeeded in his or her case; and
• any payment into court or other offers made, such as Part 36 offers.

The challenge faced by trial judges is illustrated by two recent cases. In *Widlake v BAA Ltd*[135] the original claim was for £150,000 and the claimant's final award was for just under £6,000. The trial judge decided that the defendant was the winner of the case, on the basis the claimant had exaggerated her claim, and awarded costs in the defendant's favour. The Court of Appeal overturned that decision, and found that the starting point was that the claimant was to be treated as the 'winner' having beaten the Part 36 offer but there was no order as to costs in view of the claimant's conduct.

In *Medway Primary Care Trust v Marcus*[136] the original claim was for £525,000 and the damages following a trial were £2,000. The trial

---

133 With thanks to Rajeev Thacker who drafted this accessible and user-friendly guide.
134 See CPR 44.3(5).
135 [2009] EWCA Civ 1256.
136 [2011] EWCA Civ 750.

judge ordered the defendant to pay 50 per cent of the claimant's costs. The Court of Appeal ruled that the defendant was the successful party to reflect that the substantive part of the claim had failed in its entirety and ordered the claimant had to pay 75 per cent of the defendant's costs.

Part 36 offers

Parties wishing to settle cases before they reach the trial date can do so by making offers and counter offers. Offers can be made in a number of ways, the most common is described as a 'Part 36 offer' (CPR Part 36). Part 36 offers can be made by a claimant or a defendant, they must observe certain formalities including that the offer must be in writing and specify a time period not less than 21 days within which the defendant will be liable for the claimant's costs (CPR 36.2).

If a claimant accepts a Part 36 offer, they will be entitled to the costs of proceedings up to the date on which the notice of acceptance was served (CPR 36.10). If the matter proceeds to trial, the costs consequences are as follows (CPR 36.14):

a) a claimant who fails to obtain a judgment more advantageous than a Part 36 offer (ie the defendant's offer was equal to, or better than the judgment) pays:
   i) the defendant's costs from the last date on which the part 36 offer could have been accepted, as well as interest on those costs;

b) a claimant who obtains a judgment more or at least as advantageous than his or her Part 36 offer (ie the claimant's offer was higher than or equal to the judgment), the defendant pays:
   i) interest on the damages from the last date on which the part 36 offer could have been accepted;
   ii) costs on an indemnity basis from the same date; and
   iii) interest on those costs.

As can be seen, the potential consequences for claimant and defendant are severe. For a claimant, the failure to beat a defendant's Part 36 offer may result in substantial costs being paid to the defendant, often wiping out any damages that have been awarded. A defendant, who has not accepted a Part 36 offer from a claimant, runs the risk of being subjected to substantial penalties in terms of additional costs and interest.

Calculating costs: standard or indemnity basis

When a court orders one party to pay another party's costs, they will normally be assessed on a standard basis.[137] If costs are paid on a

---

137 *Ghafoor v Cliff* [2006] EWHC 825 (Ch), para 72.

standard basis, any dispute as to whether the costs were reasonably incurred, is resolved by the judicial body in favour of the paying party (CPR 44.4(2)). Where the court orders costs to be assessed on an indemnity basis, any doubt about whether the costs were reasonably incurred will be resolved in favour of the receiving party (CPR 44.4(3)). This may make a considerable difference for legal advisers (solicitors and barristers) who represent the publicly funded party, if indemnity costs are awarded in their favour any limitations on public funding would not apply and the legal fees payable would be considerably higher. In the past it was necessary for a court to find that there had been unreasonable conduct on the part of a party in order to make an order for costs to be assessed on the indemnity basis. This is no longer necessary. The relevant principles to be applied were set out in *Three Rivers District Council v Governor and Company of the Bank of England*.[138] In essence, there must be 'some element of a party's conduct of the case which deserves some mark of disapproval'.[139]

Public funding and the statutory charge

Where a party is publicly funded, it does not mean that the issue of costs falls away. If the successful party is publicly funded, the Legal Services Commission (LSC) will want to recover their costs – for example, where a settlement agreement is reached but the losing party does not agree to pay the costs. The LSC will seek to recover their costs in any case when property is 'recovered or preserved'.[140] In practical terms, this means that if a party receives a payment of damages or other financial settlement, or retains property (such as their home), the LSC will recover the legal costs. If costs are not recovered from the other party, they can recover their costs by direct payment from the damages award or through the statutory charge, which is where the LSC register a charge against a party's home and the amount is repaid when the property is sold.

Recovering the costs of mediation

As a general rule, the cost of the mediation will be repaid to the successful party as part of their litigation costs by the unsuccessful party.

---

138 [2006] EWHC 816 (Comm).

139 *R (GG and others) v Secretary of State for the Home Department* [2006] EWHC 1111 (Admin) at para 119. See notes to CPR 44.4.2 in *Civil Procedure 2012*: The White Book (Sweet and Maxwell, 2012).

140 LSC Funding Guidelines Vol 1 para 1D-022.

Mediation and costs

Recovery of costs

Costs options

8.89   If an agreement is reached at mediation, the parties will wish to decide who will pay any legal costs incurred. Broadly speaking, the options for parties in civil mediation are that:

- each party can agree to bear their own costs; or
- the 'successful party' has its costs (or a proportion) paid by the 'unsuccessful party'.

8.90   Expecting one party to pay another's costs is not without its challenges. It is often assumed that *both* parties achieve benefits from the mediation process and so each party pays its own costs. The implications for reaching an agreement where parties pay their own costs presents particular challenges in two specific situations: CFAs and publicly funded parties. If a party wants to recover their legal costs, this should be part of the negotiations from the outset. Raising it at a late stage could derail a potential agreement.

CFAs

8.91   CFAs require solicitors (and barristers) to carry the risk of litigation. In other words, if their client loses the case, they will not be paid for their work on the case. The reward is that if the client 'wins' their case and costs are awarded in their favour, the defendant pays their fees plus an uplift depending on the level of risk.[141] Claimants have a duty to make defendants aware that they have entered into a CFA and whether they have an ATE insurance policy.[142] Parties do not need to disclose details of the success fee uplift or the ATE premium so as to keep the risk assessment confidential.

8.92   The CFA regime creates a tension between legal advisers and clients in mediations (which is likely to reduce considerably once the changes to civil litigation funding introduced by Part 2 of the LASPOA 2012 take effect).[143] This arises when the parties are able to reach agreement on the substantive issues, but the defendant is unwilling to pay (all of) the claimant's costs. If the defendant does not pay the claimant's legal costs, the solicitor will seek to recover their costs which will inevitably be deducted from any damages the

141   See paras 8.81–8.82.
142   CPR 44.3A.
143   See para 8.82.

claimant receives, possibly consuming the entire amount. Once the defendant has made their 'best' offer, the solicitor will be placed under real pressure to either recover the shortfall from their client or accept a reduction in their fees. This creates a conflict of interest between the solicitor and their client. Another difficulty arises when a solicitor is asked to disclose the CFA 'uplift' and success fee' so the defendant can consider the amount he or she is liable to pay. This is highly sensitive information which indicates to the defendant how the legal adviser assessed the strength of the case. If disclosed, it may cause the defendant to reassess an offer, and if no agreement is reached sensitive information will have been disclosed.

How to approach CFA issues

8.93   Before the mediation:
- Make the mediator aware; the other party should have already been informed.[144]
- The legal adviser should discuss this issue with their client to make them fully aware of the importance of seeking a global settlement which includes costs.
- The legal adviser should provide their client with an up to date bill of costs.
- Ensure that a partner (or senior practitioner) attends the mediation so they are in a position to make decisions about their legal fees or are available on the phone (and the ATE insurers are contactable[145]).

At the mediation:
- The legal adviser should consider in advance, what sort of concession they are willing to make on fees. If necessary they should propose an acceptable amount for costs rather than disclosing the CFA 'uplift'.
- If the legal adviser wishes to recover a shortfall in their fees from the client,[146] sufficient time should be given for an agreed figure to be reached during the mediation.[147]

144 See para 8.91.
145 Try to obtain an out-of-hours number in the event the mediation lasts into the evening.
146 The possibility of this occurring should have been made clear to the client in their 'client care letter'.
147 The Solicitors' Code of Conduct requires the client to be given requisite information about costs, and that the client has a right to have any bill made the subject of a detailed assessment – SRA Code of Conduct 2011, O(1.14): solicitors must ensure that '*clients* are informed of their right to challenge or

Publicly funded parties

8.94   Parties should be aware that if they are publicly funded and receive damages as part of a settlement agreement, they are expected to repay their costs to the LSC. If they do not recover their costs, the LSC will deduct the costs out of the damages payment. In a case involving the loss of a party's home, such as rent or mortgage arrears, the LSC would be entitled to place a statutory charge against the property to recover the costs.[148]

8.95   Defendant solicitors or unrepresented parties unfamiliar with the public funding regime may not be aware of the statutory charge. It is therefore helpful to explain the position at the outset of the mediation process (or in the position statement).

8.96   For publicly funded solicitors, a mediated settlement may also mean a substantial reduction in their fees. Legal aid rates are much lower than the hourly *inter partes* rates the unsuccessful party would have to pay if successful at trial. Where a mediated settlement agreement is reached which, if ordered by the court, would have resulted in the other party paying the solicitor's costs, a potential conflict arises where the client wishes to settle the case but the legal adviser will still want to find an agreement on costs. In privately funded cases, parties could ask the court to determine costs issues, but the LSC may not fund a hearing to recover the full costs from the other party.

8.97   How to approach public funding issues:

- Legal advisers should ensure that their client (party) understands the recovery of costs regime in publicly funded cases.
- Legal advisers or parties should set out in their position statement that they are publicly funded and any settlement should include a payment of costs, and explain why.
- Legal advisers should provide their client with an up-to-date schedule of costs.

Costs sanctions for a party's refusal to mediate

8.98   The courts have made clear that the conduct of the parties can be taken into account when deciding who pays the legal costs at the conclusion of a court case, and this includes an unreasonable refusal to consider mediation. This has been endorsed by the Jackson Review:

complain about your bill and the circumstances in which they may be liable to pay interest on an unpaid bill'.

148 See para 8.88 'Guide to costs' on public funding and the statutory charge.

The form of any costs penalty must be in the discretion of the court. However, such penalties might include (a) reduced costs recovery for a winning party; (b) indemnity costs against a losing party.[149]

It is for the party seeking a departure from the normal cost rule to show that the other party had acted unreasonably in refusing to engage in mediation and that there was a reasonable prospect that the mediation would have been successful. The Court of Appeal summarised the position:

> In deciding whether to deprive a successful party of some or all of his costs on the grounds that he has refused to agree to ADR, it must be borne in mind that such an order is an exception to the general rule that costs should follow the event. In our view, the burden is on the unsuccessful party to show why there should be a departure from the general rule. The fundamental principle is that such departure is not justified unless it is shown (the burden being on the unsuccessful party) that the successful party acted unreasonably in refusing to agree to ADR.[150]

8.99 The Court of Appeal went on to give guidance as to the circumstances in which a party's refusal to engage with ADR might be regarded as unreasonable. The following factors were identified:

a) the nature of the dispute;
b) the merits of the case;
c) the extent to which other settlement methods have been attempted;
d) whether the costs of the ADR would be disproportionately high;
e) whether any delay in setting up and attending the ADR would have been prejudicial; and
f) whether the ADR had a reasonable prospect of success.

8.100 The court pointed out that these factors are not exhaustive. It made it clear that there is no 'presumption in favour of mediation',[151] however, parties should ensure they justify any refusal to mediate in order to protect against an adverse costs award. There are a number of cases in which the courts have sought to apply these principles.

8.101 In *Dunnett v Railtrack plc*,[152] decided prior to *Halsey*, the winning party (the defendant) had refused to consider the claimant's suggestion of mediation, or any form of ADR. Rather than awarding costs in favour of the defendant, the Court of Appeal decided that the proper

---

149 Jackson LJ, *Review of civil litigation costs: final report*, December 2009, p361, para 36.3.34.
150 Dyson LJ *Halsey v Milton Keynes NHS Trust* [2004] EWCA Civ 576, para 13.
151 *Halsey v Milton Keynes NHS Trust* [2004] EWCA Civ 576, para 16.
152 [2002] EWCA Civ 302.

order on the appeal was no order as to costs. It has to be said, however, that its reasoning may have been influenced by the fact that the claimant had been acting in person up to a relatively late stage in the litigation, and was thereafter assisted pro bono.

8.102   In *Daniels v Commissioner of Police for the Metropolis*[153] it was argued by an unsuccessful claimant that costs should not follow the event because the defendant had refused a number of Part 36 offers. Dyson LJ considered the question of the circumstances in which a party's refusal would be characterised as unreasonable:

> It seems to me to be entirely reasonable for a defendant, especially a public body such as the police, to take the view that it will contest what it reasonably considers to be an unfounded claim in order to deter other, similarly unfounded, claims. It is well-known that large organisations often make payments to buy off claims which they consider to be speculative, if not wholly without foundation, in order to avoid the trouble and expense of contesting them. This propensity, coupled with the fact that claims are now funded on a 'no win no fee' basis may, in part, be responsible for fuelling what has been described in some quarters as a 'compensation culture'.[154]

8.103   If defendants, who routinely face what they consider to be unfounded claims, wish to take a stand and contest them rather than make nuisance payments, then the court should be slow to characterise such conduct as unreasonable so as to deprive defendants of their costs, if they are ultimately successful. As the judge recognised, this may mean (and in the present case did mean) that litigation is sometimes contested whose costs are wholly disproportionate to the sums claimed.

8.104   Keene LJ, in refusing permission to appeal to the unsuccessful claimant in *Hurst v Leeming*,[155] also referred to the fact that there may be cases where the character of one of the parties may mean that mediation would be hopeless:

> For my part, it seems clear that the case of Dunnett was not seeking to set out a comprehensive list of relevant factors in such matters. The judge was entitled to take the view that a party could properly decline mediation if there was no realistic prospect of it succeeding. The past conduct of the other party may sometimes give a guide as to whether or not there is such a prospect. It seems to me that it was that past conduct which was being referred to by the judge, when he made that comment towards the end of his judgment about the character and

---

153 [2005] EWCA Civ 1312.
154 [2005] EWCA Civ 1312, para 26.
155 [2002] EWCA Civ 1173.

attitude of Mr Hurst. The pre-action protocol is not intended to force to the negotiating table a party against whom a hopeless case has been brought and maintained despite clear evidence that it is indeed hopeless.

8.105 The Court of Appeal, in *S v Chapman*,[156] further referred to the fact that a party may well not act unreasonably in rejecting mediation when it does not know the nature of the case it is expected to meet:

> ... The burden of showing that there should be a departure from the general rule that costs follow the event is a burden which lies on the unsuccessful party. The fact that a party reasonably believes he has a strong case is relevant to the question whether he has acted reasonably in refusing ADR. The fact that a party reasonably believes he has a watertight case may well be sufficient for the refusal to mediate. What the unsuccessful party has to establish is to show that there was a reasonable prospect that the mediation would have been successful.

8.106 In the same case, Ward LJ referred to *Halsey* and said that it was a case which he 'had hoped would be more encouraging of mediation than discouraging of it'.[157] This reflects the fact that there is a surprising dearth of reported cases where parties have in fact been penalised for refusing to engage in ADR. With the increasing focus on controlling litigation costs, this may be changing. Recent High Court decisions show that parties need to have full and reasoned arguments for refusing to mediate. In *Rolf v De Guerin*,[158] Rix LJ determined that the defendant 'wanting his day in court' was not an acceptable reason not to mediate.

8.107 In another recent judgment, sanctions were imposed on the defendants who had not accepted the claimant's proposals to mediate.[159] The defendants were the 'successful party' but were penalised by not being awarded any of their costs. The judge placed particular emphasis on the fact that mediation had a reasonable prospect of success and the defendants had not, at the time of the offer, provided an explanation as to why mediation was unlikely to succeed. The judge rightly argued that if the defendants had done so, any concerns or inhibitions might reasonably have been overcome at the time.[160]

---

156 [2008] EWCA Civ 800.

157 [2008] EWCA Civ 800, para 48.

158 [2011] EWCA Civ 78, para 32. Also see case study 12.

159 *PGF v OMFS* [2012] EWHC 83 (TCC).

160 [2012] EWHC 83 (TCC) para 44.

Frequently asked questions answered by Beverly-Ann Rogers

8.108   The following questions have been answered by Beverly-Ann Rogers an experienced chancery and commercial barrister who qualified as a commercial mediator with CEDR in 1999 and is now a full-time mediator.

How effective are the current pre-action protocols in encouraging parties to mediate?

Not effective enough. There has been some increase in pre-litigation mediation but it seems that most parties need to experience some of the reality and pain of litigation before they are ready to mediate. At the mediation, with an understanding of what it can achieve and the reality check of the costs incurred between all parties, they often express the wish they had mediated earlier. Most individuals will engage in litigation only once in their lives. It is ironic that they have so much to gain from mediation and yet their unfamiliarity with the legal system disinclines them to use it early in the dispute. On the positive side, if parties are willing to mediate, the pre-action protocols assist by encouraging identification of the issues and exchange of key information at an early stage.

Isn't mediation an opportunity for people to avoid statutory obligations and legal duties and make deals behind closed doors?

If a claimant doesn't receive redress they can live with, they will not settle at mediation. There is a tendency, certainly amongst lawyers and often amongst litigants, to regard the law and the rights and duties it creates as a holy grail. I would suggest that a perfect society is not one where there are no disputes (differences are inevitable) but one in which those in dispute can resolve their differences consensually, ideally with wisdom and understanding. The law is a system of rules to resolve disputes which cannot be dealt with consensually (a last resort) and, however sophisticated the system, the legal answer may be far from a perfect one. Mediation potentially gives back to the parties an opportunity to take responsibility for the resolution of their dispute and to fashion a settlement which meets their needs. An example that comes to mind is a dispute between former cohabitants over their interests in their former home and whether it should be sold. He wanted to continue living there. She wanted it sold. Discussion revealed that his need was for a home in the short to medium term and her need was for additional funding and security when she retired. Once their needs were properly understood the solution was obvious!

How do I know the other party doesn't have a hidden agenda for attending the mediation?

Disputes generate suspicion. There is a wise saying that we judge ourselves by our intentions and others by the effect of their actions. Nowhere is that truer than between parties to disputes. It is the norm in mediations for each party to distrust the motives of the other party or at least doubt whether they are attending with a genuine desire to settle. One of the benefits of the plenary session at the beginning of the mediation may be an affirmation of a commitment to the process and a desire to achieve resolution by all parties, preferably directly or at least through their respective lawyers. That does not, of course, mean resolution at any cost. Although it is rarely made explicit, it is axiomatic that the claimants will want to settle but for as much as possible and defendants will want to settle but for as little as possible. Each will have a range in mind and it is likely to scope from "pie in the sky" to realistic. The mediation process enables parties to test their figures, however aspirational they may be, and eventually, when they are convinced that they have achieved the best available offer, there is a decision to be made as to whether they accept it or take the litigation route.

The suspected hidden agenda is usually that the process is being used "simply a fishing expedition." I have not encountered that, maybe because mediation would be expensive and far from certain in outcome as a fishing expedition. However it is important to remember that, although parties are precluded by confidentiality from referring to what happened at mediation, they cannot and do not wipe from their memories, information provided at mediation. It is therefore important to weigh up the pros and cons of disclosure before providing information which might be used to a party's disadvantage if the case does not settle. It is also important, both as the mediator and the recipient of a request for information, to weigh up the purpose of the request. A useful test is whether the provision of that information is likely to be conducive to settlement.

As mediator, if I perceive that a request is made for an ulterior motive, I will challenge it. Information which is often a double-edged sword is the financial position of a party. Perversely, a lack of financial worth may be an incentive to settle because victory may be pyrrhic but it may also signal the inability of the party to pursue the litigation to trial.

Even if a dispute does not resolve at mediation, parties are usually better informed as a result. That is an advantage, not a disadvantage. Information about settlement positions often leads to resolution within a short period after the mediation. Absent settlement, information about the case often leads to more streamlined litigation.

Doesn't mediation mean the claimants settling for less?

Less than what? Less than they might achieve in court on their best case scenario? Probably yes, because there is no incentive for defendants to settle for what would conversely be their worst case scenario. Less than realistically they are likely to achieve in court? Probably not, if they have done a careful and realistic risk analysis. Mediation takes place against the backdrop of legal rights and remedies and in my experience, the levels of settlement reflect that. However, the decision as to whether to settle is a complex process involving many elements other than just the numbers; an assessment of the likelihood of recovery of any award and of recovery of costs (including taking into account any offers and their potential effect on costs, the desire to avoid the cost, both financial and emotional, of ongoing litigation, the desire for closure and certainty, maybe even to rebuild relationships. The decision to settle or not is a highly personal one depending on a claimant's personal circumstances and temperament, for example their appetite for risk. Mediation hopefully provides them with a process in which they can make an informed decision and the best one for them.

Doesn't mediation create a conflict of interest between the legal adviser and client (party)?

Even though it has been said that ADR stands for an alarming drop in revenue, my overwhelming experience is that lawyers want the best result for their client and support their clients through mediation to achieve a sensible settlement whenever possible. It is not unusual for lawyers either in joint session or in private session to flag up to the clients, as a way of encouraging settlement, that the only winners, if the case proceeds, will be the lawyers. Only in a handful of cases have I suspected that a lawyer was putting his own interests ahead of those of his client. Interestingly in those cases, the clients came to the same the conclusion and in one of them, the client continued the mediation to a successful conclusion without his lawyer.

Conditional Fee Agreements undoubtedly create tensions between legal adviser and client, in particular in relation to the division of the proposed settlement pot between them. It is often necessary to conduct a mediation within a mediation on this issue. Again my overwhelming experience is that lawyers are sensible in achieving an accommodation with their client which gives the client an acceptable result.

Family mediation

continued

9.63   **Requirements to consider mediation**

9.63   Private family law

Before court proceedings • During court proceedings • After court proceedings

9.73   Public family law

9.75   **The family mediator's toolkit and strategies**

9.75   Dealing with power imbalances

Gender roles • Changing power imbalances • Extreme behaviour

9.84   Domestic violence and safeguarding

9.87   Cultural and gender sensitivity

9.89   Mediator bias and manipulation

9.93   Dealing with impasses

9.94   Arrangements for dependent children

The child's voice • Parenting plans

9.96   Financial family mediation

9.98   Reaching agreement

9.99   Closing the mediation

9.101   **Frequently asked questions answered by Margaret Pendlebury and Christopher Richards**

> ## Key points
> - Family mediation is used for a wide variety of family disputes, most commonly for relationship breakdowns.
> - The process aims to improve communication and help establish working relationships, joint decision-making between parties and effective co-parenting (and in some cases supports reconciliation).
> - Family mediation is widely accepted as better suited to resolving family disputes and relationship breakdown than going to court.
> - In family cases it is compulsory to attend Mediation Information and Assessment Meetings (MIAMs) before applying to start court proceedings.
> - Family mediators are specially trained to address power imbalances and enable parties to reach agreement about dependent children and financial issues.

Introduction

What is family mediation?

> Family mediation is a process in which those involved in family breakdown, whether or not they are a couple or other family members, appoint an impartial third person to assist them to communicate better with one another and reach their own agreed and informed decisions concerning some, or all, of the issues relating to separation, divorce, children, finance or property by negotiation.[1]

9.1   Family mediation can be used by families involved in relationship breakdown or conflicts arising from a divorce or separation. The process is ideally suited to these situations because it enables parties to reach decisions together, improve the way they communicate and address underlying psychological and emotional conflicts. Where a marriage or relationship has irretrievably broken down, mediation seeks to minimise the distress (and stress) to those involved, and helps separating couples reach decisions together about money, property and/or the care of children. Mediation does not preclude

---

1   *Code of Practice for family mediators*, Family Mediation Council (FMC), 9 September 2010 ('FMC Code of Practice') para 1.2 – see appendix J.

the possibility that a couple may reconcile and get back together,[2] but the emphasis is on restoring communication and building co-operation between parties to enable shared responsibility for children and effective parenting.

9.2   This chapter will explore family mediation for separating couples. Family mediation is an expanding field and also helps families facing issues such as a teenager leaving home, a disputed will or other intergenerational issues such as a disagreement over the care of an elderly relative.[3] It can be used effectively in international contexts, for example, child abduction cases where online mediation provides an innovative means of communication.[4] In the UK, it is starting to be used in adoption or at the end of care proceedings to support the move of a child into foster care or to rebuild relationships where a child is being placed back with its own family. However, increasing pressure on public funding may impede the progress of some of these developments.[5]

Why use family mediation?

There is a general acknowledgement that an adversarial court process is not always best-suited to the resolution of family disputes, particularly private law disputes between parents relating to children, with such disputes often best resolved through discussion and agreement, where that can be managed safely and appropriately.[6]

9.3   Adversarial court proceedings can be a long, expensive and damaging experience for families. Recent developments, such as the requirement to attend MIAMs before a legal process[7] can begin, and the removal of legal aid in private family law (with limited exceptions)[8] overshadow an ongoing shift away from court hearings towards a more family-centred approach. This follows on from a number of reports into the family justice system, such as the Finer Report on

2 Throughout the mediation mediators must keep the possibility of reconciliation of the participants under review: FMC Code of Practice para 6.3.

3 See paras 11.73–11.75.

4 For more information see www.reunite.org and the International Family Law Group at www.iflg.uk.com.

5 See paras 9.59–9.62.

6 Practice Direction 3A, Pre-Application Protocol for mediation information and assessment para 3.1 – see appendix K.

7 See paras 9.8–9.9 and 9.63–9.71.

8 See paras 9.59–9.62.

One-Parent Families[9] and later the Booth Committee,[10] both of which made recommendations to encourage mediation (also described as conciliation) rather than divorcing and separating couples resolving their issues within the court system. The final report of the long-awaited Family Justice Review – conducted by the Ministry of Justice, the Department of Education and the Welsh Assembly Government – has endorsed this view.[11]

9.4   Family mediation draws upon three core principles: First, that improving communication is helpful in overcoming the emotional and psychological hurt of family disagreements or relationship break-down, which is beneficial to all parties. Second, that families making decisions for themselves rather than court-imposed settlements pro-duces better outcomes. Third, that parenting is more effective and more beneficial for children when parents and family members can co operate together and effectively co-parent.

9.5   There are other reasons why mediation can be helpful for fami-lies. It is not uncommon for them to find that the issues preventing them from talking or making agreements together cannot be easily identified. A fluid flexible process taking place over time therefore enables families to work through a complex set of issues.

9.6   For some, mediation will not be suitable, particularly where safe-guarding concerns require the issues to be ultimately resolved by a court or where one party is so entrenched in their position that they are unable to move forward.

9.7   Commentators such as Lisa Parkinson[12] and Bouille and Nesic[13] observe that the growth and recognition of family mediation repre-sents a shift towards a new system of child-focused, participatory jus-tice. It also has the potential to give children a voice and for them to join in making decisions about their future.[14] If the proposals set out in the Family Justice Review are adopted, mediators will be given an even greater role in private law proceedings.[15]

---

9   Finer Report on One-Parent Families, 1974.

10   Booth Committee, *Report of the Committee on Matrimonial Causes*, HMSO, London 1985.

11   *Family Justice Review: final report*, November 2011 p157, para 4.94.

12   L Parkinson, *Family mediation*, Jordan Publishing, 2011, 2nd edition.

13   L Boulle and M Nesic, *Mediator skills and techniques: triangle of influence*, Bloomsbury Professional, 2010.

14   *Office of the Children's Commissioner: response to the Family Justice Review interim report*, July 2011 para 2.3.

15   *Family Justice Review: final report*, November 2011 paras 4.94–4.115.

The family mediation process

Mediation Information and Assessment Meetings

What are MIAMs?

9.8   The initial meetings between a mediator and each party are called Mediation Information and Assessment Meetings (MIAMs), also called an *intake session* or *assessment meeting*. A letter is sent inviting each party to attend a MIAM which are usually separate meetings (but can also take place with both parties present). If mediation is considered suitable, the parties will be invited to attend a series of *joint meetings*. MIAMs are now a prerequisite in private law family cases for a party wishing to make an application to court.[16]

9.9   During the meetings the mediator will find out more about the parties and their circumstances and assess their suitability for the process. He or she will also assess the parties' financial eligibility for public funding (legal aid).[17] The mediator will explain what mediation is and how it works, in particular that (with some exceptions) it is a voluntary and confidential process. This information will usually be provided in writing to the parties before the MIAMs. The benefits, and limitations, of mediation will be discussed, as well as other forms of appropriate dispute resolution (ADR). The mediator will explore the suitability of other forms of problem-solving assistance, such as collaborative law, and explain the relative costs of mediation, other forms of ADR and litigation. The parties will have an opportunity to ask questions about their situation and how mediation might work for them.

Screening for suitability

9.10   The mediator will begin the screening process before meeting the parties, using material provided in the initial enquiry from a party's solicitor or a self-referral. Where there is any concern about abusive behaviour or that pressure may have been placed on one side, the mediator will arrange separate MIAMs. Any information disclosed in these separate meetings will remain confidential and will not be passed on to the other party, unless the mediator confirms with the

---

16   Practice Direction 3A, Family Procedure Rules 2010 SI No 2955 – see appendix K.
17   FMC Code of Practice, para 6.10.

party they are happy for the information to be shared. This enables an anxious person to disclose information without fear of reprisals.

9.11   Screening and an assessment of suitability requires mediators to meet the parties face-to-face.

> Assessments can be conducted jointly or separately depending on client preference, but must include an individual element with each participant to allow mediators to undertake domestic abuse screening.[18]

9.12   There are a number of factors which would automatically indicate that mediation is unsuitable. Where there are safeguarding concerns, such as an ongoing risk of domestic abuse or child protection issues, or any concerns about an imbalance of power which cannot be addressed by the mediator, the case would have to be directly referred to the family courts.

9.13   At the conclusion of the MIAMs, a mediator may be asked to complete and sign the Family Mediation Information and Assessment form (FM1).[19] The FM1 form is a requirement for a solicitor or individual wishing to issue private law proceedings. In cases where mediation is considered suitable, screening and assessment of suitability remains under review throughout the process.

> Where mediators consider that a participant is unable or unwilling to take part in the process freely and fully, they must raise the issue and possibly suspend or terminate the mediation.[20]
> Mediators must seek to prevent manipulative, threatening or intimidating behaviour by any participant. They must conduct the process in such a way as to redress, as far as possible, any imbalance of power between the participants. If such behaviour or any other imbalance seems likely to render the mediation unfair or ineffective, mediators must take appropriate steps to seek to prevent this including terminating the mediation if necessary.[21]

9.14   Appropriate steps a mediator may take to ensure effective participation of both parties may be to suggest 'shuttle mediation'[22] or to make arrangements for parties to arrive and depart at different times, so they only meet together in the presence of a mediator.

---

18   FMC Code of Practice para 6.1.
19   See appendix K and paras 9.63–9.66.
20   FMC Code of Practice para 5.2.
21   FMC Code of Practice para 5.4.2.
22   See paras 5.13–5.4.

9.15   In assessing suitability, the mediator will also consider the following factors:

Voluntary participation

9.16   The FMC Code of Practice requires that:

> In all cases, mediators must seek to ensure that participants take part in mediation willingly and without fear of violence or harm. They must seek to discover through a screening procedure whether or not there is fear of abuse or any other harm and whether or not it is alleged that any participant has been or is likely to be abusive towards another. Where abuse is alleged or suspected mediators must discuss whether the participant wishes to take part in mediation, and information about available support services should be provided.[23]

9.17   This is particularly relevant where a risk factor such as domestic abuse has been raised. If one party has been abusive to another, the separate meeting during MIAMs is an opportunity to discuss this with them. The mediator will need to ask questions sensitively, as this is not information which will be readily disclosed, and discuss with the person whether they feel they can take part freely and voluntarily in the process. Mediators will be mindful that both men and women, and other family members, may be the perpetrators of domestic abuse.

Balance of power between parties

> Mediators must be alert to the likelihood of power imbalances existing between the participants.[24]

> Mediators must seek to prevent manipulative, threatening or intimidating behaviour by either participants during the mediation.[25]

9.18   It is important that the mediator meets the parties to assess whether both sides are able to take part in the process freely and fully. Sometimes mediation will not be appropriate if one party remains emotionally less able to cope with the relationship breakdown. In this situation the mediator may advise reconsidering after a period of time and possibly referring the party to another service such as counselling or therapy.

Safeguarding checks

9.19   Mediators are required to undertake thorough safeguarding checks. One of the challenges is that it is particularly difficult to identify

---

23 FMC Code of Practice para 5.8.2.
24 FMC Code of Practice para 5.8.1.
25 FMC Code of Practice para 5.8.4.

safeguarding concerns where the mediator is reliant on the parent sharing their concerns or disclosing information about domestic violence, child abuse or drug and alcohol addiction.[26]

Good faith

9.20 Mediators will assess whether a party has a genuine intention to enter the mediation process and discuss matters openly; factors such as non-disclosure or providing incorrect information would indicate otherwise. In cases where there is a complete lack of trust between the parties or one parent is denying all contact and apparently using the process as a tactical device to delay court proceedings, mediation would be unsuitable.

Active participation

9.21 Issues such as mental disability or mental illness, alcohol and drug abuse and other factors which may inhibit a party's ability to engage in the mediation will also be explored. Consideration should be given to the use of an intermediary in appropriate cases. Where parties communicate in a language different from that used by the mediator, using an interpreter (including a British Sign Language interpreter) should be discussed.

Conflicts of interest and impartiality

9.22 The mediator will ensure they have no personal or professional connection to the case.[27]

Joint meetings

9.23 Family mediation, as distinct from other fields of mediation, takes place over a series of joint sessions. Parties may already have appointed a solicitor, but it is not generally envisaged that their legal adviser will attend meetings. The agreements reached are non-binding[28] and the mediation remains confidential (with some exceptions),[29] in particular over financial disclosure.[30] Allowing for reasonable time intervals between meetings provides parties with the opportunity to receive legal advice, to reflect on what has been said and prepare for the next

26 See paras 8.84–9.86.
27 FMC Code of Practice para 5.
28 See para 9.34.
29 See paras 9.29–9.30.
30 See paras 9.31–9.33.

meeting. Where couples are dealing with the emotional trauma of a relationship breakdown, it is particularly important to have time to consider long-term decisions and to provide pause for thought at a time when they are stressed and emotionally vulnerable. Interim arrangements can be put in place during the intervening periods. Being able to make temporary, interim agreements has the advantage of being able to assess the implications over a period of time. Mediation should not urge couples to make decisions without thinking through the emotional and practical consequences. A series of meetings can also enable parties to shift from entrenched positions with the passage of time.

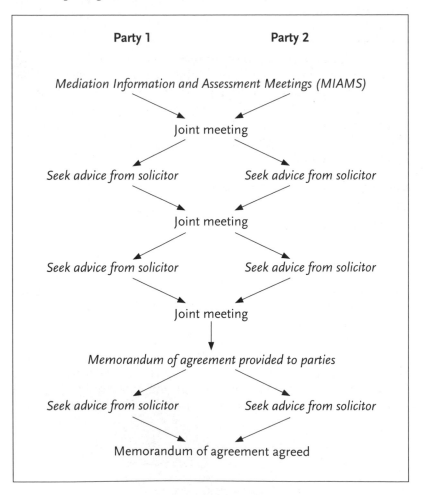

9.24 Family mediation usually takes place over a series of up to six ses-sions, each lasting around 90 minutes, where both parties meet together with the mediator. The number of sessions will depend on what issues need to be resolved. Parties can seek legal advice from a solicitor before they start mediation, and in between the meetings. It is important that mediation is not seen as a substitute for therapy or counselling and may be paused in order for a person to access these services.

9.25 The mediator will explain that he or she will *not* provide legal advice and ensures impartiality. Parties will be advised to ask their legal adviser to look through any agreement or *memorandum of understanding* before it is made into a formal court order. Mediators can explain the family court legal processes and, if the parties reach agreement, may advise them that their proposed resolution would be outside the scope of what a court might approve or order.[31]

Family mediation principles

9.26 The FMC Code of Practice[32] sets out the general principles of family mediation: voluntary participation, a neutral and impartial mediator, confidentiality and privilege which are common to all mediation.[33] Family mediation has other features which make it unique. As already explained, the mediation process takes place over a series of meetings and parties attend without lawyers. There are a number of other core principles:

Confidentiality

9.29 Family mediation is a confidential process. This means that every-thing said during sessions cannot be shared with friends, family or lawyers afterwards. In exceptional cases, where a mediator suspects that any child is suffering, or likely to suffer significant harm, they will advise parties that they are obliged to notify the local social serv-ices department.[34] Where other public policy considerations arise, such as an adult likely to suffer significant harm, mediators may

---

31 FMC Code of Practice para 5.4.3.
32 See appendix J.
33 Except where child protection and public policy considerations arise (FMC Code of Practice para 5.5) and all information relating to financial issues which is provided on an open basis (FMC Code of Practice para 5.6).
34 FMC Code of Practice paras 5.5.3 and 5.7.5.

notify the appropriate agency.[35] Parties can waive privilege and may do so if they have reached agreement on some issues and not others and it would be helpful for the mediator to summarise the position for the benefit of court proceedings.

9.30　A statement on confidentiality has been drafted by the FMC and the Family Justice Council, which includes:

> Any client entering a mediation process is asked to sign an 'Agreement to Mediate' – which sets out both the scope of and limitations to confidentiality in line with Re D[36] (and in regard to legislation relating to abuse and harm and money laundering) – and further, participants to a mediation are asked not to call the mediator to provide evidence (either as notes or in person).

> Independent mediators are therefore not able to provide information to the court as to the content of any discussions held in mediation or the reasons why proposals were not reached and/or any view as to who may have not co-operated or declined to enter or continue with a mediated process.[37]

Open financial disclosure

9.31　Mediators will explain that if there are financial issues to be discussed then full details, supported by necessary documents, will need to be provided in an open and honest way. This must be offered on an open basis and can be referred to in legal proceedings (if there are any).[38] It will be explained to the parties that this means that any financial information disclosed during mediation is *not* confidential.

9.32　There is a standard financial questionnaire, form E, which is used by the courts. Mediators use similar questionnaires to gather information – the responses and documents will be shared between the parties and can be considered by a court if necessary. As part of their role, if requested, the mediator can produce an Open Financial Statement which is a summary of the financial information provided to them. Lawyers for each party are able to go through the financial material to ensure that the agreement reached is a fair settlement.

35　FMC Code of Practice para 5.5.4.

36　*Re D (minors) (conciliation: privilege) (disclosure of information)* [1993] 1 FLR 932.

37　Family Mediation Council and Family Justice Council *Independent Mediation – Information for Judges, Magistrates and Legal Advisors* – available at www.judiciary.gov.uk/NR/rdonlyres/01F618CE-48D1-4886-9646-FEB0A886075C/0/IndependentMediationInformationforJudgesMagistratesandLegalAdvisors.pdf.

38　FMC Code of Practice para 5.6.2.

9.33   In some cases, parties may need to seek independent financial advice. Mediators should be able to provide information on how to get advice from a financial adviser or legal advice on welfare benefits.[39]

Non-binding agreements

9.34   Parties in family mediation reach written agreements or proposals which are non-binding, usually described as a *memorandum of agreement*.[40] They can then seek legal advice and the *memorandum* may form part of a legally binding agreement. As with all mediation processes, parties should not reach legally binding agreements without receiving legal advice, and will usually be encouraged to obtain legal advice after every mediation session and before any legally binding agreement is drawn up. This raises concerns about the implications of changes to legal aid, which will restrict public funding of legal advice and representation.[41]

Referral for relationship counselling or therapy

9.35   Mediators should be conscious of and attentive to the psychological and emotional needs of the parties. There may be unspoken, non-verbal signals that indicate unresolved issues or a history of abuse. Mediators are trained to direct parties to appropriate help and support. In some cases, for example where somebody is not psychologically able to participate in mediation, individual therapy may be appropriate. Mediators should be able to provide information on relationship or marital and child counselling.[42]

Children

9.36   The best interests of children lie at the heart of the family justice system and in turn mediation. In all cases, parents should be encouraged to consider their children's wishes and feelings. This reflects the principles underpinning the Children Act 1989 (England and Wales)[43] and article 12 of the UN Convention on the Rights of the Child 1989.

9.37   The child's wishes and feelings should be taken into consideration whenever a decision is made which affects them. Children can,

---

39 LSC Quality Mark Standard for Mediation, 2nd edn, September 2009 F2.3.
40 See appendix E.
41 See paras 9.59–9.62.
42 LSC Quality Mark Standard for Mediation, 2nd edn, September 2009 F2.3.
43 Children Act 1995 in Scotland.

in appropriate cases, be involved in the mediation process.[44] The mediator will discuss ways in which the child's views can be given consideration; this may involve the child meeting the mediator or even attending a mediation meeting. Mediators consulting directly with children are required to undertake specific training and have enhanced clearance from the Criminal Records Bureau ('an enhanced CRB check').[45] At all times mediators are conscious of child welfare issues, and can terminate a mediation process if necessary, making the parties aware of their duty to report any concerns regarding child welfare or risk of serious harm to the appropriate agency.

Facilities

Specialist facilities

9.38 Family mediation providers will have in place arrangements to safeguard the safety and well-being of parties. This includes separate waiting areas and arrangements for parties to arrive and leave separately, as well as an additional 'breakout room' to enable shuttle mediation or separate meetings.[46] There should also be appropriate facilities for meeting with children. In some cases Specialist Family Centres may be used.

Seating arrangements

9.39 Family mediation is less formal than civil mediation. The mediator and participants will usually sit around a table, but mediators may try to create a more relaxed atmosphere by using a room with more comfortable seats than office chairs and a low (less obtrusive) table. The mediator usually sits in the middle with the parties on either side opposite each other but facing slightly towards the mediator (to avoid them facing each other directly, which may appear confrontational).

When to mediate?

Choosing mediation

9.40 Most separating couples seeking a divorce, dissolution of a civil partnership or a legal agreement over care of children or an elderly relative will first contact a solicitor to understand their legal rights and

---

44 FMC Code of Practice para 5.7.3 and also see para 9.94..
45 FMC Code of Practice paras 5.7.2–5.7.3.
46 LSC Quality Mark Standard for Mediation, 2nd edn, September 2009, C4.

entitlements, before meeting their mediator. The solicitor is unlikely to attend the mediation meetings – however, in financial cases it may be expedient for legal advisers to attend mediation meetings.

9.41 Deciding whether mediation is the right process to resolve a particular family dispute is an individual decision, but it will be helped substantially by the initial MIAMs. The factors that make mediation suitable are present in the majority of family cases, including:

- ongoing relationship between parties;
- clear benefit to improving communication and cooperative decision-making;
- court proceedings would be stressful and likely to cause the relationship between parties to worsen;
- court unable to impose a solution that meets both parties' needs.

9.42 Where mediation may be unsuitable, factors requiring careful consideration include:

- one party unwilling to participate (or lacks any goodwill or genuine engagement in the process);
- an alternative process may be more appropriate because:
  - depression or acute distress indicate that family circumstances would benefit from counselling or therapy;
  - complex finances indicate that collaborative law or a financial dispute resolution hearing within the court structure may be more appropriate;
- power imbalances which a mediator is unable to address;
- mental illness, disability or addiction issues which may prevent one side from engaging in the process;
- threats of ongoing domestic violence or abuse which would prevent one party from participating freely without fear of harm;
- serious welfare issues which raise child protection concerns.

Timing

9.43 Even where parties have decided to mediate, it can be difficult to choose the right time. Both parties need to be ready. During the initial stages of relationship breakdown, when emotions are raw and feelings of abandonment and loss are still intense, individuals may not feel emotionally equipped to meet face-to-face to discuss the future or deal with making long-term decisions about their (and their children's) future. The family mediation process is flexible – in some cases parties may agree interim arrangements and delay further mediation meetings until both parties are ready for final decisions to be taken.

Alternatives to family mediation

Negotiation

9.44   In many cases there is no need for parties to consider mediation because communication remains intact and any issues arising from a relationship breakdown or separation can be resolved through direct communication, or lawyer-to-lawyer negotiation.

Court-referred conciliation and in-court mediation

Court-referred conciliation

9.45   Independent out-of-court mediation, as already described, needs to be distinguished from court-referred 'conciliation'. This is a settlement-seeking process addressing issues related to children conducted by family court social workers from the Children and Family Court Advisory and Support Service (Cafcass) and in some cases overseen by a judge. The process is not binding on the parties and is confidential to a limited extent, a report may be written by the conciliator and provided to the court. The conciliator and/or the Cafcass officer may be directive in seeking settlement. They may also provide a report and recommendations to the court if an agreement is not reached. The courts refer suitable cases and the conciliation often takes place at court.

9.46   The advantage of in-court conciliation is that in some cases, parties are looking for guidance on what is in the best interests of their children. It may be offered as a free service. In-court conciliation can also help in cases where levels of mistrust and hurt are such that cooperative decision-making is not possible but a decision needs to be made.

Cafcass

An independent government organisation, Cafcass advises the courts on what is in the best interests of individual children in family proceedings. A Cafcass officer (also called a court welfare officer) will prepare a report on the children, their wishes and feelings and the ability of the various adults to provide for them. This report will go to the judge and will generally have a significant impact on the final order.

In-court mediation

9.47   In-court mediation is offered to families who are already in the court system. It remains completely voluntary and is conducted by independent mediators. A pilot undertaken by the Legal Services Commission (LSC) found that 71 per cent of families reached a full agreement through this process or were able to narrow some of the key issues in dispute.[47] Parties were selected by judges who gave a certain level of judicial encouragement, for example:

> You should know your children better than anyone. Why do you think someone who doesn't know your family at all (like me) should make decisions about it? The chances are no one will like my decision. It would be better to at least try and agree something. You might well be surprised: most people manage to agree at least something and many everything.[48]

Financial dispute resolution

9.48   Once cases are inside the court system, financial dispute resolution (FDR) hearings provide an opportunity to see if financial issues can be resolved. A judge considers summaries of each party's case presented by their representative, but no evidence is heard. If either side have made *without prejudice* offers, these are shown to the judge. The judge then gives an indication on what he or she would decide if this were a final hearing. The parties are then encouraged to reach a negotiated settlement. The judge who has conducted the FDR is unable to oversee the final hearing.

Collaborative law

9.49   Collaborative law is a process in which parties instruct specially trained lawyers to work together to resolve family disputes. The parties agree not to go to court, and instead meet face-to-face alongside their lawyer to try to find solutions aimed at helping them move forward. If they are unable to reach an agreement, they must then instruct alternative lawyers to take their case to court. Although this makes the process more expensive if the case ends up going to trial and new legal advisers need to be instructed, it also means there is no incentive for collaborative lawyers to allow the process to fail.

---

47   *In-court mediation for family disputes – research and evaluation report of in-court mediation trial*, LSC, August 2010 p15.

48   *In-court mediation for family disputes – research and evaluation report of in-court mediation trial*, LSC, August 2010 p25, para 7.4.

Collaborative law is a relatively new process; it is more expensive than alternatives but reports high success rates.[49]

Counselling and therapy

9.50   Family mediators are not counsellors or therapists, although they should be able to signpost parties seeking therapeutic intervention to an appropriate service or agency.[50] In some cases the mediator may propose therapeutic input as an alternative to mediation, and make parties aware of other processes such as relationship or marriage counselling.

Practicalities

How to set up a family mediation

Finding a mediator

9.51   DirectGov provides an online search engine (formerly the Family Mediation Helpline) which can locate local family mediation services: www.familymediationhelpline.co.uk. Community Legal Advice[51] can also provide advice on finding a mediator.

9.52   Parties who may be eligible for public funding should choose a provider who is able to undertake legal aid work. The Legal Adviser Finder website has a map highlighting local mediators who have contracts to provide publicly funded mediation.[52] Only mediation services that meet the LSC Quality Mark standards are able to provide free mediation for publicly funded parties.[53]

9.53   Family mediation is self-regulated. The FMC[54] is an umbrella organisation bringing together a number of member organisations

---

49 Resolution published a research report in 2009, *Collaborative law in England and Wales: early findings*, reporting that 80 per cent of cases undertaken during 2006 and 2007 reached settlement on all issues through the collaborative process.

50 LSC Quality Mark Standard for Mediation, 2nd edn, September 2009, B1 and F2.3 – participants must be clearly advised at the outset of the nature and purpose of mediation and how it differs from other services such as marriage or relationship counselling, therapy or legal representation.

51 Tel: 0845 345 4345 – Monday to Friday 9am to 8pm, Saturday 9am to 12.30pm.

52 http://legaladviserfinder.justice.gov.uk. The website can be searched using the 'family mediation' option.

53 See para 12.41.

54 See www.familymediationcouncil.org.uk.

– the Family Mediators Association,[55] National Family Mediation,[56] Resolution,[57] the College of Mediators,[58] ADR Group[59] and the Law Society (which represents solicitors in England and Wales).[60] The FMC member organisations ensure their members meet minimum professional and training standards.[61]

Choosing a mediation model

9.54 There are a number of different models, depending on the issues raised:

a) *All issues mediation (AIM):* If there are a range of issues about children, a shared home and finances, it will probably take four to six sessions.

b) *Child only:* Mediation concerned with children can take an average of three to six hours, usually spread over two or three sessions.

c) *Property and finance only:* Dividing up joint finances and property can be complex; it is likely to take two or three sessions, sometimes longer.

In addition:

d) *Co-mediation:* This involves two mediators, so is more expensive but has certain advantages.[62]

Choosing a mediator

9.55 Family mediators undertake specialist training, so all will be trained in the specific issues faced by separating couples and relationship breakdown, but it is worth spending time finding somebody with a style that suits the parties' needs. Questions to consider when choosing a mediator include:

- Do you mind if you have a male or female mediator?
- Do you want a mediator who has a background in therapy and counselling who may encourage the parties to talk openly

---

55 See www.thefma.co.uk.
56 See www.nfm.org.uk.
57 See www.resolution.org.uk.
58 See www.collegeofmediators.co.uk.
59 See www.adrgroup.co.uk.
60 See www.lawsociety.org.uk.
61 See paras 12.33–12.41.
62 It can offer an interdisciplinary approach and gender balance. It may also be considered where there are issues of power imbalance to enable mediators to manage the process in a fair and even-handed way.

about their emotions, or a mediator with a legal background who may be able to manage complex issues and take a more systematic approach to the issues?

- Depending on whether the mediation process will be 'all issues', 'child only' or 'property and finance only', do you want a mediator with specialism in a particular area?
- Do you want a mediator who has received specialist training in seeing children during mediation?

Fees and funding

The cost of mediation

9.56 The fees for publicly funded mediation are set out below.[63] Mediation providers can charge self-funded clients independent rates, although the fees set by the Legal Services Commission (LSC) are a useful benchmark. For MIAMs, the FMC recommends its members follow the LSC rates. Some providers may offer MIAMs for free or at a discounted rate.

Assessment meetings

Activity	
Assessment alone	£87
Assessment separate	£87
Assessment together	£130

Mediation fees

Category of work	Single session	Multi-session	Agreed proposal
All issues – sole mediation	£168	£756	£252
All issues – co-mediation	£230	£1,064	£252
Property and finance – sole mediation	£168	£588	£189

63 Community Legal Service (Funding) (Amendment No 2) Order 2011 SI No 2066.

Category of work	Single session	Multi-session	Agreed proposal
Property and finance – co-mediation	£230	£834	£189
Child – sole mediation	£168	£462	£126
Child – co-mediation	£230	£647	£126

Funding the mediation

Eligibility for public funding (legal aid)

9.57 Family mediators are required to assess parties' eligibility for public funding (legal aid). Detailed questions will be asked during MIAMs in order to gather enough financial information to calculate average monthly income. Public funding is available for those in receipt of state benefits or on low incomes. Parties can independently calculate their eligibility for legal aid online.[64]

9.58 Parties eligible for public funding do not pay to attend MIAMs or subsequent mediation meetings as this will be covered by legal aid.[65] In circumstances where one party is eligible for public funding and the other is not, the non-funded party will not be charged to attend the MIAMs as this is funded by legal aid (this does not apply to subsequent mediation sessions). Whether a provider organisation is able to offer a publicly funded service is therefore an important consideration. Providers must not charge anybody who is eligible for public funding unless it has been explained to the party that they would be able to go to an alternative legal aid service, and the party have made it clear that they are willing and happy to pay privately.[66]

64 See www.legalservices.gov.uk/civil/guidance/eligibility_calculator.asp.
65 At present, mediation providers who hold contracts to provide publicly funded mediation are paid by directly by the LSC (and in the future by the Director of Legal Aid Casework) for their services.
66 Family Mediation Council, 'Notice re fees for mediation information and assessment meetings', 21 March 2011.

Public funding (legal aid)

Legal aid describes the public funding available to parties to cover their legal costs. The LSC is responsible for the administration of the legal aid scheme in England and Wales. It works in partnership with solicitors and not-for-profit organisations to help individuals access legal advice, information and help. In civil and family cases, legal aid is known as Community Legal Service funding. A funding code sets out the help that can be provided and the requirements that need to met. This includes a financial means test (and a legal merits test in civil non-family cases).

Family mediation and changes to legal aid

9.59   In the past, parties being granted legal aid in family cases, with certain exceptions, were required to attend an *assessment meeting* in order to consider whether mediation appears suitable as an alternative to court proceedings.[67] Since 6 April 2011, all potential applicants considering whether to apply for a court order in private law proceedings must first attend MIAMs,[68] with certain exceptions which include where a recent allegation of domestic violence has been investigated by police or resulted in civil proceedings.[69]

9.60   As of April 2013, public funding will no longer be available for legal costs in private law family cases (with the exception of domestic violence).[70] The government will continue to fund family mediation.[71] The implications are considerable. At present, mediation remains voluntary and there are a number of safeguards. These include the fact that agreements reached at mediation are reviewed by a legal adviser on behalf of each party. The legal adviser provides advice, reviews the financial disclosure and drafts any legally binding agreement. Where agreement cannot be reached, parties can apply to court. Without recourse to the courts or high quality legal representation and advice, a power imbalance is created and the ability of the mediator to manage a fair process will be potentially compromised.

---

67   Family Law Act 1996 s29.
68   Practice Direction 3A – Pre-application protocol for mediation information and assessment, see appendix K.
69   For all exceptions see para 9.65.
70   Legal Aid, Sentencing and Punishment of Offenders Act (LASPOA) 2012 Sch 1 Part 1 para 12.
71   LASPOA 2012 Sch 1 Part 1 para 14.

9.61   These changes mean there will be no funding for expert reports in child abuse cases arising in private law. Overall, responses to the proposals felt that the changes fail to

> ... sufficiently recognise the importance and complexity of the issues in private law cases.[72]

9.62   The government's proposals are based on figures that suggest that publicly funded family mediation costs an average of £535 per party, as compared to £2,823 for cases going to court.[73] However according to the National Audit Office (NAO) figures for 2007, on average mediation costs £753 while a court hearing costs £1,682.[74] There is no doubt that encouraging more couples to mediate is a positive step, but removing public funding will not save money – it will merely shift the financial burden of resolving family disputes to the court system, which will become clogged with self-represented parties. It may also have the unintended consequence of increasing the number of court cases and reducing opportunities to mediate. For example, parties may respond to the removal of legal aid by reporting allegations of domestic violence, which have historically been underreported, in order to bring themselves within scope for legal aid.[75]

Requirements to consider mediation

Private family law

Before court proceedings

9.63   Since 6 April 2011, Practice Direction 3A of the Pre-Application Protocol for Mediation Information and Assessment encourages any party contemplating making an application for a court order to engage with a mediator by attending a MIAM.[76] The purpose

---

72 *Family Justice Review: final report* November 2011, para 5.54.
73 MOJ figures based on legal aid data provided to the Justice Select Committee, 6th report, *Operation of Family Courts*, 28 June 2011, para 128.
74 Justice Select Committee, 6th report, *Operation of Family Courts*, June 2011, para 128.
75 See footnote 70. Domestic violence is defined as 'any incident of threatening behaviour, violence or abuse (whether psychological, physical, sexual, financial or emotional) between individuals who are associated with one another' – LASPOA 2012 Sch 1 Part 1 para 12(9).
76 For further guidance see *The Family Court Guide to family applications and Mediation Information and Assessment Meetings* (February 2011) – available at www.judiciary.gov.uk/.

of MIAMs is for parties to consider with a mediator whether their dispute may be capable of being resolved through mediation.[77] This requirement does not compel parties to mediate but is a mechanism for increasing awareness. In effect, it extends the requirement which has existed for publicly funded litigants to have attended a meeting about mediation.

> Parties are only required to attend a meeting about mediation. Once they have been to the meeting, even if the mediator believes they are excellent candidates for mediation, they are free to go straight ... to the court.[78]

9.64   Recent research suggests that before the new requirement came into force, 43 per cent of users in the family court had not previously considered mediation.[79] One year on, nationally there is wide variation in how courts are interpreting the rules.[80] The protocol has also attracted criticism because it foreshadows extensive cuts to family legal aid which could undermine a fundamental principle of mediation – that parties, separately and independently of the mediation process, should be able to seek legal advice.[81]

9.65   The pre-application protocol does not need to be followed in the following situations:[82]

> 1. The mediator is satisfied that mediation is not suitable because another party to the dispute is unwilling to attend a Mediation Information and Assessment Meeting and consider mediation.
> 2. The mediator determines that the case is not suitable for a Mediation Information and Assessment Meeting.
> 3. A mediator has made a determination within the previous four months that the case is not suitable for a Mediation Information and Assessment Meeting or for mediation.
>
> **Domestic abuse**
> 4. Any party has, to the applicant's knowledge, made an allegation of domestic Violence against another party and this has resulted in a police investigation or the issuing of civil proceedings for the protection of any party within the last 12 months.

77 See paras 9.8–9.9.
78 Justice Select Committee, 6th report, *Operation of Family Courts*, 28 June 2011, para 116.
79 *In-court mediation for family disputes: research and evaluation report of in-court mediation trial*, LSC, August 2010 p5.
80 A survey of members commissioned by Resolution to mark the first anniversary, April 2012 – at www.resolution.org.uk.
81 See paras 9.59–9.62.
82 Practice Direction 3A, annex C – see appendix K.

Bankruptcy

5. The dispute concerns financial issues and the applicant or another party is bankrupt.

6. The parties are in agreement and there is no dispute to mediate.

7. The whereabouts of the other party are unknown to the applicant.

8. The prospective application is for an order in relevant family proceedings which are already in existence and are continuing.

9. The prospective application is to be made without notice to the other party.

Urgency

10. The prospective application is urgent, meaning –

(a) there is a risk to the life, liberty or physical safety of the applicant or his or her family or his or her home; or

(b) any delay caused by attending a Mediation Information and Assessment Meeting would cause a risk of significant harm to a child, a significant risk of a miscarriage of justice, unreasonable hardship to the applicant or irretrievable problems in dealing with the dispute (such as an irretrievable loss of significant evidence).

11. There is current social services involvement as a result of child protection concerns in respect of any child who would be the subject of the prospective application.

12. A child would be a party to the prospective application by virtue of Rule 12.3(1).

13. The applicant (or the applicant's legal representative) contacts three mediators within 15 miles of the applicant's home and none is able to conduct a Mediation Information and Assessment Meeting within 15 working days of the date of contact.

9.66 To comply with this requirement, the mediator conducting the MIAMs (or having deemed such meetings unsuitable) must complete the new Family Mediation Information and Assessment Form (FM1).[83] This provides for a mediator to indicate that the MIAMs are unsuitable and therefore Practice Direction 3A need not be followed, but the form does not require the mediator to indicate that, at the conclusion of the MIAMs, they are of the opinion that mediation *is* suitable. There is therefore no compulsion for self-funded (privately paying) parties to pursue mediation having attended MIAMs. By contrast, publicly funded parties will have greater reason to pursue mediation as there will be no funding (legal aid) to enable them to initiate court proceedings.[84]

---

83 See appendix D.
84 See paras 9.59–9.62 on proposed changes to public funding.

During court proceedings

9.67   Where a party initiates court proceedings, the private law programme (as set out in Practice Direction 12B) provides for a first hearing dispute resolution appointment (FHDRA). At a FHDRA, the judge, legal adviser or magistrates, accompanied by an officer from Cafcass, will discuss with parties both the nature of their dispute and whether it can be resolved by mediation or other alternative means, and can give the parties information about services which may be available to assist them.

9.68   In appropriate cases, the FHDRA envisages that, where mediation has already taken place, a mediator discloses those discussions to the court. This requires parties to waive privilege so could not take place against their wishes.

> 4.3 The detailed arrangements for the participation of mediators will be arranged locally. These will include –
>
> (a) Arrangements for the mediator to ask the parties in a particular case to consent to the mediator seeing the papers in the case where it seems appropriate to do so.
> (b) Arrangements for the mediator to ask the parties to waive privilege for the purpose of the first hearing where it seems to the mediator appropriate to do so in order to assist the work of the mediator and the outcome of the first hearing.
> (c) In all cases it is important that such arrangements are put in place in a way that avoids any pressure being brought to bear in this connection on the parties that is inconsistent with general good mediation practice.[85]

9.69   It must be anticipated this would only be appropriate in a narrow category of cases where, for example, parties have found certain areas of agreement but wish the court to determine contentious issues. If mediators were encouraged, for example, to indicate to the court why an agreement was not reached – and provide insight as to where a lack of cooperation or genuine goodwill in the process may lie – this would clearly undermine good mediation practice.[86] Legal advice should always be sought before waiving privilege or considering such a course of action.

9.70   Those parties who have failed to follow the pre-action protocol set out in Practice Direction 3A may be referred to a meeting with a mediator before matters are allowed to proceed further. The Family

---

85   Practice Direction 12B – The Revised Private Law Programme.
86   Family Mediation Council and Family Justice Council, *Independent mediation – information for judges, magistrates and legal advisors.*

Procedure Rules[87] provide a duty for the court to consider alternative dispute resolution throughout family proceedings. This enables the proceedings to be adjourned to allow ADR to take place, or for parties to obtain information and advice about ADR. The Family Procedure Rules, Part 3 state:

Court's duty to consider alternative dispute resolution
3.2. The court must consider, at every stage in proceedings, whether alternative dispute resolution is appropriate.

When the court will adjourn proceedings or a hearing in proceedings
3.3. (1) If the court considers that alternative dispute resolution is appropriate, the court may direct that the proceedings, or a hearing in the proceedings, be adjourned for such specified period as it considers appropriate –
> (a) to enable the parties to obtain information and advice about alternative dispute resolution; and
> (b) where the parties agree, to enable alternative dispute resolution to take place.

9.71 It is important to remember that mediation can be pursued at any stage of proceedings. Research has shown that even after protracted legal proceedings, where parties appear to have become entrenched in a long-running court battle, mediation can reach an agreed outcome.[88]

After court proceedings

9.72 At the conclusion of court proceedings, mediation can be used very effectively. It can be used to fine tune existing arrangements in accordance with a family's changing needs, such as agreeing details of childcare arrangements or making the transition to a new care arrangement can benefit from mediation.

Public family law

9.73 The Practice Direction on Public Law Proceedings[89] encourages the increasing use of mediation in public law cases, such as adoption and care proceedings. Such active case management includes:

---

87 2010 SI No 2955.
88 '[M]ediation often succeeds where previous attempts to settle have failed': LJ Dyson in *Halsey v Milton Keynes General NHS Trust* [2004] EWCA Civ 576 para 20. *In-court mediation for family disputes: Research and evaluation report of in-court mediation trial*, LSC, August 2010.
89 Practice Direction 12A – Public law proceedings guide to case management.

... where it is demonstrated to be in the interests of the child, encouraging the parties to use an alternative dispute resolution procedure if the court considers such a procedure to be appropriate and facilitating the use of such procedure[90]

9.74   Family group conferences (FGCs) are offered by local authorities as an alternative to issuing care or child protection proceedings. They are meetings between professionals and members of the extended family, facilitated by a neutral third party with the aim of developing a 'care plan'. Family members, having listened to the concerns of professionals, are able to write the 'care plan' themselves, which is likely to be accepted where the proposed plan addresses the issues raised and there are no concerns that the child would be put at risk.[91]

The family mediator's toolkit and strategies

Dealing with power imbalances

Knowledge is power.[92]

9.75   Mediators are described as *neutral facilitators* who enable parties to reach decisions without 'taking sides'. This should not mean, however, that they are non-interventionist or passive.

9.76   It is particularly important that a mediator does not allow the process to perpetuate or magnify pre-existing power imbalances between the parties or permit coercion or manipulation by the stronger side.[93] For couples where one is more conciliatory and cooperative, the other may seek to take advantage of this. Where parties each have particular concerns, this may indicate that co-mediation is appropriate, as it can be effective at addressing these issues without threatening the impartiality of the process.

---

90   Practice Direction 12A – Public law proceedings guide to case management, para 3.20(14).

91   See para 11.75.

92   'There is no power relation without the correlative constitution of a field of knowledge, nor any knowledge that does not presuppose and constitute at the same time power relations': Michel Foucault, *Discipline and punish: the birth of the prison*, Penguin, 1991.

93   FMC Code of Practice paras 5.4.2, 5.8.4, 6.2.

Gender roles

9.77   One key factor contributing to inequalities of power is 'gender roles' within relationships. Research, however, does not show that mediation favours one gender over the other.[94] Fathers have often viewed the family justice system as unequal,[95] favouring mothers, so mediation may represent greater accessibility to decision-making and fairness. Mediators are alert to the fact that every individual situation will have its own particular power dynamic.

9.78   Men often have greater economic power, and it is common for the male partner to earn a higher income and have greater knowledge of financial arrangements. Mediators will be attentive to manipulative and astute partners (not necessarily always male) seeking to dictate the terms of any financial agreement. This can be addressed by ensuring that such arrangements are transparent and that the party with less knowledge is able to talk through the details with their legal adviser.

9.79   By contrast, traditionally women have other areas of control and power. They are usually the primary carers, and may seek to use this power to determine the parameters of any childcare arrangements. This may enable a mother to dictate the terms of any settlement far more easily than a man.

9.80   Mediators working with separating couples and families in conflict, particularly in the early stages of relationship breakdown, will also be mindful of the power imbalance between the initiator of a separation and the recipient. Techniques such as greater time intervals between meetings can be used to help the recipient cope better.

Changing power imbalances

9.81   Power imbalances shift and move over time. What is important is that an experienced mediator can recognise this. Mediators will monitor parties' body language and unspoken communication to assess the power dynamic and continuously assess whether mediation remains appropriate.

---

94 Parkinson Family Mediation: *Appropriate Dispute Resolution in a new family justice system* Sweet & Maxwell, 2011, 2nd edition, p329.

95 As evidenced by campaigning groups such as 'Families Need Fathers' and 'Fathers for Justice'.

Extreme behaviour

9.82 During a mediation meeting, overt intimidation or aggression should be immediately addressed. Techniques can include returning to the ground rules, coaching and modelling non-violent communication,[96] and acknowledging or 'naming' the emotions and anxiety. Where the mediator has intervened and used their power to restore balance, it will be important to build and maintain rapport with each party to maintain impartiality. Reality testing and empathy can be used, as well as time intervals between mediations, to encourage parties to reach a fair and balanced agreement.

9.83 Ultimately, a mediator can terminate the session if the power balance is too great.

Domestic violence and safeguarding

9.84 Allegations of domestic abuse do not preclude mediation. The first step is for the mediator to carry out an in-depth screening process for domestic abuse and child protection issues. The simple reality of relationship breakdown is that separation may have been triggered by infidelity or lifestyle change, but common features are also domestic violence and alcohol or drug abuse. If children are involved, partners will often want contact to continue between children and the estranged parent, but with safeguards to ensure the children are protected from harm.

9.85 Screening for welfare issues should be informed by the fact that domestic violence is an issue in one-third of cases where safeguarding concerns have been identified. The other factors[97] identified were:

- parenting capacity affected by:
  - drug abuse;
  - alcohol abuse;
  - mental illness;
  - learning difficulties;
- fear of abduction.

9.86 The mediator will sensitively explore whether these factors are present. The risk of continuing with the process when the mediator

---

96 See paras 4.35–4.37.

97 J Hunt and A Macleod, *Outcomes of applications to court for contact orders after parental separation or divorce*, Briefing Note, University of Oxford – quoted in Justice Select Committee, 6th report, *Operation of Family Courts*, June 2011, para 95.

is not aware of these issues is that the resident parent may be persuaded to agree direct contact when serious welfare concerns may suggest that greater protective measures need to be put in place to ensure the best interests of the child.

Case study 13: Court proceedings and domestic violence

Julie and Steve attended assessment meetings and agreed to mediate about contact and finance issues. At the first mediation meeting it became apparent there had been intervening violence, an injunction was now in force, and a CAFCASS report ordered in respect of contact. Nevertheless, they had attended mediation to try to make progress, Julie in good faith, Steve (who had enduring mental health issues) without any degree of trust.

Over a series of meetings, communication and a revision of the terms of the injunction were addressed. Contact was developed, and short and long term financial settlement achieved. The Court were kept informed of developments throughout and the request for the involvement of CAFCASS was rescinded.[98]

Cultural and gender sensitivity

9.87   Family mediators are sensitive to the fact that different versions of 'family' exist from the conventional notion of the two-parent model. Children can be cared for by grandparents, extended family, single parents or same-sex parents, and the primary carer can be the mother, father, grandparent, aunt, uncle or even a nanny. Separated couples may co-parent or parallel parent. Mediators should be careful not to be directive or judgmental as to which model favours children.

9.88   In the same way, cultural sensitivity requires the mediator to respect and acknowledge different cultures. Ultimately, where cultural norms dictate that a partner is co-operative and compliant, the mediator must be cautious about imposing their own values. Such roles can also function over a much wider framework covering the extended family or local community.

---

98   Case study provided by the Family Mediators Association (FMA) – www. thefma.co.uk.

Mediator bias and manipulation

9.89   Mediators are mindful of the multi-faceted power struggles that can present themselves in family mediation, and their own power within that dynamic.

9.90   One common example – described as 'triangulation' – is where one party seeks to establish an 'upper hand' or greater rapport with a particular mediator. The mediator needs to be aware of the way this can impact the process. One simple technique is to encourage parties to speak to each other, rather than to the mediator.

9.91   Ensuring balance and equality at the earliest stages of the process is also essential. If one side makes initial contact, the mediator must ensure that the other party is contacted and equal time is spent speaking to each before any *joint meeting*.

9.92   Mediators need to be self-aware, to ensure that they are not imposing their solution on the process, or allowing their own moral framework to influence their interventions. Mediators can use a number of techniques to guard against their inherent biases. This is most simply achieved through non-judgmental interventions, but also through close supervision and support from their family mediation provider organisation.

Case study 14: Unvoiced concerns

Anne and Gareth had separated and came to mediation to reach an agreement about contact with their children, Stanley and Frank. During the second mediation meeting, Anne reacts defensively when Gareth suggests he could take the children to the park or swimming every Saturday and she insists he can only have contact with their children at his mother's one bedroom flat (which has not got a garden).

An interim arrangement was put in place and the mediator arranges separate meetings with Anne and Gareth. During her private meeting Anne disclosed that Gareth drinks heavily and she only feels the children will be safe when Gareth's mother is also present. Anne did not raise this issue during her assessment meeting with the mediator and indicates she feels uncomfortable about raising this in front of Gareth as she is scared he may become angry. A skilled mediator was able to address this underlying issue in a sensitive way.

Dealing with impasses

9.93　In family breakdown, the level of mistrust, anger and hurt may mask the underlying issues. When faced with a stalemate, mediators have a number of techniques to move the process forward:

a) *Slow the pace.* This gives everybody time to think, enabling the parties to reflect on whether they are able to be more co-operative. Mediators can summarise the conflicting positions, acknowledge parties' feelings and set out the possible options.

b) *Enable the parties to solve their own problem.* This includes asking them how they feel in response to what the other party has said, building empathy or inviting parties to generate alternative solutions.

c) *Break down the problem.* Try to define the different issues, separating out feelings and emotions from practical obstacles, for example:

Angela　I can't drop Tom off on a Friday because he would be too tired after his swimming lesson.

Mediator　If he didn't have swimming on a Friday, how would you feel about him going to his father's on a Friday? What would you suggest instead? Why would that be a better arrangement from your perspective? Have you considered whether there are other options? James has suggested that he could take Tom to swimming lessons on a Saturday morning, what's your reaction to that suggestion? Are you happy to leave that option on the table?

d) *Present different scenarios.* What would happen if nothing changes?

e) *Put the contentious issue to one side.* Focus on those areas where you have agreement. It may be less of a sticking point if agreement has been reached on other things, or it may be an area where agreement cannot be reached.

f) *Take a break.* If the mediator is becoming frustrated, their ability to be impartial will start to be eroded. The parties, too, may want a chance to have some space.

g) *Educate and coach.* The mediator may be able to say, for example, 'In my experience, where one party has compromised on an issue, the other party feels able to co-operate on a different issue'.

Arrangements for dependent children

The child's voice

9.94　Mediators should enable children's views to be part of the process. This may involve private conversations between a party and the child, the mediator (with the parties' consent) speaking to the child directly, or the child attending a mediation meeting. The mediator should also be mindful that having asked the child for his or her views, they should not only be listened to but actually 'heard'.[99]

Case study 15: The child's view

A case was referred from court, where a mother had made an application for the daughter to change her name to her own (the mother's). The mediator saw both parents and they agreed that the daughter, aged 12, should be seen.

When the mediator met her, the daughter was happy with the contact arrangements with her father and his partner. In terms of the name she said that she had always been known by her father's name and she didn't want to change this, though she understood that her mother wanted her to feel a greater part of her family. She asked whether her mother's name could be a middle name. The parents met to discuss this and decided to investigate the means for this to happen formally.[100]

Parenting plans

9.95   Where parents have parental responsibility for children but are unable to make decisions easily together, it may be helpful to provide a structure and guidance about what decisions need to be made. This could include a checklist of issues they need to agree on, including:

- Who will the child(ren) live with?
- What contact will they have with each parent and other family members?
- What happens if there is an emergency? Who will be contacted?
- How will you make decisions about changing these arrangements?
- How will you share information about your children?
- How will decisions be made about schooling (eg choice of school, responsibility for homework, parents meetings)?
- How will decisions be made about discipline?

---

99 *Office of the Children's Commissioner: response to the Family Justice Review interim report*, July 2011 recommendation 2.3.

100 Case study provided by Oxfordshire Family Mediation – www.ofm.org.uk; Family Justice Review: interim report (March 2011) p165.

- How will decisions be made about holidays?
- How will decisions be made about birthdays and religious festivals?
- How will decisions be made about religious upbringing?
- How will decisions be made about sex education, drugs and alcohol?

Financial family mediation

9.96 Financial considerations can encompass deciding the future of the family home and any other property or assets, including pensions and inheritance, as well as issues of child and spousal maintenance and, commonly, debts. This is a unique, open and collaborative process. Unlike other areas of mediation the financial information in family cases is 'open' (ie not confidential) and can be used in legal proceedings if an agreement is not reached. The mediator may be asked to prepare a document on the financial position for a court.

9.97 An important aspect of open financial disclosure is that where a party is concerned that the financial information disclosed during mediation is not full and frank, a court order can be sought.

Reaching agreement

9.98 Mediators will usually draft the final proposals agreed by the parties. This is called a *memorandum of understanding*[101] (where proposals are vague or do not meet the strict legal requirements it may be called an *outcome summary*). It is described as a proposal or summary in order to distinguish it from a legally binding agreement. Mediators encourage parties to go through the proposal with their legal adviser, who will then draft a legally binding document or 'consent order'. Mediators will usually charge for drafting the mediation summary and can also summarise the financial information in what called an *open financial summary* or *open statement of financial information*.

Closing the mediation

9.99 At the end of each mediation meeting, the mediator should make a record of the issues under discussion. This includes any agreement or options for agreement which may have been discussed, including setting out areas of disagreement. If interim arrangements have

---

101 See appendix E.

been reached, these should be recorded. There is also likely to be an 'action plan' or 'task list' for each party.

9.100   Where agreement cannot be reached, summarising the areas of agreement and disagreement will be a useful exercise. Where the parties indicate that they would benefit from a judge deciding certain issues, a summary of issues could be drafted and is potentially disclosable to the court, if the parties think it will be helpful.

Frequently asked questions answered by Margaret Pendlebury and Christopher Richards

9.101   The following questions have been answered by Margaret Pendlebury and Christopher Richards. Margaret is a family mediator, supervisor and trainer and has been mediating since 1994. Christopher is a family mediator, supervisor and has his own mediation company. He has been mediating since 1986.

My ex-partner and I get on fairly well – should I contact a mediator or a lawyer?

By contacting a family mediator first, you will hear information about the range of options open to you and be helped to decide on the most realistic way forward.

   The mediator will explain and discuss how you can manage every aspect of separation and divorce. There are parental, financial and legal decisions to be made, and there may be quite specific issues of your own, which you will want to resolve. The mediator will help you to establish your priorities and identify areas of difference.

   When you need legal or other advice, the mediator will encourage you both to consult a lawyer or financial adviser. You bring the advice you receive back to the mediation and use it to inform your decisions and negotiate jointly acceptable arrangements.

I am worried my ex-partner will bully me into making the decisions she wants

The mediator will certainly ask you separately and confidentially about any such worries you may have. Mediators have a responsibility to ensure that discussion and negotiation can take place without threat, fear or intimidation. They are trained and skilled in managing the process, so that both parties can speak freely, and no one is forced to commit to anything against their will. Mediators will not allow bullying and would stop the mediation if necessary, or you would be free to withdraw.

Decisions made in mediation are not binding, so there is no incentive to 'force' agreements. Mediated arrangements work because both parties have reached fully informed decisions that they can both accept.

How will the mediator know whether my ex-husband is lying about his financial position?

The mediator is not a mind-reader or a judge, but the mediation process is rigorous!

Mediation on finances requires full and open disclosure, supported by documentary evidence. Each of you is required to provide property valuations, bank statements, business accounts, pension valuations, debt balances, income details, tax returns and so on. It is no less thorough than making financial disclosure any other way, except that in mediation you can ask questions on the spot from your ex-husband and check what the financial information actually means. The mediator will want to be sure you are as confident as you can be that financial disclosure is complete and accurate.

Once disclosure is made, you will have an 'open financial statement' which is a written summary of your financial information drawn up with you by the mediator. You will be able to show it, and the supporting evidence, to your solicitor or other advisers, before making any decisions.

CHAPTER 10

Workplace mediation

continued

Key points

- Employers are being encouraged to use workplace mediation to manage disputes in the workplace.
- Participating in mediation is voluntary and employees do not forgo their employment rights.
- Workplace mediation can be carried out by trained in-house or external mediators.
- Workplace mediation is used where the parties are continuing in an employment relationship.
- Employment mediation covers situations where the employment relationship has ended or is likely to end. Legal advisers are often present and parties will have received independent legal advice.
- Once an employment tribunal claim is made, other dispute resolution processes include: conciliation, arbitration and judicial mediation.
- There are currently a number of government proposals seeking to increase awareness and use of mediation in the workplace.

Introduction

Workplace disputes

> Three rules of work: out of clutter find simplicity; from discord find harmony; in the middle of difficulty lies opportunity.[1]

10.1   Disputes in the workplace cause disharmony, reduce productivity and are a drain on resources. If left unresolved, formal grievance or disciplinary procedures and employment tribunals are time-consuming and stressful for employers and employees alike. Stress-related illness is costly for employers – in terms of absence, sick pay, sickness cover, overtime and recruitment – and miserable for employees.[2] It's not just the financial cost – a less stressful workplace is healthier, happier and better motivated. Creating a better working environment insulates an organisation from costs of litigation and protects its reputation.

---

1   Albert Einstein.
2   *Work-related stress: What the law says*, Chartered Institute of Personnel and Development, September 2010, at www.cipd.co.uk/hr-resources/guides/work-related-stress.aspx.

10.2　　The government is set to implement measures encouraging employers to pursue early resolution of workplace disputes, thereby avoiding recourse to employment tribunals.[3] Claims to the employment tribunal have been steadily rising[4] and cost an average £3,800 for businesses and £1,500 for a claimant.[5] There are additional costs of the dispute on morale, productivity and staff turnover. Mediation offers a chance to address workplace conflict and improve working relationships without relinquishing employment rights. Workplace mediation explores how to maintain an employment relationship and should be distinguished from employment mediation, which is offered once the employment relationship has ended (or is being brought to an end).[6]

10.3　　The promotion of workplace mediation is part of a wider shift away from a strict adherence to formal procedural guidelines towards processes which enable employers to address the substance of the dispute at an early stage. The Employment Act 2008, which adopted recommendations set out in the Gibbons Review,[7] created greater procedural flexibility and encouraged a renewed emphasis on early resolution of disputes. The statutory Code of Practice is provided by the Advisory, Conciliation and Arbitration Service (ACAS) Code on Disciplinary and Grievance Procedures 2009 ('the ACAS Code')[8] and although the words 'conciliation', 'arbitration' and 'mediation' do not appear in the Code, mediation is dealt with fully in *Discipline and grievances at work: the ACAS guide.*[9]

10.4　　It will take time for familiarity and confidence of using mediation in the workplace to grow.[10] Greater awareness of workplace mediation is needed, as well as evidence of its benefits. See, for example, a recent pilot mediation scheme introduced by a large high street

---

3　*Resolving workplace disputes: government response to the consultation*, Department for Business Innovation and Skills (BIS), November 2011, para 31. See also paras 10.60–10.61.

4　Claims rose by 56 per cent to 236,000 between 2009 and 2010. However, many of these were multiple claims covering large groups of workers.

5　*Resolving workplace disputes: a consultation*, BIS, January 2011, p19.

6　See paras 10.11–10.13 on employment mediation.

7　Gibbons, *A review of employment dispute resolution*, March 2007 commissioned by the then Department of Trade and Industry.

8　The code is issued under the Trade Union and Labour Relations (Consolidation) Act 1992 s199, in force 6 April 2009.

9　Available at www.acas.org.uk/.

10　*Resolving workplace disputes: government response to the consultation*, BIS, November 2011, para 27.

clothing retailer,[11] which saw the number of grievances reduce by 50 per cent over a 12-month period.

10.5   Mediation is not a substitute for legislation recognising rights and affording protection to employees. This chapter examines how workplace disputes may be addressed by mediation and lead to a more productive workplace.

Workplace mediation

10.6   The potential for an employer to address tensions at an early stage will depend on the size of the organisation, the training and awareness of staff internally and their ability to respond swiftly. Organisations, in both the public and the private sector, are realising the cost of workplace conflict and are becoming more interested in exploring ways of capping that cost. Likewise for employees, who invest emotionally in their working life, finding more constructive ways to resolve disputes and avoid an irreconcilable breakdown in their employment relationship has obvious benefits.

Defining workplace mediation

10.7   Workplace mediation generally describes intervention by a neutral third party while there is an ongoing working relationship. Workplace mediation is sought with a view to restoring a working relationship or exploring a way in which future communication can be conducted to minimise disputes and improve a working environment. When successful, this makes the conditions at work more satisfactory not only for the parties concerned but also their colleagues, managers, families and friends; morale is boosted, performance enhanced, absenteeism reduced. Workplace mediation can be carried out by a trained in-house mediator or an external workplace mediation service. There are national provider organisations such as ACAS, Consensio, Globis, Mediation Works, and the TCM Group, as well as local providers. Workplace mediation may also be offered by some community mediation schemes.

10.8   Workplace mediation is still an emerging field. Practitioners use a variety of workplace mediation models and these are continuing to develop. Practice varies – for example, some practitioners work alone, while other practitioners find the co-mediation model effective. Where disputes are complex or exist within teams, the co-mediation

11 *Conflict management*, March 2011, report commissioned by CIPD. http://www. cipd.co.uk/hr-resources/survey-reports/conflict-management.aspx.

model is likely to be preferred as it can add strength, energy and balance to the mediation process. In some cases, where an internal mediation scheme exists, an external mediator may co-mediate alongside an in-house mediator. Most workplace mediators use a facilitative or transformative approach and, while there is currently no formal obligation for workplace mediators to be accredited or regulated, there is a voluntary registration scheme.[12]

10.9   The fundamental principles of mediation apply equally to workplace mediation as they do in other fields. As an informal and flexible process, mediation is well-equipped for dealing with challenges that can arise unexpectedly in the workplace. The process is voluntary, confidential and independently facilitated by a neutral mediator. It differs from civil mediation in two key ways: the agreements reached are non-binding and it is a non-legal process.

10.10   The agreements reached in workplace mediation are described as 'non-binding' because an employee would still be entitled to pursue a grievance or an employment tribunal claim.[13] This does not mean that a party would be entitled to rely on anything said or done during the mediation process. Mediation is private and confidential and parties can only rely on something said during the mediation in exceptional circumstances or if both parties agree.[14]

Employment mediation

10.11   Employment mediation is a more formal process than workplace mediation. It might appropriately be described as civil mediation because legal advisers are involved and any agreement reached is usually legally binding. The distinguishing feature between workplace and employment mediation is sometimes described as: whether or not the employment relationship is continuing[15] – where parties wish the employment relationship to be repaired, the process is workplace mediation; where the discussion is about how to bring the employment relationship to an end or the employee has left employment, the process is employment mediation.

---

12 See paras 12.44–12.45.
13 Subject to the limitation period (the period of time within which a claim must be brought), which in employment tribunals is three months. See para 8.64.
14 See paras 7.8, 7.16 and 7.31–7.32.
15 Clive Lewis, *The definitive guide to workplace mediation and managing conflict at work*, RoperPenberthy Publishing, 2009, p103.

Compromise agreements

A *compromise agreement* is a contract conataining some standard terms between an employer and employee (or ex-employee) under which the employee receives a negotiated financial sum (or some other consideration) in exchange for agreeing that he or she will have no further claim against the employer under any employment legislation and employees need to have taken independent legal advice before signing it.[16] A compromise agreement is tailored to the individual circumstances.

10.12 In employment mediation, the employer will be seeking to avoid the cost of an employment tribunal claim and it is important that the employee is fully advised as to the strength of any potential claim.[17] In most cases the employer will either contribute to or fully fund the cost of an employee receiving independent legal advice. Given the widespread use of compromise agreements, the government is proposing changes to create greater certainty around the use of this form of legally binding agreement.[18]

10.13 The advantages of employment mediation are that where parties do not want the employment relationship to be repaired, it will resolve matters far more quickly than alternative processes. For the employer, there is an opportunity to understand the issues more fully, including what led to the dispute. For the former employee it is a chance to vent their grievances, and, in some cases, receive an acknowledgement or apology. An agreement can be reached that includes things an employment tribunal could not or would not order such as securing a good reference.

Moving from workplace mediation to employment mediation

10.14 If at any stage during a workplace mediation the dialogue shifts towards a discussion about a compromise agreement the mediator may need to ask for a break to make a decision about whether the mediation should be brought to an end. It may still be appropriate

---

16 Employment Rights Act 1996 s203(3).

17 As above. The government proposes 'compromise agreements' will be amended to 'settlement agreements' – *Resolving workplace disputes: government response to the consultation*, BIS, November 2011, para 10.

18 *Resolving workplace disputes: government response to the consultation*, BIS, November 2011, paras 42–44.

for the mediation to continue if the parties wish. In some cases, having an informal discussion with a neutral third party may assist in reaching a satisfactory outcome for both parties. The mediator will only allow the mediation to continue if, first, they are satisfied that both parties are aware that any agreement reached will not be legally binding until the employee has received legal advice.[19] Practically speaking it may not be possible to receive legal advice on the same day, so the parties may have preliminary discussions and possibly reach a broad agreement, but the employee should still be given time to seek legal advice before a legally binding agreement is signed.[20] Second, it is essential that the people present in the mediation have the authority to reach a potential agreement (for example, two co-workers could not reach a settlement agreement, but if a manager is a participant then they may have the authority to explore potential areas of agreement, particularly sums of money). Third, the mediator will be mindful of the potential imbalance of power, and will only allow the mediation to continue if the employee is able to engage equally in the discussion. If the mediator is satisfied the mediation should continue they will signal that the process has changed and confirm the parties wish to continue.

Setting up a workplace mediation

10.15   Mediation can take place between employees whether a grievance or disciplinary procedure has begun; it may also be proposed where disagreements between employees are impacting upon their ability to do their job. In order for a mediation to be set up, the dispute must be known about and at least one of the parties concerned must have the courage to call attention to it.

What can be mediated?

10.16   Mediation can address disputes that exist between individuals, within teams, across hierarchical lines of management or between organisations. Mediation can be used before any grievance has been made. Where allegations of serious misconduct, such as harassment or bullying, have been made, care must be taken when deciding whether

19   See paras 10.11–10.13.
20   *Resolving workplace disputes: government response to the consultation*, BIS, November 2011, paras 42–51 for the government's view on the use of compromise agreements.

mediation is appropriate. As a general rule where allegations necessitate a formal investigation, mediation may not be appropriate. However, provided an investigation or formal process is not required, these sorts of cases are highly amenable to mediation. This is largely because the perception of one party's behaviour can alter during the mediation process. The essential ingredient is the willingness of the parties to want to improve the situation.

10.17 Mediation in the workplace, as in other areas, is voluntary, so both parties must agree to become involved. Where a case would normally trigger a formal investigation but for the availability of mediation, the mediation option cannot be exercised against the wishes of the person making the allegation. There may be cases where a formal investigation is halted or waived and the parties seek mediation. Alternatively, mediation may be offered at the conclusion of a formal investigation to restore communication and trust where parties still have to work together.

Who starts the mediation process?

10.18 Complaints often arrive at the door of HR personnel, many of whom are well-equipped to deal with problems, defuse tensions and encourage colleagues towards a better understanding. At times though, when a complaint is more serious or the problem is recurring, the employer may seek the assistance of a mediator in an effort to divert the threat of a grievance procedure or avoid having to use the disciplinary procedure. Obviously, in cases of gross misconduct or investigations that involve the police or other investigative bodies, mediation would not be the starting point.

10.19 It follows that it is more usually the organisation which takes the decision to try mediation. An employee may of course request mediation, particularly if this is an option within the employer's policies. As with informal procedures, the sooner the dispute is tackled the better.

When to start the mediation process?

10.20 Mediation can take place at any stage in a dispute, provided internal formal procedures are put on hold. It is generally most effective if used soon after the problem has arisen before either party's view becomes entrenched or the problem is exacerbated. Sometimes disciplinary, grievance or complaints policies have the option of mediation written into them. It is necessary to be clear which route is being chosen and whether any formal procedure is being suspended while mediation is attempted. Additionally, if formal avenues have ended, whether or not there has been an adverse finding for one of the parties, mediation can be used to rebuild a working relationship.

Case study 16: Knowing when mediation can help

This referral came from a Director of a manufacturing company with around 50 employees. There was no internal human resources (HR) function and when a dispute escalated between two office staff to the point where allegations of bullying and harassment were made the Director sought advice from an employment lawyer, who recommended mediation.

The two employees were the sole members of the finance team and shared an office. A particular incident triggered a sudden and complete breakdown in communication, which was resistant to all management intervention. From then, the finance team simply did not function effectively, posing significant risks for the company.

During mediation, the mediators discovered that the parties had previously had a good working relationship but structural changes had created uncertainty as to their exact roles and reporting relationships. This had led to mistrust, which was unwittingly made worse by management communications which at times seemed to favour one over the other.

Mediation enabled them to rebuild trust and loyalty to one another as they understood now how much of what had happened was caused by circumstances outside either of their control. At their request the final agreement was shared with management and included constructive proposals to update job descriptions and clarify procedures that they felt would improve the situation, not just for them but for the organisation as a whole.[21]

Cost

10.21   Mediation is sometimes freely available through a community mediation service and the government is exploring more ways to make mediation cost-effective. Where external mediation incurs a fee, the employer almost always pays for it. The cost of an external mediation provider varies depending on the number of parties, complexity of

---

21 Case study provided by Mediation Works – www.mediation-works.co.uk.

the dispute and surrounding factors. The average cost is £800 to £1,200 per day. These rates are likely to increase where the mediation may last longer, requires more than one mediator or involves a team mediation over a number of days.

10.22   Some larger companies and institutions are choosing to set up in-house mediation schemes. If an internal scheme exists, referral to mediation will generally be made at an earlier stage. This is dependent, however, on sufficient awareness of the availability of an in-house mediation scheme and how it can be used.

Who attends the mediation?

10.23   The parties who attend the mediation are the people who have a dispute. It may be an issue between individuals, co-workers or between a member of staff and their line manager or a more senior member of staff. If a party wishes to bring someone with them, a work colleague or trade union rep, as supporter,[22] it is important the mediator is informed beforehand in order that all parties can know and agree who will attend in advance.

Team mediation

10.24   Where there are more than two parties or a team which is not functioning well, the mediator may recommend 'team mediation'. This is a process which usually involves two or more mediators working with a whole team.[23]

Conflict resolution training and coaching

10.25   Additional aspects of coaching and training may be offered by workplace mediation organisations, addressing wider issues which emerge during the mediation process and which extend beyond the resolution of a dispute between two people.

22 See para 3.89.
23 See para 10.37.

In-house mediation schemes – a catalyst for change

Cost?

The start-up cost of embedding an in-house mediation scheme is in the region of £1,000 per mediator. It is, therefore, often only large organisations who can afford to implement such schemes. Continuing support and mentoring may be offered by the training provider at an additional cost to ensure the scheme achieves what it was established for and provide guidance in particular situations.

Benefits?

Public and private sectors have seen the benefits of training employees to mediate disputes quickly and effectively. The benefit of having an in-house mediation scheme is quantified in cost savings to the organisation by the reduced number of formal procedures, a decrease in absenteeism and a more productive workplace.

Who gets involved?

The organisation can work with the training provider to identify which employees are best placed to be trained as mediators within the organisation. This process may look at existing skills, longevity of employment and a commitment to stay, an enthusiasm for mediation and the time available to practice it in conjunction with the current role.

> *In our experience companies that have invested in setting up a mediation scheme are experiencing significant benefits – human and economic. They offer mediation as a credible alternative to costly, stressful and traditionally adversarial grievance procedures, and it works. The evidence from over 100 internal mediation schemes set up by the TCM Group suggests that mediation delivers a significant reduction in stress and absence; increases performance and productivity; reduces time spent by managers and leaders and ultimately the opportunity for the organisation and its employees to achieve their full potential.*[24]

NHS – East Lancashire set up an in-house mediation scheme in 2008. It now has 15 internal mediators. Within the first 18 months of the scheme there was a 60% reduction in formal processes (grievances and fair treatment cases) and over £200,000 in cost savings.[25]

24   David Liddle, Founder and Director of The TCM Group – www.thetcmgroup.com.
25   Trained by Consensio – www.consensiopartners.co.uk.

Higher Education Institutes (HEIs) – Leeds Metropolitan University set up its in-house mediation scheme about four years ago. Its trained mediators, drawn from staff from across the university deal with approximately 36 'disputes' each year. The disputes range from issues between members of staff as well as between students and staff. The service is now sufficiently well-established that it can now offer advice and guidance to staff on handling a number of complaints and conflict situations.

Private sector – BT Retail introduced a pilot mediation scheme which was set-up in 2008; it resulted in mediation being rolled out through the company of about 100,000 employees in 2010 and established employee engagement. It is estimated to have cut the cost of conflict by many hundreds of thousands of pounds.

Choice of mediator

10.26   There is a wide range of independent workplace mediators, including specialist workplace mediation providers[26] and some community mediation providers.[27] Alternatively, the employer may have their own mediation scheme. Where the issues are more complex or serious, an external mediator may be more appropriate or there is a perceived conflict of interest if an in-house mediator is used.

10.27   The mediator should always be independent and impartial. There are a number of safeguards to ensure the mediation process remains independent. Before the mediation, the mediator explains that the process is confidential and voluntary. No record of the discussions will be retained by the mediator or mediation provider and the parties decide what information, if any, is passed back to the employer.[28] Mediation is a voluntary process and the parties may decide not to continue with the mediation at any time. During the ground rules, the mediator will ask the parties to agree to inform him or her if they are going to leave the mediation or want the mediation to end.

10.28   It may be perceived that an in-house mediator lacks neutrality and the same concerns may be raised where an external mediation provider is being funded by the employer. In both cases, an employee

---

26 See www.cmcregistered.org – this is an online register of workplace mediation providers who meet minimum standards (also see paras 12.42–12.45 and appendix A).
27 See appendix A.
28 See para 10.39.

may feel there is an incentive for the mediator to resolve the dispute in favour of the employer. If a party's perception is that the mediator is not neutral, it will be difficult for the mediator to establish the necessary trust and rapport. If an employee has any concerns, they may wish to seek legal advice about their rights and entitlements. They can ask their employer to set out in writing the purpose of the mediation, which should always focus upon the employee's future employment.[29]

10.29   The mediation process should be conducted with equal impartiality, whether an in-house or external mediator is used. An in-house mediation scheme has the advantage of being able to respond immediately to a dispute provided there are sufficient mediators. The process may be more informal, helping the parties to be open and relaxed during the mediation, alternately more tense depending on the parties' perspective. The in-house mediator can always seek the assistance of an external mediator in appropriate cases. In cases where a dispute has been going on for some time or where the mediation is taking place after an internal grievance procedure (particularly where one party still feels aggrieved), referral to an external mediator is generally recommended.

Choice of venue

10.30   Whether an in-house or external mediator is being used, venue is important. To keep costs down, the mediation may be arranged at the place of work. In such cases, it is useful to agree boundaries and ground rules beforehand to ensure parties are as engaged as possible – for example, use a different part of the building or office from where the parties are usually based; avoid colleagues who are not directly involved in the mediation; agree that checking voicemails and emails will only be done during breaks.

The mediation process

10.31   A workplace mediation between two parties follows a similar process to other types of mediation.

---

29 See para 10.11 for the distinction between workplace and employment mediation.

Provision of information

10.32   First, information is provided in advance by the organisation referring or commissioning the workplace mediation to the mediator
being used, whether in person, by phone or by email. This provides
the mediator with the context of the dispute and many mediators prefer not to be provided with too much detail. There may be occasions
where confidential information is disclosed by the referrer and must
not be passed on to the parties. The mediator respects the confidentiality of all information provided, and any personal opinion expressed
by the referrer would not be disclosed to the parties. In most cases,
the organisation will be open about their expectations as these are
set out in the terms of referral which a mediator may request to be
disclosed to all parties. Each situation has to be looked at individually. The preliminary information enables the mediator to assess the
suitability of the dispute for mediation, gauge how long the process
is likely to take and who needs to be involved, enabling them to prepare for the individual (or pre-mediation) meetings.

Individual meetings (pre-mediation meetings)

10.33   The next stage of the mediation consists of separate meetings
between the mediator and each party, which usually last at least an
hour. These individual meetings can be described as *pre-mediation
meetings*, however they are an integral part of the mediation process.
Some mediators arrange for the individual meetings to take place
on the same day as the *joint meeting* and others allow some time to
elapse between the individual meetings and the *joint meetings*, practice varies. Sometimes more than one meeting is needed to prepare
the parties to meet each other. Sometimes a pre-mediation questionnaire[30] is used to help parties prepare for their mediation and be open
about their expectations, fears and needs. This may be designed for
the party's own private use, alternatively the answers can be supplied
to the mediator before the mediation.

10.34   The *pre-mediation meeting* gives each party an opportunity to
describe their experience of the dispute. Encouraging each party to
identify what they want the other party to hear is crucial if the *joint
meeting* is to resolve misunderstandings and develop a fresh way of
communicating. At the end of the individual meetings, each party

---

30 See appendix D, which will be adapted in each case to prompt reflection on the
circumstances surrounding the dispute.

prepares opening comments, sometimes referred to as an *opening statement*, with help from the mediator.

The joint meeting

10.35   The next stage is the *joint meeting*. The mediator makes some introductory remarks, explains the ground rules and the structure of the joint mediation before each party makes their opening comments. In some cases parties may be more comfortable to read from notes, ensuring that nothing gets forgotten. At the end of the opening comments, the mediator summarises the main issues and checks with each party that the summary is accurate before the joint discussion begins. The mediator then facilitates a dialogue between the parties with the aim of increasing mutual understanding in order to explore resolution and an acceptable outcome for both. Where the *joint meeting* takes place at a later date from the individual meetings, some time is spent re-capping before the joint mediation begins to check whether there has been any adjustment or change since the *pre-mediation meetings*.

10.36   As the discussion progresses,[31] the mediator will manage the process, encouraging the parties to reach an agreement, if this is possible. A mediator does not impose his or her solution and each party is responsible for any decision reached and any form of agreement.

Team mediation

10.37   Where a dispute has triggered a breakdown of trust and there is resentment among a group of employees, team mediation can help improve communication and rebuild positive working relationships. Team mediation may take place over several days and involves at least two mediators. Much of the preparation will be done before the *joint meeting*. This is essential as there are likely to be many layers to the dispute, and underlying issues can unexpectedly emerge or be revealed. This may necessitate a dispute being resolved between two or three people before concentrating on the group as a whole. If this process is not undertaken thoroughly enough it can jeopardise the mediation.

---

31   See paras 5.9–5.15 and 5.19 for further discussion of the mediation process.

Case study 17: The office party

Carol and James were referred to mediation following an allegation of sexual harassment. They had recently attended a work party and James had become inebriated and touched Carol inappropriately. Human resources (HR) had followed formal procedures and James was subject to a disciplinary hearing, resulting in a formal written warning. While this approach was entirely appropriate and both parties were satisfied with the formal outcome, both felt they needed the chance to speak to each other about what had happened in order to put the incident behind them.

The mediators saw Carol and James separately to explain the mediation process and ask about what had happened. This revealed important background material about a recent family bereavement James' had suffered and the stigma Carol now perceived from colleagues for reporting the incident.

The joint meeting took place three days after the initial meetings. Both parties appeared very nervous and anxious on arrival and did not make eye contact with each other at first. The mediation was a chance for James to say sorry and for Carol to talk about the impact of the incident and explain why she had made a formal allegation.

At the follow-up, four weeks later, both parties reported that things were not back to how they had been before but that they had put the incident of sexual harassment behind them and were getting on quite well in work now. Carol remarked that it takes time to rebuild trust and she felt that mediation had enabled them to begin to do this.[32]

Closing the mediation

Where an agreement is reached

10.38 A mediation may end with a handshake or a written agreement, or both. Integral to whatever settlement is reached is that it can sustain the parties in the future. The agreement will be drafted with the help of the mediator who should ensure any written agreement is SMART – specific, measurable, achievable, realistic and time-specific[33] – and is signed by the parties.

---

32 Case study provided by Bolton Mediation – www.boltonmediation.org.uk.
33 See para 7.12.

Telling the employer

10.39   The agreement must make clear what information will be passed to the employer. If the parties agree, a copy of the agreement may be sent to the employer, although the agreement may still remain confidential. Alternatively, the parties may decide that the outcome will remain private between the parties and the mediator. In some cases, it may be necessary to separate the parties' agreement from any recommendation or request which the parties wish to bring to the employer or organisation's attention. A separate document may be drafted and, as with all agreements, care must be taken to check the wording of any information which will be communicated to the referrer or employer and the document should be signed by the parties.[34]

Future working relationships and follow up

10.40   Ideally the agreement should set out how issues will be dealt with in future if any difficulties arise. The mediator will also contact the parties after the mediation to see how the agreement is working out usually after one, three, six and maybe 12 months.

Where an agreement is not reached

10.41   In some cases, the parties will not be able to reach an agreement and the mediator will bring the mediation to an end. The parties may agree on some questions or requests to be made to their employer, and if these are agreed they should be written down and signed by the parties. In other situations the discussion may move to consider a severance package or compromise agreement.

Alternatives to mediating workplace disputes

Informal procedures

10.42   Sometimes there is an absence of any procedures to deal with diffi-culties at work. This is not uncommon in small businesses, for ex-ample where there is no separate HR department or identifiable disciplinary or grievance policy or procedures (despite the employer's obligations under the ACAS code).[35] This leaves problems at work

---

34   See paras 7.8 and 7.16.
35   See www.acas.org.uk.

with no immediate route to resolution and relies on the individuals in the workplace to find a solution if possible. Sometimes a chat between colleagues can help, or a pre-existing problem surfaces in a row which alerts others to the problem. Informal procedures may be less effective if there is a power imbalance in the relative status of employees involved in a dispute, for example an administrator complaining about the team leader.

10.43   In larger organisations and business, much will depend on the skills of the manager or HR department to address issues when they arise. For example, policies to combat bullying, harassment and complaints are only effective if they are properly implemented and this will usually require managers to be trained, not just in what the policies mean but how to deal with situations in the event of apparent transgressions. Disputes can often be resolved within the workplace before any formal procedure is invoked. Understandably, without proper training or skills, managers may be reluctant to have a difficult conversation with an employee or employees, with the result that a relatively minor issue remains unaddressed and potentially becomes a bigger problem.

10.44   Training within the workplace is integral to improving the prospects of resolving conflict successfully. It can be prudent to train people who already display some of the skills and attributes necessary for mediation. Such training can allow employees who are worried about raising a dissenting voice to feel able to do so within the workplace. A useful starting point is the *Mediation: an employer's guide*[36] published by ACAS.

Formal procedures

10.45   Formal procedures may be an investigation, formal grievance or disciplinary hearings. If they are not satisfactorily resolved, this may lead to an employment tribunal hearing. Disciplinary situations cover misconduct as well as poor performance. Grievances are problems, complaints or concerns that employees raise with their employers. Within these procedures there may be opportunities to refer appropriate cases to an in-house or external mediator.

---

36   August 2008 – available at www.acas.org.uk/CHttpHandler.ashx?id=949&p=0.

Employment tribunal claim

10.46   If an employee wishes to commence a formal legal process, this will normally be in the employment tribunal. More unusually, a claim may be brought in the county court. Employment tribunals are designed to be relatively informal and a costs-free jurisdiction, although costs can be awarded against a party for, broadly speaking, unreasonable conduct. The usual remedy is compensation.

10.47   In terms of starting an employment tribunal claim, the first step is seeking legal advice, and the next step will be to complete the ET1 form. In some cases, a claimant may commence proceedings hoping that the employer will be motivated to settle the case. For a claimant motivated by resentment, anger or frustration and who wishes to 'make a point', employment tribunal proceedings rarely meet their expectations.

10.48   When an employment tribunal claim is made, ACAS are sent a copy of the claim and will explore possibilities of settling the case.[37] This does not affect the timetable of the employment tribunal which will set a hearing date regardless of whether they have heard from ACAS.

Conciliation

10.49   Conciliation is a voluntary process between employer and employee. It cannot take place unless both employer and employee agree to it. Like a mediator, the conciliator is independent, impartial and has no power to impose a solution. It differs from mediation in that a conciliator may suggest possible solutions.

10.50   Conciliation is a service provided by ACAS where a claimant is considering or has made a claim to an employment tribunal. This is described as pre-claim conciliation (PCC) and is generally conducted over the telephone although face to face meetings can be arranged. The ACAS Helpline can provide free advice on whether a case is suitable for conciliation.[38] Once a claim is made, a conciliator from ACAS contacts the claimant, the employer and any representatives involved to offer the *free* conciliation service.[39] If conciliation does not result in resolution and a claim proceeds to a hearing, the employ-

---

37   See para 10.50.
38   Tel: 08457 47 47 47, Monday to Friday 8am to 8pm and Saturday 9am to 1pm.
39   If an agreement is reached it is recorded on a COT3 form.

ment tribunal's decision is not affected by the decision to have tried conciliation.

10.51 Employers and trade unions can also enter the conciliation process on an entirely voluntary basis.

Arbitration

10.52 Arbitration, like conciliation, can be used as an alternative to an employment tribunal and can be used to resolve individual or collective problems at work, for example, when trade unions are considering strike action.

10.53 The arbitration process involves an independent and impartial expert determining the outcome of the problem. Arbitration differs from conciliation and mediation because the arbitrator acts like a judge, making a firm decision on a case. Compared to an employment tribunal, arbitration is considered faster, less formal and less stressful (because the issues are resolved more quickly). It is usually cheaper for an employer than an employment tribunal hearing and may be available free of charge.

10.54 The employee and employer must agree in writing to refer a case to arbitration. Independent legal advice will usually be sought before making this decision. Before the arbitration, the potential parties can agree, depending on the nature of the case, whether the arbitrator's decision will be legally binding. Unfair dismissal claims or requests to work flexibly are particularly likely to end in a legally binding decision from the arbitrator. If the arbitration decision is legally binding the parties cannot proceed to an employment tribunal. If it is agreed that the arbitrator's decision will not be legally binding, the case may still proceed to an employment tribunal hearing.

10.55 ACAS and some commercial organisations, including the Chartered Institute of Arbitrators,[40] offer the services of specialist arbitrators. ACAS runs a free arbitration scheme.[41]

Judicial mediation in the employment tribunal

10.56 Where employment tribunal proceedings have commenced, judicial mediation is offered in suitable cases.[42] This would be canvassed at a case management discussion (CMD). The current system began as

40 See www.ciarb.org.
41 Trade Union and Labour Relations (Consolidation) Act 1992 s212A.
42 See para 10.58.

a pilot in 2005[43] and was rolled out in England and Wales in January 2009 and in Scotland in June 2009.[44]

10.57   Judicial mediation is conducted like any other mediation except that the mediator is an employment judge who has trained as a mediator. If the judicial mediation does not result in an agreement and the case proceeds to a full hearing, it will be heard before a different employment judge and nothing referred to in the judicial mediation can be repeated in the tribunal hearing. The employment judge conducting a judicial mediation has no decision-making role and the process should not hinder private negotiated settlements. During the pilot, of those who participated in judicial mediation, 72 per cent resolved their case at the judicial mediation stage.[45]

10.58   There are broad criteria for determining whether a claim is suitable for a judicial mediation:

- the claim does not have any insolvency element;
- the claim would not involve claims to other courts or tribunals;
- the claim has a discrimination element;
- the claim would be listed for hearing for at least three full days;
- the claim involves a maximum of three claimants.

The Law Society has produced a Practice Note to assist solicitors whose clients may be offered judicial mediation.[46]

10.59   Judicial mediation should not delay the eventual outcome of a case as a date for a judicial mediation is likely to be found sooner than a hearing date for a multi-party case. Parties who attend a judicial mediation bear their own costs.

The future

10.60   When there is a clash of working practices, personalities or behaviours in the workplace, one thing is clear: ignoring it is an expensive

---

43   *Evaluating the use of judicial mediation in employment tribunals*, Ministry of Justice (MOJ) Research Series 7/10, March 2010.
44   Judicial mediation is not part of the industrial tribunal or Fair Employment Tribunal system in Northern Ireland where the Labour Relations Agency forms a similar role to ACAS.
45   *Evaluating the use of judicial mediation in employment tribunals*, Ministry of Justice (MOJ) Research Series 7/10, March 2010, p33.
46   *Judicial mediation*, Law Society, August 2010 – available at www.lawsociety.org.uk/productsandservices/practicenotes/judicialmediation/4548.article.

mistake. The government believes that for smaller businesses, increasing the use of mediation means making it more accessible and affordable.[47] To this end the Department for Business Innovation and Skills (BIS) has announced a pilot scheme for two regional mediation networks for small and medium-sized enterprises.[48] The government's response to the BIS consultation, *Resolving workplace disputes*, contains a number of proposals which seek to 'build a new approach to resolving workplace disputes so that the use of mediation to resolve disputes becomes a more accepted and trusted part of the process'.[49]

10.61   The government's aim is to reduce the number of employment tribunal claims. The proposal increasing the qualifying period for unfair dismissal to two years, reducing the number of employees eligible to take a case to the employment tribunal was brought into force on 6 April 2012.[50] The government is also considering introducing the payment of a fee by claimants wishing to make an employment tribunal claim.[51] There is an understandable fear that this will deter legitimate claimants from using the tribunal service. For mediation to function effectively, employees need to know they have recourse to the legal system to enforce their rights and entitlements.

10.62   Workplace and employment mediation are now established mechanisms for reaching meaningful resolutions of employment disputes. Much needs to be done to ensure all those facing disputes in the workplace have sufficient awareness and understanding of the mediation process.

47 *Resolving workplace disputes: government response to the consultation*, BIS, November 2011, p3.

48 Employment Relations Minister Edward Davey announced the pilot on 23 January 2012.

49 *Resolving workplace disputes: government response to the consultation*, BIS, November 2011, para 26.

50 Unfair Dismissal and Statement of Reasons for Dismissal (Variation of Qualifying Period) Order 2012 SI No 989.

51 *Resolving workplace disputes: government response to the consultation*, BIS, November 2011, paras 98–102.

Frequently asked questions answered by Marilyn Webster and Carolyn Graham

10.63   The following questions have been answered by Marilyn Webster and Carolyn Graham. Marilyn is CEO of Mediation Works and is a trained and experienced workplace and family mediator. Carolyn is a highly experienced civil mediator with substantial experience in workplace mediation and training.

How can workplace mediation ever be voluntary and neutral if it is proposed by an employer or an HR department?

Marilyn: It is important to understand the distinction between *proposed* and *imposed*. The employer is making an offer to provide resources in the hope of resolving a dispute in everyone's interests. The parties' decision to participate remains voluntary and there should never be any sanctions for refusal. Mediator neutrality and impartiality are often confused and used as interchangeable terms when they actually mean something different – and neither are affected by who makes the initial referral as long as it is made clear to the employer that they cannot force a particular outcome. Neutrality means that the mediator does not have a stake in the outcome. Impartiality means that the mediator does not favour the interests of either party above the other.

Carolyn: It is one thing to be 'encouraged' to attend a workplace mediation; it's another to participate once there. Even if someone is strongly encouraged to attend, the overt influence of the referring party ends there. Irrespective of who suggests mediation in the first instance, parties must be convinced of the worth of committing to the process. If clear about the potential benefits of mediating rather than going down the grievance route (control over the outcome, confidential, consensual, time-limited), parties will feel better able to commit to the process, whoever suggested it. Helping parties think through their alternative options (do nothing or pursue a grievance) can be one means of enabling parties to make a choice.

How can an employer monitor and implement a confidential agreement?

Marilyn: Mediators have different views on where the boundaries of confidentiality lie. In broad terms our view as a service provider is that the detail of the conversation in meetings remains with the parties, but we would encourage them to share all or part of the written agreement with their employer. This will enable the employer to provide support or make changes where needed. Sometimes the parties' agreement may request a change in procedures or practice that have contributed to the dispute (and may be having a similar effect on others). They won't have the power to implement this themselves, but bringing it to the attention of the employer can lead to changes that will benefit both them and others.

Carolyn: It can't. One of the central tenets of mediation is that it empowers the individuals involved to resolve their disputes in their own terms. What must surely follow is that responsibility for ensuring compliance with any agreement reached should rest with the parties themselves. Giving opportunity for parties to discuss what they would do, should their agreement break down will help equip them to deal with that hypothetical scenario without recourse to outside agencies. Expecting organisations to play an ongoing role in compliance potentially undermines the confidence and faith otherwise displayed by organisations who entrust parties to solve their own disputes through mediation. Having said that, parties will often choose to share written outcomes from mediation with the organisation (HR or a manager). This act of sharing can help parties commit to the delivery of what has been agreed and provides a route to further assistance if required.

In what circumstances would you say allegations of bullying or discrimination are not suitable for mediation and ought to be covered under other formal processes?

Marilyn: Bullying can be intentional or unintentional. The effect on the person experiencing the behaviour can be the same and the validity of their experience should not be questioned. The focus of the mediator, in determining suitability for mediation, should be on whether the person accused of bullying was a) aware of the effect of their behaviour and b) if not, if the person is willing to accept how it made the other person feel and do something to change it. If the person is intentionally bullying, then the matter should be dealt with formally. If it was unintentional but the person is not prepared to accept that what he or she did had that effect (though not the label), then it is doubtful whether you can mediate.

Carolyn: This is a difficult question and one to which there is no 'one size fits all' answer. Mediation might not be the best route if one or more parties feel unsafe discussing their concerns and/or if the organisation needs to respond and be seen to be responding publically to what's been happening. In my experience however, allegations of bullying and discrimination feature not infrequently in workplace conflicts (after all, one person's bullying can be another's assertive and clear management style). What mediation provides for is not only the opportunity to unpack such labels into clear and comprehensible sets of behaviours (behaviours that can be identified, discussed and potentially changed) – it also provides opportunity for the person owning the behaviours to better understand their impact on the other person as well as clarify their own intent behind them. This sharing of impact and intent, underpinned by a specific distillation of the behaviours that are creating the difficulties, is part of the powerful dialogue for increasing mutual understanding that mediation alone can provide.

How effective can workplace mediation be in rebuilding trust after a long dispute or adverse finding?

Marilyn: The essence of mediation is about rebuilding trust and communication. The longer a dispute has been allowed to escalate, the more layers of misunderstanding and miscommunication there will be for the mediator to unravel, and there is likely to be a high degree of emotional and psychological investment in the idea of 'winning' rather than 'co-operating'. But despite everything that is said about mediation being most effective at an early stage, a skilled mediator is capable of resolving even the most seemingly intractable disputes.

Carolyn: Trust cannot be rebuilt overnight, let alone over the course of a one-day mediation. What mediation can helpfully do is identify that trust – or rather the lack of it – has been an underlying issue to start with (rather than, for example, the consequence of an adverse outcome of a more formal process) and that it is likely to remain an important issue going forwards. As often as not, it's less a case of there being a loss of trust following the breakdown in a relationship but rather, the loss of trust that has contributed to the relationship breakdown in the first instance. Mediation can help flush this out like no other formal process. And having established the importance of trust, mediation gives opportunity for the parties to identify and put in place practical steps, within a realistic timeframe, to help rebuild a trusting relationship as well as preventative strategies to help prevent mistrust from re-occurring in the future.

Community mediation

continued

Key points

- Community mediation is about local people working together to help themselves.
- Most community mediation services are not-for-profit or charitable organisations which offer mediation free of charge to local people.
- Community mediators are volunteers, supported by paid staff who manage projects and undertake casework.
- People who use a community mediation organisation to resolve their dispute may be referred by housing departments, housing associations, environmental health officers, anti-social behaviour teams, social services, schools, community groups or the police.
- Those who engage with mediation use it to achieve greater understanding and to be able to talk about the impact it has had.
- Community mediation agreements are non-binding and self-enforcing.
- The wider uses of community mediation include peer mediation, restorative justice, intergenerational mediation and family group conferences.

Introduction

11.1   Community mediation services aim to help communities find better ways to resolve disputes which arise in people's everyday lives. This model of community empowerment and social justice helps build stronger more cohesive communities who are better equipped to help resolve conflicts in the future. Community mediators are, for example, helping communities come to terms with the aftermath of the 2012 riots. Community mediation has been particularly able to respond to specific issues arising between different communities and within communities.

What is community mediation?

Mediation turns a two way fight into a three way search for a solution.[1]

11.2   Community mediation developed in the UK in the 1980s with grass roots, locally run organisations starting to use mediation to address conflict in their communities. Organisations were created, such as Conflict and Change which began in Newham in 1984, Mediation Leeds which started in 1988 and Bolton Neighbourhood Dispute Service which first opened its doors in 1991.

11.3   Community mediation has developed because traditional models of dispute resolution were unable to address pressing social issues in the local community, such as problems between neighbours. Migration, immigration and urbanisation meant that people were often no longer living in communities with which they were able to identify closely[2] and people's lives were pushed ever closer together. Community groups began to use what would now be recognised as 'mediation' to address these issues, influenced by the mediation movement in the US (in particular the San Francisco Community Boards[3]) and some with the support of Quakers meetings.[4] Police, housing officers and church leaders looked to these organisations to help resolve tensions in their communities. Community leaders recognised that social issues could be resolved by enabling people to speak to each other.

> Conflict and Change was established in 1984 by local volunteers as a response to the social tensions arising from economic change and population shift in Newham, East London. They saw that people from diverse backgrounds were living side by side without knowing each other and wanted to find ways to build trust while respecting differences.[5]

11.4   Community mediation organisations are founded on the principle of local people working together to help themselves. Community mediators are volunteers who live, work or have close connections with the local area. Community mediation organisations usually rely

---

1   www.ealingmediation.org.uk/Benefits-of-Mediation-Feedback.
2   L Boulle and M Nesic, *Mediation: principle, process, practice*, Butterworths, 2001 p6.
3   For example, San Francisco Community Boards which were already well established – see http://communityboards.org.
4   For example, Lambeth Mediation was founded with support from the Streatham Quaker Meeting.
5   See www.conflictandchange.co.uk/whoweare/history.

on a variety of funding sources which include referral agencies,[6] such as housing associations, local authorities (councils), schools and the police, as well as funding from donors and grant-giving bodies such as the National Lottery. Most community mediation is delivered by not-for-profit or charitable organisations who provide the service free of charge to users. Community mediation usually shares the following features:

- free to users;
- service available for disputes to be addressed at an early stage;
- parties are neighbours or in an ongoing relationship;
- delivered by volunteer mediators using the co-mediation model (supported by paid case workers who manage the referral and may also undertake mediations with volunteers);
- focuses on improving communication and restoring relationships and neighbours living peacefully with each other;
- strong emphasis on receiving peer feedback from co-mediators, mentoring and supervision of mediators.

11.5   Community mediation organisations have evolved according to local need. The pressures on funding and a need for income generation are also leading organisations to diversify the services they provide. Community mediation covers a broad spectrum of services and users, which include:

- neighbourhood mediation;
- homelessness prevention;
- community issues (group mediation);
- outreach with young people (street mediation);
- hate crimes;
- gangs;
- conflict resolution training.

Community mediation providers may also offer:

- peer mediation in schools;
- restorative justice;
- family mediation (intergenerational, family group conferences);
- workplace mediation
- civil mediation.

---

6   Funding is usually arranged through service level agreements between the community mediation service and the referral agency.

11.6   The work of community mediation providers can be quite varied; for example, Mediation Leeds[7] offers services including mediation for the community care sector. Unite,[8] a large community mediation organisation working in the North East of England, provides community mediation services as well as workplace mediation, homelessness prevention and anger management. Alongside community mediation organisations there is also a growing body of professional community mediators and dispute resolution consultants.

Why use community mediation?

> Whether it's the individual that has a debt, or the business that is trying to get back what it believes it is owed, or the homeowner that might be facing repossession, too often disputes get bogged down in the legal system that could have been resolved outside it.[9]

11.7   Community mediation has the potential to enable people to resolve arguments or disputes without recourse to the courts. This in itself has huge cost savings. It also signals a shift away from a litigation or 'blame' culture and provides individuals with conflict resolution strategies to minimise the impact of future disagreements.

11.8   In 2003, researchers compared the cost and effectiveness of mediation with legal interventions in dealing with anti-social behaviour. Community mediation cost on average £121 (rising to nearly £500 in some complex cases) while anti-social behaviour orders (ASBOs) cost around £2,250 and repossession actions approximately £9,000.[10] Perhaps most significantly, an earlier study had also found that while the average cost spent by a local authority on a neighbour dispute cases was £50, compared with between £81 and £251 for community mediation. The cost of formal action which was in the region of £800 for a housing transfer and nearly £4,000 for a possession order.[11] Cases where ASBOs or other legal enforcement action were required are not only more costly. They also only temporarily 'solve' the problem by the perpetrator moving away or being imprisoned, rather than providing a long-term solution.

7   See www.mediationleeds.org.uk.

8   See www.unite-mediation.org.

9   *Solving disputes in the county courts: creating a quicker, simpler and more proportionate system – the government response*, TSO, February 2012, p3.

10   *The role of mediation in tackling neighbour disputes and anti-social behaviour*, Scottish Executive Social Research, 2003 para 8.

11   J Dignan, A Sorsby, J Hibbert *Neighbour disputes – comparing the cost-effectiveness of mediation and alternative approaches*, Centre for Criminological and Legal Research, University of Sheffield, 1996.

11.9   Increasingly local authorities and fund-giving charitable organisations have been persuaded of the benefits of community mediation projects. It is therefore extremely worrying that the economic pressures on local and central government are seeing cuts to funding of these organisations. By way of example, Bolton, Bromley and Southwark are all well-established community mediation organisations who have seen substantial amounts of their finding withdrawn and are faced with closing their service in 2012. Other services such as Hillingdon Mediation have closed completely.

Case study 18: Trouble on your street

Complaints were being made about young people playing football on a grassed area. Residents living in flats for elderly people were complaining about noise and property damage and as a result wanted a 'no ball games' sign to be erected. The young people felt they were entitled to play on the grass near to where they live as it was safe and the younger children could join in. The situation deteriorated as the Local Residents Association considered the request to forbid ball games and local residents started to verbally abuse each other about the issue. This case was referred to the local mediation service by the local Police Community Support Officer.

Letters were sent to all the homes surrounding the area to let them know about the referral to Mediation and invite them to meet the mediators and get involved. The mediators met with the adults separately in their own homes to find out the problems from their own perspective. Some of the residents were fearful of getting involved but after meeting the mediators they were reassured and agreed to come. The young people preferred to meet as a group so a meeting was held at a local community centre for young people and parents. Likewise some of the younger people were frightened due to an incident where an adult resident had struck one of the young people.

After bringing the parties together, a mutual understanding and respect was achieved. The younger parties had not realised the impact on and the fear that playing football induced in the elderly residents. The older residents did not know how frightened the young people were of some of the older residents and why. They were also surprised at how polite and friendly the young people were. An agreement was reached that both parties were happy with.[12]

---

12 Case study provided by Bolton Mediation – www.boltonmediation.org.uk.

Types of community mediation

11.10   Community mediation is used in a wide range of issues and disputes. It can be helpful to explore and understand some common issues to provide an overview of this field of work:

Neighbourhood mediation

11.11   Disputes between neighbours arise most commonly over noise, lifestyle differences and the use of shared or communal spaces. Many of our homes were built long before the invention of televisions, stereos or washing machines, parts of our everyday routine that can easily interfere with the lives of those living next door. In some cases, properties will have been poorly fabricated or designed without consideration of noise transference. Equally, period properties which have been converted into flats were not constructed with any regard to different families living on each floor, or families with young children living above retired couples.

11.12   People are often unaware that noise from their everyday routines is causing their neighbour distress. This may then be compounded when neighbours follow different lifestyles, for example, where a neighbour works shifts and needs to sleep during the day lives below a family with young children who wake up early. Where one neighbour enjoys loud music or another has a dog, lifestyle clashes can become intolerable. Lack of awareness about religious or cultural rituals may also inadvertently cause offence. Intolerance and fear of living near somebody who is 'different' from themselves can also lead to hostility (and deliberate targeting) of people living in the same community. In our busy modern lives, neighbours often do not communicate with one another, so that unexplained noises from an upstairs flat or the neighbouring property may sound deliberate. A faulty hot water system, for example, may sound to a neighbour like a person deliberately hammering a pipe.

11.13   Use of shared space is often a particular issue, such as staircases, hallways, driveways or gardens. Neighbours may be unable amicably to resolve issues ranging from a dispute over parking in the street or use of residents' designated bays, to the use of a shared hallway for the storage of belongings. Use of communal or shared gardens, how they are maintained and by whom can be another source of tension. Boundary disputes over the maintenance of a shared path, wall or fence, issues over tall hedges or large trees obstructing light or causing damage can also cause disproportionate levels of stress.

11.14   Most people consider their homes to be their own personal space and don't think about how their daily lives impact on their neighbours. In some cases, a lack of awareness or consideration may mean a neighbour being disturbed by the vibration of a washing machine late at night or the sound of a television being watched in the early hours. For another, regularly hearing raised voices from next door may cause an intolerable strain. Cultural and lifestyle differences can impact upon neighbours: issues such as culinary aromas, noisy sex, parking, pets and recycling are all moments where lives overlap and tensions arise. In some cases, prejudice and racist or narrow-minded views mean that frustrations and annoyance becomes abuse against sexual orientation, religion or race. It can also be the way in which a person complains which turns a legitimate grievance into a 'neighbour dispute'.

11.15   Wider community problems such as serious group offending commonly referred to in urban areas as gangs[13] or groups of teenagers causing anti-social behaviour[14] also arise in community mediation.

Homelessness prevention

11.16   Homelessness mediation refers to mediation services provided for young people and their families. In particular, mediation is offered because local authorities have a duty to provide young people aged under 18 with accommodation who are considered (unintentionally) homeless.[15] Many local authorities fund mediation schemes provided by local community or family mediation services.[16] When difficulties arise for families, communication breakdown and conflict can quickly escalate – for example, a young person may feel they are no longer able to live at home, or be asked to leave. Most people only consider somebody to be homeless if they are sleeping on the street – in fact, someone may be considered homeless if they are sleeping on a friend's sofa or living in an overcrowded property or if there is something that makes their living conditions inadequate.

11.17   Homelessness mediation may improve the relationship between a young person and their family so that they are able to remain in their family home; equally it may enable a young person to make

13 See paras 11.26–11.30.
14 See paras 11.19 and 11.20.
15 Children Act 1989 s17.
16 See, for example, www.nfm.org.uk/about/other-support-services/homelessness-mediation.

a positive transition to independent living arrangements. Alone in London,[17] a charity supporting young people and preventing homelessness, provides mediation to help young people and their families resolve conflict and make informed choices.

11.18　　Some mediation providers offer mediation between tenants and landlords to prevent homelessness. The issues may include the threat of eviction because of rent arrears or breach of the tenancy agreement. The tenant may have a complaint about their landlord because the flat or building may have fallen into disrepair, require some work or maintenance. Whatever the cause, a breakdown in the relationship between landlord and tenant can result in deadlock or the potential loss of a home.

Community issues (group mediation)

11.19　　Group mediation facilitates discussions between groups within the same community or representatives of different communities.[18] This may involve, for example, creating a dialogue between Muslims and non-Muslims, or between the Somali community and the indigenous white British community. It may involve resolving disputes that have arisen between two different groups within the same community or it may help address conflict which has arisen within an organisation.

Outreach with young people (street mediation)

11.20　　Street mediation involves trained mediators (these are often experienced youth workers) visiting an area where complaints have arisen, engaging with groups of young people meeting in public spaces and then, where appropriate, arranging a mediation. This process often identifies areas of need which are not being met by local services, and may provide the opportunity for young people to influence service provision in the future. It aims to challenge anti-social behaviour and improve relationships between young people and adults. It has the potential to enable communities to work together to help themselves.

17 See www.aloneinlondon.org.
18 See, for example, work by Conflict and Change at www.conflictandchange.co.uk.

Hate crimes mediation

11.21 Work in this field has been particularly successful at tackling racial harassment and homophobia in the community.[19] 'Hate crime' is distinguishable from anti-social behaviour as it involves the deliberate targeting of victims on the grounds of identity: age, race, faith, gender, sexual orientation or disability.

11.22 Hate crimes mediation involves a high degree of planning, preparation, and ongoing dialogue with the parties before a *joint meeting* is achieved. It aims to bring parties together successfully in a joint mediation but also uses shuttle mediation where parties decide not to meet or where the mediator decides this would not be appropriate. It requires a high-risk management assessment framework, and is likely to involve multi-agency partnership work and extended monitoring. Mediators undertaking this work use a transformative approach.

11.23 One example of this work is the Southwark Hate Crimes Project[20] which began in 2000 and, until its funding was withdrawn in 2011, worked with residents who had experienced spitting, egg-throwing, name-calling and violence. This project has been externally evaluated and shown that it has a high resolution rate and is successful in keeping recidivism rates low.[21]

11.24 Those who engage in hate crimes mediation use it to discover why they were targeted, to let those causing the harm know the impact of their actions, and to get guarantees from those causing the harm that incidents will stop. These are incidents which often get reported to the police but no identifiable crime has been committed, or are difficult to investigate due to a lack of evidence. Parties are also reluctant to see perpetrators prosecuted as they fear reprisals and further victimisation.

11.25 Hate crimes mediation works with adults, young people and children and is most effective when there are wider community programmes to raise awareness and increase understanding of race, culture and identity.

---

19 See, for example, work by CALM (Confidential and Local Mediation) at www.calmmediation.org; the Centre for Peaceful Solutions at www.centreforpeacefulsolutions.org; Specialist Mediation in Lancashire East (SMILE) at www.smilemediation.co.uk.

20 Using a model which was developed by Elena Noel (former manager of the Hates Crimes Project, Southwark Mediation).

21 M Walters and C Hoyle, *International review of victimology: exploring the everyday world of hate victimisation*, Sage, November 2011.

Gang mediation

11.26   Gang mediation is one of the newest forms of mediation in the UK. It was developed in Birmingham in response to shootings which occurred during the 1990s. Gang mediation is very high-risk mediation – working with young people who carry weapons and live by the code: *'kill or be killed'*. Its purpose is to save lives and reduce loss of life by helping young people reduce conflict and leave gangs safely.

11.27   Community gang mediators are reliant upon good information and intelligence to ensure their safety. The pace and dynamics of working with gangs is fast moving – it may involve work on the streets as well as communities to address community tensions and gang rivalry and reprisals, especially in the aftermath of an incident or death.

11.28   The principles of gang mediation remain the same as with all community mediation, using a co-mediation model and working towards a *joint meeting* between the main protagonists where a written agreement is reached. Mediators will also use family intervention work underpinned by a partnership approach, working with families, siblings, peers and professionals such as youth offending teams. Mediators may use shuttle or indirect mediation before parties are ready to meet in a *joint meeting*. They make a contract with participants about not having weapons present at a *joint meeting*. Conflict management and risk assessment plays a significant part in gang mediation and safety of all involved is paramount.[22] Mediators are insured and receive clinical supervision.

11.29   Gang mediation is primarily solution-focused. Many of the young people involved in gangs (and their families and peers) have experienced higher than average levels of bereavement. It is important that trust is built and the independence of the mediators established (to address the risk that mediators will be perceived as police informants). As with all mediation, the meetings remain confidential unless a threat to take someone's life or cause serious injury has been made.[23]

---

22   Any venues used have to be risk-assessed for the potential of ambush, and *joint meetings* require support staff as additional security. Well ahead of any *joint meetings*, the arrival and departure routes have to be planned and checked so that any potential risks are minimised for the participants and mediators.

23   In these circumstances, for reasons of safeguarding, it must be reported to the co-ordinator of the mediation service. Also see paras 12.60 and 12.64.

Conflict resolution training

11.30 Community mediation organisations work closely with their local communities and referral agencies. When issues arise, training programmes can be developed to help local people use mediation skills and techniques and conflict resolution strategies to address local disputes and communty concerns.

The community mediation process

How community mediation works

11.31 The community mediation process begins with a self-referral or a referral from a third-party agency or community group. Referral agencies include: housing departments, housing associations, environmental health officers, anti-social behaviour teams, social services, schools and the police. As a result, referral may be dependent on the view of an individual responding to issues arising from the dispute. In some cases the referral will be made at an early stage, in others only once parties are entrenched and emotions are running high (which makes the task of mediation more difficult).

11.32 Broadly speaking, the mediation can be divided into two parts: the pre-mediation and the *joint meeting*. These may take place on two separate days.[24] There are various models for community mediation – most use co-mediation as an approach. The co-mediators will spend time preparing together before meeting the parties.

Contacting the parties

11.33 Once the referral is made, both parties will be contacted by the mediation service. There is often a member of paid staff who arranges the mediation meetings and it is not unusual for community mediation coordinators or administrators to be trained mediators. They are well placed to explain the mediation process and help parties to find out more about mediation and discuss any individual issues or concerns. Community mediation is voluntary even where parties have been referred to a mediation service. Parties are not placed under any pressure to participate in mediation and there should be no consequences if they decide they do not wish to participate. Mediators must be independent and impartial of either party.

24 See para 11.45.

11.34   Mediators will explain to parties that all discussions that take place during the mediation process are confidential. It is for the parties to decide whether any mediation agreement reached should remain confidential or whether they wish a copy to be sent to their referrer. Any mediation agreement is entered into voluntarily.

11.35   The initial pre-mediation appointment is arranged even where a party expresses some reluctance.[25] The mediation provider will consider the most appropriate time and place for this meeting, and additional requirements such as an interpreter are usually funded by the mediation service, local authority, housing provider or referring body. Other needs can be assessed at this early stage, such as whether a disability needs to be accommodated or appropriate support can be identified for vulnerable parties.

11.36   It is important for everyone to speak for themselves, and moral support is sometimes needed for parties to have the confidence to do this. Parties are able to bring someone with them to the mediation, such as a friend or family member, who is described as a *supporter*. This person can also be a professional such as a mentor, support worker, GP or counsellor. Supporters don't take an active role and would not be invited to speak, but they can provide a particularly important role in community mediation and can offer support to parties during the mediation process.[26] Professionals can also attend as *experts*, to provide specific information that can inform the mediation process – for example, both parties may agree to a structural engineer being present to discuss sound insulation and transference.[27] Some community mediators will ask parties whether anyone else is affected by the conflict and invite them along.[28]

Screening

11.37   The initial contact with the parties on the telephone is an opportunity to assess whether the situation is appropriate for mediation. The referrer will be asked to provide the community mediation service with some background information, if statutory agencies have been involved, the mediation service may contact them for further information. The administrator will speak with each party and discuss the mediation process and whether they would be willing to meet the

---

25 See paras 11.39–11.40.
26 See para 3.89.
27 See para 3.88.
28 See para 11.47.

other party. The screening will include asking whether there have been any incidents in which they felt threatened or either party has been violent or aggressive. In such cases, the mediation provider would have to satisfy themselves that a *joint meeting* could take place safely without putting either party or the mediators at foreseeable risk.

11.38   If the administrator perceives that there are any risk factors, such as power imbalances, these are issues to be considered by the mediators during the *pre-mediation meeting*.

Case study 19: Putting a spring in your step

Rajeev had lived in the flat beneath his neighbour Sonali for four years. For the last three years he had gone to bed with ear-plugs. Sonali had two children and although Rajeev could hear the children playing this did not disturb him, however between about 3 and 5 am each morning there was the noise of furniture being scraped across the floor.

The parties were referred to mediation after Rajeev had made a number of complaints to the building manager and his housing officer. Sonali had received letters from the council warning that if she made unreasonable noise between 10 pm and 6 am then she could be in breach of her tenancy. At the pre-mediation meeting she was frightened she might lose her home. She also believed that the complaints were because her children were making too much noise.

At the joint mediation, Rajeev explained that he was not disturbed by the children and Sonali's relief was visible. Sonali was able to have an open and frank discussion which revealed that it was probably Sonali's bed that was making the noise because the frame and mattress were very old. Sonali could not afford a new bed but after the mediation she made arrangements to borrow a new bed from a relative. Rajeev and Sonali left the mediation chatting happily to each other. Several weeks later when the mediation service made their follow-up call, they learnt that after months of deep anxiety for both parties, a new mattress had cured the problem!

Pre-mediation meetings (first visit, home visits)

11.39   *Pre-mediation meetings* are separate meetings with each party. In neighbour disputes these meetings often take place in the parties' homes. The purpose of the meeting is for the mediators to listen, and to ensure they have a good understanding of the nature of the dispute. Mediators will explain the mediation process and aim to gain the trust of the parties who are given time to be listened to. At an appropriate stage, the mediators will discuss the possibility of a *joint meeting*. Mediators are alert to risk factors and will review whether a *joint meeting* would be suitable.

11.40   If one party has indicated a reluctance to mediate, mediators can provide information about the mediation process and address concerns which may lead the party to change their mind or be open to re-considering mediation at some time in the future. If a party does not wish to participate in a *joint meeting*, the mediators will encourage the party to think about how they could improve the situation in the future and consider what other options they have for resolving the dispute. When both parties agree to a *joint meeting*, it will be arranged with the same co-mediators. At the end of the *pre-mediation meeting*, the mediators will help prepare the party for the joint mediation meeting.

The joint meeting

11.41   The *joint meeting* will usually last two to three hours (and in some cases longer). It takes place at a neutral, local venue which may be at the mediation service, a local community centre or church hall. The timing of the meeting and location should be convenient and accessible to the parties.

11.42   The *joint meeting* is a chance for the parties to hear each other's point of view, and to work together on a resolution that they both find acceptable. It is a conversation facilitated by skilled co-mediators. The process follows the stages which are discussed in chapter 5.[29] It is likely to be more informal than mediation involving a civil or workplace dispute. It is even open to the mediators to attend the parties' homes in a dispute over noise, for example, and undertake a *sound observation* where the neighbours listen to the sounds as heard in each other's homes and to look for creative solutions, such as moving a washing machine or re-postioning a stereo.

29 See paras 5.10–5.63.

11.43   Towards the end of the meeting, the mediators record any agreements which may have been reached, as far as possible in the parties'
own words.[30] The mediators will also manage the parties' expectations so that parties anticipate that any changes which have been
agreed may take time.

Variations in the process

Visits only

11.44 Many community mediations do not reach a *joint meeting* – either
because the parties do not wish to meet together, or because it would
be considered unsafe. The process of mediators visiting parties can
still be powerful in encouraging them to see the other person's point
of view, providing the potential for reducing the cause of tensions
and the possibility of improved communication.

Combined process

11.45 In some instances, the entire community mediation process will take
place in one day at a neutral venue. These are described as a fast-
track[31] or all-in-one[32] mediations. This would involve, for example,
the *pre-mediation meetings* taking place in the morning and a *joint
meeting* in the afternoon. There are a number of advantages to this,
not least it increases the chances of parties attending the *joint meeting* as there are fewer barriers to this happening and the parties have
already invested a considerable amount of their time to the process.
The disadvantages are that the mediators do not visit the parties'
homes and there is less time for the parties to prepare for the *joint
meeting*, although some preparatory work will have been done on the
phone by the mediation administrator.

Shuttle mediation (indirect mediation)

11.46 In exceptional cases, a mediation provider may work with parties who
would like to use mediation but they are unable to be in the same
room as each other. If the parties consider that mediation could be
beneficial, a mediation could be arranged where the parties remain
in separate rooms and the mediator would move between them. Mediators would encourage parties to meet in one room for the opening
and uninterrupted speaking time before moving to separate rooms.

30 See paras 11.48–11.51 on the agreement.
31 See, for example, Confidential and Local Mediation (CALM) at www.
    calmmediation.org.
32 See, for example, Ealing Mediation Service at www.ealingmediation.org.uk.

This model may be appropriate where there have been threats of violence or racist abuse, but the parties are open to mediation.

Multiple parties

11.47   Some disputes involve a number of people or parties. Mediators will vary the process to respond to enable them to speak to parties separately and to meet together in one room. This may mean speaking with a representative from each group, or, the whole group. The *joint meeting* may require people to sit in a large circle. Alternatively, in a dispute where there is an issue affecting a number of people, and one perceived perpetrator, mediators may feel the power imbalance is too great, however, if resolution can be found it will be more effective if all affected parties are able to attend.

The agreement

11.48   Community mediation agreements are created by the parties. The agreement will usually be written down by one of the mediators,[33] as far as possible using the words spoken by the parties. Mediators need to be attentive throughout the process, to parties making suggestions or offers. When an offer is made, the mediators should make sure the other party has heard it and then write it down. Towards the end of the process, the mediators will encourage parties to think about an agreement and any offers will be discussed.

11.49   As the agreement is being written, the wording should be agreed with the parties. Once complete, it is checked by the parties who are usually invited to sign the agreement. Agreements must be balanced so that both parties make offers about their future conduct. Generally, mediators will try to frame the agreement in positive terms, for example: 'Stanley agrees only to play his music between 8am and 8pm; Frank agrees to speak to Stanley before contacting their housing officer or the police in future.' The agreement will be 'SMART': specific, measurable, achievable, realistic and time-limited.

11.50   Community mediation agreements, as with other fields of mediation, are future-focused. The mediators help the parties reach an agreement about the current problem – as well as try to help them agree on how they will communicate in future. Will it be face-to-face, by text, speaking through an intercom, leaving a message with a third party or posting a note through a letter-box? The simplicity of

---

33   When mediators prepare for the mediation, they will agree who will write the agreement – see para 6.20.

resolving ongoing communication issues means that parties have a strategy to address any future problems which may arise.

11.51 Community mediation agreements are made voluntarily, in good faith and are non-binding. The parties themselves are responsible for ensuring that the terms of the agreement are followed. The agreement, as well as whatever has been said during the mediation, remains confidential. If the parties agree, a copy of the agreement may be sent to the referrer, such as the housing officer. The agreement is non-binding so there is no power to enforce the agreement but experience shows that mediation agreements are self-enforcing, in other words, parties are more likely to keep to the agreement because they created it. Generally, there are high levels of compliance for self-generated agreements.[34]

Follow-up

11.52 The mediation provider will contact the parties in the weeks following the mediation, to find out how the agreement is working. The parties will also be asked to provide feedback and evaluation of the mediators' performance.

Peer feedback

11.53 At the conclusion of the mediation, it is good practice for co-mediators to give each other feedback. Mediators should give feedback sensitively and compassionately and the non-violent communication (NVC) model of communication[35] can be used if mediators wish to address an aspect of the mediation which could have been done differently. They should be honest, as all feedback enables a mediator to develop their skills.

How to give peer feedback

11.54 Usually co-mediators will take it in turns to give feedback using two questions:

- What worked well?
- What could have been done better or differently?

11.55 The mediator receiving the feedback can then discuss the strategies which they felt were effective and those which were less successful, and then discuss their *learning points*.

34 See paras 2.19–2.20.
35 See paras 4.35–4.37.

How to set up a community mediation

11.56   Parties can set up a community mediation by contacting their local provider or by asking their housing officer or a local agency to refer them. Community mediation can be provided by a:

- community mediation service or provider;
- independent mediation provider;
- independent mediator.

11.57   A community mediation service is a charitable or not-for-profit organisation that has specially trained mediators. Some are able to offer free mediation to anyone living within their borough or local area. Others can only offer a free service through a direct referral. Parties can usually locate a community mediation provider through their local council. Until 2006, an organisation called Mediation UK acted as an umbrella body for over 120 community mediation organisations.[36] Since then, there is no national body representing community mediation.[37]

11.58   An independent mediation provider is usually a commercial business offering mediation and dispute resolution services, some have mediators who have specialist training and expertise in community mediation.

11.59   An independent mediator may have particular knowledge or expertise of issues relevant to the particular dispute such as 'hate crime' or anti-social behaviour.

Fees and funding

11.60   Most community mediation is provided free of charge to users and is funded by referral agencies or grants. In cases where the mediation will be self-funded, community mediation providers may offer a discounted rate.[38] Some mediators may be willing to work for free (pro bono).[39] Parties should explore free or low-cost mediation schemes.[40] Legal aid may be available in certain situations where legal proceedings are contemplated or legal obligations are involved, such as a

---

36   In October 2006, Mediation UK went into voluntary liquidation.
37   For a list of community mediation providers, see appendix A.
38   See, for example, Wandsworth Mediation Service at www. wandsworthmediation.co.uk.
39   See, for example, LawWorks at www.lawworks.org.uk.
40   See paras 8.10–8.33.

young person leaving home or where a person is at risk of losing their home.

When to mediate

11.61 The best time to mediate is in the early stages of a conflict when both parties have indicated a willingness to try and sort things out. Many parties are unaware that mediation is available and the challenge for community mediation is to raise its profile to ensure all those who could benefit are given the opportunity. Once a suggestion or proposal is put forward by a referral agency – such as a landlord, police officer or adviser – parties can make the decision whether to mediate. Parties may have questions or concerns which the mediation provider can address in an initial telephone call, allaying fears and encouraging parties to feel confidence in the process.

11.62 Referral agencies are encouraged to refer parties at an early stage, however the issues are only likely to be raised with a third party once relations have deteriorated and at least one of the parties has sought help or assistance. Community mediation providers who are able to promote their services direct to their clients are likely to be more effective in helping parties and avoiding an escalation of an argument or disagreement. Housing officers and other referrers should continue to be encouraged to refer cases at an early stage.

And when not to mediate

11.63 Mediation may not be suitable if there are issues of drug and alcohol abuse or mental health which would prevent one party actively participating in the process. Referrals are assessed on a case-by-case basis. If either party has used physical violence or made threats of violence, or where a party has used racial or homophobic abuse, the mediation service will consider carefully whether mediation would be appropriate. There are some situations where alternative forms of dispute resolution – such as legal proceedings or a formal complaints process – may be discussed. If one party is using mediation to seek to avoid a statutory duty or legal obligation, such as a landlord, then mediation is unlikely to be appropriate. Equally, mediation may not be suitable where the underlying issues involve the responsibilities of a third party, although it is open to the parties or the mediation provider to engage them in the process.

Wider uses of community mediation

Peer mediation

11.64   Peer mediation projects work with children and young people within schools, their local community and young offender institutions. They train young people as peer mediators who are able to use their mediation skills to resolve their own conflicts as well as help their friends and peers resolve disputes. They introduce young people to 'peaceful and creative ways of dealing with conflict among their peers and in their own lives'.[41]

11.65   Peer mediation is effective because young people are able to resolve disputes without involving staff or teachers and therefore reducing resources devoted to this by schools, the police and local authorities. It is used to address bullying, violence and racism in schools, and in work with young people involved in gangs and knife crime.[42] Peer mediators gain valuable skills, they develop their communication skills as well as a greater understanding of co-operation and empathy. Peer mediation aims to reduce conflict and violence in young people's lives and promotes a wider social agenda of living in a more cooperative and peaceful society.

11.66   There are a large number of organisations running peer mediation projects in the UK. In 2000, Leap[43] set up the country's first national network of young mediators, the Young Mediators Network (YMN), and in 2006 established the PeerLink project to promote and support peer mediation. The Peer Mediation Network (PMN)[44] brings together conflict resolution practitioners and others committed to promoting peer mediation in schools and the wider community. LawWorks,[45] a national charity offering free civil mediation, has established a programme 'Talking Works in Schools'[46] which uses professional mediators to deliver mediation skills training in schools.

---

41   See www.peermediationnetwork.org.uk.
42   See, for example, www.nspcc.org.uk/inform/publications/downloads/peermediationintheuk_wdf48055.pdf.
43   See www.leapconfrontingconflict.org.uk.
44   See www.peermediationnetwork.org.uk.
45   See www.lawworks.org.uk.
46   See www.twis.org.uk.

Case study 20: Peer mediation – from failing school to peace leader

South Leeds High School was the result of a merger between a predominantly Asian School and a predominantly White school in an area which had been the home of one the 7/7 bombers. The 2005 terrorist attacks had left the community polarised and seen a dramatic increase in violence and racism. The BNP were highly active in the area, and were trying to engage and influence students including leafleting students as they were leaving school. A number of local agencies had tried to intervene at the school.

A Peer Leadership model was introduced in the school. Over the course of three years, the Foundation for Peace worked with 198 young people from across the school year groups and trained staff from the school and wider school support agencies. Training for staff and young people included talking about identity, prejudice and discrimination and exploring alternative approaches to managing conflict that arose in the school, particularly in relation to race and faith. Peer leaders were instrumental in leading focus groups exploring issues of racism and conflict within school; supporting their peers in cohesion projects; mediating between peers and delivering education sessions exploring those issues that threatened to cause negative conflict in their school including race and religion. In addition, projects were undertaken in feeder primary schools to promote the values and attitudes that the school wished to promote to younger pupils preparing to start at the school. Pupil led events included pupil take over days promoting anti-racism and community cohesion. This enabled the school and wider community to increase their capacity and responses to external and internal threats to cohesion; as well as to ensure that responses to those threats were consistent and impactful.

A follow up evaluation with the school found that 'alternative dispute resolution' techniques including mediation had been incorporated into school policy and were being practiced by staff and delivered by young people when conflict occurred. This was enabling disputants to find meaningful and effective solutions to their conflicts and therefore impacting positively on levels of cohesion within school.[47]

47 Case study provided by The Tim Parry Jonathan Ball Foundation for Peace – www.foundation4peace.org/. The Foundation for Peace works with those affected by political, racial or faith based conflict and helps to prevent violence in their own communities and beyond through peace and reconciliation.

Restorative justice

What is restorative justice?

> Restorative processes bring those harmed by crime or conflict, and those responsible for the harm, into communication, enabling everyone affected by a particular incident to play a part in repairing the harm and finding a positive way forward.[48]

11.67 Restorative justice conferences involve victims and offenders meeting together, where victims get the chance to tell offenders about the real impact of their crime (also described as *victim–offender mediation*). Restorative processes are well-established in the criminal justice system and are increasingly being used in schools, care homes and the wider community to address conflict, build understanding and strengthen relationships with young people.

Restorative justice in the criminal justice system

11.68 Restorative justice has been proven to reduce re-offending, provide high victim satisfaction and offer value for money.[49] Government research into victim–offender mediation shows a reduction in the frequency of re-offending of 27 per cent and for every £1 spent on restorative justice, £9 of savings are made.[50] Restorative practices are used to improve dialogue between communities and the police, described as *restorative policing*.[51] Police can divert cases out of the criminal justice system using *community conferences* and *conditional cautions*.[52] Courts can sentence offenders to reparation orders as part of their community sentence. Important restorative justice work is also undertaken in prisons. The government is exploring ways to develop provision of restorative justice for victims of crime.[53]

48 Restorative Justice Council at www.restorativejustice.org.uk.

49 J Shapland, G Robinson and A Sorsby, *Restorative justice in practice*, Routledge, 2011. Also see M Wright, *Towards a Restorative Society: a problem-solving response to harm*, Make Justice Work, April 2010.

50 J Shapland and others, *Restorative justice: does restorative justice affect reconviction*, Ministry of Justice Research (MOJ) Series 10/08, 2008, Fourth Report.

51 See www.restorativejustice.org.uk/what_is_restorative_justice/in_criminal_justice/restorative_policing/.

52 See www.cps.gov.uk/legal/p_to_r/restorative_justice/.

53 Ministry of Justice consultation, Getting it right for victims and witnesses, 30 January 2012 – www.justice.gov.uk/consultations.

11.69　　Restorative practices are increasingly being used within youth offending teams (YOTs),[54] local authorities and by the police. Youth conferencing or family group conferencing[55] is where victim–offender mediation is followed by the offender's family having private time to come up with a plan for reparation and for the future. Referral orders are available for young people who plead guilty to offences and are overseen by youth offender panels using restorative practices including victim–offender mediation and have been shown to have a lower re-conviction rate than other disposals.[56]

Restorative justice in schools

11.70　A restorative approach in schools can help to address specific incidents of conflict involving students, staff and parents and can help strengthen the school community and reduce the need to exclude children. A two-year Restorative Justice pilot in Hull led to 73 per cent fewer classroom exclusions, 81 per cent fewer fixed term exclusion days, a reduction in verbal abuse between pupils and verbal abuse towards staff of over 70 per cent.[57]

11.71　　Restorative justice in schools uses a range of processes including conflict resolution skills, circle time, peer mentoring, school councils, peer mediation and restorative conferencing. This may require a 'whole-school approach'[58] to ensure its whole policy reflects a shared commitment to the values and principles of restorative justice.[59]

Neighbourhood resolution panels

11.72　This is a form of restorative justice where the victim and offender meet, facilitated by a community volunteer in cases when an offender has admitted responsibility for an offence which is not sufficiently serious to justify a prosecution and both they and the victim consent. Community justice panels already exist, for example, in South Somerset, Sheffield and Manchester. The government is exploring

---

54　See, for example, the work of youth offending teams in Bristol, Cardiff, Ceredigion, Hull, Kent, Norfolk, Oxfordshire, Salford, Surrey, Walsall and Wigan.

55　See para 11.75.

56　*Criminal Justice and Immigration Bill Regulatory Impact Assessments*, MOJ, June 2007 p41.

57　www.restorativejustice.org.uk/what_is_restorative_justice/in_criminal_justice/with_youngpeople.

58　See, for example, B Hopkins, *Just schools: a whole school approach to restorative justice*, Jessica Kingsley Publishers, 2003.

59　M Liebmann, *Restorative justice*, Jessica Kingsley Publishers, 2007 p118.

the possibility of establishing neighbourhood resolution panels nationally.[60] There are a number of issues including the lack of government funding, the interrelationship between a community-run programme and the criminal justice system and the extent to which non-criminal civil disputes could be resolved in this way.

Family mediation

11.73   Family mediation, as discussed in chapter 9, describes family mediation processes concerned with separating couples and divorce. It runs alongside the family court system and exists within a legal framework, supporting separating couples to resolve the issues concerning finances, property and children. In addition to this more formal process, there are other areas where mediation can help support families.

Intergenerational family mediation

11.74   Intergenerational family mediation addresses conflicts and disagreements which arise within families and if left unresolved may lead to civil legal proceedings or family members left without a support network and in some cases homeless. Community mediation providers may offer intergenerational family mediation to address conflicts faced by their local community which commonly arise when there are inter-generational clashes of lifestyle. Teenagers leaving home,[61] living with in-laws or extended family, girls becoming pregnant, decisions about the care of an elderly relative are all issues which can benefit from improving communication and restoring relationships so that parties are able to make informed choices and joint decisions.

Family group conferences

11.75   Local authorities offer family group conferences (FGCs) as an alternative to issuing care or child protection proceedings.[62] They can also be used for young people who have problems such as truanting or as an alternative to a criminal prosecution.[63] The process begins with a meeting where professionals explain their concerns to the family and the resources available. This is followed by private family time,

60   Testing neighbourhood resolution panels: a specification to inform expressions of interest, MOJ, 29 July 2011.
61   See paras 11.16–11.18.
62   See para 9.74.
63   See para 11.69.

where the family meet on their own to develop a plan that addresses the concerns that have been raised. The plan is then presented to the professionals who should support it if their concerns are met and it does not put the child at risk. The meetings are facilitated by independent, third parties.

The future

11.76 The scope of community mediation and its measurable benefits are proven. It could be envisaged that every borough would have a community mediation service that provides mediation free of charge for a range of disputes. Making community mediation freely available could substantially reduce public expenditure on local policing, environmental health teams, social workers and housing officials and reduce civil claims and criminal prosecutions. The challenge is persuading local and national governments to invest in the long-term futures of their communities. There is also a need for accrediting, monitoring and standard setting in the community mediation field. Without a national voice for community mediation in the UK and in financially austere times, this is not without its challenges.

11.77 Real differences could be introduced by small changes. Information about resolving issues between neighbours using mediation could appear in tenants' manuals. Housing officers and environmental health officers could have more training on when to refer cases to mediation. Since the first mediation organisation began in the UK in 1985, community mediation has come a long way. There are currently 60 or more community mediation organisations and many more using mediation.

Frequently asked questions answered by Elena Noel

11.78 The following questions have been answered by Elena Noel. Elena is a leading restorative justice practitioner and mediator in hate crime. She has been a practitioner for over 15 years and is a consultant advising government on tackling hate crime and community conflict. She is the founder of Empowering People for Excellence.[64]

---

64 Empowering People for Excellence, Liberty House, 9–11 Cottage Green, London SE5 7ST.

What is a successful community mediation?

One where the parties, however sceptical, come with an open mind and a willingness to hear another account (that they may disagree with) but are willing to participate, get their needs met and let those causing them harm learn about their impact. Where parties are able to explore hurtful, uncomfortable and embarrassing elements of the conflict and experience optimism that change is possible. When the parties tell me at the end of the *joint meeting* how successful the mediation was and they could not have conceived the outcomes reached when they entered the room at the beginning of the meeting. Especially when they shake hands and are smiling at the end.

Mediations which increase participant's awareness of themselves and others and leads to a sustainable change of behaviour and attitude. When after six months to a year of post mediation monitoring, there are no further incidents and those who experience harm are living free from fear, are empowered and see the community as a place where they belong.

How professional is a volunteer mediator?

I have managed and supervised volunteers for over ten years and in my experience volunteer mediators are very professional. Much still depends on the professionalism of service to which the mediator volunteer belongs and the policies and practice of the organisation, as well as the mediator's commitment to their own learning and development. Key to this is regular formal supervision, informal support, guidance and mandatory Continuing Professional Development training. Recently trained mediators should, for example, co-mediate with more experienced mediators. It is important that mediation services 'invest' in their volunteer mediators in order to attain highest mediator competence by providing quality volunteering opportunities.

Mediation organisations need to be 'fit for purpose'. Mediation work is not only about home visits and joint meetings – much of it is about administration, reports, record-keeping, processing data accurately, maintaining confidentiality and building good agency partnership work and relationships with funders and stakeholders. Unprofessional conduct by paid staff or volunteers undermines or prevents this from occurring.

How could the principles of community mediation be extended more broadly?

More work needs to done in schools that will prevent gangs and help young people and adults to manage conflict more positively. All young people should be trained in mediation as a tool and skill for life, as part of their self-development and a strategy for managing conflict.

The government and criminal justice agencies need to look at how disaffected communities can be included and heard to build positive communities for the future. Successful community mediation provides important data which can inform future policy as well illustrate its cost benefits. Embracing the principles of community mediation should be strategically developed alongside more traditional approaches to offending behaviour and crime.

PART IV

Professional standards

CHAPTER 12

Training, accreditation and ethics

continued

Key points

- Mediation accreditation and training varies across the different specialist areas – civil, family, workplace and community.
- There are a large number of trained mediators in the UK.
- Although there is no formal regulatory body setting universal requirements for the training of mediators, there are common standards of good practice.
- The Civil Mediation Council (CMC) accredit civil mediation providers and set standards for the training and supervision of individual civil mediators.
- Family mediators are accredited by the member organisations of the Family Mediation Council (FMC).
- There is a voluntary registration scheme for workplace mediators, overseen by the CMC.
- Community mediation organisations usually provide in-house training which rely on external assessment such as the Open College Network (OCN).
- Ethical considerations which arise during mediation include: conflicts of interest, when to terminate a mediation and when a mediators has a duty to disclose confidential information.

Mediators' training and qualifications

12.1   Mediation training and accreditation has emerged at different rates in the areas of family, community, civil and workplace mediation in the UK. Of the different areas, family mediation has the most established accreditation scheme. At present, for all other areas of mediation, there is no national accreditation or regulation of individual mediators. There are a number of commonly agreed minimum standards, and increasingly there is a shift towards greater quality assurance and regulation.

Training to be a mediator

12.2   There are a large number of 'would be' mediators in the UK. It is a marketplace where the number of mediators is disproportionate to the quantity of mediations. People wishing to train as a mediator should be cautious to invest large sums of money on a training course, unless they can be sure of getting the opportunity to observe mediations and build an established practice. The length of time it takes to qualify as a mediator should also be measured. In family mediation the accreditation requirements are likely to take most trainee mediators up to two years. In other fields, even once the training is complete, trainee mediators are required to observe mediations. It can be a real challenge to complete the observerships and then get exposure to work as a mediator, unless a trainee has a niche specialism or expertise.

12.3   The largest of the training providers for civil mediation are the Centre for Effective Dispute Resolution (CEDR),[1] ADR Group,[2] the Academy of Experts,[3] the Chartered Institute of Arbitrators (CIArb)[4] and the School of Psychotherapy and Counselling Psychology (SPCP) at Regent's College London. The International Mediation Institute (IMI)[5] also offers mediator certification to mediators worldwide.

12.4   In family mediation, the national training providers are the ADR Group, National Family Mediation (NFM),[6] Resolution[7] and the Family Mediators Association (FMA),[8] while the College of Mediators[9] approve Family Mediation Council (FMC) recognised training.

12.5   In workplace mediation, the established training providers are the Advisory, Conciliation and Arbitration Service (ACAS), CEDR, the TCM Group[10] and Globis,[11] although this is an emerging field. Community mediation services provide in-house training for their volunteer mediators.

Common standards

12.6   Accredited mediators undertake ongoing training and ensure that their practice includes opportunities for supervision, mentoring, peer review and self-development. In the absence of regulation, and in some areas of the profession a lack of individual accreditation, the

1   See www.cedr.com.
2   See www.adrgroup.co.uk.
3   See www.academy-experts.org.
4   See www.ciarb.org.
5   See http://imimediation.org.
6   See www.nfm.org.uk.
7   See www.resolution.org.uk.
8   See www.thefma.co.uk.
9   See www.collegeofmediators.co.uk.
10 See www.thetcmgroup.com.
11 See www.globis.co.uk.

following areas of good practice should be common to all mediators and mediation providers.

Code of conduct

12.7 A code of conduct provides guidance to the profession on ethical issues, and sets out a framework for issues which arise during the mediation process. There are two commonly agreed standards:

a) EU Code of Conduct for Mediators 2004 (see appendix H);

b) FMC Code of Practice (see appendix I).

Competence

12.8 All mediators should undertake a foundation training which includes an external assessment process combined with ongoing mentoring and supervision which is designed to ensure all accredited mediators are competent mediators. This will include evaluation of practical skills as well as assessing competency through written work. Mediators should have sufficient experience, such as observing mediations and conducting supervised mediations, before mediating without supervision.

Supervision

12.9 A process of continuing assessment and appraisal should be overseen by either the mediation provider or an individual supervisor. Supervision requirements or other mechanisms should measure an existing practitioner's skills and ability and provide guidance on training and self development. This is all the more important in a profession which is not open to public scrutiny, the confidential nature of mediation means that only the participants are able to assess the competence of a mediator.

Training and skill development

12.10 As a mediator's skills and abilities will always be evolving. A mediator will undertake ongoing training and professional development, also described as continuing professional development (CPD) by writing articles and presenting papers, as well as attending training events, lectures, seminars, discussions and conferences.[12]

---

12 For CPD requirements in family mediation, see para 12.40.

Self-reflective practices

12.11   Self-reflective practices enable a mediator to build on their experience and develop and improve the way they mediate. A mediator should be conscious of themselves and their presence during a mediation. Mediators who are self-aware are able to acknowledge their biases and prejudices which means they are better equipped to remain impartial.

12.12   Self-reflective practices include:

- peer feedback or peer review;
- keeping a reflective journal;
- completing a self appraisal of mediations;
- sharing and learning groups (mediators meet to share experience and practice).

Peer review

12.13   Having opportunities to debrief and reflect on what took place during a mediation enables mediators to increase their self-awareness, ability to maintain their neutrality and ability to act in a non-judgmental way. When mediators have been co-mediating or acting as a lead or assistant mediator, time should be set aside to give feedback to each other. This should be done in a structured and supportive way.[13] Supervisors and observers can also give feedback, although this should be discussed before the mediation and feedback should be provided in a structured way.

Record-keeping

12.14   The confidential and privileged nature of mediation means that mediators are not required to keep their notes or paperwork once a mediation has concluded.[14] It remains good practice for the mediation provider to keep a record of the parties (including contact details – and this may include details of the communication between the mediation provider and parties before the mediation), the date, venue, time started and closed, a copy of any *agreement to mediate* and a brief note of the dispute and outcome.

12.15   In family mediation, those who hold contracts to provide publicly funded work have to meet LSC Quality Mark standards which are quite stringent for record-keeping.

13 See para 11.53–11.55.
14 See paras 7.31–7.32.

Complaints and feedback

12.16 All mediators should have a formal complaints process which is clearly set out in their paperwork and on their website. The complaint may be with regards to the mediator, or the mediation provider.

12.17 All mediators and mediation providers should have a method for parties to provide feedback on the process. Feedback enables a mediation provider or prospective party to appraise the skills and abilities of the mediator.

Areas of mediation

Civil mediation

Generally

12.18 The national administrating body for civil and commercial mediators is the Civil Mediation Council (CMC). Established in 2003, the CMC aims to ensure high standards in the delivery of mediation and promote its use. The CMC accredit 'mediation providers' and set the standard for the training requirements of individual civil and commercial mediators working within a provider's panel.

12.19 There are a number of alternative accreditation schemes for civil mediators, including the Law Society Civil and Commercial Mediation Accreditation Scheme.[15]

12.20 It is anticipated that self-regulation and increased quality assurance will emerge in the light of recent government proposals to increase the use of mediation in civil disputes.[16]

The Ministry of Justice will continue to work with the Civil Mediation Council (CMC) to make the accreditation process for mediation providers more robust, together with possible measures to enable individual mediators to also be accredited by the CMC, or another body.

12.21 The EU Mediation Directive[17] places an emphasis on parties having mutual trust in the process of mediation through 'ensuring the quality of mediation' and encourages 'the training of mediators and the introduction of effective quality control mechanisms concerning the

---

15 See www.lawsociety.org.uk. Also see the Law Society of Scotland's Accredited Commercial Mediators Scheme – www.lawscot.org.uk.

16 *Solving disputes in the county courts: creating a quicker, simpler and more proportionate system: the government response* February 2012 para 28.

17 See appendix G.

provision of mediation services'[18] and the development of voluntary codes of conducts:

Article 4
Ensuring the quality of mediation
1. Member States shall encourage, by any means which they consider appropriate, the development of, and adherence to, voluntary codes of conduct by mediators and organisations providing mediation services, as well as other effective quality control mechanisms concerning the provision of mediation services.
2. Member States shall encourage the initial and further training of mediators in order to ensure that the mediation is conducted in an effective, impartial and competent way in relation to the parties. [19]

CMC accreditation of civil mediation

12.22   The CMC oversee the accreditation of mediation providers who must have a panel at least six civil or commercial mediators who meet the CMC accreditation requirements. The government's Civil Mediation Online Directory[20] (formerly the National Mediation Helpline), launched in October 2011, requires all mediation providers to be CMC-accredited.

Accreditation of mediation providers

12.23   The CMC set minimum requirements of accredited civil mediation providers:
- mediator panel of at least six suitably qualified mediators with adequate mediator training;[21]
- code of conduct;[22]
- complaints procedure;[23]
- supervision and mentoring;
- insurance;
- efficient administration;
- allocation of mediators.

12.24   Applications for accreditation are considered annually.

18 EU Mediation Directive, recital (16).
19 EU Mediation Directive article 4.
20 See www.civilmediation.justice.gov.uk.
21 See para 12.25.
22 Consistent with the standards set by the EU Code of Conduct for Mediators 2004 – see appendix H.
23 If not satisfactorily resolved, parties may be able to use the CMC's Complaints Resolution Service which enables the dispute to be mediated by an experienced mediator and is provided free for members.

Panel mediators

12.25   CMC-accredited mediation providers are required to ensure that their civil mediators:[24]

a) have completed an accredited civil mediation training course;[25]
b) adhere to the EU Code of Conduct (and any additional code of conduct instituted by the provider organisation);
c) are provided with adequate and appropriate supervision (including mentoring and monitoring) and peer working (such as observerships and peer review);
d) undertake CPD;[26]
e) adhere to a clear complaints procedure;
f) hold relevant insurance.

Supervision and monitoring

12.26   The CMC require accredited providers to offer panel members adequate and appropriate supervision. Mediators should have a 'mentor' or a more experienced mediator to enable mediators to consult a senior practitioner before, during and after their mediation.[27] Supervision should include monitoring, although no guidance is given as to how this should be carried out.

12.27   Mediation providers should give panel mediators the opportunity for peer working. This may include observerships as well as opportunities for peer review.[28]

Accreditation of independent mediators

12.28   The CMC does not accredit individual mediators. The CMC offers individual membership but makes it clear this is not a 'quality mark' or an accreditation process. The CMC promotes professional mediation practice and individual mediators have to demonstrate they have completed a mediation training course conforming to the CMC training requirements (at the time the training was undertaken).

Article 2.4 of the CMC Constitution
... a 'Mediator' is defined as an individual who conducts a professional mediation practice in England and Wales, whether solely or in

24 CMC Provider Accreditation Scheme, as revised and approved by the Board on 11 January 2012.
25 See para 12.30.
26 See para 12.31.
27 CMC Provider Accreditation Scheme, January 2012, paras 7(d) and 8E(3).
28 See para 12.13.

conjunction with other business or professional pursuits, and who is qualified in accordance with such standards as to training accreditation or otherwise as the Board may publish from time to time.

The Eligibility Standards for Individual Membership
A mediator will comply with the Board's requirements under paragraph 2.4 of the Constitution if he or she shows either that they (a) have been accredited by and currently hold accreditation from an Accredited Mediation Provider or (b) have completed and passed a mediation training course conforming to the training requirements required by the Council to be applied by Accredited Mediation Providers to their panel members (or which would have conformed at the time to such requirements as were then current).[29]

12.29   This means that CMC membership does not provide any assurance of ongoing training or good practice. In other words, CMC members who are independent mediators (and not a member of an accredited mediation provider panel) have no requirement to undertake ongoing professional development or training. Equally, there are no preconditions for mediation providers who wish to join the CMC (accreditation of mediation providers is a separate process).[30]

Qualification requirements

12.30   The CMC set out the minimum standards for all newly qualifying mediators who form part of an accredited mediation providers panel. Training courses must meet the following standards:[31]

- A minimum of 40 hours training with face-to-face tuition and role-play (excluding breaks), followed by a formal assessment. The training should include not less than 20 hours of role-play, of which ten hours should be supervised.[32]
- Formal assessment by an accredited mediator separate to those delivering the training.[33]
- Course will include: ethics, mediation theory, mediation practice, negotiation, role play, basic contract law (for non-lawyers).

---

29   Eligibility Standards for Individual Membership, passed by the Board on 5 January 2011 pursuant to article 2.4 of the CMC Constitution.
30   See paras 12.23–12.27.
31   CMC Provider Accreditation Scheme, January 2012, para 8(B).
32   The training should not exceed 40 delegates.
33   The assessment phase should include one continual assessment of a minimum one hour, and at least two assessments carried out on separate days.

- Assessment criteria will include that:
  - an appropriate and safe environment is set by the participant-mediator which is conductive (sic) to problem-solving;
  - the role of mediator is fully and properly articulated;
  - the principles of confidentiality, neutrality and facilitation is evidenced;
  - trust and rapport is established;
  - necessary skills to explore issues, interests and options are applied;
  - the ability to manage the parties and the process is clear;
  - the ability to advance resolution through the application of negotiation and communication skills is seen;
  - proper consideration of ethical issues as they arise is given.

Continuing professional development

12.31 The annual training requirements for mediators on a CMC-accredited mediation provider's panel are:[34]

- to have observed or conducted at least two civil or commercial mediations, one of which may be a role play. Newly qualified mediators must observe at least three mediations in the first 12 months to become eligible for appointment as a lead mediator;[35]
- to have undertaken at least six hours of mediation-specific training/CPD.[36] These hours may include:
  - courses offering practical role-plays;
  - attendance at seminars, conferences, tutorials and debates on mediation;
  - writing articles on mediation;
  - presenting mediation training, seminars or similar events;
- to have insurance of not less than £1,000,000 (or as high as the value of the claim being mediated).

---

34 CMC Provider Accreditation Scheme, January 2012, paras 8E and 8F.
35 Where a panel mediator is on maternity leave or long-term sick leave, this period may be extended to 18 months.
36 At present there is no accreditation of training courses or seminars.

Publicly funded work

12.32 The Legal Services Commission (LSC) requires civil mediators to be on a CMC-accredited mediation provider panel, or have appropriate training and expertise.[37]

Family mediation

Generally

12.33 Family mediation is self-regulated and the training and accreditation process is the most rigorous of all the fields of mediation. The Family Mediation Council (FMC) acts to oversee family mediators. It was established in 2007 with the aim of harmonising standards, promoting best practice, raising public awareness and access to mediation services. The FMC works closely with the Ministry of Justice (*MOJ*) and the LSC. The LSC has done much to develop protocols and good practice. The LSC Quality Mark Standard[38] and funding code provide guidance and minimum standards for publicly funded work. This sets a high benchmark for standards in family mediation.

12.34   The FMC is formed of six member organisations:
- National Family Mediation (NFM);
- The Family Mediators Association (FMA);
- Resolution;
- ADR Group;
- The Law Society;
- College of Mediators.

FMC accreditation

12.35 The founder organisations of the FMC keep a register of all family mediators who have attained the relevant levels of training and accreditation, and NFM administer the competence assessment scheme (on behalf of the FMC).

12.36   The FMC member organisations regulate their individual memberships[39] ensuring that their family mediators:[40]

a) have successfully completed an FMC-recognised family mediator foundation training;

---

37 Funding Code: Decision Making Guidance (LSC) Part C 3C-101, 7.6 1.
38 2nd edn, September 2009.
39 Members must all adhere to the FMC Code of Practice – see appendix I.
40 FMC Code of Practice para 3.

b) adhere to the FMC Code of Practice;

c) have successfully demonstrated personal aptitude for mediation and competence to mediate;

d) agree to maintain and improve their skills through FMC-accredited CPD;

e) receive FMC-recognised supervision from a professional practice consultant (PPC);

f) mediators may only undertake direct consultation with children when they have had two years' experience, successfully completed specific training and have received specific clearance from the Criminal Records Bureau (an enhanced CRB check);

g) adhere to a clear complaints procedure;

h) hold relevant professional indemnity insurance;

i) undertake additional specialist training where required;

j) have effective equal opportunities policies.

Professional Practice Consultancy

12.37　Every practising family mediator is supervised by a qualified PPC.[41] PPCs provide supervision for a minimum of four hours per year, and provide supervision for trainee mediators until they have successfully completed their competence assessment.[42]

Competence assessment

12.38　Once family mediators have completed their foundation training, there are three levels of FMC competence. Mediators can be assessed as competent to undertake (a) MIAMs;[43] (b) privately-funded work (this is described as 'readiness to practice');[44] and (c) publicly-funded work.

12.39　Family mediators wishing to undertake publicly-funded work must successfully complete the FMC Assessment of Professional Competence (APC) scheme[45] (or have practitioner membership of

---

41　FMC Constitution para 5.4.

42　PPCs receive training and are required to be registered with an FMC member organisation.

43　'Agreed Minimum Requirements for Mediators Carrying Out Information and Assessment Meetings' (February 2011) – www.familymediationcouncil.org. uk/resources/agreed+MIAMs+requmnts+0211.pdf.

44　New mediators who are assessed by the PPC as being competent, this means they are able to take the lead on publicly-funded cases (with support from an experienced mediator who has successfully completed the APC scheme).

45　www.familymediationcouncil.org.uk/resources/APC+spec+final+040412.pdf.

the Law Society Family Mediation Panel[46]). The APC scheme takes as long as two years to complete and requires candidates to complete at least three mediation cases[47] for their portfolio under the supervision of their PPC.

Continuing professional development

12.40   Family mediators must gain ten CPD points per year to ensure that their skills and training are up-to-date. Five points must be FMC-approved training events (category A) and the other half may include attending meetings, presenting case files or self-directed learning eg reading (category B).

Publicly funded work

12.41   The LSC requires family mediators to be members of a FMC member organisation and to have successfully completed an LSC-approved competence assessment to be eligible to undertake publicly funded mediation.[48] There are set criteria to enable less experienced mediators who have not completed their full accreditation to be approved by their PPC to undertake MIAMs.[49]

Workplace mediation

Generally

12.42   In 2009, the CMC set up a voluntary registration scheme of workplace mediation organisations. The purpose is that ACAS and other organisations concerned with workplace matters will be encouraged to use CMC Registered Workplace Organisations.

12.43   In the light of the recommendations from the Department for Business Innovation and Skills (BIS),[50] it is likely that the CMC, working in partnership with organisations such as ACAS and the Chartered Institute of Personnel and Development (CIPD), will develop a more formal accreditation process.

---

46   See www.lawsociety.org.uk.
47   These are fully completed mediations rather than observed mediations, intake sessions or MIAMs.
48   See para 12.39.
49   See para 12.38.
50   *Resolving workplace disputes: government response to the consultation*, BIS, November 2011.

Registration requirements

12.44 The 'CMC Registered' scheme requires the organisation to agree to information about the workplace organisation to be displayed on the CMC Registered Workplace Organisation Pilot Scheme's website.

12.45 A CMC Registered Workplace Mediation Organisation must have:[51]

a) a minimum of two 'workplace mediators';

b) a minimum of £1,000,000 professional indemnity insurance for the organisation, or other appropriate arrangements for public bodies;

c) a code of conduct;[52]

d) an internal complaints procedure;

e) a panel of mediators who have completed a minimum of 24 hours' training together with a successful assessment and who the organisation requires to undertake a minimum of six hours' workplace mediation-specific CPD annually;

f) a formal commitment to diversity and anti-discrimination.

Community mediation

12.46 Until 2006, an organisation called Mediation UK acted as an umbrella body for over 120 community mediation organisations and had developed a mediator accreditation process for community mediation including an LSC Quality Mark.[53] Accreditation was based on observed practice, feedback from co-mediators and service managers, and a written portfolio based on mediations carried out.

12.47 Based on this accreditation model, the College of Mediators[54] has continued to offer 'approved mediator' status[55] for community mediators. Most providers, however, oversee the training and supervision of their mediators themselves. Often using the OCN (Open College Network) framework to provide independent qualification and external assessment. The candidates' practical skills are assessed and a proportion of the assessment is based upon written work. While there is a great deal of good practice, at present there is no national requirement for accreditation or competency of community mediators. The LSC Quality Mark for community mediation providers was

---

51 CMC Registered Workplace Mediation Organisation Pilot Scheme 2009.

52 Consistent with the standards set by the EU Code of Conduct for Mediators 2004 – see appendix H.

53 In October 2006, Mediation UK went into voluntary liquidation.

54 See www.collegeofmediators.co.uk.

55 Formerly 'recognised mediator' status.

subsequently withdrawn and is no longer used. As a result there is no common benchmark to offer guidance and provide quality assurance for users of community mediation.

12.48   Community mediation providers promote competency and CPD by encouraging their mediators to attend training events and conferences. Additional training may include mediation skills and theory, diversity and equality training, drug awareness and anti-social behaviour.

Scotland and Northern Ireland

Scotland

12.49   The Scottish Mediation Network (SMN) has practice standards for all mediators in Scotland. Mediators are required to have:

a) adequate training – at least 40 hours of training, of which at least 20 hours or more is spent in role-play or practical experience including formal assessment;

b) sufficient experience – at least two mediations in the past year and/or not less than six hours conducting mediations as a principal mediator;

c) post-training CPD – a minimum of 12 hours per year and practice support;

d) a portfolio of evidence[56] – which contains the mediator's initial training certificate, a log of mediations (mediation hours) and CPD hours, certificates of insurance and an annual training and development plan;

e) a code of conduct consistent with the EU Code of Conduct;

f) a clear complaints procedure or system for addressing concerns and handling complaints;

g) appropriate professional indemnity insurance.

12.50   All mediators listed on the Scottish Mediation Register[57] meet the SMN Benchmark Standards. Family mediators must comply with the practice standards set by Relationship Scotland[58] and community mediators must comply with the practice standards of the Scottish

---

56 A verification process in which random checks on 10–15 per cent of mediators is conducted by the SMN each year.

57 See www.scottishmediation.org.uk/find-a-mediator.

58 See www.relationship-scotland.org.uk.

Community Mediation Network.[59] Accreditation is also offered by the Law Society of Scotland.[60]

Northern Ireland

12.51 Northern Ireland does not have its own accreditation system. Family mediators, for example, can be accredited by FMC member organisations.

Ethics

What happens if a conflict of interest arises during a mediation?

12.52 Information may be revealed during a mediation which places a mediator in a conflict of interest. For example, they become aware that one of the parties is related to a close friend, relative or close neighbour. Or, it is revealed that one of the parties has a commercial relationship with a business the mediator is also associated with.

12.53 First, the mediator must decide whether this compromises their neutrality. If the answer is 'yes', they must stop the mediation. If the answer is 'no', the mediator must explain the situation which has arisen and obtain the consent of both the parties to continue.

When must a mediator withdraw from a mediation?

12.54 The are a few situations when a mediator may need to withdraw from a mediation:

- where they become unwell or are unable to mediate effectively;
- where a conflict of interest arises and they are unable to maintain their neutrality;[61]
- where something is said or done during the mediation which prevents them from maintaining their impartiality or independence.

---

59 See www.scmcsacro.org.uk/html/scmn.html.
60 See www.lawscot.org.uk.
61 See paras 12.52–12.53.

When must a mediation be brought to an end?

12.55   The following are situations in which a mediator would need to terminate the mediation:

- there is an imbalance of power that the mediator has been unable to address – for example, the mediator believes it is not possible for one of the parties to reach a freely negotiated agreement;
- the mediator believes that one party is acting dishonestly, or is deliberately misleading the other party – for example, they have failed to give the other party relevant information which they are under duty to disclose;
- there is a serious risk to human life or safety by continuing the mediation;.
- the mediator believes that a child/children would be put at risk by continuing the mediation;
- the mediator believes the mediation agreement is an attempt to conceal criminal or fraudulent behaviour – for example, the mediation is being used as a pretext for agreeing the acquisition, retention use or control of criminal property;
- the mediator believes that the proposed mediation agreement would be unlawful;
- one or both of the parties requires legal advice.

12.56   In appropriate situations, the mediator may raise their concerns with the party(ies), and if the situation is remedied then the mediation can continue. If the mediator's concern is not addressed then the mediator will end the mediation.

How does a mediator stop a mediation?

12.57   The mediation ends when an agreement is made, the time allowed for the mediation has elapsed or the mediator has explained to the parties that they are of the view that mediation cannot assist the parties any further in resolving their dispute.

12.58   In all other situations, the mediator will explain to the parties that they need to end the mediation but they are unable to explain why. This is to ensure the confidentiality of the mediation process. In the event that the reason for ending the mediation is no fault of the parties, the mediator may offer to waive their fees and explain that the parties will be contacted by the mediation provider to appoint another mediator.

When can a mediator disclose confidential information?

12.59 Anything said or done during a mediation is, under normal circumstances, confidential. Any document that is shown during the mediation process is also confidential. However, any information that the parties already knew before the mediation process began, is not made confidential just because it is mentioned or referred to during the mediation process.[62]

12.60 In certain exceptional circumstances, mediators have a duty to disclose information given to them during the mediation process which would otherwise be confidential:[63]

- the mediation is being used as an attempt to commit a crime or conceal a crime, or a dishonest act such as money laundering or tax evasion;[64]
- there is a risk of serious harm (physical or psychological injury) to another person, whether or not they are a party to the mediation;[65]
- child protection issues or safeguarding concerns arise.[66]

What are a mediator's duties and obligations?

12.61 The Proceeds of Crime Act 2002 created a duty to report any knowledge or suspicion relating to the involvement of the proceeds of crime (including tax evasion) and a criminal offence of 'tipping off', which precludes informing the parties of an intention to report them. The legal position has subsequently been clarified by the Court of Appeal in the case *Bowman v Fels*.[67]

12.62 In certain circumstances, it will be ethical for a mediator to withdraw from a mediation having first given the parties the opportunity to rebut any suspicions:

a) where there are no existing or contemplated legal or arbitration proceedings or where the link between the mediation and such proceedings is tenuous;

b) where (even if there are existing or contemplated proceedings) the settlement did 'not reflect the legal and practical merits of the

---

62 *Aird v Prime Meridien Ltd* [2006] EWCA Civ 1866.
63 Also see paras 7.34–7.36.
64 See paras 12.61–12.64.
65 See para 12.64.
66 See para 12.64.
67 [2005] EWCA Civ 226.

parties' respective positions in the proceedings and was known or suspected to be no more than a pretext for agreeing on the acquisition, retention, use or control of criminal property'.[68]

12.63   Except for those situations set out above, where legal proceedings are in existence or contemplated, the principles set out in *Bowman v Fels*[69] suggest that a mediator undertaking their duties to facilitate a consensual resolution of a legal dispute does not have to report suspicions of money laundering or tax evasion.

12.64   In cases involving children, a mediator who suspects that any child is suffering, or likely to suffer, significant harm, is under a duty to notify the local social services department having first advised parties they are under a duty to do so.[70] Where the mediator becomes aware a risk of serious harm (physical or psychological injury) to another person whether or not they are a party to the mediation, mediators may notify the appropriate agency.[71]

How can a party complain about their mediator?

12.65   Mediation is a non-binding and voluntary process, so if parties feel that the mediation process is not working, they can withdraw at any time. If a party then wishes to complain, all mediators and mediation providers should have a clearly accessible complaints policy which is available to those who are not satisfied with the service they receive. The initial complaint is usually made to the mediator or mediation provider and dealt with under their complaints policy and procedures. Where possible, issues should be raised with the mediator as they arise.

12.66   For civil mediators who are members of the CMC there is a Complaints Resolution Service which enables the dispute to be mediated by an experienced mediator and is provided free for members and their clients.[72] If the mediator is also a barrister or solicitor and the complaint is that they have breached their professional code of conduct, for example, this may mean they failed to keep information confidential, acted dishonestly or discriminated against a participant because of their race, sex, disability, religion or belief, sexual

---

68 CMC Guidance Note No 2: The obligations of mediators under the Proceeds of Crime Act 2002 – available from www.civilmediation.org/downloads/.
69 [2005] EWCA Civ 226.
70 FMC Code of Practice paras 5.5.3 and 5.7.5.
71 See, for example, FMC Code of Practice para 5.5.4.
72 See www.civilmediation.org/governance/13/complaints-resolution-service.

orientation, gender reassignment, age or marital/civil partnership status. Parties may be able to make a complaint through the Bar Standards Board[73] or the Solicitors Regulation Authority.[74]

12.67   In family mediation, if the mediator is working within a mediation provider, any initial complaint would go to their mediation service or provider organisation and be dealt with under their complaints policy and procedures. If a satisfactory outcome is not achieved, then the complainant could go to the FMC member organisation (NFM, The FMA, Resolution, The Law Society, ADR Group or College of Mediators). The member organisation would then investigate whether the appropriate procedures were followed (but does not investigate the original complaint). After this, they may make recommendations on either procedural matters or the original complaint (or both). If the mediator is working on their own then the party should contact the appropriate FMC member organisation who would investigate and deal with the complaint.

Frequently asked questions answered by Lesley Saunders and Lawrence Kershen

12.68   The following questions have been answered by Lesley Saunders and Lawrence Kershen. Lesley is a family mediator, supervisor and trainer and has been mediating since 1993. She also has experience of community, special educational needs (SEN), disability and workplace mediation. Lawrence has been mediating commercial disputes since 1994 and is an experienced criminal and civil litigator and Queen's Counsel. He is the current chair of the Restorative Justice Council. Both are experienced trainers in mediation, conflict resolution and management.

---

73   See www.barstandardsboard.org.uk; tel: 020 7611 1444.
74   See www.sra.org.uk; tel: 0870 606 2555.

How can I make sure that I get a competent mediator?

Lawrence: Standards of competence in mediation can be ensured by choosing a mediator who has an appropriate qualification. What that appropriate qualification might be depends to some extent on the nature of the mediation, the scale and complexity and the sector in which it is taking place. Broadly, parties will want to choose a mediator who has gone through a training and assessment process which ensures that they have attained a minimum standard of competency. Accreditation and continuing professional development together with a code of conduct also helps to ensure minimum standards of practice and reassure parties they have chosen a competent mediator.

In my opinion, competency is also acquired with experience, so another consideration when looking for a mediator is whether they have undertaken a number of mediations. Of course, a mediator's reputation is also a good guide.[75]

Lesley: In family mediation the LSC fund certain clients in mediation. There is an LSC Quality Mark which sets out standards for family mediation. The LSC competency includes minimum training and competence standards which are set by the FMC working with the LSC and MOJ for mediators doing publicly funded work. As of 1 May 2012, revised LSC competence standards were introduced and there are proposals for these standards to become the universal baseline within family mediation and the minimum requirements for all family mediation provision. Mediators offering publicly funded mediation are monitored through regular LSC audits which cover both quality and contract compliance (with the written permission of any paying client in each case). All family mediators belonging to a member organisation of the FMC subscribe to a Code of Practice which sets out minimum standards.

If a mediator thinks the agreement is 'unfair' on one party, what can they do?

Lawrence: First of all, prepare for success. This means managing the process to ensure that any agreement is fairly reached. It is important to get the right people at the mediation by making sure that the parties are as well supported as they can be and that they've received legal advice. I find it helpful before the mediation

---

75　See paras 3.53–3.73 on choosing a mediator.

to ask parties whether there is anyone else they'd like to attend, or someone they'd want to discuss the potential agreement with before reaching a settlement. Having a friend, associate or professional adviser at the mediation can be key to reaching a resolution and ensuring a party's peace of mind.

Second, I would be really concerned if I thought that the agreement was unfair because there was an unaddressed power imbalance, which may be caused by gender or economic resource, for example. Some of these things you cannot do anything about, but it is the mediator's duty to ensure that there is as level a playing field as possible. For example, ensuring that parties are given equal time to speak. Or, where parties are representing themselves, I would suggest that they seek legal advice before signing a settlement agreement (particularly where the other party has a legal adviser present).

Ultimately, fairness in the outcome is not something the mediator can address. In facilitative mediation, parties control the outcome and have responsibility for any agreement reached at mediation. A mediator will never know the full picture or be aware of all the background facts and so they are not in a position to make a judgment on the 'fairness' of the outcome.

Lesley: I absolutely agree with Lawrence – the mediator has no responsibility for any agreement reached in mediation as long as they have ensured that the process is fair and equitable. However, in family mediation we do have a responsibility to ensure that clients leave with a financial agreement which can be formalised. For this reason, if client proposals are unusual or unorthodox, cannot be sufficiently explained and/or do not meet the legal requirements[76] we have a duty to explain our concerns to them and propose that they seek legal advice and, in rare cases, write their proposals in the form of an outcome summary rather than a memorandum of understanding.

Is mediation sufficiently well regulated?

Lawrence: Mediation is an evolving field. In the UK, mediation is self-regulated and I would not wish that to change. At present, however, anyone can call themselves a mediator. I think that members of the public would like to know that mediators are

---

76 The criteria set out in section 25 of the Matrimonial Causes Act 1973 (Principles Applicable in Dividing the Matrimonial Assets).

required to complete a professional qualification and attain minimum standards of competency. For this reason, I would like to see an overarching professional body to oversee training standards in civil and commercial mediation. The natural progression for the CMC would be to hold a practitioner register of all suitably qualified civil and commercial mediators as the Restorative Justice Council does for restorative practitioners.

I think it would be desirable to have a code of conduct for civil and commercial mediators as well as a more formalised system of individual accreditation, including professional development and supervision to help maintain minimum standards and shared good practice. Ethical issues do arise in mediation and a single professional body can provide guidance and establish good practice.

In Scotland, the SMN Benchmark Standards are a shared minimum practice standard for all mediators – parties can use the Scottish Mediation Register[77] to find mediators who meet these standards.

Lesley: All family mediators who belong to a member organisation of the FMC must subscribe to the FMC Code of Practice for mediators which sets out minimum practice standards. The FMC also approve initial family mediator training as a pre-requisite to competence assessment. As of 1 May 2012, the FMC have introduced the Assessment of Professional Competence (APC) for all mediators wishing to undertake publicly funded work. There are proposals to introduce these requirements as the standard accreditation requirement for all family mediators.

I recognise that family mediators who belong to FMC member organisations are committed to mediation and want to work to the highest standards. I am also aware that some mediators who undertake family mediation work have had very little, if any, formal training. They currently operate outside any regulatory framework. I would therefore support the proposals to introduce the APC scheme (or similar) as a standard, universal qualification for all family mediators.

---

77   See www.scottishmediation.org.uk/find-a-mediator; Scottish Mediation Helpline, tel: 0131 556 1221.

APPENDICES

Mediation providers

USEFUL CONTACTS

ADR Now
Web: www.adrnow.org.uk

Bar Council
289–293 High Holborn
London WC1V 7HZ
Tel: 020 7242 0082
Web: www.barcouncil.org.uk

Civil Justice Council
Judicial Office
11th floor, Thomas More Building
Royal Courts of Justice
Strand
London WC2A 2LL
Web: www.judiciary.gov.uk/about-the-judiciary/advisory-bodies/cjc

Civil Mediation Council (CMC)
The International Dispute Resolution Centre
70 Fleet Street
London EC4Y 1EU
Tel: 020 7353 3227
Web: www.civilmediation.org

Civil Mediation Online Directory
Web: www.civilmediation.justice.gov.uk

Court of Appeal Mediation Scheme (CAMS)
Web: www.justice.gov.
uk/courts/rcj-rolls-building/court-of-appeal/civil-division/mediation

Family Justice Council
11th Floor, Thomas More Building
Royal Courts of Justice
Strand
London WC2A 2LL
Tel: 020 7947 9333
Web: www.judiciary.gov.uk/about-the-judiciary/advisory-bodies/fjc

Family Mediation Council
PO Box 593
Exeter EX1 9HG
Web: www.familymediationcouncil.org.uk

International Mediation Institute
Web: www.imimediation.org.uk

Law Society of England & Wales
The Law Society's Hall
113 Chancery Lane
London WC2A 1PL
Tel: 020 7242 1222
Web: www.lawsociety.org.uk

Law Society of Scotland
26 Drumsheugh Gardens
Edinburgh EH3 7YR
Tel: 0131 226 7411
Web: www.lawscot.org.uk

LawWorks
National Pro Bono Centre
48 Chancery Lane
London WC2A 1JF
Tel: 020 7092 3940
Web: www.lawworks.org.uk

Scottish Mediation Network and Scottish Mediation Register
18 York Place
Edinburgh EH1 3EP
Tel: 0131 5561221
Web: www.scottishmediation.org.uk

Standing Conference of Mediation Advocates (SCMA)
1 Chancery Lane
London WC2A 1LF
Tel: 020 7092 2924
Web: www.mediationadvocates.org.uk

ACCREDITED CIVIL MEDIATION PROVIDERS

The following organisations meet the accreditation standards set by the Civil Mediation Council (CMC), as of 1 April 2012.

Academy of Experts
3 Gray's Inn Square
London WC1R 5AH
Tel: 020 7430 0333
Web: www.academy-experts.org/

ADR Group
Grove House
Grove Road
Redland
Bristol BS6 6UN
Tel: 0117 946 7180
Web: www.adrgroup.co.uk/

Association of Cambridge Mediators
Sheraton House
Castle Park
Cambridge CB3 0AX
Tel: 01223 370063
Web: www.cambridgemediators.co.uk/

Association of Midlands Mediators
P O Box 14188
Birmingham B2 2HJ
Tel: 0800 633 5460
Web: www.midlandsmediators.co.uk/

Association of Northern Mediators
ICON Business Centre
4100 Park Approach
Thorpe Park
Leeds LS15 8GB
Tel: 0113 397 0826
Web: www.northernmediators.co.uk/

Association of South West Mediators
Milsted Langdon
Winchester House
Dean Gate Avenue
Taunton TA1 2UH
Tel: 01823 445566
Web: www.aswm.org.uk/

Berkeley Square Mediation Ltd
23 Berkeley Square
London W1J 6HE
Tel: 07730 982140
http://berkeleysquaremediation.com/

BL Resolve
Blake Lapthorne
New Kings Court
Tollgate
Chandler's Ford
Eastleigh
Hampshire SO53 3LG
Tel: 023 8090 8090
Web: www.bllaw.co.uk/services_for_businesses/mediation.aspx

Canterbury Christ Church University
North Holmes Road
Canterbury
Kent CT1 1QU
Tel: 01227 863026
Web: www.canterbury.ac.uk/social-applied-sciences/crime-and-policing/
mediation-clinic/Home.aspx

CEDR Solve
International Dispute Resolution Centre
70 Fleet Street
London EC4Y 1EU
Tel: 020 7536 6060
Web: www.cedr.com/solve/

Centre for Peaceful Solutions
96 Tubbs Road
London NW10 4SB
Tel: 020 8453 0086
Web: www.centreforpeacefulsolutions.org/

Clerksroom
Equity House
Blackbrook Park Avenue
Taunton
Somerset TA1 2RA
Tel: 0845 083 3000
Web: www.clerksroom.com/mediators.php

Commercial & Medical Dispute Solutions LLP (CMDS)
The Base
Dartford Business Park
Victoria Road
Dartford
Kent DA1 5FS
Tel: 01322 314820
Web: www.cmds.org.uk/

Devon & Somerset Law Society (DASLS)
Aston Court
Pynes Hill
Exeter EX2 5AZ
Tel: 01392 366333
Web: www.dasls.com/uploads/Mediation

Dispute Mediation Consultancy (DMC) LLP
113b High Street
Cowes
Isle of Wight PO31 7AX
Tel: 07540 333340
Web: www.dispute-mediation.co.uk/

Effective Dispute Solutions Ltd (EDSL)
41 Hanover Road
Birmingham B65 9EB
Tel: 0121 533 2793
Web: www.effectivedisputesolutions.co.uk/

Eternal Alliances
3 More London Riverside
London SE1 2RE
Tel: 020 3283 4260
Web: www.eternalalliances.com/

FCMS (Field Court Mediation Service)
Field Court Chambers
5 Field Court
Gray's Inn
London WC1R 5EF
Tel: 020 7405 6114
Web: www.fieldcourt.co.uk/mediation.htm

Focus Commercial Mediation
Ashton House
417 Silbury Boulevard
Milton Keynes MK9 2AH
Tel: 01908 231132
Web: www.focus-mediation.co.uk/

Garden Court Mediation
Garden Court Chambers
57–60 Lincolns Inn Fields
London WC2A 3LJ
Tel: 020 7993 7600
Web: www.gardencourtmediation.co.uk/

Global Mediation Ltd
Elwood House
42 Lytton Road
Barnet
Herts EN5 5BY
Tel: 020 8441 1355
Web: www.globalmediation.co.uk/

Globis Mediation Group
1 Wheatstone Court
Waterwells Business Park
Quedgeley
Gloucester GL2 2AQ
Tel: 0330 100 0809
Web: www.globis.co.uk/

Grays Mediation Services LLP
Richmond Station
Station Yard
Richmond DL10 4LD
Tel: 0844 264 1880
www.graysmediationservices.co.uk

Greater London and East Anglia Mediation LLP
St Martin's House
63 West Stockwell Street
Colchester
Essex CO1 1HE
Tel: 01206 217133
Web: www.gleamed.co.uk/

IDRS Ltd
International Dispute Resolution Centre
70 Fleet Street
London EC4Y 1EU
Tel: 020 7520 3800
Web: www.idrs.ltd.uk/

InterMediation
International House
1 St Katherine's Way
London E1W 1UN
Tel: 020 7977 0600
Web: www.inter-resolve.com/home/mediation/why-mediation

KIDS London SEN Mediation Service
49 Mecklenburgh Square
London WC1N 2NY
Tel: 020 7837 2900
Web: www.kids.org.uk/information/100885/100924/mediation/

Landmark Chambers
180 Fleet Street
London EC4A 2HG
Tel: 020 7430 1221
Web: www.landmarkchambers.co.uk/mediation

LawWorks Mediation
National Pro Bono Centre
48 Chancery Lane
London WC2A 1JF
Tel: 020 7092 3940
Web: www.lawworks.org.uk/

Lyons Davidson Limited Solicitors
Victoria House
51 Victoria Street
Bristol BS1 6AD
Tel: 0117 904 6000
Web: www.lddr.co.uk/

Mediation-1st
73 The Close
Norwich
Norfolk NR1 4DD
Tel: 01603 281128
Web: www.mediation-1st.co.uk/

Mediation Cumbria
6 Victoria Place
Carlisle
Cumbria CA1 1ES
Tel: 0845 052 3667
Web: mediationcumbria.com/

Mediation Solve
20 High Beech Lane
Chepstow
Monmouthshire NP16 5BQ
Tel: 020 7993 6869
Web: www.mediationsolve.co.uk/

Middlesex & Thames Valley Mediators
7 Lambscroft Way
Chalfont St Peter
Buckinghamshire SL9 9AY
Tel: 01753 888023
Web: www.mtvm.org/

Northern Dispute Resolutions Ltd
c/o JK Property Consultants LLP
Rotterdam House
116 Quayside
Newcastle upon Tyne NE1 3DY
Tel: 0191 406 0038
Web: www.northerndisputeresolution.co.uk/

North West Mediation Solutions
29 West Leigh Road
Blackburn
Lancashire BB1 8JR
Tel: 01254 720278
Web: www.nwmediationsolutions.co.uk/

Oxford Mediation
c/o 3 PB
23 Beaumont Street
Oxford OX1 2NP
Tel: 01865 793736
Web: oxford-mediation.com/

Rapproche Civil and Commercial Mediation
Purdy House
Wickmere
Norwich NR11 7LU
Tel: 01263 768607
Web: www.rapproche.co.uk/services/dispute-mediation/

Royal Institution of Chartered Surveyors
Surveyor Court
Westwood Way
Coventry CV4 8JE
Tel: 020 334 3806
Web: www.rics.org/drs

Solent & Wessex Civil Mediation
Biscoes Solicitors
Boyces Cottage
The Square
Wickham
Hampshire PO17 5JN
Tel: 01329 833249
Web: www.solentmediation.com/

Southern Mediators
Sawyers
Green Lane
Jevington
East Sussex BN26 5QD
Tel: 01273 311221
Web: www.southernmediators.co.uk/

Specialist Mediators LLP
Forest Hollow
Nursery Lane
Nutley
East Sussex TN22 3NP
Tel: 0845 868 8912
Web: www.specialistmediators.org/

Talk Mediation Ltd
41 Bridge Street
Hereford HR4 9DG
Tel: 01432 344666
Web: www.talkmediation.co.uk/

UK Mediation Ltd
8 Green Lane
Belper
Derbyshire DE56 1BY
Tel: 01773 829982
Web: www.ukmediation.net/

Wandsworth Mediation Service
St Mark's, Durie Hall
Battersea Rise
London SW11 1EJ
Tel: 020 7223 7744
Web: www.wandsworthmediation.co.uk/

FAMILY MEDIATION PROVIDERS

England & Wales

The Family Mediation Council (FMC) is formed of the following member organisations that accredit individual mediators

ADR Group
Grove House
Grove Road
Redland
Bristol BS6 6UN
Tel: 0117 946 7180
Web: www.adrgroup.co.uk

College of Mediators
3rd Floor, Alexander House
Telephone Avenue
Bristol BS1 4BS
Tel: 0845 65 85 258 (Local rate)
Web: www.collegeofmediators.co.uk

Law Society of England & Wales
The Law Society's Hall
113 Chancery Lane
London WC2A 1PL
Tel: 020 7242 1222
Web: www.lawsociety.org.uk

Law Society Office in Wales
Capital Tower
Greyfriars Road
Cardiff CF10 3AG
Tel: 029 2064 5254
Email: wales@lawsociety.org.uk

National Family Mediation (NFM)
Margaret Jackson Centre
4 Barnfield Hill
Exeter
Devon EX1 1SR
Tel: 0300 4000 636
Web: www.nfm.org.uk

Resolution
Central Office
PO Box 302
Orpington
Kent BR6 8QX
Tel: 01689 820272
Web: www.resolution.org.uk

Scotland

Family Mediators Association (FMA)
Glenfinnan Suite
Braeview House
9/11 Braeview Place
East Kilbride G74 3XH
Tel: 01355 244 594
Web: www.thefma.co.uk

Relationships Scotland
18 York Place
Edinburgh EH1 3EP
Tel: 0845 1192020
Web: www.relationships-scotland.org.uk

The Law Society of Scotland
26 Drumsheugh Gardens
Edinburgh EH3 7YR
Tel: 0131 226 7411
Web: www.lawscot.org.uk

Northern Ireland

Family Mediation Northern Ireland
7 University Street
Belfast BT7 1FY
Tel: 028 9024 3265
Web: www.familymediationni.org.uk

WORKPLACE MEDIATION PROVIDERS

ACAS
22nd Floor, Euston Tower
London NW1 3JJ
Tel: 08457 383736
Web: www.acas.org.uk

ADR Group
Grove House
Grove Road
Redland
Bristol BS6 6UN
Tel: 0117 946 7180
Web: www.adrgroup.co.uk

Alliance Mediation Management Ltd
Mercury House
Nottingham NG7 7FN
Tel: 0115 971 8129
Web: www.alliancemediation.co.uk

Angel Productions Ltd
8 Hillside Gardens
London N6 5ST
Tel: 08444 1555 34
Web: www.angelproductions.co.uk

Association of Cambridge Mediators
Sheraton House
Castle Park
Cambridge CB3 0AX
Tel: 01223 370063
Web: www.cambridgemediators.co.uk

ATOS Healthcare
Axis Beta Building
4–5 Woodlands
Almondsbury
Bristol
Somerset BS32 4JT
Tel: 01454 284 651
Web: www.atoshealthcare.co.uk

Centre for Effective Dispute Resolution (CEDR)
International Dispute Resolution Centre
70 Fleet Street
London EC4Y 1EU
Tel: 020 7536 6060
Web: www.cedr.com

Centre for Peaceful Solutions
96 Tubbs Road
London NW10 4SB
Tel: 020 8453 0086
Web: www.centreforpeacefulsolutions.org

Civitas Dispute Resolution
Global Reach
Celtic Gateway
Cardiff
Glamorgan CF11 0SN
Tel: 0845 071 3007
Web: www.civitaslaw.com

CMP Resolutions
Low Farm
Brook Road
Bassingbourn
Royston
Herts SG8 5NT
Tel: 0844 504 8874
Web: www.cmpresolutions.co.uk

Conflict Resolution Centre
13 Corringway
London NW11 7ED
Tel: 0845 434 9542
Web: www.conflictresolutioncentre.co.uk

Consensio
51 Musard Road
London W6 8NR
Tel: 020 7831 0254
Web: www.consensiopartners.co.uk

Consensus Mediation Ltd
82 King Street
Manchester M2 4WQ
Tel: 0844 561 1763
Web: www.consensusmediation.co.uk

Eternal Alliances
91 Belmont Hill
London SE13 5AX
Tel: 0845 271 2828
Web: www.eternalalliances.com

Focus Commercial Mediation
Ashton House
471 Silbury Boulevard
Milton Keynes MK9 2AH
Tel: 01908 231132
Web: www.focus-mediation.co.uk

Geoff Lawday Associates – Team Concept
The Old Mill House
95 Park Road
Stevington
Beds MK43 7QG
Tel: 01234 823333

Global Mediation
Elwood House
42 Lytton Road
Barnet
Herts EN5 5BY
Tel: 020 8441 1355
Web: www.globalmediation.co.uk

Globis Ltd
Ground Floor
26 Eccleston Square
London SW1V 1NS
Tel: 0330 100 0809
Web: www.globis.co.uk

Greater London and East Anglia Mediation LLP (GLEAMED)
St Martin's House
63 West Stockwell Street
Colchester
Essex CO1 1HE
Tel: 01206 217133
Web: www.gleamed.co.uk

InterMediation
International House
1 St Katherine's Way
London E1W 1UN
Tel: 020 7977 0600
Web: www.intermediation.com

JIB Mediation Services
Kingswood House
47/51 Sidcup Hill
Sidcup
Kent DA14 6HP
Tel: 020 8302 0031
Web: www.jibms.org.uk

Lamb Building Mediation Group
Chambers of Ami Feder
London EC4Y 7AS
Tel: 020 7797 7811
Web: www.lambbuilding.co.uk

Lorraine Bramwell Associates
Windmill Hill Business Park
Whitchill Way
Swindon
Wiltshire SN5 6QR
Tel: 01793 887227
Web: www.bestwayforward.com

Lyons Davidson Dispute Resolution (LDDR)
St Martin's House
Britannia Street
Leeds
West Yorkshire LS1 2DZ
Tel: 0113 368 6164
Web: www.lddr.co.uk

McCormick & Wood Ltd
22 Woodside Road
London N22 5HU
Tel: 07736 736933
Web: www.mccormickandwood.co.uk

Mediation 1st
73 The Close
Norwich
Norfolk NR1 4DR
Tel: 01603 281144
Web: www.mediation-1st.co.uk

Mediation at Work
PO Box 272
Bristol BS99 1RN
Tel: 0117 373 9192
Web: www.mediationatwork.co.uk

Mediation Works
16 Queen Street
Wellington
Telford
Shropshire TF1 1EH
Tel: 01952 520091
Web: www.mediation-works.co.uk

MTVM
7 Lambscroft Way
Chalfont St Peter
Bucks SL9 9AY
Tel: 01753 888023
Web: www.mtvm.org

Oxford Mediation
23 Beaumont Street
Oxford OX1 2NP
Tel: 01865 793736
Web: www.oxford-mediation.com

Paradigm Campbell Associates
Iona House
172 New Bridge Street
Newcastle Upon Tyne NE1 2TE
Tel: 0191 230 3777
Web: www.paradigmcampbell.co.uk

People Resolutions Ltd
Commerce House
1 Oakhill Close
Milton Keynes MK5 6JP
Tel: 01908 524110
Web: www.peopleresolutions.com

Personal Performance Consultants UK Ltd
4200 Nash Court
John Smith Drive
Oxford OX4 2RU
Tel: 01865 397000
Web: www.ppcworldwide.com

Solent and Wessex Civil Mediation
c/o Biscoes
Boyces Cottage, The Square
Wickham
Hampshire PO17 5JN
Tel: 01329 833249
Web: www.solentmediation.com

Steve Hindmarsh Ltd
St Brandon's House
29 Great George Street
Bristol BS1 5QT
Tel: 0800 028 3866
Web: www.stevehindmarsh.co.uk/mediation-standards/

Talk Mediation
41 Bridge Street
Hereford HR4 9DG
Tel: 01432 344666
Web: www.talkmediation.co.uk

TCM Ltd (Total Conflict Management)
1st Floor, New House
67–68 Hatton Garden
London EC1N 8JY
Tel: 020 7404 7011
Web: www.tcmsolutions.co.uk

COMMUNITY MEDIATION PROVIDERS

These are charitable or not-for-profit community mediation services who offer mediation free of charge to local users.

London area

CALM (Confidential and Local Information)
Unit 10 Berghem Mews
Blythe Road
London W14 0HN
Tel: 020 7603 4014
Web: www.calmmediation.org

Camden Mediation Service
11–17 The Marr
Camden Street
London NW1 OHE
Tel: 020 7383 0733
Web: www.camdenmediation.org.uk

Common Ground (formerly Tower Hamlets Mediation Service)
St Margaret's House
21 Old Ford Road
Bethnal Green
London E2 9PL
Tel: 020 7702 8305
Web: www.findcommonground.org.uk

Conflict and Change
2A Streatfield Avenue
East Ham
London E6 2LA
Tel: 020 8552 2050
Web: www.conflictandchange.co.uk

Croydon Community Mediation
17–20 Ramsey Court
122 Church Street
Croydon
Surrey CR0 1RF
Tel: 020 8686 6084
Web: www.croydonmediation.org.uk

Ealing Mediation Service
Greenford Community Centre (room 17)
170 Oldfield Lane South
Greenford
London UB6 9JS
Tel: 0208 575 9500
Web: ealingmediation.org.uk

Lambeth Mediation Service
Ilex House
1 Barrhill Road
London SW2 4RJ
Tel: 020 8678 6046
Web: www.lambethmediation.org

LAMP (Lewisham Action on Mediation Project)
Old Fire Station,
340 Lewisham High Street
London SE13 6LE
Tel: 020 8690 1133
Web: lampmediation.wordpress.com

Southwark Mediation Centre
92 Camberwell Road
London SE5 0EG
Tel: 0207 708 4959
Web: www.southwarkmediation.co.uk

The Mediation Centre UK
The Mediation Centre (UK) Ltd
Fortis House
160 London Road
Essex IG11 8BB
Tel: 020 7511 0111
Web: www.mediationcentreuk.com

Wandsworth Mediation Service
St Mark's, Durie Hall
Battersea Rise
London SW11 1EJ
Tel: 020 7223 7744
Web: www.wandsworthmediation.co.uk

East Anglia

Cambridge and District Community Mediation Service
Llandaff Chambers
2 Regent Street
Cambridge CB2 1AX
Tel: 01223 302514
Web: www.cdcms.org.uk

North East

Bliss Services
Eric Tolhurst Centre
3–13 Quay Road
Blyth
Northumberland NE24 2AS
Tel: 01670 540979
Web: www.blissmediation.co.uk

UNITE
Southlands Centre
Ormesbury Road
Middlesborough TS3 0HB
Tel: 01642 311633
Web: www.unite-mediation.org

North West

Bolton Mediation
2–16 Mayor Street
Bolton BL3 5HT
Tel: 01204 335260
Web: www.boltonmediation.org.uk

Crown Mediation
47 Egremont Court
Wildserpool Causeway
Warrington WA4 6LB
Tel: 08006 123 523
Web: www.crownmediation.co.uk

Mediation Services
Abraham Moss Centre
Crescent Road
Crumpsall
Manchester M8 5UF
Tel: 0161 908 8375
Web: www.manchester.gov.uk

Resolve Mediation Service
Mobet Building
40 Peart Road
Derwent Howe
Workington
Cumbria CA14 3YT
Tel: 01900 603229
E-mail: resolve.mediation@yahoo.co.uk

Specialist Mediation in Lancashire East (SMILE)
The School House
Smurthwaite Street
Burnley BB11 4AZ
Tel: 01282 436989
Web: www.smilemediation.co.uk

Wirral Mediation Service
Royal Standard House
334 New Chester Road
Birkenhead CH42 1LE
Tel: 0151 645 5500
Web: www.involvenorthwest.org.uk

Midlands

Broxtowe Borough Mediation Service
14 Devonshire Avenue
Beeston
Nottinghamshire NG9 1BS
Tel: 01159 173736
Web: www.broxtowe.gov.uk

Central Mediation Services
Canalside House
67/68 Rolfe Street
Smethwick B66 2AL
Tel: 0121 525 4659
Web: www.centralmediation.co.uk

Change Agency
37 Grove Hill Road
Handsworth
Birmingham
West Midlands B21 9PA
Tel: 07779 158 623

Focus Mediation
C/o Information Shop for Young People
Mansfield Library
Westgate
Mansfield
Nottinghamshire NG18 1NH
Tel: 01623 657077
E-mail: infoshop.enquiries@nottscc.gov.uk

Mediation First Ltd
8 Centre Court, Vine Lane
Halesowen
West Midlands B63 3EB
Tel: 0121 550 1667
Web: www.mediationfirstltd.co.uk

Talk 2 Sort
The Bridge
38 Leicester Road
Loughborough
Leicestershire LE11 2AG
Tel: 01509 260 500
Web: www.bridgehousingservices.com

West Midlands Quaker Peace Education Project
46 Parkway Road
Dudley
West Midlands DY1 2QA
Tel: 01384 234113
Web: www.peace-education.org.uk/west-midland-quaker-peace-education-project

South East

Ashford Mediation Service
The Annexe
Tufton Street
Ashford
Kent TN23 1BT
Tel: 01233 663488
Web: www.ashfordmediation.co.uk

East Surrey Community Mediation
PO Box 187
Reigate
Surrey RH2 0FT
Tel: 01737 248559
Web: www.eastsurreycommunitymediation.co.uk

Hastings & Rother Mediation
St Nicholas Centre
66 London Road
St Leonards on Sea
East Sussex TN37 6AS
Tel: 01424 446808
Web: www.hrmediation.org

Mediation North Surrey
PO Box 279
Cobham
Surrey KT11 2JR
Tel: 0870 751 4311
Web: www.mediate.me.uk

Medway Mediation
77a High Street
Chatham
Kent ME4 4EE
Tel: 01634 832285
Web: www.medwaymediation.co.uk

Rushmoor Community Mediation Services
The Community Centre
Meudon Avenue
Farnborough
Hampshire GU14 7LE
Tel: 07825 999 026
Web: www.rushmoormediation.co.uk

SEAMS Mediation
PO Box 5303
Braintree
Essex CM7 1SA
Tel: 01376 331511
Web: www.seamsmediation.co.uk

Shepway & Dover Mediation
3–5 Shorncliffe Road
Folkestone
Kent CT20 2SH
Tel: 01303 227296
Web: www.mediationsoutheast.btck.co.uk

The Mediation Service
171–172 John Wilson Park
Whitstable
Kent CT5 3RB
Tel: 01227 262049
Web: www.themediationservice.co.uk

West Kent Mediation
25 Bevan Place
Swanley
Kent BR8 8BH
Tel: 01322 615774
Web: www.wkm.org.uk

West Sussex Mediation Service
Alphacom House
8A Oakhill Road
Horsham
West Sussex RH13 5SB
Tel: 01403 258900 / 267800
Web: www.wsms.org.uk

South West

Bath Area Mediation
Tel: 01225 571296
Web: www.bathareamediation.co.uk

Devon Mediation Service
The Red House
St Lawrence Green
Crediton
Devon EX17 3LN
Tel: 01363 777734
Web: www.devon-mediation.org.uk

Gloucestershire Mediation
27 Brunswick Square
Gloucester GL1 1UN
Tel: 01452 411843
Web: www.gloucestershiremediation.co.uk

Mediation Dorset
49–51 Charles Street
Dorchester
Dorset DT1 1EE
Tel: 01305 257717
Web: www.mediationdorset.co.uk

Mediation Somerset
Victoria House
Victoria Street
Taunton
Somerset TA1 3FA
Tel: 01823 352210

Somerset Youth Offending Team
5–7 West End
Street
Somerset BA16 0LG
Tel: 01458 440820
Web: wwwmediationsomerset.co.uk

Wales

Conflict Resolution Team
PO Box 1031
Cardiff CF24 3ZT
Tel: 02920 480254
E-mail: conflict.resolutionteam@ntlworld.com

Mediation Plus
34 Y Weirglodd
Denbigh LL16 3JS
Tel: 07708 057448
E-mail: cjmediation@yahoo.co.uk

Yorkshire

Bradford Community Mediation Service
2nd Floor, Trust House
5 New Augustus Street
Bradford
West Yorkshire BD1 5LL
Tel: 01274 254272

Community Accord
Carlisle Business Centre
60 Carlisle Road
Bradford BD8 8BD
Tel: 01274 431222
Web: www.communityaccord.co.uk

Mediation Leeds
Oxford Chambers
Oxford Place
Leeds
West Yorkshire LS1 3AX
Tel: 0113 242 4110
Web: www.mediationleeds.org.uk

Mediation Yorkshire
Field House
15 Wellington Road
Dewsbury
West Yorkshire WF13 1HF
Tel: 01924 520818
Web: www.mediationyorkshire.co.uk

Northern Ireland

Mediation Northern Ireland
83 University Street
Belfast
County Antrim BT7 1HP
Tel: 02890 438614
Web: www.mediationnorthernireland.org

Scotland

Community Mediation Team
Citizens Advice Bureaux
Market House
14 Market Street
Lerwick
Shetland ZE1 0JP
Tel: 01595 743934
Web: shetland-communities.org.uk/subsites/CMT/community-mediation.html

Dundee and Angus Community Mediation
Unit E
Market Mews
Market Street
Dundee DD1 3LA
Tel: 01382 459252
Web: www.sacro.org.uk

Edinburgh Community Mediation Service
21 Abercromby Place
Edinburgh EH3 6QE
Tel: 0131 557 2101
Web: www.sacro.org.uk

OTHER USEFUL COMMUNITY MEDIATION ORGANISATIONS

Centre for Peaceful Solutions
12 Chamberlayne Road
London NW10 3JD
http://centreforpeacefulsolutions.org/

College of Mediators
3rd Floor, Alexander House
Telephone Avenue
Bristol BS1 4BS
Tel: 0845 6585258
Web: www.collegeofmediators.co.uk/

Empowering People for Excellence
Liberty House
9–11 Cottage Green
London SE5 7ST
Tel: 07958 452149

Leap Confronting Conflict
Wells House (Unit 7)
5–7 Wells Terrace
London N4 3JU
Tel: 020 7561 3700
Web: www.leapconfrontingconflict.org.uk

Peer Mediation Network
Web: www.peermediationnetwork.org.uk

Mediation Works
Tel: 01952 520091
Web: mediation-works.co.uk/

Restorative Justice Council
Beacon House
113 Kingsway
London WC2B 6PP
Tel: 020 7831 5700
Web: www.restorativejustice.org.uk/

The Tim Parry Jonathan Ball Foundation for Peace
Peace Drive
Great Sankey
Warrington WA5 1HQ
Tel: 01925 581231
Web: www.foundation4peace.org

Specialist advisers

Advice Now
Web: www.advicenow.org.uk

Citizens Advice
Web: www.citizensadvice.org.uk and www.adviceguide.org.uk/

Community Legal Advice
Web: www.communitylegaladvice.org.uk
Tel: 0845 345 4 345 (Monday to Friday 9.00 am to 8.00 pm, Saturday 9.00 am to 12.30 pm). Alternatively, text 'legalaid' and your name to 80010 and an operator will call you back.

Consumer Credit Counselling Service
Web: www.cccs.co.uk
Tel: 0800 138 111 (Mon to Fri 8am–8pm and Sat 9am–3pm)

Law Centres Federation
Web: www.lawcentres.org.uk/

Legal Adviser Finder
Web: http://legaladviserfinder.justice.gov.uk/
Tel: 0845 345 4 345

National Debtline
Web: www.nationaldebtline.co.uk
Tel: 0808 808 4000 (Mon to Fri 9am–9pm and Sat 9.30am–1pm)

Relate (counselling services)
Web: www.relate.org.uk
Tel: 0300 100 1234

Agreement to mediate

LAWWORKS MEDIATION AGREEMENT[1]

Dated

PARTIES
xxx (name) of xxx (address) and xxx (name) of xxx (address)

DISPUTE
The dispute ('the Dispute') between the parties results from xxx

THE MEDIATOR/S
xxx (name) of xxx (address) [and xxx (name) of xxx (address)]

The Parties and the Mediator/s agree to the mediation of the Dispute on the following terms:

1. The Parties agree that xxx (name) will be the Mediator/s and will cooperate in good faith with him and each other during the mediation. The Mediator/s is independent of the Parties and does not give legal advice.
2. The person signing this Agreement on behalf of each Party warrants having authority to bind that Party and all other persons present on that Party's behalf at the Mediation to observe the terms of this Agreement, and also having authority to bind that Party to the terms of any settlement.
3. Neither the Mediator/s nor LawWorks shall be liable to the Parties for any act or omission in relation to the Mediation unless the act or omission is proved to have been fraudulent or involved wilful misconduct.
4. The Parties will supply a copy of a bundle of agreed documents to the Mediator by xxx (date), and, if they wish to do so, a short position paper by the same date.
5. The mediation meeting will take place at xxx (address) . It will last for three hours starting at xxx (time)

Confidentiality and without prejudice status
6. Every person involved in the Mediation:
6.1 Mediation, including the fact and terms of any settlement, but not including the fact that the Mediation is to take place or has taken place or where disclosure is required by law to implement or to enforce terms of settlement; and

---

1 Provided by LawWorks – www.lawworks.org.uk. For other examples see www.cedr.com, www.ciarb.org and www.coresolutions.org.

6.2 acknowledges that all such information passing between the Parties, the Mediator/s and/or LawWorks, however communicated, is agreed to be without prejudice to any Party's legal position and may not be produced as evidence or disclosed to any judge, arbitrator or other decision-maker in any legal or other formal process, except where otherwise disclosable in law.

7. Where a party privately discloses to the Mediator/s any information in confidence before, during or after the Mediation, the Mediator/s will not disclose that information to any other Party or person without the consent of the Party disclosing it, unless required by law to make disclosure.

8. The Parties will not call the Mediator/s or any employee or volunteers of Law-Works as a witness, nor require them to produce in evidence any records or notes relating to the Mediation, in any litigation, arbitration or other formal process arising from or in connection with their dispute and the Mediation; nor will the Mediator/s nor any LawWorks' employee or volunteer agree to act as a witness, expert, arbitrator or consultant in any such process. If any Party does make such an application, that Party will fully indemnify the Mediator/s or the employee or volunteer of LawWorks in respect of any costs any of them incur in resisting and/or responding to such an application, including a reasonable provision for their time spent in resisting and/or responding to such application.

9. The mediation will continue during the agreed period until agreement is reached, or one of the parties decides to stop the process, or the mediator informs the parties that in their opinion further attempts would not be worthwhile or appropriate.

10. The Mediator/s [insert fees and cancellation policy / does not charge any fees or expenses for his work]. The Parties agree that they will each have to take personal responsibility for any costs or expenses that they incur.

Settlement formalities

11. No terms of settlement reached at the Mediation will be legally binding until set out in writing and signed by or on behalf of each of the Parties.

Legal Status and effect of the Mediation

12. This agreement is governed by English Law and the courts of England and Wales shall have exclusive jurisdiction to decide any matters arising out of or in connection with this Agreement and the Mediation.

13. The referral of the Dispute to mediation does not affect rights under Article 6 of the European Convention on Human Rights. If the Dispute is not settled, the parties' rights to a fair trial will not be affected.

Signed

Party _____

Party _____

Mediator _____

Supporter/Expert _____

Pre-mediation questionnaire

QUESTIONS TO THINK ABOUT WHEN PREPARING FOR A MEDIATION[1]

The mediator may often ask parties to prepare in advance or at the beginning of the mediation day by addressing some specific questions. These may include the following:

- What are your overall objectives?

- What in particular are you seeking to achieve?

- What is in dispute? What do parties have in common?

- What are your strengths? What are your weaknesses?

- What are your needs? What are your concerns?

- What might the other party's needs be? Their concerns?

- What do you think the other side need to hear from you? What might you say to the other side?

- If you do not reach agreement, what are the alternatives?

- What costs have you incurred to date? If you do not reach agreement, what costs will you incur in future?

- If you do not reach agreement, what other consequences will there be? For you? For the other party?

- What are the options for resolving this matter?

- How will you assess any proposals put by the other party?

- What proposals might you make?

Mediation settlement agreements

NON-BINDING AGREEMENT[1]

This agreement is established by the following named parties:

_____

_____

The following mediators were present:

_____

_____

Third Parties present: _____

Interpreter: _____

This agreement is made in good faith, and is not legally binding upon the parties.

This is a summary of the main points of agreement:

-
-
-
-
-
-

Mediation Service

- The case worker/mediation administrator agrees to contact the parties in 12 weeks to assess the progress of the agreement.
- The parties agree that a copy of the agreement should be sent to the referrer. / The parties agree that the agreement would remain confidential between themselves.

BINDING AGREEMENT

SETTLEMENT AGREEMENT / CONSENT ORDER

Court: [if relevant]

Claim Number: [if relevant]

Claimant/Party A: _____

Defendant/Party B: _____

On _____ [date] the Parties agreed that:

Terms

1. _____ will pay _____ the sum of _____
no later than [time, date] to _____ by cheque/cash/banker's
draft/bank transfer.

2.

3.

4. The Action will be dismissed with no order as to costs.

5. This Agreement is in full and final settlement of any causes of action the
parties to this dispute have against each other.

6. This Agreement supersedes all previous agreements between the parties.

7. If any dispute arises out of this agreement, the parties will first attempt
to settle it through the mediator, but if no legally binding settlement of
this dispute is reached within 28 days from the date of the notice to the
Mediator, either party may institute court proceedings.

8. [The parties will keep the information contained in this agreement
confidential and not use it for any collateral or ulterior purposes.] Other
than a final written agreement, any information – whether written in
a document prepared for mediation or written or spoken during the
mediation – can only be used for the purpose of mediation and cannot be
referred to in any court action unless the parties agree. The parties agree
that they will not call the mediator to give evidence in any court action.

TOMLIN ORDER

Court:

Claim Number:

Claimant: _____

Defendant: _____

IT IS BY CONSENT ORDERED

That all further proceedings in this claim be stayed except for the purpose of carrying such terms into effect, the parties having agreed to the terms set out in the attached schedule

AND for that purpose the parties have permission to apply.

IT IS FURTHER ORDERED that (payment of money out of court is as follows)

AND IT IS FURTHER ORDERED that (each party bear it own costs / payment of costs and assessment of costs is as follows)

Signed: Date:

Claimant: _____   _____

Defendant: _____   _____

Mediator: _____   _____

SCHEDULE OF TERMS OF AGREEMENT:

1.

2.

3.

MEMORANDUM OF UNDERSTANDING (FAMILY MEDIATION)

This Memorandum is a summary of the outcome of mediation and proposals for settlement reached by [Party 1] and [Party 2].

This Memorandum is legally privileged and 'without prejudice'. It does not record or create a legally binding agreement between the parties.

It is intended to assist [Party 1] and [Party 2].in obtaining independent professional advice. The mediator(s) has recommended they receive legal advice before entering into a binding agreement, at the moment no such binding agreement exists between them.

[Party 1] and [Party 2].understand that the financial information they have given may be produced to the Court (unlike this Memorandum) and they have had the necessity for full and complete disclosure explained to them and recorded to them in writing. The Memorandum may of course, be produced to legal advisors upon the basis that it is and remains a legally privileged document.

1. Background information
They have [   ] children. [   ] aged [   ] dob [   ] and [   ] aged [   ] dob [   ].
The children live with [   ]. [   ] is renting until able to purchase a property.

2. Separation
Clean break? Deed of Separation? Legal costs

3. Shared parental responsibility
Grandparents, other family members, school events. Description of children's needs if appropriate

4. The Family Home
The family home was bought in joint names on [   ] for [   ] with a repayment mortgage of [   ]. For negotiation purposes, X and Y agree the valuation of [   ] which leaves the current equity of [   ].

5. Loans and credit cards
Joint loans/credit card debts and plan to discharge them. Joint bank account

6. Additional property/assets
Include if any.

7. Pensions
Include pensions within settlement or have pension claims waived?

8. Proposals for settlement

9. Inheritance

10. Wills

11. Next Steps

Dated _____
Signed _____
Family Mediator
(Name and address of mediation service)

Mediation contract clause

SIMPLE MEDIATION CONTRACT CLAUSE

If any dispute arises in connection with this agreement, the parties will first attempt to settle it through mediation. To initiate the mediation a party must give notice in writing to the other party[ies] involved requesting a mediation. A copy should be sent to the proposed mediator/mediation provider. The mediation should start no later than [ ] days after the date of the notice.

MULTI TIERED MEDIATION CONTRACT CLAUSE[1]

I2: Dispute Resolution

I2.1 The Parties shall attempt in good faith to negotiate a settlement to any dispute between them arising out of or in connection with the Contract within 20 Working Days of either Party notifying the other of the dispute and such efforts shall involve the escalation of the dispute to the [finance director (or equivalent)] of each Party.

I2.2 Nothing in this dispute resolution procedure shall prevent the Parties from seeking from any court of competent jurisdiction an interim order restraining the other Party from doing any act or compelling the other Party to do any act.

I2.3 If the dispute cannot be resolved by the Parties pursuant to clause I2.1 the Parties shall refer it to mediation pursuant to the procedure set out in clause I2.5 unless (a) the Client considers that the dispute is not suitable for resolution by mediation; or (b) the Contractor does not agree to mediation

I2.4 The obligations of the Parties under the Contract shall not cease, or be suspended or delayed by the reference of a dispute to mediation (or arbitration) and the Contractor and the Staff shall comply fully with the requirements of the Contract at all times.

I2.5 The procedure for mediation and consequential provisions relating to mediation are as follows:

(a) a neutral adviser or mediator (the '**Mediator**') shall be chosen by agreement between the Parties or, if they are unable to agree upon a Mediator within 10 Working Days after a request by one Party to the other or if

---

1 Dispute Resolution Commitment – Guidance for Government Departments and Agencies, Ministry of Justice, May 2011, Annex A, pp 16–17.

the Mediator agreed upon is unable or unwilling to act, either Party shall within 10 Working Days from the date of the proposal to appoint a Mediator or within 10 Working Days of notice to either Party that he is unable or unwilling to act, apply to [an appropriate mediation provider] to appoint a Mediator.

(b) The Parties shall within 10 Working Days of the appointment of the Mediator meet with him in order to agree a programme for the exchange of all relevant information and the structure to be adopted for negotiations to be held. If considered appropriate, the Parties may at any stage seek assistance from [an appropriate mediation provider] to provide guidance on a suitable procedure.

(c) Unless otherwise agreed, all negotiations connected with the dispute and any settlement agreement relating to it shall be conducted in confidence and without prejudice to the rights of the Parties in any future proceedings.

(d) If the Parties reach agreement on the resolution of the dispute, the agreement shall be recorded in writing and shall be binding on the Parties once it is signed by their duly authorised representatives.

(e) If the Parties fail to reach agreement in the structured negotiations within 60 Working Days of the Mediator being appointed, or such longer period as may be agreed by the Parties, then any dispute or difference between them may be referred to the Courts / [unless the dispute is referred to arbitration pursuant to the procedures set out in clause ...].

EU Mediation Directive

DIRECTIVE 2008/52/EC OF THE EUROPEAN PARLIAMENT AND OF THE COUNCIL
of 21 May 2008
on certain aspects of mediation in civil and commercial matters

THE EUROPEAN PARLIAMENT AND THE COUNCIL OF THE EURO-PEAN UNION,

Having regard to the Treaty establishing the European Community, and in particular Article 61(c) and the second indent of Article 67(5) thereof,

Having regard to the proposal from the Commission, Having regard to the Opinion of the European Economic and Social Committee,

Acting in accordance with the procedure laid down in Article 251 of the Treaty,

Whereas:

(1) The Community has set itself the objective of maintaining and developing an area of freedom, security and justice, in which the free movement of persons is ensured. To that end, the Community has to adopt, inter alia, measures in the field of judicial cooperation in civil matters that are necessary for the proper functioning of the internal market.

(2) The principle of access to justice is fundamental and, with a view to facilitating better access to justice, the European Council at its meeting in Tampere on 15 and 16 October 1999 called for alternative, extra-judicial procedures to be created by the Member States.

(3) In May 2000 the Council adopted Conclusions on alternative methods of settling disputes under civil and commercial law, stating that the establishment of basic principles in this area is an essential step towards enabling the appropriate development and operation of extrajudicial procedures for the settlement of disputes in civil and commercial matters so as to simplify and improve access to justice.

(4) In April 2002 the Commission presented a Green Paper on alternative dispute resolution in civil and commercial law, taking stock of the existing situation as concerns alternative dispute resolution methods in the European Union and initiating widespread consultations with Member States and interested parties on possible measures to promote the use of mediation.

(5) The objective of securing better access to justice, as part of the policy of the European Union to establish an area of freedom, security and justice,

should encompass access to judicial as well as extrajudicial dispute resolution methods. This Directive should contribute to the proper functioning of the internal market, in particular as concerns the availability of mediation services.

(6) Mediation can provide a cost-effective and quick extrajudicial resolution of disputes in civil and commercial matters through processes tailored to the needs of the parties. Agreements resulting from mediation are more likely to be complied with voluntarily and are more likely to preserve an amicable and sustainable relationship between the parties. These benefits become even more pronounced in situations displaying cross-border elements.

(7) In order to promote further the use of mediation and ensure that parties having recourse to mediation can rely on a predictable legal framework, it is necessary to introduce framework legislation addressing, in particular, key aspects of civil procedure.

(8) The provisions of this Directive should apply only to mediation in cross-border disputes, but nothing should prevent Member States from applying such provisions also to internal mediation processes.

(9) This Directive should not in any way prevent the use of modern communication technologies in the mediation process.

(10) This Directive should apply to processes whereby two or more parties to a cross-border dispute attempt by themselves, on a voluntary basis, to reach an amicable agreement on the settlement of their dispute with the assistance of a mediator. It should apply in civil and commercial matters. However, it should not apply to rights and obligations on which the parties are not free to decide themselves under the relevant applicable law. Such rights and obligations are particularly frequent in family law and employment law.

(11) This Directive should not apply to pre-contractual negotiations or to processes of an adjudicatory nature such as certain judicial conciliation schemes, consumer complaint schemes, arbitration and expert determination or to processes administered by persons or bodies issuing a formal recommendation, whether or not it be legally binding as to the resolution of the dispute.

(12) This Directive should apply to cases where a court refers parties to mediation or in which national law prescribes mediation. Furthermore, in so far as a judge may act as a mediator under national law, this Directive should also apply to mediation conducted by a judge who is not responsible for any judicial proceedings relating to the matter or matters in dispute. This Directive should not, however, extend to attempts made by the court or judge seised to settle a dispute in the context of judicial proceedings concerning the dispute in question or to cases in which the court or judge seised requests assistance or advice from a competent person.

(13) The mediation provided for in this Directive should be a voluntary process in the sense that the parties are themselves in charge of the process and may organise it as they wish and terminate it at any time. However, it should be possible under national law for the courts to set time-limits for a mediation process. Moreover, the courts should be able to draw the parties' attention to the possibility of mediation whenever this is appropriate.

(14) Nothing in this Directive should prejudice national legislation making the use of mediation compulsory or subject to incentives or sanctions provided that

such legislation does not prevent parties from exercising their right of access to the judicial system. Nor should anything in this Directive prejudice existing self-regulating mediation systems in so far as these deal with aspects which are not covered by this Directive.

(15) In order to provide legal certainty, this Directive should indicate which date should be relevant for determining whether or not a dispute which the parties attempt to settle through mediation is a cross-border dispute. In the absence of a written agreement, the parties should be deemed to agree to use mediation at the point in time when they take specific action to start the mediation process.

(16) To ensure the necessary mutual trust with respect to confidentiality, effect on limitation and prescription periods, and recognition and enforcement of agreements resulting from mediation, Member States should encourage, by any means they consider appropriate, the training of mediators and the introduction of effective quality control mechanisms concerning the provision of mediation services.

(17) Member States should define such mechanisms, which may include having recourse to market-based solutions, and should not be required to provide any funding in that respect. The mechanisms should aim at preserving the flexibility of the mediation process and the autonomy of the parties, and at ensuring that mediation is conducted in an effective, impartial and competent way. Mediators should be made aware of the existence of the European Code of Conduct for Mediators which should also be made available to the general public on the Internet.

(18) In the field of consumer protection, the Commission has adopted a Recommendation establishing minimum quality criteria which out-of-court bodies involved in the consensual resolution of consumer disputes should offer to their users. Any mediators or organisations coming within the scope of that Recommendation should be encouraged to respect its principles. In order to facilitate the dissemination of information concerning such bodies, the Commission should set up a database of out-of-court schemes which Member States consider as respecting the principles of that Recommendation.

(19) Mediation should not be regarded as a poorer alternative to judicial proceedings in the sense that compliance with agreements resulting from mediation would depend on the good will of the parties. Member States should therefore ensure that the parties to a written agreement resulting from mediation can have the content of their agreement made enforceable. It should only be possible for a Member State to refuse to make an agreement enforceable if the content is contrary to its law, including its private international law, or if its law does not provide for the enforceability of the content of the specific agreement. This could be the case if the obligation specified in the agreement was by its nature unenforceable.

(20) The content of an agreement resulting from mediation which has been made enforceable in a Member State should be recognised and declared enforceable in the other Member States in accordance with applicable Community or national law. This could, for example, be on the basis of Council Regulation (EC) No 44/2001 of 22 December 2000 on jurisdiction and the recognition and enforcement of judgments in civil and commercial matters or Council Regulation (EC) No 2201/2003 of 27 November 2003 concerning jurisdiction

and the recognition and enforcement of judgments in matrimonial matters and the matters of parental responsibility.

(21) Regulation (EC) No 2201/2003 specifically provides that, in order to be enforceable in another Member State, agreements between the parties have to be enforceable in the Member State in which they were concluded. Consequently, if the content of an agreement resulting from mediation in a family law matter is not enforceable in the Member State where the agreement was concluded and where the request for enforceability is made, this Directive should not encourage the parties to circumvent the law of that Member State by having their agreement made enforceable in another Member State.

(22) This Directive should not affect the rules in the Member States concerning enforcement of agreements resulting from mediation.

(23) Confidentiality in the mediation process is important and this Directive should therefore provide for a minimum degree of compatibility of civil procedural rules with regard to how to protect the confidentiality of mediation in any subsequent civil and commercial judicial proceedings or arbitration.

(24) In order to encourage the parties to use mediation, Member States should ensure that their rules on limitation and prescription periods do not prevent the parties from going to court or to arbitration if their mediation attempt fails. Member States should make sure that this result is achieved even though this Directive does not harmonise national rules on limitation and prescription periods. Provisions on limitation and prescription periods in international agreements as implemented in the Member States, for instance in the area of transport law, should not be affected by this Directive.

(25) Member States should encourage the provision of information to the general public on how to contact mediators and organisations providing mediation services. They should also encourage legal practitioners to inform their clients of the possibility of mediation.

(26) In accordance with point 34 of the Interinstitutional agreement on better law-making (3), Member States are encouraged to draw up, for themselves and in the interests of the Community, their own tables illustrating, as far as possible, the correlation between this Directive and the transposition measures, and to make them public.

(27) This Directive seeks to promote the fundamental rights, and takes into account the principles, recognised in particular by the Charter of Fundamental Rights of the European Union.

(28) Since the objective of this Directive cannot be sufficiently achieved by the Member States and can therefore, by reason of the scale or effects of the action, be better achieved at Community level, the Community may adopt measures in accordance with the principle of subsidiarity as set out in Article 5 of the Treaty. In accordance with the principle of proportionality, as set out in that Article, this Directive does not go beyond what is necessary in order to achieve that objective.

(29) In accordance with Article 3 of the Protocol on the position of the United Kingdom and Ireland, annexed to the Treaty on European Union and to the Treaty establishing the European Community, the United Kingdom and Ireland have given notice of their wish to take part in the adoption and application of this Directive.

(30) In accordance with Articles 1 and 2 of the Protocol on the position of Denmark, annexed to the Treaty on European Union and to the Treaty establishing the European Community, Denmark does not take part in the adoption of this Directive and is not bound by it or subject to its application,

HAVE ADOPTED THIS DIRECTIVE:

Article 1: Objective and scope

1. The objective of this Directive is to facilitate access to alternative dispute resolution and to promote the amicable settlement of disputes by encouraging the use of mediation and by ensuring a balanced relationship between mediation and judicial proceedings.
2. This Directive shall apply, in cross-border disputes, to civil and commercial matters except as regards rights and obligations which are not at the parties' disposal under the relevant applicable law. It shall not extend, in particular, to revenue, customs or administrative matters or to the liability of the State for acts and omissions in the exercise of State authority (acta iure imperii).
3. In this Directive, the term 'Member State' shall mean Member States with the exception of Denmark.

Article 2: Cross-border disputes

1. For the purposes of this Directive a cross-border dispute shall be one in which at least one of the parties is domiciled or habitually resident in a Member State other than that of any other party on the date on which:
   (a) the parties agree to use mediation after the dispute has arisen;
   (b) mediation is ordered by a court;
   (c) an obligation to use mediation arises under national law; or
   (d) for the purposes of Article 5 an invitation is made to the parties.
2. Notwithstanding paragraph 1, for the purposes of Articles 7 and 8 a cross-border dispute shall also be one in which judicial proceedings or arbitration following mediation between the parties are initiated in a Member State other than that in which the parties were domiciled or habitually resident on the date referred to in paragraph 1(a), (b) or (c).
3. For the purposes of paragraphs 1 and 2, domicile shall be determined in accordance with Articles 59 and 60 of Regulation (EC) No 44/2001.

Article 3: Definitions

For the purposes of this Directive the following definitions shall apply:

(a) 'Mediation' means a structured process, however named or referred to, whereby two or more parties to a dispute attempt by themselves, on a voluntary basis, to reach an agreement on the settlement of their dispute with the assistance of a mediator. This process may be initiated by the parties or suggested or ordered by a court or prescribed by the law of a Member State.

It includes mediation conducted by a judge who is not responsible for any judicial proceedings concerning the dispute in question. It excludes attempts made by the court or the judge seised to settle a dispute in the course of judicial proceedings concerning the dispute in question.

(b) 'Mediator' means any third person who is asked to conduct a mediation in an effective, impartial and competent way, regardless of the denomination or profession of that third person in the Member State concerned and of the way in which the third person has been appointed or requested to conduct the mediation.

Article 4: Ensuring the quality of mediation

1. Member States shall encourage, by any means which they consider appropriate, the development of, and adherence to, voluntary codes of conduct by mediators and organisations providing mediation services, as well as other effective quality control mechanisms concerning the provision of mediation services.
2. Member States shall encourage the initial and further training of mediators in order to ensure that the mediation is conducted in an effective, impartial and competent way in relation to the parties.

Article 5: Recourse to mediation

1. A court before which an action is brought may, when appropriate and having regard to all the circumstances of the case, invite the parties to use mediation in order to settle the dispute. The court may also invite the parties to attend an information session on the use of mediation if such sessions are held and are easily available.
2. This Directive is without prejudice to national legislation making the use of mediation compulsory or subject to incentives or sanctions, whether before or after judicial proceedings have started, provided that such legislation does not prevent the parties from exercising their right of access to the judicial system.

Article 6: Enforceability of agreements resulting from mediation

1. Member States shall ensure that it is possible for the parties, or for one of them with the explicit consent of the others, to request that the content of a written agreement resulting from mediation be made enforceable. The content of such an agreement shall be made enforceable unless, in the case in question, either the content of that agreement is contrary to the law of the Member State where the request is made or the law of that Member State does not provide for its enforceability.
2. The content of the agreement may be made enforceable by a court or other competent authority in a judgment or decision or in an authentic instrument in accordance with the law of the Member State where the request is made.
3. Member States shall inform the Commission of the courts or other authorities competent to receive requests in accordance with paragraphs 1 and 2.
4. Nothing in this Article shall affect the rules applicable to the recognition and enforcement in another Member State of an agreement made enforceable in accordance with paragraph 1.

Article 7: Confidentiality of mediation

1. Given that mediation is intended to take place in a manner which respects confidentiality, Member States shall ensure that, unless the parties agree otherwise, neither mediators nor those involved in the administration of the mediation process shall be compelled to give evidence in civil and commercial judicial proceedings or arbitration regarding information arising out of or in connection with a mediation process, except:

(a) where this is necessary for overriding considerations of public policy of the Member State concerned, in particular when required to ensure the protection of the best interests of children or to prevent harm to the physical or psychological integrity of a person; or

(b) where disclosure of the content of the agreement resulting from mediation is necessary in order to implement or enforce that agreement.

2. Nothing in paragraph 1 shall preclude Member States from enacting stricter measures to protect the confidentiality of mediation.

Article 8: Effect of mediation on limitation and prescription periods

1. Member States shall ensure that parties who choose mediation in an attempt to settle a dispute are not subsequently prevented from initiating judicial proceedings or arbitration in relation to that dispute by the expiry of limitation or prescription periods during the mediation process.

2. Paragraph 1 shall be without prejudice to provisions on limitation or prescription periods in international agreements to which Member States are party.

Article 9: Information for the general public

Member States shall encourage, by any means which they consider appropriate, the availability to the general public, in particular on the Internet, of information on how to contact mediators and organisations providing mediation services.

Article 10: Information on competent courts and authorities

The Commission shall make publicly available, by any appropriate means, information on the competent courts or authorities communicated by the Member States pursuant to Article 6(3).

Article 11: Review

Not later than 21 May 2016, the Commission shall submit to the European Parliament, the Council and the European Economic and Social Committee a report on the application of this Directive. The report shall consider the development of mediation throughout the European Union and the impact of this Directive in the Member States. If necessary, the report shall be accompanied by proposals to adapt this Directive.

Article 12: Transposition

1. Member States shall bring into force the laws, regulations, and administrative provisions necessary to comply with this Directive before 21 May 2011, with the exception of Article 10, for which the date of compliance shall be 21 November 2010 at the latest. They shall forthwith inform the Commission thereof.

   When they are adopted by Member States, these measures shall contain a reference to this Directive or shall be accompanied by such reference on the occasion of their official publication. The methods of making such reference shall be laid down by Member States.

2. Member States shall communicate to the Commission the text of the main provisions of national law which they adopt in the field covered by this Directive.

Article 13: Entry into force

This Directive shall enter into force on the 20th day following its publication in the Official Journal of the European Union.

Article 14: Addressees

This Directive is addressed to the Member States.

European Code of Conduct for Mediators

This code of conduct sets out a number of principles to which individual mediators can voluntarily decide to commit, under their own responsibility. It is intended to be applicable to all kinds of mediation in civil and commercial matters.

Organisations providing mediation services can also make such a commitment, by asking mediators acting under the auspices of their organisation to respect the code. Organisations have the opportunity to make available information on the measures they are taking to support the respect of the code by individual mediators through, for example, training, evaluation and monitoring.

For the purposes of the code mediation is defined as any process where two or more parties agree to the appointment of a third-party – hereinafter "the mediator" – to help the parties to solve a dispute by reaching an agreement without adjudication and regardless of how that process may be called or commonly referred to in each Member State.

Adherence to the code is without prejudice to national legislation or rules regulating individual professions.

Organisations providing mediation services may wish to develop more detailed codes adapted to their specific context or the types of mediation services they offer, as well as with regard to specific areas such as family mediation or consumer mediation.

1. COMPETENCE AND APPOINTMENT OF MEDIATORS

1.1 Competence
Mediators shall be competent and knowledgeable in the process of mediation. Relevant factors shall include proper training and continuous updating of their education and practice in mediation skills, having regard to any relevant standards or accreditation schemes.

1.2 Appointment
The mediator will confer with the parties regarding suitable dates on which the mediation may take place. The mediator shall satisfy him/herself as to his/her background and competence to conduct the mediation before accepting the appointment and, upon request, disclose information concerning his/her background and experience to the parties.

1.3 Advertising/promotion of the mediator's services
Mediators may promote their practice, in a professional, truthful and dignified way.

2. INDEPENDENCE AND IMPARTIALITY

2.1 Independence and neutrality

The mediator must not act, or, having started to do so, continue to act, before having disclosed any circumstances that may, or may be seen to, affect his or her independence or conflict of interests. The duty to disclose is a continuing obligation throughout the process.

Such circumstances shall include

- any personal or business relationship with one of the parties,
- any financial or other interest, direct or indirect, in the outcome of the mediation, or
- the mediator, or a member of his or her firm, having acted in any capacity other than mediator for one of the parties.

In such cases the mediator may only accept or continue the mediation provided that he/she is certain of being able to carry out the mediation with full independence and neutrality in order to guarantee full impartiality and that the parties explicitly consent.

2.2 Impartiality

The mediator shall at all times act, and endeavour to be seen to act, with impartiality towards the parties and be committed to serve all parties equally with respect to the process of mediation.

3. THE MEDIATION AGREEMENT, PROCESS, SETTLEMENT AND FEES

3.1 Procedure

The mediator shall satisfy himself/herself that the parties to the mediation understand the characteristics of the mediation process and the role of the mediator and the parties in it.

The mediator shall in particular ensure that prior to commencement of the mediation the parties have understood and expressly agreed the terms and conditions of the mediation agreement including in particular any applicable provisions relating to obligations of confidentiality on the mediator and on the parties.

The mediation agreement shall, upon request of the parties, be drawn up in writing.

The mediator shall conduct the proceedings in an appropriate manner, taking into account the circumstances of the case, including possible power imbalances and the rule of law, any wishes the parties may express and the need for a prompt settlement of the dispute. The parties shall be free to agree with the mediator, by reference to a set of rules or otherwise, on the manner in which the mediation is to be conducted.

The mediator, if he/she deems it useful, may hear the parties separately.

3.2 Fairness of the process

The mediator shall ensure that all parties have adequate opportunities to be involved in the process.

The mediator if appropriate shall inform the parties, and may terminate the mediation, if:

- a settlement is being reached that for the mediator appears unenforceable or illegal, having regard to the circumstances of the case and the competence of the mediator for making such an assessment, or
- the mediator considers that continuing the mediation is unlikely to result in a settlement.

3.3 The end of the process

The mediator shall take all appropriate measures to ensure that any understanding is reached by all parties through knowing and informed consent, and that all parties understand the terms of the agreement.

The parties may withdraw from the mediation at any time without giving any justification.

The mediator may, upon request of the parties and within the limits of his or her competence, inform the parties as to how they may formalise the agreement and as to the possibilities for making the agreement enforceable.

3.4 Fees

Where not already provided, the mediator must always supply the parties with complete information on the mode of remuneration which he intends to apply. He/she shall not accept a mediation before the principles of his/her remuneration have been accepted by all parties concerned.

4. CONFIDENTIALITY

The mediator shall keep confidential all information, arising out of or in connection with the mediation, including the fact that the mediation is to take place or has taken place, unless compelled by law or public policy grounds. Any information disclosed in confidence to mediators by one of the parties shall not be disclosed to the other parties without permission or unless compelled by law.

Practice Direction: Pre-action conduct

SECTION I – INTRODUCTION

1. AIMS

1.1 The aims of this Practice Direction are to –
  (1) enable parties to settle the issue between them without the need to start proceedings (that is, a court claim); and
  (2) support the efficient management by the court and the parties of proceedings that cannot be avoided.

1.2 These aims are to be achieved by encouraging the parties to –
  (1) exchange information about the issue, and
  (2) consider using a form of Alternative Dispute Resolution ('ADR').

2. SCOPE

2.1 This Practice Direction describes the conduct the court will normally expect of the prospective parties prior to the start of proceedings.

2.2 There are some types of application where the principles in this Practice Direction clearly cannot or should not apply. These include, but are not limited to, for example –
  (1) applications for an order where the parties have agreed between them the terms of the court order to be sought ('consent orders');
  (2) applications for an order where there is no other party for the applicant to engage with;
  (3) most applications for directions by a trustee or other fiduciary;
  (4) applications where telling the other potential party in advance would defeat the purpose of the application (for example, an application for an order to freeze assets).

2.3 Section II deals with the approach of the court in exercising its powers in relation to pre-action conduct. Subject to paragraph 2.2, it applies in relation to all types of proceedings including those governed by the pre-action protocols that have been approved by the Head of Civil Justice and which are listed in paragraph 5.2 of this Practice Direction.

2.4 Section III deals with principles governing the conduct of the parties in cases which are not subject to a pre-action protocol.

2.5 Section III of this Practice Direction is supplemented by two annexes aimed at different types of claimant.
  (1) Annex A sets out detailed guidance on a pre-action procedure that is likely to satisfy the court in most circumstances where no pre-action protocol

or other formal pre-action procedure applies. It is intended as a guide for parties, particularly those without legal representation, in straightforward claims that are likely to be disputed. It is not intended to apply to debt claims where it is not disputed that the money is owed and where the claimant follows a statutory or other formal pre-action procedure.

(2) Annex B sets out some specific requirements that apply where the claimant is a business and the defendant is an individual. The requirements may be complied with at any time between the claimant first intimating the possibility of court proceedings and the claimant's letter before claim.

2.6 Section IV contains requirements that apply to all cases including those subject to the preaction protocols (unless a relevant pre-action protocol contains a different provision). It is supplemented by Annex C, which sets out guidance on instructing experts.

3. DEFINITIONS

3.1 In this Practice Direction together with the Annexes –

(1) 'proceedings' means any proceedings started under Part 7 or Part 8 of the Civil Procedure Rules 1998 ('CPR');

(2) 'claimant' and 'defendant' refer to the respective parties to potential proceedings;

(3) 'ADR' means alternative dispute resolution, and is the collective description of methods of resolving disputes otherwise than through the normal trial process; (see paragraph 8.2 for further information); and

(4) 'compliance' means acting in accordance with, as applicable, the principles set out in Section III of this Practice Direction, the requirements in Section IV and a relevant pre-action protocol. The words 'comply' and 'complied' should be construed accordingly.

SECTION II – THE APPROACH OF THE COURTS

4. COMPLIANCE

4.1 The CPR enable the court to take into account the extent of the parties' compliance with this Practice Direction or a relevant pre-action protocol (see paragraph 5.2) when giving directions for the management of claims (see CPR rules 3.1(4) and (5) and 3.9(1)(e)) and when making orders about who should pay costs (see CPR rule 44.3(5)(a)).

4.2 The court will expect the parties to have complied with this Practice Direction or any relevant pre-action protocol. The court may ask the parties to explain what steps were taken to comply prior to the start of the claim. Where there has been a failure of compliance by a party the court may ask that party to provide an explanation.

Assessment of compliance

4.3 When considering compliance the court will –

(1) be concerned about whether the parties have complied in substance with the relevant principles and requirements and is not likely to be concerned with minor or technical shortcomings;

(2) consider the proportionality of the steps taken compared to the size and importance of the matter;

(3) take account of the urgency of the matter. Where a matter is urgent (for example, an application for an injunction) the court will expect the parties to comply only to the extent that it is reasonable to do so. (Paragraph 9.5 and 9.6 of this Practice Direction concern urgency caused by limitation periods.)

4.4 The court may decide that there has been a failure of compliance by a party because, for example, that party has –

(1) not provided sufficient information to enable the other party to understand the issues;

(2) not acted within a time limit set out in a relevant pre-action protocol, or, where no specific time limit applies, within a reasonable period;

(3) unreasonably refused to consider ADR (paragraph 8 in Part III of this Practice Direction and the pre-action protocols all contain similar provisions about ADR); or

(4) without good reason, not disclosed documents requested to be disclosed.

Sanctions for non-compliance

4.5 The court will look at the overall effect of non-compliance on the other party when deciding whether to impose sanctions.

4.6 If, in the opinion of the court, there has been non-compliance, the sanctions which the court may impose include –

(1) staying (that is suspending) the proceedings until steps which ought to have been taken have been taken;

(2) an order that the party at fault pays the costs, or part of the costs, of the other party or parties (this may include an order under rule 27.14(2)(g) in cases allocated to the small claims track);

(3) an order that the party at fault pays those costs on an indemnity basis (rule 44.4(3) sets out the definition of the assessment of costs on an indemnity basis);

(4) if the party at fault is the claimant in whose favour an order for the payment of a sum of money is subsequently made, an order that the claimant is deprived of interest on all or part of that sum, and/or that interest is awarded at a lower rate than would otherwise have been awarded;

(5) if the party at fault is a defendant, and an order for the payment of a sum of money is subsequently made in favour of the claimant, an order that the defendant pay interest on all or part of that sum at a higher rate, not exceeding 10% above base rate, than would otherwise have been awarded.

5. COMMENCEMENT OF PRE-ACTION PROTOCOLS

5.1 When considering compliance, the court will take account of a relevant pre-action protocol if the proceedings were started after the relevant pre-action protocol came into force.

5.2 The following table sets out the pre-action protocols currently in force and the dates that they came into force –

Pre-Action Protocol	Came into force
Personal Injury	26 April 1999
Clinical Disputes	26 April 1999
Construction and Engineering	2 October 2000
Defamation	2 October 2000
Professional Negligence	16 July 2001
Judicial Review	4 March 2002
Disease and Illness	8 December 2003
Housing Disrepair	8 December 2003
Possession Claims based on rent arrears	2 October 2006
Possession Claims based on Mortgage Arrears etc.	19 November 2008

SECTION III – THE PRINCIPLES GOVERNING THE CONDUCT OF THE PARTIES IN CASES NOT SUBJECT TO A PRE-ACTION PROTOCOL

6. OVERVIEW OF PRINCIPLES

6.1 The principles that should govern the conduct of the parties are that, unless the circumstances make it inappropriate, before starting proceedings the parties should –

(1) exchange sufficient information about the matter to allow them to understand each other's position and make informed decisions about settlement and how to proceed;

(2) make appropriate attempts to resolve the matter without starting proceedings, and in particular consider the use of an appropriate form of ADR in order to do so.

6.2 The parties should act in a reasonable and proportionate manner in all dealings with one another. In particular, the costs incurred in complying should be proportionate to the complexity of the matter and any money at stake. The parties must not use this Practice Direction as a tactical device to secure an unfair advantage for one party or to generate unnecessary costs.

7. EXCHANGING INFORMATION BEFORE STARTING PROCEEDINGS

7.1 Before starting proceedings –

(1) the claimant should set out the details of the matter in writing by sending a letter before claim to the defendant. This letter before claim is not the start of proceedings; and

(2) the defendant should give a full written response within a reasonable period, preceded, if appropriate, by a written acknowledgment of the letter before claim.

7.2 A 'reasonable period of time' will vary depending on the matter. As a general guide –

(1) the defendant should send a letter of acknowledgment within 14 days of receipt of the letter before claim (if a full response has not been sent within that period);

(2) where the matter is straightforward, for example an undisputed debt, then a full response should normally be provided within 14 days;

(3) where a matter requires the involvement of an insurer or other third party or where there are issues about evidence, then a full response should normally be provided within 30 days;

(4) where the matter is particularly complex, for example requiring specialist advice, then a period of longer than 30 days may be appropriate;

(5) a period of longer than 90 days in which to provide a full response will only be considered reasonable in exceptional circumstances.

7.3 Annex A sets out detailed guidance on a pre-action procedure that is likely to satisfy the court in most circumstances where no pre-action protocol applies and where the claimant does not follow any statutory or other formal pre-action procedure.

7.4 Annex B sets out the specific information that should be provided in a debt claim by a claimant who is a business against a defendant who is an individual.

8. ALTERNATIVE DISPUTE RESOLUTION

8.1 Starting proceedings should usually be a step of last resort, and proceedings should not normally be started when a settlement is still actively being explored. Although ADR is not compulsory, the parties should consider whether some form of ADR procedure might enable them to settle the matter without starting proceedings. The court may require evidence that the parties considered some form of ADR (see paragraph 4.4(3)).

8.2 It is not practicable in this Practice Direction to address in detail how the parties might decide to resolve a matter. However, some of the options for resolving a matter without starting proceedings are –

(1) discussion and negotiation;

(2) mediation (a form of negotiation with the help of an independent person or body);

(3) early neutral evaluation (where an independent person or body, for example a lawyer or an expert in the subject, gives an opinion on the merits of a dispute); or

(4) arbitration (where an independent person or body makes a binding decision), many types of business are members of arbitration schemes for resolving disputes with consumers.

8.3 The Legal Services Commission has published a booklet on 'Alternatives to Court', CLS Direct Information Leaflet 23 (www.clsdirect.org.uk) which lists a number of organisations that provide alternative dispute resolution services. The National Mediation Helpline on 0845 603 0809 or at www.nationalmediationhelpline.com can provide information about mediation.

8.4 The parties should continue to consider the possibility of reaching a settlement at all times. This still applies after proceedings have been started, up to and during any trial or final hearing.

SECTION IV – REQUIREMENTS THAT APPLY IN ALL CASES

9. SPECIFIC PROVISIONS

9.1 The following requirements (including Annex C) apply in all cases except where a relevant preaction protocol contains its own provisions about the topic.

Disclosure

9.2 Documents provided by one party to another in the course of complying with this Practice Direction or any relevant pre-action protocol must not be used for any purpose other than resolving the matter, unless the disclosing party agrees in writing.

Information about funding arrangements

9.3 Where a party enters into a funding arrangement within the meaning of rule 43.2(1)(k), that party must inform the other parties about this arrangement as soon as possible and in any event either within 7 days of entering into the funding arrangement concerned or, where a claimant enters into a funding arrangement before sending a letter before claim, in the letter before claim. (CPR rule 44.3B(1)(c) provides that a party may not recover certain additional costs where information about a funding arrangement was not provided.)

Experts

9.4 Where the evidence of an expert is necessary the parties should consider how best to minimise expense. Guidance on instructing experts can be found in Annex C.

Limitation Periods

9.5 There are statutory time limits for starting proceedings ('the limitation period'). If a claimant starts a claim after the limitation period applicable to that type of claim has expired the defendant will be entitled to use that as a defence to the claim.

9.6 In certain instances compliance may not be possible before the expiry of the limitation period. If, for any reason, proceedings are started before the parties have complied, they should seek to agree to apply to the court for an order to stay (i.e. suspend) the proceedings while the parties take steps to comply.

Notifying the court

9.7 Where proceedings are started the claimant should state in the claim form or the particulars of claim whether they have complied with Sections III and IV of this Practice Direction or any relevant protocol.

Transitional Provision

9.8 The amendments to paragraph 9.3 do not apply to a funding arrangement entered into before the 1st October 2009 and paragraph 9.3 in force immediately before that date will continue to apply to that funding arrangement as if paragraph 9.3 had not been amended.

ANNEX A
GUIDANCE ON PRE-ACTION PROCEDURE WHERE NO PREACTION PROTOCOL OR OTHER FORMAL PRE-ACTION PROCEDURE APPLIES

1. General

1.1 This Annex sets out detailed guidance on a pre-action procedure that is likely to satisfy the court in most circumstances where no pre-action protocol or other formal pre-action procedure applies. It is intended as a guide for parties, particularly those without legal representation, in straightforward claims that are likely to be disputed. It is not intended to apply to debt claims where it is not disputed that the money is owed and where the claimant follows a statutory or other formal pre-action procedure.

2. Claimant's letter before claim

2.1 The claimant's letter should give concise details about the matter. This should enable the defendant to understand and investigate the issues without needing to request further information. The letter should include –
(1) the claimant's full name and address;
(2) the basis on which the claim is made (i.e. why the claimant says the defendant is liable);
(3) a clear summary of the facts on which the claim is based;
(4) what the claimant wants from the defendant;
(5) if financial loss is claimed, an explanation of how the amount has been calculated; and
(6) details of any funding arrangement (within the meaning of rule 43.2(1)(k) of the CPR) that has been entered into by the claimant.

2.2 The letter should also –
(1) list the essential documents on which the claimant intends to rely;
(2) set out the form of ADR (if any) that the claimant considers the most suitable and invite the defendant to agree to this;
(3) state the date by which the claimant considers it reasonable for a full response to be provided by the defendant; and
(4) identify and ask for copies of any relevant documents not in the claimant's possession and which the claimant wishes to see.

2.3 Unless the defendant is known to be legally represented the letter should –
(1) refer the defendant to this Practice Direction and in particular draw attention to paragraph 4 concerning the court's powers to impose sanctions for failure to comply with the Practice Direction; and
(2) inform the defendant that ignoring the letter before claim may lead to the claimant starting proceedings and may increase the defendant's liability for costs.

3. Defendant's acknowledgment of the letter before claim

3.1 Where the defendant is unable to provide a full written response within 14 days of receipt of the letter before claim the defendant should, instead, provide a written acknowledgment within 14 days.

3.2 The acknowledgment –
(1) should state whether an insurer is or may be involved;

(2) should state the date by which the defendant (or insurer) will provide a full written response; and

(3) may request further information to enable the defendant to provide a full response.

3.3 If the date stated under paragraph 3.2(2) of this Annex is longer than the period stated in the letter before claim, the defendant should give reasons why a longer period is needed.

3.4 If the defendant (or insurer) does not provide either a letter of acknowledgment or full response within 14 days, and proceedings are subsequently started, then the court is likely to consider that the claimant has complied.

3.5 Where the defendant is unable to provide a full response within 14 days of receipt of the letter before claim because the defendant intends to seek advice then the written acknowledgment should state –

(1) that the defendant is seeking advice;

(2) from whom the defendant is seeking advice; and

(3) when the defendant expects to have received that advice and be in a position to provide a full response.

3.6 A claimant should allow a reasonable period of time of up to 14 days for a defendant to obtain advice.

4. Defendant's full response

4.1 The defendant's full written response should –

(1) accept the claim in whole or in part; or

(2) state that the claim is not accepted.

4.2 Unless the defendant accepts the whole of the claim, the response should –

(1) give reasons why the claim is not accepted, identifying which facts and which parts of the claim (if any) are accepted and which are disputed, and the basis of that dispute;

(2) state whether the defendant intends to make a counterclaim against the claimant (and, if so, provide information equivalent to a claimant's letter before claim);

(3) state whether the defendant alleges that the claimant was wholly or partly to blame for the problem that led to the dispute and, if so, summarise the facts relied on;

(4) state whether the defendant agrees to the claimant's proposals for ADR and if not, state why not and suggest an alternative form of ADR (or state why none is considered appropriate);

(5) list the essential documents on which the defendant intends to rely;

(6) enclose copies of documents requested by the claimant, or explain why they will not be provided; and

(7) identify and ask for copies of any further relevant documents, not in the defendant's possession and which the defendant wishes to see.

4.3 If the defendant (or insurer) does not provide a full response within the period stated in the claimant's letter before claim (or any longer period stated in the defendant's letter of acknowledgment), and a claim is subsequently started, then the court is likely to consider that the claimant has complied.

4.4 If the claimant starts proceedings before any longer period stated in the defendant's letter of acknowledgment, the court will consider whether or not the longer period requested by the defendant was reasonable.

5. Claimant's reply

5.1 The claimant should provide the documents requested by the defendant within as short a period of time as is practicable or explain in writing why the documents will not be provided.

5.2 If the defendant has made a counterclaim the claimant should provide information equivalent to the defendant's full response (see paragraphs 4.1 to 4.3 above).

6. Taking Stock

6.1 In following the above procedure, the parties will have a genuine opportunity to resolve the matter without needing to start proceedings. At the very least, it should be possible to establish what issues remain outstanding so as to narrow the scope of the proceedings and therefore limit potential costs.

6.2 If having completed the procedure the matter has not been resolved then the parties should undertake a further review of their respective positions to see if proceedings can still be avoided.

ANNEX B
INFORMATION TO BE PROVIDED IN A DEBT CLAIM WHERE THE CLAIMANT IS A BUSINESS AND THE DEFENDANT IS AN INDIVIDUAL

1. Where paragraph 7.4 of the Practice Direction applies the claimant should –
   (1) provide details of how the money can be paid (for example the method of payment and the address to which it can be sent);
   (2) state that the defendant can contact the claimant to discuss possible repayment options, and provide the relevant contact details; and
   (3) inform the defendant that free independent advice and assistance can be obtained from organisations including those listed in the table below.

INDEPENDENT ADVICE ORGANISATIONS

Organisation	Address	Telephone Number	e-mail Address
National Debtline	Tricorn House 51–53 Hagley Road Edgbaston Birmingham B16 8TP	FREEPHONE 0808 808 4000	www. nationaldebtline. co.uk
Consumer Credit Counselling Service (CCCS)		FREEPHONE 0800 138 1111	www.cccs.co.uk

Organisation	Address	Telephone Number	e-mail Address
Citizens Advice	Check your local Yellow Pages or Thomson local directory for address and telephone numbers		www. citizensadvice. org.uk
Community Legal Advice (formerly Community Legal Services Direct)		0845 345 4345	www.clsdirect. org.uk

2. The information set out in paragraph 1 of this Annex may be provided at any time between the claimant first intimating the possibility of court proceedings and the claimant's letter before claim.

3. Where the defendant is unable to provide a full response within the time specified in the letter before claim because the defendant intends to seek debt advice then the written acknowledgment should state –
   (1) that the defendant is seeking debt advice;
   (2) who the defendant is seeking advice from; and
   (3) when the defendant expects to have received that advice and be in a position to provide a full response.

4. A claimant should allow a reasonable period of time of up to 14 days for a defendant to obtain debt advice.

5. But the claimant need not allow the defendant time to seek debt advice if the claimant knows that –
   (1) the defendant has already received relevant debt advice and the defendant's circumstances have not significantly changed; or
   (2) the defendant has previously asked for time to seek debt advice but has not done so.

ANNEX C
GUIDANCE ON INSTRUCTING EXPERTS

1. The CPR contain extensive provisions which strictly control the use of experts both before and after proceedings are started. These provisions are contained in –
   (1) CPR Part 35;
   (2) Practice Direction 35; and
   (3) the Protocol for the 'Instruction of Experts to give Evidence in Civil Claims' which is annexed to that Practice Direction.

2. Parties should be aware that once proceedings have been started –
   (1) expert evidence may not be used in court without the permission of the court;
   (2) a party who instructs an expert will not necessarily be able to recover the cost from another party; and

(3) (it is the duty of an expert to help the court on the matters within the expert's scope of expertise and this duty overrides any obligation to the person instructing or paying the expert.

3. Many matters can and should be resolved without the need for advice or evidence from an expert. If an expert is needed, the parties should consider how best to minimise the expense for example by agreeing to instruct –

(1) a single joint expert (i.e. engaged and paid jointly by the parties whether instructed jointly or separately); or

(2) an agreed expert (i.e. the parties agree the identity of the expert but only one party instructs the expert and pays the expert's costs).

4. If the parties do not agree that the nomination of a single joint expert is appropriate, then the party seeking the expert evidence (the first party) should give the other party (the second party) a list of one or more experts in the relevant field of expertise whom the first party would like to instruct.

5. Within 14 days of receipt of the list of experts, the second party may indicate in writing an objection to one or more of the experts listed. If there remains on the list one or more experts who are acceptable, then the first party should instruct an expert from the list.

6. If the second party objects to all the listed experts, the first party may then instruct an expert of the first party's own choice. Both parties should bear in mind that if proceedings are started the court will consider whether a party has acted reasonably when instructing (or rejecting) an expert.

Family Mediation Council
Code of Practice

CODE OF PRACTICE FOR FAMILY MEDIATORS
Agreed by the member organisations: version approved 9.9.10

1 DEFINITIONS

1.1 This Code of Practice applies to all family mediation conducted or offered by mediators who are members of the Member Organisations of the Family Mediation Council.

1.2 Family mediation is a process in which those involved in family breakdown, whether or not they are a couple or other family members, appoint an impartial third person to assist them to communicate better with one another and reach their own agreed and informed decisions concerning some, or all, of the issues relating to separation, divorce, children, finance or property by negotiation.

1.3 This Code applies whether or not there are or have been legal proceedings between the participants and whether or not any, or all of them, are legally represented.

1.4 In this Code, "mediation" means the family mediation to which this Code applies. "Mediator" means any person offering such mediation. "Participant" means any family member taking part in mediation.

2 AIMS AND OBJECTIVES

2.1 Mediation aims to assist participants to reach the decisions they consider appropriate to their own particular circumstances.

2.2 Mediation also aims to assist participants to communicate with one another now and in the future and to reduce the scope or intensity of dispute and conflict within the family.

2.3 Where a marriage or relationship has irretrievably broken down, mediation has regard to the principles that the marriage or relationship should be brought to an end in a way that
- minimises distress to the participants and to any children;
- promotes as good a relationship between the participants and any children as is possible;
- removes or diminishes any risk of abuse to any of the participants or children from the other participants; and
- avoids any unnecessary cost to participants.

3 QUALIFICATIONS AND TRAINING

3.1 Mediators must have successfully completed such training as is approved by a Member Organisation and accredited by the Council to qualify them to mediate upon those matters upon which they offer mediation.

3.2 Mediators must be a member of a Member Organisation and must therefore have successfully demonstrated personal aptitude for mediation and competence to mediate.

3.3 Mediators must satisfy their Member Organisation that they have made satisfactory arrangements for regular professional practice consultancy with a professional practice consultant who is a member of and approved for the purpose by a Member Organisation.

3.4 Mediators must agree to maintain and improve their skills through continuing professional development courses approved by a Member Organisation and/or the Council.

3.5 Mediators may only undertake direct consultation with children when they have successfully completed specific training approved by their Member Organisation and/or the Council and have received specific clearance from the Criminal Records Bureau.

3.6 Mediators undertaking publicly funded mediation must have been assessed as competent to do so by a recognised assessment scheme.

3.7 Mediators must not mediate upon any case unless they are covered by adequate professional indemnity insurance.

3.8 Mediators must abide by the complaints and disciplinary procedures laid down by the Member Organisation of which they are a member.

4 SCOPE OF MEDIATION

4.1 Mediation may cover any or all of the following matters

4.1.1 options for maintaining or ending the marital or other relationship between the adult participants and the consequences of doing so;

4.1.2 arrangements for dependant children :– with whom they are to live; what contact they are to have with each parent and other family members; any other aspect of parental responsibility such as, but not exhaustively, schooling, holidays, religious education;

4.1.3 the future of the family home and any other property or assets, including pensions, belonging to the adult participants; issues of child maintenance and spousal maintenance; issues relating to debts;

4.1.4 how adjustments to these arrangements are to be decided upon in the future;

4.2 Participants and mediators may agree that mediation will cover any other matters which it would be helpful to resolve in connection with relationship breakdown between the participants and which the mediators consider suitable for mediation.

5 GENERAL PRINCIPLES

5.1 Impartiality and Conflicts of Interest

5.1.1 It is the duty of the mediator at all times to ensure that he or she acts with impartiality and that that impartiality is not compromised at any time by any conflict of interest, actual or capable of being perceived as such.

5.1.2 Mediators must not have any personal interest in the outcome of the mediation.

5.1.3 Mediators must not mediate in any case in which they have acquired or may acquire relevant information in any private or other professional capacity.

5.1.4 Mediators must not act or continue to act if they or a member of their firm has acted for any of the parties in issues not relating to the mediation.

5.1.5 Mediators must not accept referrals from any professional practice with whom they are employed, in partnership or contracted, on a full or part-time basis and which is involved in advising one of the participants on matters which relate or are capable of relating to the mediation, even though the practices are separate legal entities.

5.1.6 Mediators must not refer a participant for advice or for any other professional service to a professional practice with whom they are employed, in partnership or contracted, on a full or part-time basis on matters which relate or are capable of relating to the mediation even though the practices are separate legal entities.

5.1.7 Mediation must be conducted as an independent professional activity and must be distinguished from any other professional role in which the mediator may practise.

5.2 Voluntary Participation

Participation in mediation is voluntary at all times and participants and the mediator are always free to withdraw. Where mediators consider that a participant is unable or unwilling to take part in the process freely and fully, they must raise the issue and possibly suspend or terminate the mediation.

5.3 Neutrality

Mediators must remain neutral as to the outcome of a mediation at all times. Mediators must not seek to impose their preferred outcome on the participants or to influence them to adopt it, whether by attempting to predict the outcome of court proceedings or otherwise. However, if the participants consent, they may inform them that they consider that the resolutions they are considering might fall outside the parameters which a court might approve or order. They may inform participants of possible courses of action, their legal or other implications, and assist them to explore these, but must make it clear that they are not giving advice.

5.4 Impartiality

5.4.1 Mediators must at all times remain impartial as between the participants and conduct the mediation process in a fair and even-handed way.

5.4.2 Mediators must seek to prevent manipulative, threatening or intimidating behaviour by any participant. They must conduct the process in such a way as to redress, as far as possible, any imbalance of power between the participants. If such behaviour or any other imbalance seems likely to render the mediation unfair or ineffective, mediators must take appropriate steps to seek to prevent this including terminating the mediation if necessary.

5.5 Confidentiality

5.5.1 Subject to paragraphs 5.5.3, 5.5.4 and 5.5.5 below mediators must not disclose any information about, or obtained in the course of, a mediation to anyone, including a court welfare officer or a court, without the express consent of each participant, an order of the court or where the law imposes an overriding obligation of disclosure on mediators.

5.5.2 Mediators must not discuss the mediation or correspond with any participant's legal advisor without the express consent of each participant. Nothing must be said or written to the legal advisor of one party regarding the content of the discussions in mediation which is not also said or written to the legal advisor(s) of the other.

5.5.3 Where it appears necessary so that a specific allegation that a child has suffered significant harm may be properly investigated or where mediators suspect that a child is suffering or is likely to suffer significant harm, mediators must ensure that the relevant Social Services department is notified.

5.5.4 Mediators may notify the appropriate agency if they consider that other public policy considerations prevail, such as an adult suffering or likely to suffer significant harm.

5.5.5 Where mediators suspect that they may be required to make disclosure to the appropriate government authority under the Proceeds of Crime Act 2002 and/or relevant money laundering regulations, they must stop the mediation immediately without informing the clients of the reason.

5.6 Privilege and Legal Proceedings

5.6.1 Subject to paragraph 5.6.2 below, all discussions and negotiations in mediation must be conducted on a legally privileged basis. Before the mediation commences the participants must agree in writing that discussions and negotiations in mediation are not to be referred to in any legal proceedings, and that mediators cannot be required to give evidence or produce any notes or records made in the course of the mediation, unless all participants agree to waive the privilege or the law imposes upon mediators an overriding obligation of disclosure upon the mediator.

5.6.2 Participants must agree that all factual information material to financial issues must be provided on an open basis, so that it can be referred to in legal proceedings.

5.6.3 All information or correspondence provided by either participant should be shared openly and not withheld, except any address or telephone number or as the participants may agree otherwise.

5.6.4 Privilege will not apply in relation to communications indicating that a child or other person is suffering or likely to suffer significant harm, or where other public policy considerations prevail.

5.7 Welfare of children

5.7.1 At all times mediators must have special regard to the welfare of any children of the family. They should encourage participants to focus on the needs and interests of the children as well as on their own.

5.7.2 Mediators must encourage participants to consider the children's wishes and feelings. If appropriate they may discuss with them whether and to what extent it is proper to consult the children directly in order to ascertain their wishes and feelings.

5.7.3 Where mediators and both participants agree that it is appropriate to consult any children directly, the consent of the children must first be obtained.

Mediators consulting directly with any children must have been specifically trained to do so and have received specific enhanced clearance from the Criminal Records Bureau. Such mediators must provide appropriate facilities for direct consultation.

5.7.4 Where qualified mediators undertake direct consultation with any child, they must offer that child confidentiality as to any disclosure that that child may make to them. This must be explained to the participants before they agree to the direct consultation. Confidentiality in direct consultation with children must always be exercised subject to paragraphs 5.5.3, 5.5.4, 5.5.5, and 5.6.4 above.

5.7.5 Where mediators suspect that any child is suffering or likely to suffer significant harm, they must advise the participants to seek help from the appropriate agency. Mediators must also advise the participants that, in any event, they are obliged to report the matter to the appropriate agency in accordance with paragraph 5.5.3.

5.7.6 Where mediators consider that the participants are or are proposing to act in a manner likely to be seriously detrimental to the welfare of any child of the family or family member, they may withdraw from the mediation. The reason for doing this must be outlined in any further communication.

5.8 Abuse and power imbalances within the family

5.8.1 Mediators must be alert to the likelihood of power imbalances existing between the participants.

5.8.2 In all cases, mediators must seek to ensure that participants take part in the mediation willingly and without fear of violence or harm. They must seek to discover through a screening procedure whether or not there is fear of abuse or any other harm and whether or not it is alleged that any participant has been or is likely to be abusive towards another. Where abuse is alleged or suspected mediators must discuss whether a participant wishes to take part in mediation, and information about available support services should be provided.

5.8.3 Where mediation does take place, mediators must uphold throughout the principles of voluntary participation, fairness and safety and must conduct the process in accordance with this section. In addition, steps must be taken to ensure the safety of all participants on arrival and departure.

5.8.4 Mediators must seek to prevent manipulative, threatening or intimidating behaviour by either participant during the mediation.

6 CONDUCT OF THE MEDIATION

6.1 All assessments for suitability for mediation must be conducted at meetings on a face-to-face basis. Assessment meetings can be conducted jointly or separately depending on client preference, but must include an individual element with each participant to allow mediators to undertake domestic abuse screening.

6.2 Mediators must manage the mediation process. They should consult the participants on management decisions such as the ordering of issues and the agenda for each mediation session but must not relinquish control of the process to the participants.

6.3 Throughout the mediation mediators must keep the possibility of reconciliation of the participants under review.

6.4 Participants must be clearly advised at the outset of the nature and purpose of mediation and how it differs from other services such as marriage or relationship counselling, therapy or legal representation.

6.5 Participants must be informed of all the general principles set out in Section 5 above, including the nature and limits of the principles of confidentiality and privilege and mediators' special concern for the welfare of any children of the family.

6.6 Participants must be informed of the extent of any disclosure which will be required in cases relating to their property and finances.

6.7 Each participant must be supplied with written information covering the main points in this Code and given the opportunity to ask questions about it.

6.8 Mediators must ensure that the participants agree the terms and conditions regulating the mediation before dealing with the substantive issues. This must be in the form of a written agreement which reflects the main principles of this Code. The agreement must also set out the client fees.

6.9 Participants must be requested to notify any legal advisors acting for them of the appointment of a mediator.

6.10 Where during a privately funded mediation, mediators become aware that one or more of the participants may qualify for public funding, they must inform the client of this and, if they do not undertake publicly funded work, of the potential services of a mediation practice with an LSC contract.

6.11 Mediators must assist participants to define the issues, identify areas of agreement, explore the options and seek to reach agreement upon them.

6.12 Mediators must seek to ensure that participants reach their decision upon sufficient information and knowledge. They must inform participants of the need to give full and frank disclosure of all material relevant to the issues being mediated and assist them where necessary in identifying the relevant information and supporting documentation.

6.13 Mediators must ensure each participant is given the opportunity to make enquiries about information disclosed by any other participant and to seek further information and documentation when required. They must promote the participants' equal understanding of such information before any final agreement is reached.

6.14 Mediators must make it clear that they do not themselves make further enquiries to verify the information provided by any participant, that each participant may seek independent legal advice as to the adequacy of the information disclosed before reaching a decision; that in any court proceedings a sworn affidavit, written statement or oral evidence may be required and that authoritative calculations of liability under the Child Support Act 1991 can only be made by the Child Support Agency or may replacement organisation established under the Child Maintenance and Other Payments Act 2008.

6.15 Mediators must inform participants of the advantages of seeking independent legal or other appropriate advice whenever this appears desirable during the course of the mediation. They must advise participants that it is in their own interests to seek independent legal advice before reaching any final agreement and warn them of the risks and disadvantages if they do not do so.

6.16 Mediation meetings are commonly conducted without lawyers present. However, solicitors or counsel acting for the participants may be invited to participate in the mediation process and in any communications if the participants agree and the mediator considers that it would be appropriate.

6.17 When appropriate and with the consent of both participants, arrangements may be made for the attendance of professional third parties other than lawyers, such as interpreters, accountants, actuaries, independent financial advisors, and other advisors.

6.18 When appropriate and with the consent of both parties, arrangements may be made for the attendance of third parties with an interest in the proceedings, such as new partners, parties with a legal or beneficial interest in property that is the subject of dispute, or other family members.

6.19 Mediators must seek to ensure that agreements reached by participants are fully informed and freely made. Participants must have as good an understanding as is practicable of the consequences of their decisions for themselves, their children and other relevant family members.

Practice Direction 3A: Pre-application Protocol for Mediation Information and Assessment
Family Mediation Information and Assessment Form (FM1)

PRACTICE DIRECTION 3A: PRE-APPLICATION PROTOCOL FOR MEDIATION INFORMATION AND ASSESSMENT

This Practice Direction supplements FPR Part 3

Introduction

1.1 This Practice Direction applies where a person is considering applying for an order in family proceedings of a type specified in Annex B (referred to in this Direction as 'relevant family proceedings').

1.2 Terms used in this Practice Direction and the accompanying Pre-action Protocol have the same meaning as in the FPR.

1.3 This Practice Direction is supplemented by the following Annexes –

    (i)   Annex A: The Pre-application Protocol ('the Protocol'), which sets out steps which the court will normally expect an applicant to follow before an application is made to the court in relevant family proceedings;

    (ii)   Annex B: Proceedings which are 'relevant family proceedings' for the purposes of this Practice Direction; and

    (iii) Annex C: Circumstances in which attendance at a Mediation Information and Assessment Meeting is not expected.

Aims

2.1 The purpose of this Practice Direction and the accompanying Protocol is to –

    (a) supplement the court's powers in Part 3 of the FPR to encourage and facilitate the use of alternative dispute resolution;

    (b) set out good practice to be followed by any person who is considering making an application to court for an order in relevant family proceedings; and

    (c) ensure, as far as possible, that all parties have considered mediation as an alternative means of resolving their disputes.

Rationale

3.1 There is a general acknowledgement that an adversarial court process is not always best-suited to the resolution of family disputes, particularly private 453 law disputes between parents relating to children, with such disputes often best resolved through discussion and agreement, where that can be managed safely and appropriately.

3.2 Litigants who seek public funding for certain types of family proceedings are (subject to some exceptions) already required to attend a meeting with a mediator as a pre-condition of receiving public funding.

3.3 There is growing recognition of the benefits of early information and advice about mediation and of the need for those wishing to make an application to court, whether publicly-funded or otherwise, to consider alternative means of resolving their disputes, as appropriate.

3.4 In private law proceedings relating to children, the court is actively involved in helping parties to explore ways of resolving their dispute. The Private Law Programme, set out in Practice Direction 12B, provides for a first hearing dispute resolution appointment ('FHDRA'), at which the judge, legal advisor or magistrates, accompanied by an officer from Cafcass (the Children and Family Court Advisory and Support Service), will discuss with parties both the nature of their dispute and whether it could be resolved by mediation or other alternative means and can give the parties information about services which may be available to assist them. The court should also have information obtained through safeguarding checks carried out by Cafcass, to ensure that any agreement between the parties, or any dispute resolution process selected, is in the interests of the child and safe for all concerned.

3.5 Against that background, it is likely to save court time and expense if the parties take steps to resolve their dispute without pursuing court proceedings. Parties will therefore be expected to explore the scope for resolving their dispute through mediation before embarking on the court process.

The Pre-application Protocol

4.1 To encourage this approach, all potential applicants for a court order in relevant family proceedings will be expected, before making their application, to have followed the steps set out in the Protocol. This requires a potential applicant except in certain specified circumstances, to consider with a mediator whether the dispute may be capable of being resolved through mediation. The court will expect all applicants to have complied with the Protocol before commencing proceedings and (except where any of the circumstances in Annex C applies) will expect any respondent to have attended a Mediation Information and Assessment Meeting, if invited to do so. If court proceedings are taken, the court will wish to know at the first hearing whether mediation has been considered by the parties. In considering the conduct of any relevant family proceedings, the court will take into account any failure to comply with the Protocol and may refer the parties to a meeting with a mediator before the proceedings continue further.

4.2 Nothing in the Protocol is to be read as affecting the operation of the Private Law Programme, set out in Practice Direction 12B, or the role of the court at the first hearing in any relevant family proceedings.

ANNEX A

The Pre-application Protocol

1. This Protocol applies where a person ('the applicant') is considering making an application to the court for an order in relevant family proceedings.

2. Before an applicant makes an application to the court for an order in relevant family proceedings, the applicant (or the applicant's legal representative) should contact a family mediator to arrange for the applicant to attend an information meeting about family mediation and other forms of alternative dispute resolution (referred to in this Protocol as 'a Mediation Information and Assessment Meeting').

3. An applicant is not expected to attend a Mediation Information and Assessment Meeting where any of the circumstances set out in Annex C applies.

4. Information on how to find a family mediator may be obtained from local family courts, from the Community Legal Advice Helpline – CLA Direct (0845 345 4345) or at www.direct.gov.uk.

5. The applicant (or the applicant's legal representative) should provide the mediator with contact details for the other party or parties to the dispute ('the respondent(s)'), so that the mediator can contact the respondent(s) to discuss that part''s willingness and availability to attend a Mediation Information and Assessment Meeting.

6. The applicant should then attend a Mediation Information and Assessment Meeting arranged by the mediator. If the parties are willing to attend Together, the meeting may be conducted jointly, but where necessary separate meetings may be held. If the applicant and respondent(s) do not attend a joint meeting, the mediator will invite the respondent(s) to a separate meeting unless any of the circumstances set out in Annex C applies.

7. A mediator who arranges a Mediation Information and Assessment Meeting with one or more parties to a dispute should consider with the party or parties concerned whether public funding may be available to meet the cost of the meeting and any subsequent mediation. Where none of the parties is eligible for, or wishes to seek, public funding, any charge made by the mediator for the Mediation Information and Assessment Meeting will be the responsibility of the party or parties attending, in accordance with any agreement made with the mediator.

8. If the applicant then makes an application to the court in respect of the dispute, the applicant should at the same time file a completed Family Mediation Information and Assessment Form (Form FM1) confirming attendance at a Mediation Information and Assessment Meeting or giving the reasons for not attending.

9. The Form FM1, must be completed and signed by the mediator, and countersigned by the applicant or the applicant's legal representative, where either –
   (a) the applicant has attended a Mediation Information and Assessment Meeting; or
   (b) the applicant has not attended a Mediation Information and Assessment Meeting and
      (i) the mediator is satisfied that mediation is not suitable because another

party to the dispute is unwilling to attend a Mediation Information and Assessment Meeting and consider mediation;

   (ii) the mediator determines that the case is not suitable for a Mediation Information and Assessment Meeting; or

   (iii) a mediator has made a determination within the previous four months that the case is not suitable for a Mediation Information and Assessment Meeting or for mediation.

10. In all other circumstances, the Form FM1 must be completed and signed by the applicant or the applicant's legal representative.

11. The form may be obtained from magistrates' courts, county courts or the High Court or from www.direct.gov.uk.

ANNEX B

Proceedings which are 'relevant family proceedings' for the purposes of this Practice Direction

1. Private law proceedings relating to children, except –
   - proceedings for an enforcement order, a financial compensation order or an order under paragraph 9 or Part 2 of Schedule Al to the Children Act 1989;
   - any other proceedings for enforcement of an order made in private law proceedings; or
   - where emergency proceedings have been brought in respect of the same child(ren) and have not been determined.

('Private law proceedings' and 'emergency proceedings' are defined in Rule 12.2)

2. Proceedings for a financial remedy, except –
   - Proceedings for an avoidance of disposition order or an order preventing a disposition;
   - Proceedings for enforcement of any order made in financial remedy proceedings.

('Financial remedy' is defined in Rule 2.3(1) and 'avoidance of disposition order' and 'order preventing a disposition' are defined in Rule 9.3(1))

ANNEX C

A person considering making an application to the court in relevant family proceedings is not expected to attend a Mediation Information and Assessment Meeting before doing so if any of the following circumstances applies:

1. The mediator is satisfied that mediation is not suitable because another party to the dispute is unwilling to attend a Mediation Information and Assessment Meeting and consider mediation.

2. The mediator determines that the case is not suitable for a Mediation Information and Assessment Meeting.

3. A mediator has made a determination within the previous four months that the case is not suitable for a Mediation Information and Assessment Meeting or for mediation.

Domestic abuse

4. Any party has, to the applicant's knowledge, made an allegation of domestic Violence against another party and this has resulted in a police investigation or the issuing of civil proceedings for the protection of any party within the last 12 months.

Bankruptcy

5. The dispute concerns financial issues and the applicant or another party is bankrupt.
6. The parties are in agreement and there is no dispute to mediate.
7. The whereabouts of the other party are unknown to the applicant.
8. The prospective application is for an order in relevant family proceedings which are already in existence and are continuing.
9. The prospective application is to be made without notice to the other party.

Urgency

10. The prospective application is urgent, meaning –
    (a) there is a risk to the life, liberty or physical safety of the applicant or his or her family or his or her home; or
    (b) any delay caused by attending a Mediation Information and Assessment Meeting would cause a risk of significant harm to a child, a significant risk of a miscarriage of justice, unreasonable hardship to the applicant or irretrievable problems in dealing with the dispute (such as an irretrievable loss of significant evidence).
11. There is current social services involvement as a result of child protection concerns in respect of any child who would be the subject of the prospective application.
12. A child would be a party to the prospective application by virtue of Rule 12.3(1).
13. The applicant (or the applicant's legal representative) contacts three mediators within 15 miles of the applicant's home and none is able to conduct a Mediation Information and Assessment Meeting within 15 working days of the date of contact.

Family Mediation Information and Assessment Form (FM1)

<u>Family Mediation Information and Assessment Form FM1</u>
This form is to be used in connection with family proceedings to which Practice Direction 3A applies. It should be completed in accordance with the Pre-application Protocol annexed to the Practice Direction and be filed with the court with any application made in proceedings to which the Practice Direction applies.

Where either Part 1 or Part 2 applies, the form must be completed and signed by the mediator concerned and counter-signed by the applicant or the applicant's solicitor.

Where either Part 3 or Part 4 applies, the form must be completed and signed by the applicant or the applicant's solicitor

Part 1
☐   The applicant has attended a Mediation Information and Assessment meeting

Part 2
The applicant has not attended a Mediation Information and Assessment meeting because:

☐   The mediator is satisfied that mediation is not suitable because another party to the dispute is unwilling to attend a Mediation Information and Assessment Meeting and consider mediation.

☐   The mediator determines that the case is not suitable for a Mediation Information and Assessment Meeting.

☐   A mediator has made a determination within the previous four months that the case is not suitable for a Mediation Information and Assessment Meeting or for mediation.

Part 3
The applicant has not attended a Mediation Information and Assessment meeting because:
☐ A party has, to the applicant's knowledge, made an allegation of domestic violence against another party and this has resulted in a police investigation or the issuing of civil proceedings for the protection of any party within the last 12 months.
   (Please attach evidence confirming the date of any civil proceedings or police investigation)

☐   The dispute concerns financial issues and the applicant or another party is bankrupt.

☐   The parties are in agreement and there is no dispute to mediate.

☐ The whereabouts of the other party are unknown to the applicant.

☐ The prospective application is for an order in relevant family proceedings which are already in existence and are continuing.

☐ The prospective application is to be made without notice to the other party.

☐ The prospective application is urgent, meaning:
(a) there is a risk to the life, liberty or physical safety of the applicant or his or her family or his or her home; or
(b) any delay caused by attending a Mediation Information and Assessment Meeting would cause a risk of significant harm to a child, a significant risk of a miscarriage of justice, unreasonable hardship to the applicant or irretrievable problems in dealing with the dispute (such as an irretrievable loss of significant evidence).

> *Please give details here:*

☐ There is current social services involvement as a result of child protection concerns in respect of any child who would be the subject of the prospective application.

☐ A child would be a party to the prospective application by virtue of the Family Procedure Rules 2010, r 12.3(1).

☐ The applicant (or the applicant's solicitor) has contacted three mediators within 15 miles of the applicant's home and none has been able to conduct a Mediation Information and Assessment Meeting within 15 working days of the date of contact.

Part 4

☐ The applicant has not complied with the Pre-application Protocol and has not attended a Mediation Information and Assessment meeting for the following reason (not being a reason specified in Parts 2 or 3 of this Form).

> *Please state reason here:*

Signed..................................[solicitor for] the applicant

Signed..................................mediator

Address..

Index